FACT IN FICTION

KRISTIN STAPLETON

Fact in Fiction

1920s China and Ba Jin's Family

STANFORD UNIVERSITY PRESS
STANFORD, CALIFORNIA

Stanford University Press
Stanford, California

©2016 by the Board of Trustees of the Leland Stanford Junior University. All rights reserved.

No part of this book may be reproduced or transmitted in any form or by any means, electronic or mechanical, including photocopying and recording, or in any information storage or retrieval system without the prior written permission of Stanford University Press.

Printed in the United States of America on acid-free, archival-quality paper

Library of Congress Cataloging-in-Publication Data is available upon request.

ISBN 978-0-8047-9869-3 (cloth)
ISBN 978-1-5036-0106-2 (pbk.)
ISBN 978-0-8047-9973-7 (e-book)

Cover image: Chengdu's new Chunvi Road in 1924; courtesy of the Mullett family.
Typeset by Bruce Lundquist in 10/14 Janson

Contents

	List of Illustrations	vii
	Acknowledgments	ix
	Introduction: Ba Jin's Fiction and Twentieth-Century Chinese History	1
1	Mingfeng: The Life of a Chinese Slave Girl	17
2	The Patriarch: Chengdu's Gentry	48
3	Juexin's City: The Chengdu Economy	82
4	Sedan-Chair Bearers, Beggars, Actors, and Prostitutes: The Worlds of the Urban Poor	111
5	Students, Soldiers, and Warlords: Protest and Warfare in the City	131
6	Qin: Chengdu and the "New Woman"	155
7	Juehui: Revolution, Reform, and Development in Chengdu	184
	Epilogue: Family and City in China's Twentieth-Century Revolutions	215
	Appendix 1: Timeline of Chengdu's History and Ba Jin's Life	221
	Appendix 2: List of Turbulent Stream *Characters, with Pinyin and Wade-Giles Romanizations*	225
	Notes	227
	Glossary	251
	Works Cited	253
	Index	269

Illustrations

Table 3.1	Frequency of occupations or places of employment reported by Chengdu residents in the 1909 census	89
Table 5.1	Political and military commanders in Sichuan, 1915–1924	134
Figure I.1	Ba Jin with his second-eldest brother, Li Yaolin, in 1925	9
Figure 1.1	Slave girl contract dated June 21, 1919	29
Figure 1.2	Chengdu's southern wall	35
Figure 2.1	Li Yong, Ba Jin's grandfather, with Ba Jin's eldest brother, Li Yaomei	52
Figure 2.2	A cover of *Amusing Accounts* (*Yuxianlu*)	63
Figure 2.3	Diagram of Ba Jin's childhood home	66
Figure 3.1	Construction crew on the campus of West China Union University	93
Figure 3.2	Chengdu's Chunxi Road commercial zone shortly after construction in 1924	106
Figure 3.3	Aerial view of Chengdu, 1934	107
Figure 4.1	One of Chengdu's gates, circa 1920s	128
Figure 5.1	Message from Liu Cunhou to the US Consulate in Chongqing (April 25, 1917)	136

Figure 5.2	Xiong Kewu at the wedding of one of his officers in 1923	137
Figure 5.3	Report on a clash between students and soldiers in Shaocheng Park on November 27, 1920	149
Figure 6.1	Image in *Popular Pictorial* (*Tongsu huabao*) in 1912; lightning punishes a woman	160
Figure 6.2	A young married couple in Chengdu in the 1920s	166
Figure 7.1	Li Jieren and *Sichuan Masses*	189
Figure 7.2	Editorial in the *Citizens' Gazette* (*Guomin gongbao*) praising the patriotism of Beijing students who protested the Versailles Treaty on May 4, 1919	191
Figure 7.3	Ba Jin and his eldest brother, Li Yaomei, in Shanghai in 1929	197
Figure 7.4	Lu Zuofu	210
Figure 7.5	The Chengdu Popular Education Institute	211
Map 1.1	Sichuan Province, circa 1919	32
Map 1.2	Chengdu, circa 1919	34

Acknowledgments

I am glad to have the opportunity to express my deep gratitude to all those who supported this work: colleagues, students, family, friends. Special thanks go to all those in Chengdu and elsewhere who helped me understand the world of Ba Jin's youth including, among many others, He Xingqiong 贺兴琼, Yi Aidi 易艾迪, Li Shihua 李诗华, Tan Xingguo 谭兴国, Wang Jialing 王嘉陵, Wang Lüping 王绿萍, Zhang Zhiqiang 张志强, Jiang Shanshan 蒋姗姗, Shen Zaiwang 申再望, Lei Bing 雷兵, Jerome Chen 陈志让, and the children and grandchildren of 1920s Chengdu residents who shared their photographs and family memories. Members of the Association for Asian Studies Committee on Teaching about Asia—especially Roberta Martin, Kathleen Woods Masalski, Lynn Parisi, Lesley Solomon, and Diana Marston Wood—gave me much-appreciated encouragement as I worked on this book. Craig Shaw kindly shared his translations of the 1930s version of *Family*. In the final stages, Ling Ma provided critical assistance. Greg Epp helped see it through from beginning to end.

FACT IN FICTION

INTRODUCTION

Ba Jin's Fiction and Twentieth-Century Chinese History

When student demonstrations in Beijing on May 4, 1919, turned unexpectedly violent, the incident created a political crisis in China. Chinese across the country vented deep frustration at the failure of the young Chinese Republic (not yet a decade old) to change Chinese society and improve China's status in the world. In the years before 1919, intellectuals had begun urging the creation of a "New Culture" to replace traditional values. The May Fourth incident and the publicity surrounding it put the question of the need for fundamental social reform on the national agenda. In the years that followed, reformers advocated (and sometimes tested) diverse solutions to the evils they saw in Chinese life. Many agreed that the patriarchal extended family—the basic unit of Chinese society—lay at the root of the problem, along with the value system that supported it.

An affluent teenager in Chengdu, capital city of the populous interior province of Sichuan, was among those stirred by this spirit of reform in the 1920s. Later, under the pen name Ba Jin, he wrote three novels—*Family*,

Spring, and *Autumn*—that so vividly dramatized both the evils of the old culture and the 1920s thirst for reform that their storylines became a key element of popular understandings of China's New Culture movement. These novels, known as the *Turbulent Stream* trilogy, continue to influence how the May Fourth/New Culture era is remembered.[1]

In 1977, Ba Jin wrote that *Family*, the first and most famous of the *Turbulent Stream* novels, had "played out its historical role" and perhaps should best be forgotten. Ten years earlier, at the beginning of Mao's Cultural Revolution, all of Ba Jin's writings had been declared "poisonous weeds" not fit to be read by true revolutionaries.[2]

But *Family* and its sequels continue to be read. The 1956 movie based on *Family* can be found in video stores across China and viewed on the Internet. Two TV miniseries based on the trilogy have been produced, in 1988 and 2007. The English translation of *Family* is frequently assigned in courses on modern Chinese history in the United States. Since they were first published between 1931 and 1940, the novels have appealed strongly to youthful readers who feel ensnared in a social world where they have little control over their lives. The plots center on the suffering Ba Jin considered common in patriarchal families. Over the course of the trilogy, the Gao family, well off and rigidly hierarchical, gradually falls apart as the young generation rebels against the oppression, corruption, and hypocrisy of the elders.

Because of its popularity, the *Turbulent Stream* trilogy has played a major role in shaping how China's history in the first few decades of the twentieth century has been understood, both in China and abroad. The novels are set in the early 1920s, just after the May Fourth incident, when students publicly protested China's national weakness and more and more people began to blame Chinese culture for that weakness. In particular, the moral principles that were supposed to govern Chinese family life—a system of beliefs and rituals often referred to in English as "Confucianism"[3]—came under attack. One of Ba Jin's teachers, Wu Yu, became a leader of the New Culture movement that criticized Chinese tradition in the years around 1919. Wu Yu claimed that the moral rules requiring that the young defer to the old had created generations of weak, subservient people. Children raised in this style, he argued, were easily manipulated as adults by authoritarian rulers who pictured the nation as a large family and claimed the role of national patriarch.[4] Ba Jin's *Turbulent Stream*, and particularly the story of Juexin—the eldest son in the younger generation of the Gao family, who is crushed by the expectations of his grandfather—expressed that idea in the most emotional of terms. The trilogy thus became an important part of the New Culture movement's attack on old Chinese culture and Confucian values. *Family* and its sequels became a key manifesto for the new May Fourth generation of political and social activists.

The novels in the trilogy are all set in Ba Jin's hometown, Chengdu. Many aspects of life in that large, inland city are described to some extent throughout the novels. But Ba Jin did not set out to offer his readers a realistic portrait of a particular city. He wanted the Gao family to be seen as representative of a type of patriarchal family common across China. By limiting his focus to interactions among members of the family, he highlighted the familial power structure sustained by Confucian thought that could be so damaging to the lives of all members of the family, but particularly to the young and weak.

Ba Jin's strong commitment to social change contributed to the emotional intensity of his novels. In regard to the history of the May Fourth era, though, the trilogy conceals as much as it reveals. To really understand the turbulent social dynamics dramatized in *Family* and its sequels, we must look beyond the novels themselves and into the historical record. This book does just that—looks at the history behind Ba Jin's fiction. It carefully examines the social setting that inspired Ba Jin's fiction: Chengdu during the May Fourth era. For those who have not read Ba Jin's fiction, Chengdu's 1920s history is worth exploring for its own sake and for the comparisons that can be drawn to the experiences of eastern Chinese cities such as Beijing and Shanghai. All across the world, the 1920s was a decade of considerable technological, social, and cultural change, but none of the changes occurred uniformly and evenly across the globe. The case of Chengdu presented here illustrates the complexity of the reactions to some of these changes—including calls for democracy and women's liberation, the arrival of new institutions such as Western-style schools and hospitals, growing militarization, and economic instability—in a large provincial town in inland China, complexity that Ba Jin left out of his trilogy. Thus, this book reconnects the issues dramatized in Ba Jin's novels to the real city that inspired his fictional one. By a close examination of the historical record, it presents a more complete portrait of that city, paying attention not only to landowners like the Gao family of the trilogy but to many others who made up the urban community. For those familiar with the novels or their film versions and for those studying them, this detailed portrait permits deeper appreciation of both Ba Jin's achievements and the limitations of his work as history.

When he finished *Autumn* in 1940, Ba Jin planned to write a fourth volume in the series, to be titled "Qun," which can be translated as "the group" or "the collective" or "the masses." Ba Jin may have intended "Qun" as his response to critics of the first three novels who pointed out that the members of the Gao family had been depicted in too much isolation from their surroundings—the city they lived in, the landlord system that supported their lifestyle, and a young and fractured republic buffeted by global events.

Ba Jin never wrote "Qun," however. After the establishment of the People's Republic of China (PRC) by the Communist Party in 1949, he threw himself into the spirit of "New China" and composed essays about socialist heroes emerging from the ranks of the workers and peasants. In 1952 and 1953 he spent months with Chinese troops in northern Korea chronicling what in China is called the War to Resist American Imperialism and Aid Korea. Throughout the 1950s, he also revised his earlier novels—especially *Family*—simplifying the grammar and subtly altering the political stance of the book to conform better to the Communist understanding of history.

Especially since "Qun" was never written, readers of *Family* and the trilogy as a whole get a very partial view of the community within which the story is set. This is unfortunate. As many scholars have pointed out, the iconoclasm of May Fourth writers led them to misrepresent Chinese history and culture—overemphasizing China's "backwardness" to justify their schemes to transform Chinese life.[5] This radical rejection of China's past reached its peak during the Cultural Revolution of 1966–1976, when *Turbulent Stream* itself was banned as not revolutionary enough and Ba Jin was forced to condemn it and his other writings.

Since the late 1970s, citizens of the PRC have been able to read *Turbulent Stream* again, and *Family* is again a popular novel among the young. But times have changed, and no one in China has experienced life as Ba Jin describes it in the trilogy. Industrialization has changed the nature of Chinese cities, as have the many campaigns launched by the Communist Party since 1949. Extended families no longer play mahjong and watch opera performances in their sprawling compounds, sending servants out to collect the rent that allows them to live in luxury. Patriarchs no longer arrange marriages between young people who have never met. Young women no longer fear to cut their hair short.

The danger for today's readers of Ba Jin's gripping fiction, whether or not they live in China, is that they may too readily accept Ba Jin's depiction of "Old China" as historically accurate. They may assume that most people living in China in the 1920s and 1930s experienced family life as did the Gao children of the novels: as isolating, oppressive, deadening, and even deadly. In the trilogy, Ba Jin deliberately exaggerated dark aspects of his childhood to sharpen his indictment of the patriarchal family. And, by having his young heroes and heroines, such as Gao Juehui and Gao Shuying, escape from their (and his) gloomy hometown to a life of freedom in Shanghai, Ba Jin contributed to an emerging conception that a huge cultural gap existed between coastal cities like Shanghai, where foreign influence was strong and innovation flourished, and other parts of China, whose culture was seen as stagnant. This book calls that conception into question.

Ba Jin played a significant role in helping to create a stereotypical "traditional" China that could be attacked by political and social activists of the 1930s and 1940s.[6] Readers of the *Turbulent Stream* trilogy today must keep in mind that the novels were written to serve this specific political role. On the other hand, Ba Jin drew most of what he depicted from Chengdu life, and he was a talented, empathetic writer whose characters appeal to readers worldwide. Conflict between generations within a family is a common theme across cultures. Ba Jin's work can easily draw us into a deeper experience of life in early twentieth-century China, a fascinating time when conventional wisdom was violently challenged, social institutions collapsed, and new political parties competed to impose their own visions on a country in transition.

As already noted, many details of Ba Jin's childhood life in Chengdu appear in the novels. If we widen our reading of *Family* and its sequels to take in more than the tragic family drama, we will see the outlines of an urban community lurking around the edges of the grim household of the Gao patriarch. The goal of this book is to shine a light on the city within which Ba Jin grew up. Doing so allows us to understand how he made selective use of his childhood experiences to craft a powerful indictment of the social order of the time. At the same time, by illuminating Chengdu, we can appreciate the challenges of Chinese urban life in the 1920s from alternative perspectives that are not reflected in the novels, the works of May Fourth writers, or the historical narrative they popularized.

Because *Turbulent Stream* continues to help form readers' understanding of pre-1949 China, it deserves periodic reevaluation. Access to more materials and new perspectives allows us to take a fresh look at the Gao family's world and make the works more comprehensible to new generations of readers. What made the younger people so dependent on the domineering grandfather? How did soldiers come to be fighting in the middle of a city? What job opportunities existed in the local economy of that era? Why would a young lady bring shame to her mother by cutting her hair? By examining the historical record from the formative years of Ba Jin's youth, the period in which the novels are set, this book sheds light on these and many more such questions about the social and political situation of Chengdu.

As suggested above, an equally important aspect of this study is to highlight the limitations of the trilogy as a history of China in the May Fourth era. The power of great novels to influence later generations' understanding of historical events should not be underestimated. How many people outside the United States first learned about the American Civil War via *Gone with the Wind*, either the novel or the film? For those who did, how could they avoid receiving an impression that, as an event, the war's major legacy was the tragic loss of an elite Southern way of life? Debates about the historical accuracy of fiction set in the United States are common: for instance, the bestseller *The Help* inspired many conversations among historians and others about how well and/or badly the novel and the film adapted from it depict the lives and perspectives of black female domestic workers in 1960s Mississippi.[7]

The *Turbulent Stream* trilogy has certainly shaped many people's understanding of Chinese culture and twentieth-century Chinese history, most particularly Chinese family dynamics and the history of the New Culture movement. In that sense, the trilogy has played a significant historical role of its own. This book takes a critical—though still appreciative—look at Ba Jin's interpretations of the society and world in which he grew up. In addition to offering a particularly bleak view of Chinese family life, Ba Jin's writing slights social history in favor of emotional impact. A telling contrast to Ba Jin's fiction is that of Li Jieren, who also published a trilogy of novels set in Chengdu in the early twentieth century. His work is much less well known inside and outside China than *Turbulent Stream*, largely because it lacks the emotional punch that Ba Jin gave his writing. But Li Jieren is a far better social historian; his depiction of life in early twentieth-century Chengdu is more realistic and conveys a better sense of why different characters act as they do, by showing how they are enmeshed in social networks and how their options are constrained by custom and formal law.[8]

Unlike Li Jieren, Ba Jin left it to others to fill in the historical background necessary for readers to understand the setting within which his characters lived. This book does so. We will have occasion to compare Li Jieren's perspective on the times with that of Ba Jin. However, most of the book is based on the extensive historical record that exists to document the social, cultural, and political history of early twentieth-century China, especially as it relates to life in Chengdu. As a cultural and political center in western China, Chengdu produced many prominent twentieth-century personalities in addition to Ba Jin, and this book sheds light on their formative experiences. The richness with which the city's history has been preserved in local archives and other records allows for the creation of an intimate portrait of a city that seemed far from the center of national politics of the day and yet clearly felt the forces of—and also contributed to—the turbulent stream of Chinese history.

The next section of this introductory chapter presents a biographical sketch of Ba Jin that provides context for the history of the publication and reception of the *Turbulent Stream* trilogy. The introduction concludes with an initial discussion of major topics that will be discussed throughout the book: patriarchy and the "Confucian" family, militarist politics and Chinese cities, the nature of the revolutions in cultural values and social structure during the early twentieth century, and their effects on Chinese families and on Chinese cities.

Ba Jin and Turbulent Stream

Ba Jin's life and his best-known works are intertwined with one another and with the history of China's tumultuous twentieth century: the story of the creation and reception of the *Turbulent Stream* trilogy shows both how historical events influenced the several incarnations of the trilogy and how the story became a central narrative of cultural change. Ba Jin often insisted that readers should not see his own life reflected in that of Gao Juehui, the protagonist of *Family*. Yet the outlines of their lives are similar in many ways.[9]

As a child, Ba Jin was called Li Yaotang; Ba Jin is the pen name he adopted as an adult. Like the fictional Gao Juehui, he grew up in a wealthy family in Chengdu, capital of Sichuan Province. Ba Jin's father, like Juehui's father, was the eldest son in his generation and an official in the final years of the Qing dynasty (1644–1911). His mother, like Juehui's mother, died young. Both real-life and fictional fathers died soon after remarrying. Their children grew up in extended families with stern and distant grandfathers, surrounded by many uncles, aunts, cousins, and servants. Ba Jin's eldest brother, like the fictional Gao Juexin, was expected to carry on the family line and take responsibility for the extended family, under the direction of his grandfather. Like Gao Juehui, Ba Jin left Chengdu and traveled to eastern China as a young man. In the final scene of the novel *Family*, Juehui makes a dramatic break with his family in the early 1920s as he boards a boat heading for Shanghai. In Ba Jin's case, the rupture with his family took a long time to gestate—it was announced publicly via the first installments of the novel itself, serialized in a newspaper in Shanghai in 1931–1932.

Why did Ba Jin decide to write a series of novels that condemned the values and behavior of the Chinese social elite—and which were immediately read as autobiographical, given the many parallels between his family and the fictional Gao family? He himself answered that question frequently over the years in the many essays he published about his fiction and career. In 1937, a letter he wrote to his cousin appeared in one of his essay collections. In it he explained: "I wrote the book so that other young people don't have to 'spend their days in the prison of family ritual' [a phrase he had used in his short story "Under the Street Gate"]. . . . Not for revenge but to attack the system."[10] He was disgusted by what he considered the elder generation's hypocritical appeals to Confucian morality to control people and suppress any protests against its own bad behavior. When *Family* became a bestseller, he wrote two sequels. The first, *Spring*, is very similar to *Family*, except this time a young female protagonist breaks out of the prison of familial convention and coercion. *Turbulent Stream* is above all an appeal to young people not to accept the lot in life that their elders arrange for them, but to struggle to achieve their dreams and create a more just social order.

Ba Jin also wrote these novels to express his love for the enthusiasm of youth, which he thought could easily be stifled in the context of a rigid family life but kindled in the company of like-minded friends. In a 1933 essay called "Friends," Ba Jin credited his own friends with helping him to go on living in moments of despair. Friends, he wrote, are more valuable than family. But brothers can be best friends. Ba Jin's relationships with his two elder brothers demonstrated this point, and his bonds to Li Yaolin (Figure I.1) and Li Yaomei (see Figure 7.3) provided the model for the close relationship of the three Gao brothers: Juehui, Juemin, and Juexin.[11]

Figure I.1 Ba Jin (*right*) with his second-eldest brother, Li Yaolin, in 1925. Courtesy of the Ba Jin Research Association.

The place of sisters and women in general in personal relationships seems to have been more of a puzzle to Ba Jin. As subsequent chapters discuss, for the most part he avoided the topic of sex or associated it with debauchery. In his fiction, the male-female relationship never quite attains the emotional comradely ideal that his young male characters sometimes enjoy. For men and women of the same generation there is sometimes the complicated—and often troublesome—element of romance in such relationships, with accompanying infatuation or jealousy or regret or even fear. Ba Jin himself married when he was thirty-nine; his twenty-three-year-old bride Chen Yunzhen (later called Xiao Shan) had written him a fan letter when she was a student, and the two grew to be close friends in the years before their marriage. Perhaps his relationship with Xiao Shan helped him compose the love story of Gao Juexin and the slave girl Cuihuan, which gives *Autumn* its rather implausible happy ending.

The need to struggle against the oppression and hypocrisy so common in family and social life, the promise of a more just future world, the beautiful enthusiasm of youth, the search for comradeship and love: these are Ba Jin's themes. As he wrote in his introduction to the trilogy, he aimed to help readers appreciate the turbulent stream of life flowing out of the dark mountainous wastes of Chinese society and creating a new path for itself.

Ba Jin's inspiration and models as a professional writer were numerous.[12] When he was a child, his father took him to performances of Chinese operas and discussed the stories with him. He was an avid reader from a very young age, memorizing poems and studying the Confucian classics as well as enjoying classical Chinese fiction. As a fifteen-year-old, he read an essay called *An Appeal to Youth* by the Russian philosopher Peter Kropotkin, which had been translated into Chinese and distributed by an anarchist society. By his own account, he was tremendously moved by Kropotkin's call for young people from wealthy families to sacrifice their personal comfort in order to help the poor and create a more just world. Ba Jin was introduced to revolutionary literature and learned about the work of social activists via the many periodicals founded in Beijing and Shanghai in the 1910s, including the famous *New Youth* magazine.[13] He even wrote a passionate letter to the editor of *New Youth*, Chen Duxiu, pledging to work to overthrow China's old culture and asking for advice on how best to do it.

Chen Duxiu did not write back; he probably received hundreds of such letters between 1919 and 1921. But Ba Jin found comrades locally. He joined an anarchist group called the Equity Society (Junshe) and served as editor and writer for its journal. Like more famous east-coast Chinese periodicals, the Equity Society's journal criticized militarists and argued for women's emancipation. After Ba Jin moved to eastern China in 1923, he continued to read and write essays calling for cultural and social change and explaining the principles of anarchism. He became active in Shanghai literary circles and also began to correspond with Emma Goldman, the American anarchist, then living in exile in Europe.

In 1927, Ba Jin traveled to France, where he attempted to educate himself about the international anarchist movement, working on a translation of Kropotkin's *Ethics: Origin and Development* as he studied French and published essays on Chinese politics. He also began his career as a fiction writer. His novella *Destruction*, set in Shanghai among labor organizers, appeared in print in Shanghai's most prestigious literary journal while he was still in France. As he was leaving France to return to China in 1928, he read Émile Zola's series of novels about the extended Rougon-Macquart family during

France's Second Empire. These helped inspire him to take his own family as the topic of his first full-length novel, which grew to become the *Turbulent Stream* trilogy. Back in Shanghai, he began work on the project. His eldest brother, Li Yaomei, encouraged him in letters from Chengdu, urging him to abandon all fear and reveal the ugly truths of life in families like theirs. The first segment of *Family* appeared in the literary supplement of Shanghai's *Eastern Times* (*Shibao*) in 1931. The novel was revised and published in book form in 1933.

Family was a hit. By 1936 the novel had been printed four times and tens of thousands of copies were in circulation. Ba Jin further revised the text, and a new edition appeared that year, again with strong sales that justified numerous reprintings. One more revised version (the tenth edition) was published in 1937 and again reprinted many times. By this time, Ba Jin was working on a sequel to *Family* to satisfy the demands of his huge audience of readers. The first chapters of *Spring* appeared as a serial in 1935–1936. When authorities shut down the newspaper it ran in, Ba Jin put his manuscript aside, then finished it just as the Japanese began their conquest of eastern China in autumn 1937. He stayed in Shanghai's French Concession as the Japanese took control of the Chinese sectors of Shanghai. After a trip to south and central China in 1938 and 1939, he returned to Shanghai to finish writing the final novel in *Turbulent Stream*, *Autumn*. Soon after it was published, the French government surrendered to the Nazis in Europe, and the new Vichy regime began collaborating with the Japanese in Asia. Ba Jin left Shanghai at this time and spent the remaining war years in southwestern China, which remained under the control of the Nationalist government of Chiang Kai-shek. In the wartime capital, Chongqing, Ba Jin's friend Cao Yu adapted *Family* for the stage and presented it to enthusiastic crowds.

At war's end, Ba Jin returned to Shanghai. When the victorious Communists entered that city in 1949, he stayed and worked with the new government as one of the founders of the Shanghai Writers' Federation. One of his assignments was to chronicle the heroism of the Chinese Volunteer Army fighting American troops in Korea. During the 1950s, he also substantially revised all his fiction, including *Turbulent Stream*, and the Foreign Languages Press published an English-language version of *Family*, translated by the Beijing-based American expatriate Sidney Shapiro. Whereas the revisions Ba Jin made to *Family* in the 1930s were primarily to correct typos and remove repetitive passages, the 1950s revisions were politically motivated—

passages critical of the apathy of the urban population were dropped, references to anarchism removed, and the student activists made more resolute than they were in the 1933 edition.[14] Ba Jin was also influenced in his revisions to some extent by the script of the play Cao Yu had based on *Family*.

In the 1950s, film versions of *Turbulent Stream* were produced in the PRC and in Hong Kong. The 1956 PRC film version of *Family* was particularly successful. It starred accomplished actor Sun Daolin as the conflicted eldest brother Gao Juexin. Zhang Ruifang played his wife, Ruijue, the character she had portrayed in Cao Yu's stage production in the 1940s.

By the early 1960s, the fame of *Turbulent Stream*, greatly assisted by the film versions, had made Ba Jin one of the most prominent writers in the PRC, even though he had published no new novels and very few stories in the 1950s. During the Cultural Revolution, beginning in 1966, the attacks on him were devastating.[15] His works were banned in China; he himself was forced to undergo "reeducation" and to criticize himself and his novels for their incorrect political standpoint. He admitted to having written under the influence of his "petty bourgeois" background, expressing far too much sympathy for young intellectuals and ignoring the working masses.

A veteran of the violent political struggles of the 1920s and 1930s, Ba Jin might have taken the Cultural Revolution strife more in stride, except that it claimed a victim in his immediate family. His wife and he had lived together happily in Shanghai in the 1950s, raising a daughter and a son. They all suffered with him when he came under attack. In 1972, his wife died of cancer, denied treatment that might have saved her life. In the early 1980s Ba Jin wrote a powerful essay about her death and his devastation, condemning the Cultural Revolution and the inhumanity it had caused. In the last decades of the twentieth century, cultural critics in China and abroad frequently repeated his call for the creation of a museum to document the crimes of the Cultural Revolution, commemorate its victims, and analyze its causes.[16]

The Cultural Revolution ended when Chairman Mao died in 1976; within a few years, Ba Jin's *Turbulent Stream* was once more popular reading among Chinese youth. The 1956 film *Family* was among the first pre-1966 films to reappear after Mao's death, and it was greeted more enthusiastically than it had been when it was first released.[17] In 1981 Ba Jin became chairman of the China Writers' Association, succeeding Mao Dun, one of very few twentieth-century novelists whose fame rivaled his own. A graphic novel version of the *Turbulent Stream* trilogy appeared in 1982, a television miniseries based on all three novels followed in 1988, and another miniseries, a 21-part television adaptation of *Family*, aired in 2007.

Beginning in the 1970s, Ba Jin was nominated repeatedly, but unsuccessfully, for the Nobel Prize in literature. He received the inaugural Fukuoka Asian Culture Prize in 1990. He played a significant role in establishing the National Museum of Modern Chinese Literature, which opened in Beijing in 1985, and donated his papers and other artifacts to the museum.[18] Afflicted by Parkinson's disease, he spent the last years of his life in a Shanghai hospital, dying at the age of one hundred in October 2005. His death brought renewed attention to his legacy. Much of his work is now available to download from the Internet. Chinese scholars have published dozens of books and hundreds of articles about his life and fiction. The Chinese Ministry of Education identified *Family* as one of the thirty most significant books for Chinese middle school students to read.[19] Ba Jin's *Turbulent Stream* flows on.

The Approach, Organization, and Major Themes of This Book

Turbulent Stream centers on the psychological drama of a large family being torn apart and collapsing during a time of political and cultural upheaval. This book, on the other hand, expands the frame of view and brings the novel's backdrop of political and cultural upheaval in a large inland Chinese city front and center. I use the historical record to sketch other stories playing out in the Chengdu of the May Fourth era. In the process, I highlight the significant issues with which different groups of people wrestled, in different ways, in early twentieth-century China. My approach is designed to cut across the social spectrum of a single city to embrace not only intellectuals and activists but also merchants, soldiers, slave girls, and others. As we shall see, most people in Ba Jin's hometown did not share his belief that the patriarchal family was at the root of their troubles—they did not make the connection he made between Confucian culture and oppression.

The dynamics of the May Fourth/New Culture era in China have been well examined by historians, but research has focused largely on eastern China, where New Culture theorists and publishers were concentrated and where the political institutions that emerged from the new social currents were headquartered. Also, because of the eventual triumph—after long years of struggle and war—of the Chinese Communists, who indeed remade Chinese society thoroughly after 1949, a major thrust of research has been to trace effects of May Fourth ideas and events on the course of the Chinese Revolution that ultimately led to the foundation of the PRC. And, understandably, scholarship places a strong emphasis on the experiences of intellectuals who articulated what was wrong with traditional Chinese culture and what form a new, stronger Chinese society might take.

My volume has a different set of goals: to reveal how this era was experienced in Chengdu, and to do so by plotting several transects through the historical record, so as to detect waves and ripples of social change not only in the thoughts and lives of the educated class but also in other subsets of the urban population: entrepreneurs, merchants, laborers, beggars and slaves, soldiers, students, and the small foreign community. By drawing on *Turbulent Stream* as an entree into an urban community at a pivotal moment in world history, this book explores China's early twentieth-century struggles over culture, social order, and national identity from a fresh perspective. By examining the lives and struggles of people in various social and economic groups, this book offers a broad vision of social dynamics in one particular provincial Chinese city, opening comparisons with both the coastal cities and the May Fourth/New Culture construction of "backward" China in that era. The changes, challenges, and choices Chengdu residents faced in the 1920s and 1930s were far more complex than a debate about intergenerational power within the family: my portrait of the city puts the attack on the "Confucian family" into perspective as just one of many issues contributing to social turbulence, one that was central to certain activists but not to many others in the community.

Each chapter of this book employs one or more of the characters in the trilogy as a starting point, exploring how Ba Jin's description of him, her, or them corresponds to what the historical record tells us about real people in similar social positions. Collectively, the chapters give substance to the layered cultural, political, and physical landscape of Chengdu, as an exemplar of inland, urban China during the May Fourth era.

We begin with the most unfortunate but most beloved character in *Family*—Mingfeng, the intelligent and affectionate slave girl who kills herself to avoid becoming an old man's concubine. Among the many questions addressed in the chapter inspired by Mingfeng, the most basic is "what was a slave girl?" Chapter One examines the legal and social status of slave girls and of concubines. Chapter Two takes the Gao patriarch as a starting point for examining the gradual disappearance of the cultural sphere to which he belonged. Ba Jin was highly critical of the beliefs and behavior of his elders and their friends in Chengdu's gentry community. This chapter aims to look beyond Ba Jin's depiction to see gentry culture from the perspective of people who admired and lived it. Chapter Three explores the nature of Chengdu's economy in the 1920s, showing how its families—including Ba Jin's—supported themselves. Industrialization was not widespread, and political uncertainty created economic instability. Still, the products of industrial manufacturing found ready consumers in Chengdu as elsewhere in China. Chapters Four and Five examine the lives of people whom Ba Jin passed over in his fiction, but who made up a significant part of the community: the urban poor, such as the beggars and street musicians who made a precarious living off of such people as the Gao family, and soldiers, most of them recruited from among landless farm families by militarists vying to control the cities. These chapters highlight the costs of the warfare and political turbulence of the time, and some of the reasons for it. Chapters Six and Seven focus on the people who constituted Ba Jin's generation and his original audience—young ladies and men who had the educational and financial resources to make choices about how to live their lives in a time of cultural upheaval.

Each chapter describes and discusses the types of historical sources—and specific documents—that can help us reach conclusions about the nature of 1920s Chengdu society and which may support or challenge Ba Jin's portrait of the city in *Turbulent Stream*. At times we will focus in on sections of the trilogy to take a critical look at Ba Jin's influential representation of patriarchy and the Confucian family, as well as his depiction of social classes, the restrictions on elite women, and the street fighting that terrorized him as a child. Several other themes are also central to this study. First is the physical transformation that Chinese cities were undergoing in the early decades of the twentieth century. Each chapter examines aspects of the infrastructure and architecture of Chengdu and discusses how changes in city form affected the lives of people there. Second is the nature of militarist politics in the 1910s through the 1930s, and how warfare and political insecurity affected the city and the families in it. And, third is the impact of the May Fourth movement itself in Chengdu. *Turbulent Stream* is a key text in that movement. How and to what extent were the new cultural values and social reform it called for welcomed in the city that inspired Ba Jin's famous work?

The case of Chengdu in the May Fourth era illustrates a common phenomenon at that time in world history. New media spread messages across the globe that radical change was possible and desirable. Some people inspired by that message tried to act on it, particularly educated youth, who may have had less at stake in the status quo or, at any rate, were more willing to trade it for a vision of progress. National weakness and local instability were widely recognized as serious problems in Chengdu, but there was disagreement about what caused them. Radicals like Ba Jin blamed the old order and its culture, while most of his elders and some of his contemporaries blamed the abandonment of the old moral code, among other factors. This war of words and ideas during the 1920s and 1930s tended to overshadow what was actually going on in communities such as Chengdu, where there was a diversity of thought and action. Between the extremes of radical antitraditionalism and reactionary condemnation of everything new, many people sought and found other paths. As we shall see over the course of this book, Chengdu was changing significantly in the years around 1920, although not in ways that satisfied the passionate author of *Turbulent Stream*.

CHAPTER ONE

Mingfeng

The Life of a Chinese Slave Girl

This chapter begins our exploration of 1920s Chengdu not with the most powerful but with the most vulnerable members of the traditional household structure, slave girls, whose status was surprisingly little affected by the tide of social change in the early twentieth century. Here we take a closer look at the realities behind the character at the emotional heart of *Family*—Mingfeng, the pure and gentle slave girl who has the misfortune to fall in love with the novel's hero, Gao Juehui. When the family patriarch gives her as a concubine to an old friend, Mingfeng first seeks Juehui's help and then, desperate, drowns herself in the lake in the family's compound.

Many readers have found the story of Mingfeng the most moving part of the trilogy. The playwright Cao Yu featured it prominently in his popular 1941 stage adaptation. Relations between poor slave girls and their masters form a recurrent theme in *Spring* and *Autumn*, the later novels of Ba Jin's trilogy. The unfortunate Wan'er, who is sent to the old man in Mingfeng's place, returns to visit her former home looking haggard and breaks down in tears when discussing her married life. Qian'er, a slave girl who serves Fourth Uncle Gao Ke'an's family, is mistreated by Ke'an's wife until she falls ill. Her mistress refuses to have a doctor called, and Qian'er dies. Xi'er, who serves Fifth Uncle Gao Keding's branch of the family, submits to—perhaps even encourages—the sexual advances of Keding, who later tries to make her his concubine. The young sons of two uncles harass and grope Chunlan, another poor girl serving the Gao family. And, at the end of the trilogy, Juehui's long-suffering eldest brother Juexin marries the loving and capable slave girl Cuihuan, with all expectation of living happily ever after.

Were there people like Mingfeng, Wan'er, Qian'er, Xi'er, Chunlan, and Cuihuan in China in the 1910s and 1920s? It is harder to answer this question for these characters than for any other major characters in the trilogy, for three main reasons. First, Ba Jin admitted that, although many of the upper-class characters in the book were modeled closely on members of his own family, he made up the characters of Mingfeng, Cuihuan, and the other girls. Second, although Ba Jin's family certainly acquired and made use of slave girls, his position in the social order was far removed from theirs, and it would have been difficult for him to gain a good understanding of their worldview and motivations. He did spend considerable time with male servants in the household, listening to their stories. He was also close to several older married female servants who took care of him and his siblings. But his memoirs tell us little about the unmarried girls who worked for his family, and, as some critics have pointed out, his depiction of slave girls in *Turbulent Stream* may owe more to his reading of the classic novel *Dream of the Red Chamber* than to his knowledge of real people in that position.[1] Finally, and most critically, evidence to document the lives of slave girls in China in the first decades of the twentieth century is hard to come by.

Despite the difficulty of understanding the world of slave girls, there are ways to approach the topic that can help us appreciate the environment in which they lived and to imagine how they might have responded to the difficulties they faced. Reconstructing the history of this social status helps us strive for a new perspective on city and family life—that of the many rural girls who were brought into the city and sold into gentry households. This chapter thus begins with a discussion of "slave girl" status in Chinese history and then turns to an overview of the ancient city of Chengdu and its hinterlands as a penniless girl might have experienced them. It then moves on to other subjects essential for understanding both slave girl life and Ba

Jin's depiction of Mingfeng, including religious beliefs and the status of concubines. It ends by addressing the question of why slave girls' status changed so little in the first half of the twentieth century, despite calls to abolish the status and despite Ba Jin's sympathetic portrayal of the slave girl Mingfeng.

What Was a "Slave Girl" in 1920s China?

Mingfeng does work for the Gao family that most of today's readers would recognize as that of a maid. Wealthy Chinese families in the early twentieth century, however, distinguished between types of female servants based more on their marital status than on the work they did. Married women who worked as maids (or cooks, nannies, or wet nurses) were paid wages and, although they often lived with their employers, were free to leave the residence when they were not on duty and to quit their jobs, if they wished. Unmarried girls, on the other hand, received no wages and were always on duty, in the sense that they were always subject to the commands of their masters and mistresses. The legal term for such girls was *binü*; in Ba Jin's novels, the narrator uses that term to refer to Mingfeng and the other girls. When characters in the novels refer to *binü*, they use the more colloquial and general term for young girls: *yatou* (丫頭), in which *tou* means "head" and the *ya* is a symbol representing the single braid unmarried girls wore down their backs. In his 1958 English translation of *Family*, Sidney Shapiro translated *binü* and *yatou* as "bondmaid." Many other translators, including the famous Shanghai writer Eileen Chang, prefer the term "slave girl," given the extreme dependency of such girls on their masters.[2] We shall follow their example.

The history of *binü* in China before the twentieth century is still not very well understood. Evidence on such fundamental questions as how many slave girls there were at various points in history, the nature of the market in slave girls and how it changed over time, the ways slave girls interacted with other servants and the surrounding community, and what masters and mistresses did with their slave girls when their years of bondage were over has not yet been systematically gathered and assessed. And it is quite possible that not enough evidence remains in the historical record to ever give us a very clear picture.

We do know that, from the perspective of legal formalities, sales of human beings were allowed by the legal codes of Chinese dynasties, including the

Qing (1644–1911), but with many restrictions. Basically, heads of households were only allowed to sell dependents to save themselves and other family members from starvation. From the perspective of legal practice, however, the restrictions of the codes seem not to have been enforced most of the time. Sales of male and female children commonly occurred at all periods of Qing rule, often accompanied by formal documents assigning all control over the children to the buyers. Officials seem rarely to have intervened in the process.

In the early Qing, some slaves were the children of hereditary slaves (*nubi*), thus the property of their masters from birth, and some were purchased via contracts. Hereditary slavery declined after the first decades of Qing rule, according to historians of the phenomenon.[3] The growing commercialization of the economy in the early eighteenth century made it relatively easy for adult slaves to run away and find ways to support themselves. In the 1730s, the Yongzheng emperor abolished the legal designation of "base people," which had kept many people confined to certain socioeconomic roles, including hereditary servants.[4] Almost all slave girls in the latter part of the dynasty thus were purchased as children via contracts.

The standard slave girl contract in the nineteenth and early twentieth centuries specified the number of years a girl would serve in her master's household, generally from the time she was handed over (usually when five to ten years old) to the time she was of most value for purposes of childbearing, at about twenty years old. A girl whose labor was sold by her parents—or who was kidnapped and sold by others—was given over to the absolute control of her master and mistress, who could sell her contract to someone else without notifying her birth family.

After a slave girl had served the agreed-upon number of years, most contracts assigned the master the responsibility to "choose a mate" (*zepei*) for the girl—often with no obligation to consult her birth family.[5] Thus, in *Family*, the Gao patriarch acted according to custom when he decided to send Mingfeng to another family as a concubine. That he chose to give her to an old man adds to the tragedy of the tale. Ba Jin may have been inspired by a real-life case when he wrote this part of the story. One of Chengdu's most prominent citizens in the early twentieth century, a distinguished scholar and teacher by the name of Liu Yubo, took a seventeen-year-old girl as a concubine when he was in his late fifties in 1926.[6] Apparently, this was seen as rather shocking at the time. But Liu Yubo nevertheless retained his reputation as a sagely man. We will examine his life and career further in Chapter Two.

In the discussion above, the term "birth family" is employed to highlight the fact that, according to social scientists who have studied them, slave girls were considered by officials and most Chinese people in general to be part of their masters' *jia* (family/household—the word Ba Jin chose as the title of the first volume in *Turbulent Stream*). Before and into the twentieth century, historian Johanna Ransmeier explains, Chinese families were defined partly in coresidential terms—no matter your blood relationship to the master, if you lived under his roof, you were part of his household and under his authority as a matter of law.[7] A slave girl was given a new name, either by the agent who arranged the contract or by her master and mistress when she entered their household. Mingfeng and the other slave girls in the Gao household would have had different given names before they were sold, and they clearly lack family names of their own. The older women servants, some of whom may have been slave girls before marriage, are called by their husbands' family names: Zhang Sao, for example, literally means older-sister-in-law from the Zhang family.

Being part of the master's household did not imply a warm emotional bond between master-mistress and slave girl. Anthropologist Hill Gates coined the term "patricorporations" for extended Chinese families since they were often managed like a business by the patriarch, who could sell off family assets, including women and children, in hard times or buy additional people to expand the household when economic conditions warranted.[8] On the other hand, many well-off families understood taking in children whose birth families could not support them to be a charitable act; the image of the patricorporation headed by a coldly calculating, profit-maximizing patriarch was not how most Chinese understood extended families in the nineteenth and early twentieth centuries.[9] Ba Jin himself recalled that his family had taken in a young girl named Cuifeng, the niece of an old male servant of theirs, as what was called a *jifan*, a charity case: she lodged (*ji*) at their house and worked as a maid in return for the rice (*fan*) it would cost to keep her alive. When the girl grew to marriageable age, one of Ba Jin's distant relatives wanted to make her his concubine, but she refused. In that case, because the family had not bought her via a contract, she was allowed to say no. Ba Jin commented that his family was amazed that she preferred to be a poor man's wife rather than a rich man's concubine, but they admired her for it too.[10]

Sometimes a young boy was purchased to provide a legal heir to a branch of a family, which was essential to maintaining control over land and other property and for carrying out the proper rituals for the family ancestors (on family rituals, see Chapter Two). This sort of adoption to establish an heir was supposed to be arranged among brothers or cousins of the same surname. For example, in *Autumn*, the Gao patriarch's concubine plans to adopt one of Gao Ke'an's sons formally as her grandson and heir. But sometimes there were not enough boys available within extended families. Although adoption of an heir through purchase of a boy from a different family was banned in the law codes, officials generally did not prevent it.[11]

Sometimes a girl was brought into a household as a child bride, engaged to a young boy in the family. Her birth family would be paid a bride price, and her future husband's family would feed her, train her, and put her to work. Frequently the work included serving as her husband's nanny, since child brides were often a few years older than their fiancés.[12]

There are no child brides in Ba Jin's *Turbulent Stream*; daughters in the Gao family and their circle are educated at home and married into their husband's households in their late teens. In the early twentieth century, and perhaps in previous centuries as well, the practice of taking in child brides seems to have been common in some rural areas; there is less evidence for it in the cities.[13] Each of the branches of the Gao family, however, does have a slave girl.

Why would families buy slave girls? Some historians argue that the growth of the commercial economy in the eighteenth and early nineteenth centuries led to a strong demand for status markers such as slave girls. Wealthy patriarchs could practice conspicuous consumption by buying slave girls as maids and companions for their wives, daughters, and concubines. Fang Bao, an eighteenth-century scholar-official who opposed the practice, blamed his own wife and other elite women for making slave girls a necessary fashion accessory.[14] Anthropologist James Watson gives another "demand side" argument for a growth in the slave girl phenomenon during the Qing: the growing popularity of bound feet: "People in many parts of South China made a direct connection between *mui-jai* servants [the southern Chinese colloquial term for *binü*] and mistresses with bound feet who, because of their stylish deformities, were not expected to perform domestic labor."[15] Some south China families bought slave girls for their daughters when they started binding their feet, according to Maria Jaschok.[16] Coming from poor families, slave girls were much less likely to have their feet bound and could carry heavy trays and stand in one place longer than their bound-footed mistresses (see Chapter Six for more discussion of footbinding).

All writers on the sale of women and children in Chinese history also stress the supply side. Steady population growth during the Qing—from an estimated one hundred million in the seventeenth century to close to four hundred million by 1900—helped create a large pool of people who could not be supported on the land, particularly during droughts, serious floods, and other crises. Rural unrest due to warfare, very common in the late nineteenth and early twentieth centuries, made kidnapping relatively easy.[17] Opium and gambling addiction sent more children to dealers.[18]

How opium addiction could lead to child selling is described in detail by Old Mrs. Ning, a woman who grew up poor in north China and was interviewed by social worker Ida Pruitt in Beijing in the 1930s. Mrs. Ning's addict husband sold one of their young daughters in 1889 for a small quantity of opium and sweet potatoes; when he came home, Mrs. Ning forced him to help her track down and recover the girl. But he later sold her again, this time to a childless woman who said she would treat the girl like a daughter. Since this woman promised to allow her to visit the girl, Mrs. Ning went along with the deal. The girl's new family moved out of town a few years later, and Mrs. Ning lost all contact with her daughter, but she was satisfied that at least she had seen they were treating the girl well.[19]

It is clear that by the early twentieth century many families across China purchased slave girls. A 1909 memorial on slavery, submitted by an official to the emperor, noted that slave girls could be found not only among the large clans of high officials but even in all middling and modest households.[20] In 1921 the British colonial government of Hong Kong—which ruled a population of 625,000 people, almost all immigrants from south China—required masters to register their slave girls. More than 8,600 were reported, most between the ages of ten and fourteen. It is likely many more went unreported.[21] James Watson concludes from field research in Hong Kong's New Territories that the sale of children was routine in the early twentieth century. "Members of the regional elite ... actively bought and sold children according to the needs of their domestic units."[22]

Unlike Mrs. Ning's daughter, most slave girls were probably unable to stay in touch with their birth families at all. Arrangements to buy and sell children were handled by agents, often women, many of whom also earned a modest livelihood as matrimonial matchmakers. Agents tried to keep the exchange simple by preventing contact between the two sides.[23] Many children were taken far from their homes to make the break even more irreversible. In the eighteenth century, government officials reported that there were long-distance networks of child-marketers, including kidnappers as well as entrepreneurs who made a profession out of buying and rearing children for sale as maids, actors, prostitutes, and concubines.[24] Johanna Ransmeier, who examined many legal cases involving slave girls in Beijing in the early twentieth century, points out that long-distance trade in girls was boosted by new transportation technologies such as steamships and trains.[25] A commentator writing in 1932 asserted that six cities on the east and south China coasts were headquarters for the "flourishing business" of female slave trafficking.[26] Some girls were even sent from south China to serve families in Singapore and other overseas Chinese communities.[27]

If, as seems likely, their birth families were unable to monitor how they were treated in their new households, what other protections existed for slave girls? The consensus among historians is that they depended almost entirely on the benevolence of their masters and mistresses and the extent to which masters valued the reputations of their households and/or feared supernatural retribution. Although Ba Jin only hints at this theme in *Turbulent Stream*, Mingfeng's suicide fits into a pattern that has been observed across the last several centuries of Chinese history, in which young women and other people driven to desperation kill themselves at the residences of their tormentors, hoping that their ghosts will take revenge. Belief in the power of vengeful ghosts was strong enough that a family that had experienced such a suicide might make offerings to the soul of the dead girl and hire monks to say prayers in order to appease her ghost and persuade it not to harm the family.[28] In the novel, Mingfeng does not have revenge against her masters in mind when she jumps, but Huang Ma, the older woman who takes care of Juemin and Juehui, tells them she is reluctant to stay at the Gao residence, since Mingfeng's death has made it "muddy water" (*hunshui*), a term meaning morally and socially degraded, hence vulnerable to tragedies that tend to visit those who do wrong.

Physical punishment of slave girls was part of their lives and could sometimes be taken to extremes. In the late nineteenth century, a Qing official by the name of Jiyun wrote about his visit to a friend's house, where he learned how the friend's wife trained newly bought slave girls: they were forced to kneel for a long time while receiving instructions and then beaten so they knew what it felt like to be punished. If they made noise, they were beaten harder.[29] The fact that Jiyun found this conduct notable indicates that it was unusual. Nevertheless, it was apparently acceptable among high society in Beijing.

Occasionally the murder of a slave girl resulted in a trial and/or formal punishment. Early in the nineteenth century, a high-ranking imperial official named Wang Geng was tried for beating his slave girl to death when she denied having stolen a snuff bottle. Found guilty, he was sentenced to one hundred lashes and three years of exile, which he avoided when his son paid 1,000 ounces of silver to commute the sentence.[30] Old Mrs. Ning told Ida Pruitt that she knew of a case in the eastern province of Shandong in the late nineteenth century where an official was removed from his position because he murdered a slave girl; his daughter had to settle for a less advantageous marriage than had been planned.[31]

Such punishment, if common, would certainly have been a deterrent to slave-girl abuse, but historians familiar with the Chinese legal records think it more likely that abuse frequently occurred and was rarely detected or prosecuted. Unless a family had fallen afoul of officials for some other reason, it was unlikely that their conduct relative to their slave girls would be questioned. So the fact that the tragic deaths of two slave girls (Mingfeng in *Family* and Qian'er in *Autumn*) lead to no official investigation of the Gao family is not at all implausible. Still, rumors about their heartless treatment of slave girls would have circulated within their community, spread by the older married servants who went in and out of the family compound relatively freely to do the shopping and other errands and to visit their own families. As we shall see in Chapters Two and Six, family reputation mattered a great deal in the community within which *Turbulent Stream* is set.

Sexual exploitation of slave girls—such as the seduction of Xi'er by Gao Keding and the abuse of Chunlan by the young Gao cousins in Ba Jin's novels—was probably common, and perhaps even expected. In his study of how sexual offences were defined and dealt with in the Qing legal system, historian Matthew Sommer notes that, before the Qing, a master was not prevented by law or custom from having sex with a slave girl. In the Qing, however,

> the legal standing of female domestic slaves . . . is somewhat ambiguous. Certainly, they continued to be sexually available to their masters; however, in Qing law, a *bi* who had been sexually intimate with her master was no

longer considered an ordinary slave but rather a sort of secondary spouse, regardless of whether he himself recognized her as such.[32]

Anthropologist Maria Jaschok's account of Hong Kong slave girl life, which she based on interviews with many former slave girls, describes one who was purchased by an infertile wife and lived out most of her life as a servant (until she ran away), despite having given birth to six children by the master. Her children were taught to consider the master's wife as their mother.[33] Janet Lim, a woman from south China who was sold as a girl in the early 1930s to a Chinese family in Singapore, writes that her elderly master believed he could prolong his life by having sex with young virgins, and his second wife, herself a former servant, bought a series of slave girls for this purpose.[34]

In Chengdu, Ba Jin's hometown, slave girls were vulnerable as well. According to Liu Bogu, a member of the family that included the prominent scholar Liu Yubo mentioned above, the lineage rules established by the Liu patriarchs to guide the conduct of family members prohibited the purchase of slave girls, precisely because they were recognized as a strong sexual temptation for the men in the family. He insisted that the only female servants in the Liu family in the nineteenth and early twentieth centuries were older married women.[35] As we know from Liu Yubo's case, however, Liu men were able to bring concubines into the household.

The real-life Chengdu writer and legal scholar Wu Yu makes a brief appearance in Ba Jin's *Family*, when the boys in the younger generation discover that Wu Yu has been hired to teach Chinese literature at their school.[36] Wu Yu, whose essays attacking the values and rituals of the "Confucian family system" were influential during the New Culture movement, was Ba Jin's teacher in the early 1920s, and Wu Yu's mother came from the same Liu family as Liu Yubo. Wu Yu kept a detailed diary that is a wonderful source of information on life in Chengdu in the early twentieth century. Despite his support for the New Culture movement and family reform, Wu Yu himself was "addicted to buying people," according to cultural critic Ran Yunfei: he bought slave girls and concubines throughout his adult life.[37] And, like the fictional Gao patriarch, he considered it his responsibility and prerogative to rename his slave girls and then find appropriate husbands for them when they got older. Wu Yu relates in his diary for January 1920 that he had to fire his servant Old Peng for improper conduct. According to one of his neighbors, Old Peng's wife had instructed her husband to bring Wu Yu's slave girl, Meixi, over to their house so she could talk with the girl about her marriage prospects. Wu Yu commented: "Without consulting the head of the household [himself], Old Peng and his wife privately arranged for Meixi to go outside and discuss matrimony. This clearly is similar to enticement [*gouyin*; a crime in the legal code], and the evil consequences could be grave. I consider it totally inappropriate."[38] Wu Yu put himself in the role of Meixi's protector, suggesting that Mrs. Peng might have led the girl astray, but it is clear that he also claimed complete authority over her future. It is this aspect of the life of a *binü*, the reality that even her marriage is controlled by a person who has paid money for her, that makes "slave girl" seem an appropriate translation of the term. Marriages were arranged for sons and daughters, as well, but the nature of the emotional bonds between them and their parents and the role of their marriages in maintaining the status of their families meant that marriages of daughters and sons were far less likely to be for purely financial benefit or, as with Mingfeng in *Family*, the personal convenience of the patriarch.

A Slave Girl Contract from Chengdu, 1919

As is apparent from the story of Wu Yu's Meixi, slave girls were being bought and sold, put to work, and married off by their masters in Ba Jin's community in the early 1920s. The local archives include copies of slave girl contracts. The following is the text of one of these, translated into English:

> Report Form
> To report the following matter for the record: A resident of CHENGDU county, YONGXING street, named LI XINGSHUN, is willing to contract his daughter BY BIRTH by the name of DONGMEI who at present is TWELVE years old to serve CHENG FANXING as a maid for EIGHT years only. When the time limit has been reached, then CHENG FANXING will choose a mate for her. Agreement has been reached that the price of the contract will be FOURTEEN MEXICAN silver dollars. In addition to ordering the employment agent MRS. LI, NÉE WANG and the guarantor LIAO WENXING to affix their seals to show their responsibility in this matter, charging the officially approved fee, and issuing a permit, I submit this report to your esteemed office for its inspection.
> West Main Office of the Provincial Police
> TWENTY-FIRST day, SIXTH month, EIGHTH year of the Republic of China
> WEST MAIN BRANCH office BRANCH OFFICIAL LIN YUNCAO

This document (Figure 1.1) is similar to examples of slave girl contracts that have been preserved from earlier times and from other places in China. It lists the name of the person offering the girl, the name of the person buying her service, her own name, the name of the go-between or agent, and the name of a "guarantor," who attests to the good reputation of the agent. It gives the age of the girl and how long she is contracted to serve in her master's household. It states how much money is changing hands. And it specifies that, after Dongmei's eight years of service are up, her master will arrange a marriage for her. What sort of marriage is not specified—the expression "choose a mate" allows for either a husband-wife or a master-concubine relationship. It would not allow for her to be sold into a brothel, although that certainly happened to some unfortunate slave girls.

This contract is from the eighth year of the Republic of China—1919. Ba Jin was fifteen years old that year, and the stories in *Turbulent Stream* are set just a few years later. Some parts of this document show certain changes in slave girl contracts since the fall of the Qing dynasty in 1911. First, unlike earlier such contracts, it is a printed form, with spaces to write in the pertinent information (the handwritten information on this contract is in italicized capital letters in the translation above). This type of form came into being after the creation of a Western-style police force in the first decade of the twentieth century. Police stations were set up around the city and police were charged with investigating and maintaining records on all households in their districts.[39] Before the establishment of the new professional police, hand-copied contracts for slave girls were supposed to be registered at the local county magistrate's office. As with marriage agreements and other family matters, though, many people chose to avoid dealing with officialdom. Most kept their written contracts, if they had them, at home, to be brought out in case of a legal dispute. The new police, however, tried to insist on registration of all changes within a household (birth, deaths, marriages, adoptions, etc.). One reason for this was that registration fees were an important source of police income. Also, police training stressed the need to know who belonged where in the community, and who did not belong at all, to more easily identify thieves and kidnappers and other miscreants.

The requirement to list the agent and guarantor and the address of the family providing the girl points to concern over the possibility that the slave girl had been kidnapped. This was not a new feature of slave girl contracts. One might hypothesize, though, that the fact that the new police took a

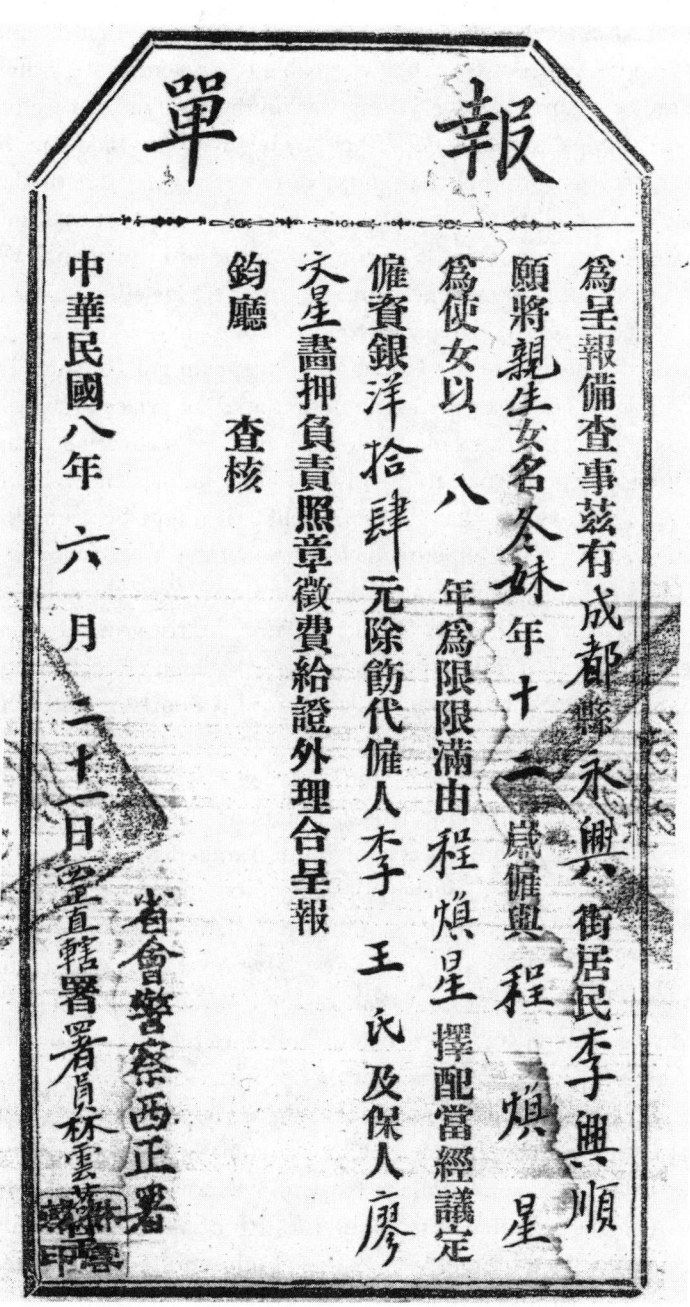

Figure 1.1 Slave girl contract dated June 21, 1919. Chengdu Municipal Archives, fond 93, file 964.

closer interest in slave girl registration beginning in the first decade of the twentieth century meant that they were able to prevent more kidnappings. Did the police ensure that everything was on the level in the case of Dongmei? Was Li Xingshun really her father "by birth"? (This blank on the form, by the way, seems to imply that adoptive fathers or masters of slave girls could also legally sell the labor of their young girls.) Did officer Lin Yuncao investigate the trustworthiness of the guarantor and the agent? We don't know, but the historical evidence does not offer strong support for the idea that the police were effective protectors of young girls.

Reports of the work of the Chengdu police from fall 1903 until the end of the dynasty in late 1911 are available in the Qing palace archives in Beijing.[40] Police officers earned many more merits for "recovering escaped servants" and apprentices than they did for foiling kidnappings. Though not conclusive, this suggests that the police (like, it might be argued, professional police everywhere) spent much of their time protecting the "property" of the better-off members of the community. After the collapse of the Qing dynasty, as we will see in Chapter Five, militarist governors came and went frequently, making funding the police a challenge. Poorly funded professional police forces are often corruptible, and a corrupt system tends to favor powerful insiders. Political instability in Chinese cities in the 1910s and 1920s fostered the growth of gangs, which often supported themselves via the opium trade, gambling dens, brothels, and kidnapping.[41] Thus, it is quite possible that Dongmei was a victim of trafficking.

In such an atmosphere, perhaps it is also not a surprise that eight years of a girl's life could be bought for fourteen dollars. "Mexican silver dollar" is the English translation of the Chinese *yang* (overseas) *yuan* (round coin or dollar)—a type of silver coin that was first brought to China as a result of the Manila galleon trade between the silver-rich Spanish colonies of the New World and Asian markets. Various provinces under the Qing began minting similar coins in the 1890s, and the early governments of the Republic of China did too, but these Chinese coins in the Spanish style were still often called "overseas" dollars. In 1919, when Dongmei became a slave girl, fourteen silver dollars was about a fourth of Wu Yu's monthly salary for teaching Chinese literature at Ba Jin's high school; he budgeted living expenses for his family of ten to fifteen people at 12 dollars a month.[42] As another comparison, in *Turbulent Stream*, Gao Juexin's monthly salary as a manager of a commercial arcade in the early 1920s (see Chapter Three) is

24 silver dollars. In an essay about *Family*, Ba Jin explained that this really was the amount that his eldest brother earned at that job and said it was considered a very modest salary. Still, Juexin would have been able to buy two new slave girls to replace Mingfeng and Wan'er for little more than a month's salary.

Given the evidence, we can be confident that there were indeed many people in Chengdu in the early 1920s who occupied the status held by Mingfeng, Cuihuan, and other slave girls in Ba Jin's fiction. Understanding how they looked at the world, though, is a much greater, indeed an insurmountable, challenge, given the lack of direct evidence. But we might begin to get a sense of a slave girl's perspective by imagining how such a girl would have experienced life in the city.

The City from Mingfeng's Perspective

In the opening pages of *Family*, the two brothers Gao Juemin and Gao Juehui walk through the snow-swept streets of their hometown and through the large gate that leads to their family's compound.[43] On each side of the gate stands a stone lion. Lacquered wooden boards attached to the walls behind the lions read "Benevolent rulers, happy family; long life, good harvests." Nothing is visible of the dwelling place within, just a dark tunnel. Ba Jin sets the scene for the trilogy by emphasizing how shut off the inner life of the Gao household is from the world around it. The signs advertise a happy family, but what—the reader wonders—really goes on inside?

Fifteen-year-old Mingfeng, who meets the two brothers on the other side of the gate on that snowy night, entered it herself, we are told in *Family*'s chapter 4, as a child of nine or ten, after her mother died and her father was unable to care for her.[44] Most likely a slave girl like her would have come from a village somewhere in Sichuan Province (Map 1.1). In the early 1910s, Sichuan had a population of some forty million. About 350,000 of them lived inside the high walls of the provincial capital, Chengdu. About the same number lived in Chongqing, the great Yangzi River port city a ten-day walk south and east of Chengdu. One hundred and forty or so other walled cities—county seats—were scattered around the province, as well as many unwalled market towns. But the majority of the population lived in villages or isolated farmhouses. Farmers took their rice, vegetables, pigs and

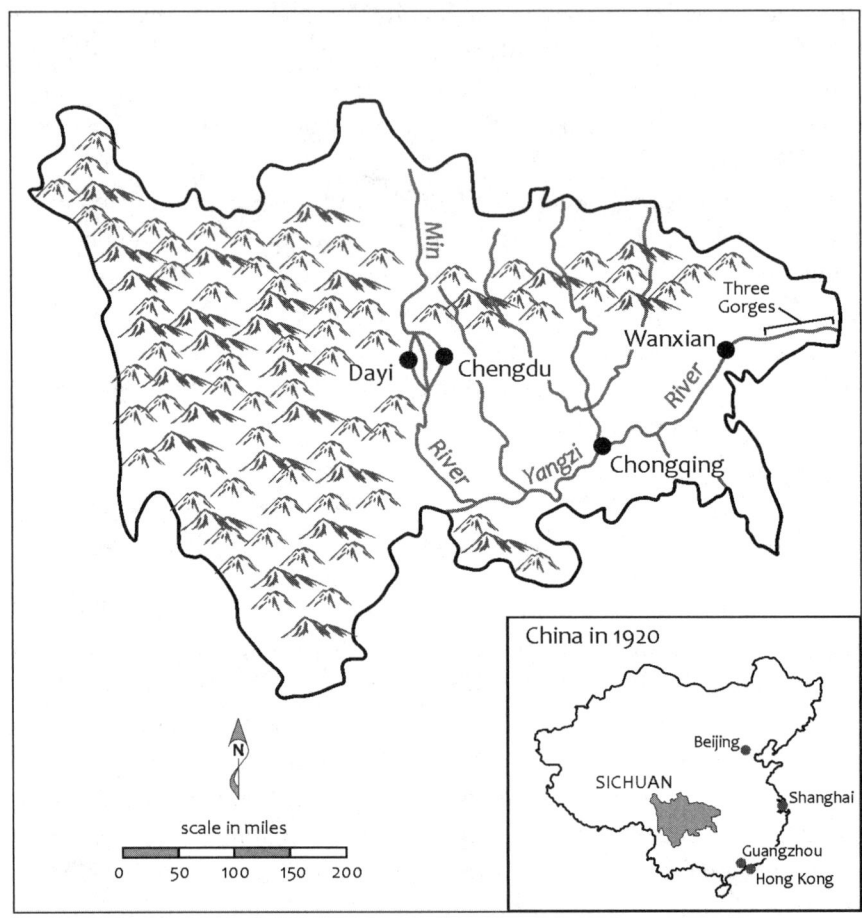

Map 1.1 Sichuan Province, circa 1919
Cartography: Debbie Newell.

chickens, raw silk, and handicrafts to the local market town to sell, buying there the household items and farm tools they couldn't make themselves. Itinerant merchants—traveling salesmen and peddlers—also connected the farmers to the markets. Among these were matchmakers, who kept an eye out for families in need of a bride or willing to send a child into service in some other household.

Political events rocking China in the late nineteenth and early twentieth centuries brought unrest to Sichuan's rural areas. The Taiping War (1850–1864) disrupted trade routes, and the opening of the port of Chongqing to foreigners—British, American, Japanese—in 1891 increased markets for Sichuan products like pig bristles and tung oil. The opening of the port also brought American and European Christian missionaries into Sichuan, making the culturally conservative elite uneasy. A 1904 British expedition from India to Tibet, just to the west of Sichuan, promoted a growing sense that the Qing government was incompetent. At about the same time, the government tried to follow the Meiji Japanese example for building national power—promoting industry and setting up new police, a new army, and a new school system. These new, mostly urban institutions needed funding, so farmers were subjected to new taxes on pork, alcohol, and many other products. Outraged farmers gathered in county seats to protest, sometimes violently.

Rural uprisings across Sichuan helped overthrow the Qing dynasty in 1911, but the republican government that replaced it failed to provide political stability or rural security. Chengdu itself managed to avoid much of the strife, but some parts of Sichuan were cut off from markets and ravaged by fighting between the armies of rival militarists, who plundered stores of food, conscripted soldiers and laborers, and raped women. This is the turbulent background from which many slave girls arrived in Chengdu in the 1910s. Most likely they would have been brought by an agent in a cart or on foot along the roads that led to the four great gates of the walled city (Map 1.2). Figure 1.2 shows the city wall (see Figure 4.1 for an image of one of the city gates). If they arrived after the gates had been closed in the evening, they could stay the night in one of the cheap inns outside the walls.

Families that wished to buy a slave girl in Chengdu in the early twentieth century sent a trusted servant to an area near the South Gate. Police reports indicate that this was where "employment agents" (*daiguren hu*) congregated, usually in teahouses. These agents were more popularly known as "people sellers" (*ren fanzi*).[45] The police census of 1909 lists forty-seven of them, some of whom may have specialized in supplying male laborers such as porters or sedan-chair bearers. The servant might choose among the available girls or perhaps accompany the agent back to the family's residence with several girls for the master or mistress to inspect. Wu Yu dealt directly with several agents, whom he received in his house in the southwestern part of the city.[46]

After being separated from her family, transported to the big city, cleaned up and given basic obedience training by an agent, and inspected by her future master's household manager, a young girl would be taken to her prospective master's home. In Ba Jin's youth, the transportation options within

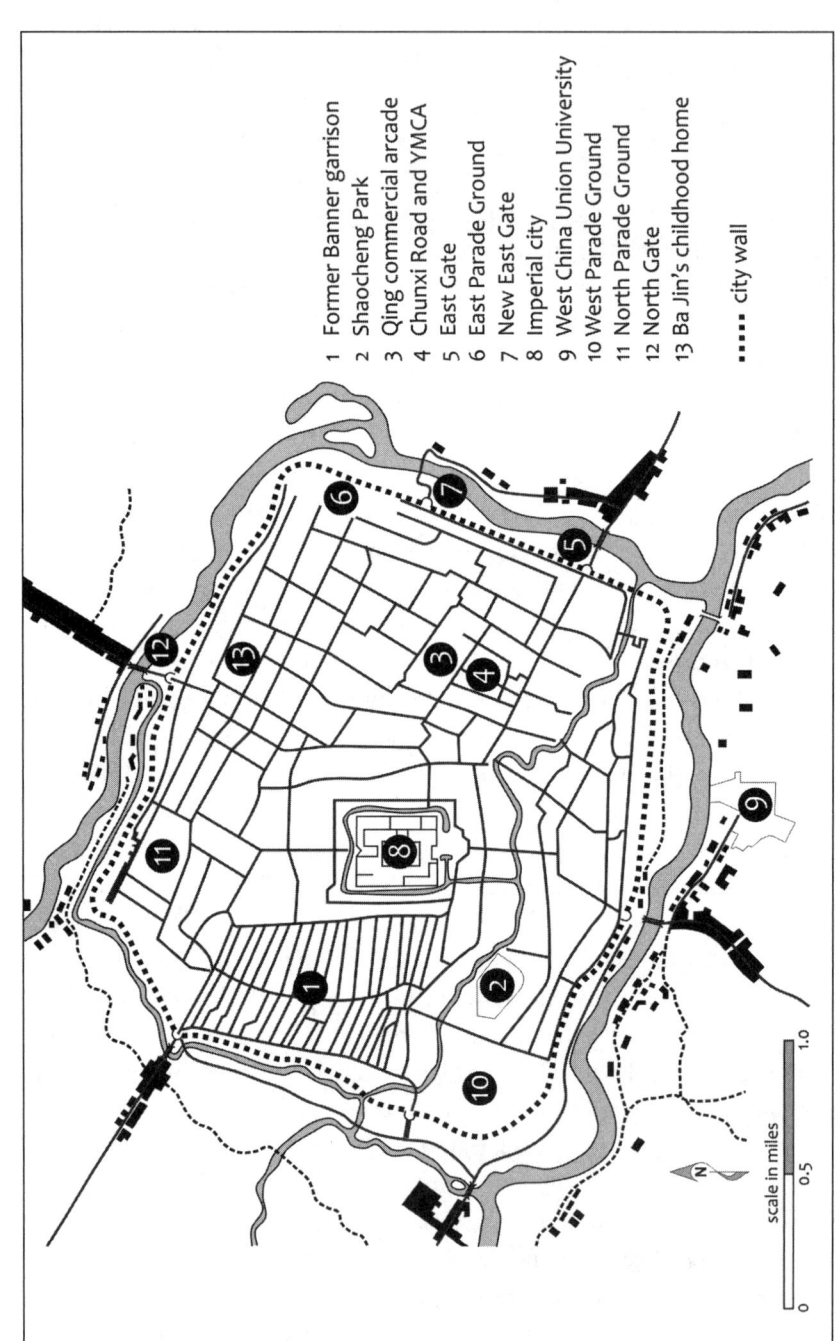

Map 1.2 Chengdu, circa 1919
Cartography: Debbie Newell.

Figure 1.2 Chengdu's southern wall, 1910s or early 1920s. Courtesy of the Willmott family.

the walls of Chengdu were limited. A very few people rode horses, and many more were carried in palanquins, also known as sedan chairs—boxes made of lacquered wood with a seat inside. Poles attached to the box allowed servants to carry it around the city (there were long-distance sedan chairs, as well, to travel from the city to a country residence or another city). Typically, two men carried a sedan chair, one in front and one behind (see Figure 1.2). Officials, though, might have six or more carriers for their sedan chairs, to make a proper show. Other servants walked in front to clear the way, carrying signs with the title of their master and commands to the multitude to be quiet and respectful. Hundreds of sedan chairs were available for rent in the city. Wealthy families generally had several of their own private chairs carried by their own servants, which they preferred for reasons of cleanliness and prestige. Less well-off families might have their own sedan chairs but hire porters whenever they needed to go somewhere.

Rickshaws were invented in Japan in the 1870s and quickly afterward brought to cities on China's east coast. In 1909 a city merchant tried to introduce them to Chengdu, but most of the streets were too narrow, uneven, and crowded to accommodate wheeled vehicles. Also, some Chengdu residents opposed rickshaws because they only required half the labor of a sedan chair and threatened to throw carriers out of work. Others saw them as a foreign object and opposed them for that reason. It was not until Chengdu experienced a road-widening campaign in 1924 that they took hold there; their use continued through the 1940s, even after automobiles had arrived in the city.

But rickshaws, like sedan chairs, were expensive. Most people in the Chengdu of Ba Jin's youth walked. The area within the walls of the city was not huge. From the "human market" near the South Gate to the northeast part of town where Ba Jin grew up was about a mile and a half. A slave girl being led along that route would have first walked through streets full of people and shops; the areas inside the South and East Gates were particularly congested. Further north, just south of Great East Street, which led from the center of town to the East Gate, she might have seen the walls surrounding the offices of the Sichuan provincial government guarded by soldiers. North of Great East Street, part of the old parade grounds for Qing military units stationed in the city had been sold to the Young Men's Christian Association (YMCA) right after the 1911 Revolution. Young men like Ba Jin went there to watch movies and practice their English, and even a slave girl, who would not have been allowed to visit it, would probably have recognized that its two-story dark brick building was very unlike the typical low-rise wood constructions lining the commercial streets in Chengdu. Just north of the YMCA was the grand commercial arcade built in 1908, during the last years of the Qing. This is where Ba Jin's eldest brother (and his fictional counterpart Gao Juexin) worked, and it is discussed in Chapter Three. Northeast of the arcade lay the part of the city where Ba Jin grew up and which he described at the beginning of *Family*: quiet streets paved with stone and lined on each side with the tall gates of the well-off families who lived within. After her escort had called out to the gateman to open the gate, the slave girl would have been led into the compound, no doubt exhausted from the long walk and new sights and completely terrified, wondering what lay ahead for her.

The Duties of Slave Girls and Other Servants

Fiction such as *Turbulent Stream* is the richest source of information on the roles servants played within Chinese households in the time of Ba Jin's youth, but there are other sources, as well. As noted above, Americans and other foreigners began to make their way to Sichuan after 1891 as Christian missionaries, and they found it necessary to set up households that followed local customs, at least to some extent. Judging from their own writings, they did not employ slave girls, but some missionary writers were interested in the phenomenon, seeing the emancipation of slave girls as part of their calling.[47] Missionary families did hire other servants, including gatemen, sedan-chair bearers, cooks, laundresses, and men who did miscellaneous work and helped the master and mistress manage the other servants. These last they called, in the colonial style, "boys" regardless of their age.

In Chinese households, the generic Chinese term for servant, *puren*, was supplemented with other colloquial expressions. As noted above, the common term for slave girls like Mingfeng was *yatou*, a visual reference to their braided hairstyle. Older women were usually called by their surnames and *sao* (elder sister-in-law), if not *ma* or *niang*, both of which mean "mother." A wet nurse was a *naima*—milk mother. Male servants, depending on their age and rank among the servants, might be referred to by their surnames and either the prefix "young" (*xiao*) or "old" (*lao*), depending on seniority. Wu Yu's servant, Lao Peng, had probably been with the family a long time before being fired for involving himself improperly in Meixi's matrimonial affairs.

Grace Service, the wife of Robert Service, the founder in 1909 of the Chengdu YMCA, wrote quite a bit about hiring and firing Chinese servants in her memoirs. For her family of two adults and three children, she hired a "boy," who managed the household and did much of the cooking from 1907 to 1920 and then started his own business, with support from the Service family. She also had a "table-boy" to help the cook, one or two amahs (nannies) to look after the children, and a gardener. Her husband employed a "horse coolie" to take care of the horse he needed to visit friends in outlying towns. They also hired a gateman, who was stationed at the main entrance of their modified Chinese residence near the Huayang County Confucius Temple in the southwest part of the walled city.[48]

The Services had considerable difficulty learning the culture of Chinese servants and trying to get them to meet the expectations of American employers, particularly in regard to hygiene. Grace Service hosted Chinese ladies in her home and visited their homes on occasion. Here is her assessment of the differences in household management:

> Most of them [her Chinese visitors] . . . thought we wasted too much time trying to be clean; clean kitchens and clean floors were no necessity to them. . . . Their kitchens were in what we would call sheds. Most of their floors were dingy brick or grimy wood. Frequent expectoration, together

with the habit of allowing babies to urinate freely on the floor anywhere and everywhere, made for unhygienic conditions and offensive odors. Cobwebs never seem to bother Chinese.

But, she notes, their servants did a great job polishing the surfaces of furniture and picture frames.[49] It would be interesting to learn how Mrs. Service's Chinese visitors compared their homes to hers, but here we run into another hole in the historical record. Old Mrs. Ning did work as a servant for missionaries in eastern China, however, and at times she was frustrated at their uncivilized ways. She was most angry at being asked to wash the bloody underclothes of her menstruating mistress, Mrs. Burns; Chinese ladies took care of that disagreeable task, she observed, and so did not force their servants to contaminate themselves.[50]

When they visited the Service household, according to Grace, her Chinese friends sometimes brought their grown daughters and children with them, along with their amahs—their older married female servants. These ladies would all have traveled in sedan chairs, so as not to be seen by the public. They would most likely not have brought their slave girls, who attended to the needs of the family at home. Like the "table-boy," slave girls did miscellaneous jobs, serving at table, delivering tea and other necessities to sitting rooms, helping their mistresses with their makeup and possibly giving them massages. Judging from all fictional accounts, including those of Chengdu writers Ba Jin and Li Jieren, slave girls were always at the beck-and-call of their mistresses and had very little time to themselves.[51] Most of them probably never left the family residence until their years of service were at an end and they went out to become wives or concubines. The ones who became wives of poor men might return to work for a salary in their former masters' households as amahs or wet nurses, or even in essentially the same role they had had previously (as the young, widowed Xi'er does in *Turbulent Stream*).

In one scene of *Family*, Ba Jin depicts Mingfeng in a cramped but drafty room near the rear of the Gao residence, worrying about her future while the older female servant with whom she shares the tiny sleeping space snores like a grunting pig. The disadvantages to being a live-in servant are clear—very little control over one's time and living space. On the other hand, Old Mrs. Ning's memoirs give us some idea of the possible advantages—a measure of security. When Mrs. Ning worked for American and British missionaries, she lived in a room she rented in another part of town and had to pay for her own food. She was an employee instead of a member of a household and was kept busy all the time while on duty. When she worked for a Chinese family, she was able to save more of her wages and tips since her room and board were provided, she had more leisure during the day, and some of her Chinese mistresses allowed her to keep her young daughter with her.[52]

Slave Girls and Concubines

If Mingfeng, the helpless victim of patriarchy, is the most beloved character in *Family*, among the most despised is the Gao patriarch's concubine, called by Juexin and his cousins "Chen Yitai," which means something like "great-aunt from the Chen family." Slave girls and concubines had a lot in common within Chinese households in the early twentieth century.[53] Although, according to Gao family gossip, grandfather's Miss Chen had been a courtesan or prostitute before she entered the family, slave girls also become concubines in the story. Mingfeng avoids that fate by killing herself, but Wan'er is forced to take her place. Xi'er aims to become Keding's concubine in *Spring*, and only the fact that the household is in mourning for the patriarch delays her marriage.

The term "concubine" entered the English language, via Latin, as a way to refer to a "secondary wife" in societies where polygamy was legal, such as among the ancient Hebrews and Romans. It is used as a translation for the Chinese term *qie*, which indicates a legally married woman whose status is lower than a *qi* (translated as "wife"). In the Qing legal code, a man could only have one wife (*qi*) at a time, but as many concubines (*qie*) as he wanted and could acquire. In general, all his children would pay respects to his wife as their mother, regardless of whether she or a concubine had given birth to them. All the boys had the right to inherit a share of the family wealth, all the girls to receive marriage settlements. Concubines were considered necessary by many Chinese families to provide male heirs if a wife did not. That is why Wu Yu, Ba Jin's teacher, purchased concubines—his wife gave birth to eight daughters and only one son, who died in infancy.

Sometimes the wife, particularly if she was the senior woman in a household (if her mother-in-law had died), chose a concubine for her husband in order to get a son. Wu Yu's wife, for example, a well-educated woman whom he adored, played a central role in buying and educating his concubines before she died in 1917. Well-off men also acquired concubines themselves as what we might today call trophy wives and sexual companions. Their first marriages, like Gao Juexin's, had usually been arranged by their parents and grandparents. The legality and social acceptability of concubines meant that, if they had the necessary resources, men could choose their own. As may be imagined, this could easily become a source of tension within the household. In 1912, an enraged elderly mother dragged her son into a police station in Chengdu and complained to the police official that her son had married a concubine who was wasting the family money and being rude to her. According to the newspaper report of this incident, the police officer ordered the man to be more respectful to his mother and get rid of the concubine.[54] As a young man, Wu Yu criticized his own father for squandering family resources on a profligate concubine. In the Hong Kong region, Maria Jaschok interviewed the daughter of a woman she calls Moot Xiao-li, who had been a concubine in the early twentieth century. Moot Xiao-li's daughter described how she was picked on and ostracized by her father's other children, who resented his infatuation with her mother. In conversation with Jaschok, she endorsed the depiction of life within an extended family in *Turbulent Stream*: "It is difficult in large Chinese families. Ba Jin told it so well. Much quarrel and strife goes on all the time."[55]

Ba Jin depicts the patriarch's concubine, Miss Chen, as a vain, vindictive, and vulgar woman. The slave girl Xi'er, who is angling to become a Gao family concubine, also is clearly manipulative, devious, and very unlike the pure, angelic Mingfeng. *Turbulent Stream* was written before the advent of feminist theory, which has led to critical analysis of the "angel/whore" dichotomy in female literary characters that may be found to some extent in his fiction.[56] Clearly Mingfeng, Xi'er, and Miss Chen are rather one-dimensional characters. But when judging the plausibility of Ba Jin's account, we must keep in mind that both slave girls and concubines were extremely dependent on other people in the family, far more so than wives and sons and even other sorts of servants, who could leave the family and seek other employment. In the case of Miss Chen, her future depends on maintaining respect for the patriarch and his family rules, even after his death.

Maria Jaschok's interviews with former slave girls and concubines in Hong Kong led her to argue that their sense of self had been formed in an environment that made it impossible for them to imagine themselves as the equals of their masters. That did not make them passive, necessarily, but limited their ambitions and produced certain patterns of behavior. Some tried to secure their places in their masters' families and hearts by dedicated and selfless service. Some used sex to attach themselves to powerful men. Their socialization into this system of gendered oppression was so complete, Jaschok writes, that they could not challenge it themselves and often their "scheming" behavior lost them the support of people who might otherwise have sympathized with them.

No one has carried out studies of concubines and slave girls in other parts of China that are comparable to Jaschok's in Hong Kong. Early twentieth-century writers describing slave girls, however, do tend to depict their psychological state in similar ways: either sweet and vulnerable or vulgar and self-serving. The female soldier and war reporter Xie Bingying recalls feeling great pity for a slave girl serving in the home of a Hunan general in 1921 and published a poem about her in the newspaper *Dagongbao*. On the other hand, when writing about how she herself hired a woman in Beijing in 1930 to look after her daughter, Xie is less sympathetic: "Like most servants, she looked out for herself and would rather work like a horse or a buffalo for a powerful, wealthy family than to work for an average person who respected her and treated her as an equal."[57]

Hu Lanqi, one of Xie's classmates at the Nationalist's Central Military Academy in Wuhan in 1927, wrote in her own memoir that the Sichuan militarist Yang Sen hired her in the early 1920s to teach two of his concubines in Chengdu to read, an unusual step for the time, since very few concubines received any formal education (unless they had been brought up for a career as a courtesan). Yang Sen was rumored to have had more than a dozen concubines and actually sent one to study at Radcliffe College in the United States. The two whom Hu Lanqi taught had originally entered his household as slave girls and continued to be called by the names they were given when purchased—Jiagui ("Our family's cassia") and Jiafeng ("Our family's phoenix"). In a memoir written more than fifty years later, Hu Lanqi remarked approvingly on their simplicity and innocence.[58] Old Mrs. Ning, on the other hand, while sympathetic to slave girls, believed that they generally did not receive proper moral training. Over the course of her life working as a domestic servant, one of her employers, a former slave girl whom the master took as concubine, ordered Mrs. Ning to behave in what she thought was an improper manner. She refused and the mistress's face turned red with anger: "She had been a slave girl and I had been brought up in a family," Mrs. Ning observes.[59]

With regard to both slave girls and concubines, it was clear to all that their birth families could not offer them a proper home and that their masters' families had bought and paid for them. While some of them were no doubt able to overcome, through luck and their own wits, the disadvantages that such a background forced on them, many more probably spent their days trying to avoid offending those who could so easily humiliate and hurt them.

"Fate" and the Worldview of Dependent Women

Greater understanding of the physical world in which slave girls lived—and of the nature of domestic service in well-off Chengdu families and of anthropologists' analyses of slave girl mentality—certainly makes it more possible to evaluate Ba Jin's depictions of slave girls and concubines. It would also be helpful to know more about certain beliefs that Ba Jin attributes to characters such as Miss Chen and Mingfeng. For example, when the Gao patriarch falls ill near the end of *Family*, Miss Chen summons a *wushi* (often translated as "vernacular priest" or "ritual specialist") to exorcise the evil spirits she thinks might be causing the old man's illness.[60] After he dies, she insists that Juexin's pregnant wife Ruijue leave the city to have her baby; if the baby is born too near the corpse of the old man, she says, the "blood glow" (*xueguang*) from the birth might interfere with the soul of the patriarch as it makes its journey to the underworld, with bad consequences for its rebirth. In contrast to the educated young heroes and heroines of the novels, who try to analyze social conditions rationally and fix the problems they see in their world, Mingfeng, the other servants and concubines, and the older generation of women in the family all tend to attribute their problems to "fate"—the notion that their life courses are determined from the time they are born and that resistance to decisions made by those in authority is useless and even morally wrong. In *Spring*, the widowed Madam Zhou counsels the young Gao women to accept their arranged marriages as part of their preordained fate and tells them that she prays that she won't be reborn as a woman in her next life.[61]

Chapter Two will discuss early twentieth-century medical practices and folk notions like the "blood glow." These subjects form part of a web of beliefs shared by many people in the Chengdu of Ba Jin's youth about the way the world was organized and how people should act within it. Shaped by

Buddhist and Daoist doctrine, Confucian teachings, and a rich folklore, this web of beliefs had a strong influence on Ba Jin, even as he criticized many aspects of it. What was valuable in Chinese culture and what should be rejected was not always clear, even to New Culture activists committed to getting rid of "superstition" and Confucian patriarchy. Wu Yu, for example, went to an enormous amount of trouble and expense to buy concubines in an attempt to beget a son (without success), even though he was a leading critic of Confucian culture as it had evolved by the early twentieth century. Near the end of his life, he immersed himself in Buddhist teachings, perhaps in part to find a connection to the cosmos and an understanding of what lay beyond death that did not center on the establishment of a legacy through a male heir.[62]

According to Ida Pruitt's record of her conversation, Old Mrs. Ning frequently turned to "fate" as a way to explain why bad things happened. She also consulted fortune-tellers when she made major decisions such as whom her daughter should marry. Like Mrs. Ning's hometown in eastern China, Chengdu had a large community of fortune-tellers and other religious specialists to advise people and help them carry out life rituals. The 1909 police census lists 263 Buddhist temples and three Daoist monasteries, with a total of 597 Buddhist monks, 113 Buddhist nuns, 269 Daoist priests, 89 exorcists of the sort who visited the Gao residence when the patriarch was ill, and 32 *yinyang* masters, hired by families who wanted to know how to arrange their residences and grave sites in accordance with fengshui principles.

Newspaperman Fu Chongju, who compiled an encyclopedia of Chengdu life in 1909, claimed that a large majority of the people in the city who had received a classical Confucian education also believed in Buddhism, whereas a much smaller number patronized Daoist institutions.[63] In regard to exorcists, he noted that they were much more popular in small towns and villages than in the city. As a self-consciously "rational man," Fu ridiculed the work of exorcists:

> If a family merely calls in a doctor when someone in the house is ill, and doesn't call in one of them [an exorcist], then their relatives and neighbors will all criticize them. Therefore, they send out a sedan chair and receive him [the exorcist] as an honored guest, and he then adopts an air of authority, mouthing all sorts of nonsense, stinking up the heavens with a lighted torch, and shaking the earth with a metal drum. The whole family, young and old, is dazed and confused by the noise and spectacle, and all the sick person lying on a bed can do is wait for death. If by chance the patient recovers, then

everyone says it is because of the effort of the exorcist. The fee may amount to more than ten thousand copper coins or even several tens of thousands. Even though the person didn't die, the family may well be bankrupted.

Fu Chongju called on local officials to ban exorcism, fortune-telling, and the like, which he denounced as scams.[64] In the last years of the Qing, police officials who shared Fu's views tried to force religious practitioners such as exorcists to register with the government, intending to regulate (and tax) their work. But that effort was abandoned after the 1911 Revolution. Such practices were far too popular, among officialdom as well as the general population. In the years around 1920, slave girls like Mingfeng certainly would have been taught by the older servants and their mistresses that it was their fate to obey those above them, and also that defiance of fate and of the authority of their masters would be punished in a multitude of frightful ways, in this life and the next.[65]

Slave Girls and the Era of Reform

Beginning in the last years of the Qing, various advocates of social change in China, including Ba Jin, called for the abolition of slave girl status and concubinage. This reform effort made very little progress in the first half of the twentieth century, however, so that both slave girls and concubines remained ingrained in Chengdu's social structure right up until the founding of the PRC in 1949. In 1909 imperial officials appointed to a commission to rewrite China's legal code clarified that young girls could only enter servitude via contractual arrangements with a limited term—they were not to be treated as the property of their masters. China's international image and not the welfare of slave girls appears to have been the prime motivation for these revised legal requirements, since they were justified by the observation that tolerating slavery could undermine the new law codes and that "buying and selling humans has long been rejected and ridiculed by the Western countries."[66] A senior Qing official argued the case in this way:

> Recently, Europe and America have made great advances in government and are aware of the barbaric nature of slavery. England spent tens of millions of gold coins to free the slaves in its country; America fought a war for years to emancipate its slaves. As news of these honorable acts spreads, each country has followed their lead. We should, too.[67]

Under the new legal framework, terms that had appeared in the Qing Code before, such as *nubi* (male and female slaves) and *jianren* (base people), were eliminated. Poor families could still send their children, no matter how old, to other families to work, but they were to do so under labor contracts, not outright sales. Contracts could not extend past the child's twenty-fifth year, at which point boys were free to establish themselves in a profession or sign annual contracts to work for their masters' families. Girls were to be returned to their parents or closest relatives to be married; if no relatives could be located, their masters would choose mates for them without accepting any bride price in return. If a master abused a child, the parents had the right to pay back the contract fee and retrieve the child. These recommendations were approved by an edict of January 31, 1910.[68]

The officials who advocated these limited changes may have been aware that antislavery forces in England had been criticizing the colonial government of Hong Kong since the 1860s for tolerating child selling. In her history of the Po Leung Kuk (Baoliangju in Mandarin), established in Hong Kong in 1878 to take in "wayward" girls, Elizabeth Sinn interprets the founding of that institution as an attempt on the part of Hong Kong's elite to protect Chinese patriarchy from challenges by British activists concerned about kidnapping and prostitution.[69]

Whereas late Qing officials at the national level seem to have been mainly concerned about slavery because of its impact on China's reputation, local officials considered it primarily from the point of view of local order. New police regulations promulgated in Chengdu in the first decade of the twentieth century, for example, required that "people sellers" be registered with the police and take steps to ensure that people passing through their hands had not been kidnapped. Mistreatment of slave girls was banned. Police received merit points for returning runaway slave girls to their masters. In the late Qing and the early Republic, despite the ban on sales in new law codes, Chengdu police still operated as they had ten years earlier, trying to discourage kidnappings and abuse of slave girls but accepting the right of people to transfer children to other families for a fee. Police archives from the early Republic show that people continued to register transfers of girls and young women at local police offices, as we saw earlier in this chapter. The Qing legal commission's 1909 emphasis on the right of parents to redeem their children and the responsibility of masters to return girls to their relatives after their service had been completed is nowhere evident in local documents from the republican period. At the local level, the status of slave girls remained essentially unaltered.

In the May Fourth era, some writers advocated the "liberation" of slave girls. In 1920, Hu Huaichen published an article in *Funü zazhi* (Women's magazine) in which he noted that "everyone affected by the new thinking" knows that the purchase and use of slave girls is bad. Slave girls are often treated as if they are not human, and, in consequence, they tend to have little self-respect, he said, and this makes them prone to laziness and craftiness; they steal from their masters and waste the family's resources. The solution to the slave girl problem is twofold, he argued. First, women should not purchase slave girls anymore. Second, slave girls already purchased should probably not be returned to their families, who are likely to resell them. Rather, they should be treated as little sisters—sent to school, taught how to be a good person, and, if they have reached the proper age, given away in marriage. When arranging their marriages, Hu warned his audience, do not do so for financial benefit; think only of the good of the girls themselves.[70] The second part of Hu's plan for the liberation of slave girls, perhaps not coincidentally, bears a close resemblance to the Qing legal commission's reform policy. The underlying logic of both is that poor families will sell their daughters and that the best that can be done for such girls is to treat them kindly and find respectable husbands for them at the proper time.

Despite Hu Huaichen's advice, sales of slave girls continued throughout the republican period and may well have increased. In 1927, the Nationalist government based in Guangzhou passed legislation declaring that all purchased girls would be treated by law as adopted daughters and requiring their masters to register them with the police. British consular officers reported to their home government that the law was not carried out.[71] Over the decade of the 1930s, national and provincial laws banned the sale and purchase of slave girls, but observers noted widespread lack of compliance.[72]

The question of slave girls continued to have some visibility among reform circles throughout the republican period, but the problem was considered simply too intractable to address, given the state of social disorder and the poverty of the countryside. An essayist writing in *Eastern Miscellany* (*Dongfang zazhi*) in 1932 echoed arguments made decades before by the Hong Kong elite studied by Elizabeth Sinn: girls are sold because their families cannot afford to keep them. If we ban sales, there will not be enough charity institutions to support them. If good people refuse take them in as slave girls, the most likely alternative is the brothel. The liberation of girls can only occur when the economy has been transformed.[73]

The chaotic political and economic conditions that prevailed near Chengdu and elsewhere in China between the 1910s and 1940s meant that many rural families were unable to support and protect all of their family members. Selling a girl to an urban family that had the means to feed her continued to be considered acceptable until after the Communist Party took control of China in 1949 and began radically and rapidly transforming both its economy and its social order. During the May Fourth era, some more-prosperous women did achieve greater independence and new roles in society, but the patterns of life changed little for women like Mingfeng. In this area, the existing culture—reinforced by economic conditions—was resistant to change, much as Ba Jin and other reformers asserted, but that was true both before and after May Fourth and not only in cities like Chengdu but throughout China.

CHAPTER TWO

The Patriarch

Chengdu's Gentry

The character of the Gao patriarch in *Family* is a mystery to his grandson Gao Juehui. As the dying old man's heart softens toward his rebellious grandson at the end of that novel, Juehui regrets not having been able to get to know him better earlier—he is clearly much more than the stern enforcer of family rules who thwarts the love lives of the younger members of the household. Throughout the trilogy, Ba Jin gives us glimpses of the cultural world that his own grandfather and uncles lived in and enjoyed, although his descriptions are often harshly critical. This chapter explores aspects of that world more fully, with the aim of understanding both what made it attractive to men like the Gao patriarch and why it seemed reprehensible in the eyes of younger people like Ba Jin. We will find evidence that local culture was not unchanging before the 1920s and also that Chengdu's elite society embraced new ideas and institutions even as it resisted other aspects of the May Fourth agenda.

The chapter begins with a discussion of the nature of the upper class in Chengdu at the time of Ba Jin's youth—how did one become a member of it and how were the elite expected to behave? The 1911 Revolution, which toppled the Qing and established an initially weak Republic of China, offered the Chengdu elite prominent roles in political life, even as the changing sociopolitical order led to the rise of militarism. After a discussion of these developments, we turn to the geography of elite life in Chengdu, including the elaborate residences of the wealthy and the parks, teahouses, and theaters where friends gathered to share poems and patronize actors. New schools, hospitals, and other such institutions—inspired by foreign models and sometimes even run by foreigners—began to become an accepted part of elite life during Ba Jin's youth, and we will consider how older ideas about education and medicine accommodated this development. The chapter ends with a discussion of family rituals—the core of the old culture Ba Jin so reviled—and the nature and significance of the debates over their role in Chinese life. Ba Jin's view that these rituals hindered social progress was not shared by most people in Chengdu in the 1920s: many of them continued to think them an integral part of civilized life.

What Did It Take to Become a Shenshi?

In a scene early in *Family*, Gao Juemin and his younger brother Juehui argue about the parts they have been assigned in a play their school is putting on, a play based on Robert Louis Stevenson's novel *Treasure Island*. Juehui says he prefers playing the part of Black Dog, a rough sailor, to playing Doctor Livesay, who is "only a *shenshi*." Juemin replies, "What's that supposed to mean? . . . Won't you be a *shenshi* in the future, too?" Juehui responds bitterly: "Yes, yes. Our grandfather is a *shenshi*, as was our father, so we should be, too, right?" The young Juehui, who has just been teased for his refusal to exploit his fellow man by riding in a sedan chair, is expressing his dissatisfaction with the class structure of the society around him. He is a member of the elite, but he is not comfortable with it.

His grandfather, on the other hand, is not only comfortable as a *shenshi* but also very proud of having achieved that status and determined to see that his descendants maintain it. The term *shenshi* is often translated as "gentry," because historians have seen parallels between the elite in pre-Communist Chinese society and the landed gentry of early modern Europe.[1] But there are significant distinctive qualities to the "Chinese gentry." Ba Jin did not need Juemin and Juehui to discuss these qualities in the novel, because his Chinese readers all understood what being a *shenshi* meant.

To be recognized as part of the Chinese gentry, families needed to control significant resources, and, for most of them, ownership of farmland was the key resource. We will discuss gentry income—land ownership and the relationship between the gentry and their farmer-tenants, as well as gentry involvement in commerce and industry—in more detail in Chapter Three. In addition to land ownership, though, a particular sort of education and cultural knowledge were at the center of the image of the Chinese gentry as it developed over the centuries. To be a member of the gentry implied a familiarity with, if not a mastery of, a body of classical literature that included poetry, annals, and writings on ritual from the Zhou period (circa 1046 to 256 BCE), before the time of Confucius (551–479 BCE), as well as Confucius's own teachings as written down by his students in the *Analects* and the essays of his most influential followers, such as Mencius. Other important texts for the gentry were the histories of all the Chinese dynasties written by generations of Confucian scholars, essays on statecraft by famous officials, and poetry from all eras. The core texts in this massive body of writings are often referred to in English as the "Confucian canon."

China was not unique in having an elite whose identity was bound up to some degree with classical learning. This was also true of European gentry—think of the relationship between the English elite and the sort of classical education that developed at such public schools as Eton and at England's famous universities. A good education in the Chinese classics, however, was even more important to the elite in nineteenth-century China than study of Latin texts was in nineteenth-century England. The essential role of classical education in defining the pre-twentieth-century elite in China was due in large part to the ingenious civil service examination system that had its origins in the Han dynasty (206 BCE to 220 CE) and was promoted during the Tang (618–907 CE) and subsequent dynasties as the most important path to becoming a government official.[2]

From early on, Chinese rulers came to rely heavily on a professional bureaucracy, in addition to their military forces, to rule over the vast and diverse territories they claimed as their domains. To ensure that the bureaucracy would be loyal as well as effective, emperors had to attract talented officials and ensure these officials felt they had a stake in the system and thus would be willing to work within it instead of challenging it. The remarkably successful solution to this problem was the civil service examination system. Two features of the system are critical to understanding how it worked. First, the state devoted a substantial amount of its resources to the promotion of ruler-friendly, state-centered interpretations of the Confucian canon. For example, Confucius's teachings—which emphasized, above all, ethical conduct within the family, i.e., sons paying respect to their fathers, fathers guiding and teaching their sons, etc.—were extrapolated and interpreted in state-sponsored essays to lay great stress on the loyalty that officials owed to the emperor, their father figure. Second, the state promised honored positions in the bureaucracy to those who did well in examinations on the officially sanctioned texts. Because the status and potential income of government officials was very high for most periods in Chinese history, many people wanted their sons and grandsons to get the sort of education that would help them succeed in the exams.

By the nineteenth century, the number of men who participated in the exams far exceeded the number of positions available in the bureaucracy. Even though it was clear that the vast majority of exam takers would never be awarded the high degrees necessary to be eligible for an official position, by that time the exam system had firmly shaped people's conception of what a good education was. An education in the Confucian canon and participation in the exam system became a part of gentry life for generations of boys. Few families could afford to give their boys the very demanding education required for the exams—but any family that was able to, whatever the source of their fortune, almost certainly wanted to. The civil service exam thus helped create a certain kind of gentry culture and drew the newly wealthy into it, but many years, even generations, of hard study were required to master it.

Ba Jin came from a long line of exam-takers. His great-great-grandfather, Li Wenxi, was classically educated. In 1818, Li Wenxi moved to Sichuan from his home in eastern China's Zhejiang Province to take up an official post. His sons and grandsons took the civil service examinations, too, and some of them did well enough to be eligible for official appointment, including Ba Jin's grandfather Li Yong (Figure 2.1).

By this time, near the end of the nineteenth century, the Qing court was in dire financial straits. It had recruited sizeable armies to put down the massive Taiping uprising and, in the process of putting it down, had devastated its richest tax base, the lower Yangzi River basin around the

Figure 2.1 Li Yong, Ba Jin's grandfather (*right*), with Ba Jin's eldest brother, Li Yaomei (*left*), circa 1919. Courtesy of the Ba Jin Research Association.

wealthy cities Suzhou and Hangzhou. Several decades of on-and-off warfare with rising powers Britain and France beginning in 1839 had also been extremely expensive. To deal with its financial problems, the Qing court raised funds by requiring would-be officials who had done well on the exams to make donations in order to win appointment.[3] Somehow or other—relying on family connections and other patrons, most likely—Ba Jin's grandfather was able to put together the necessary funds and served in various positions in the Sichuan provincial administration. Over several decades, he amassed a personal fortune that allowed him to buy a considerable amount of farmland in the region around Chengdu and a large residential compound in the northeast part of the city. He also bought commercial property in Chengdu to rent out and collected antiques, art, and books.[4]

Li Yong's eldest son, Ba Jin's father, Li Daohe, also qualified for official appointment in the last years of Qing rule. Ba Jin's biographer Chen Sihe believes that the story Gao Juexin tells his younger brothers in chapter 12 of *Family* about their deceased father's career was based on Li Daohe's life; it is known that Ba Jin's eldest brother sent him letters after he left Chengdu that touched on their family history. If Chen is right, then Li Daohe served briefly as an official in charge of police matters (equivalent to a sheriff) in the eastern Sichuan Chongqing region in 1902, during the tumultuous period after the Boxer uprising. He was removed from office abruptly and then traveled to Beijing to seek promotion to the rank of county magistrate via a financial donation and an audience with the emperor. After a delay that caused much anxiety within the family (Chen Sihe points out that Ba Jin's mother would have been pregnant with him during this stressful time), Li Daohe was promoted and returned to Chengdu. In 1909 he was appointed magistrate of Guangyuan County, in northern Sichuan. He served there for two years, until a few months before the fall of the Qing dynasty in 1911, when he returned to the Li family home in Chengdu, having made enough money to buy forty *mu*—some six acres—of farmland.[5]

As a family of classically educated landowners that had produced a number of local officials, the Li family into which Ba Jin was born clearly belonged in the category of *shenshi*—gentry. There were several dozen other families in early twentieth-century Chengdu who could boast the same level of wealth and accomplishments, some of them registered as natives of Sichuan and others, like the Li family, who considered themselves natives of other parts of China.[6] Whether or not it was their official native place, these people definitely saw themselves—and were seen by others—as the elite of Chengdu. Until the Qing collapse in 1911 and the establishment of the Republic of China, holding examination degrees conferred a number of valuable benefits aside from eligibility for official positions. These included tax breaks and opportunities to meet with provincial and local officials on a basis of relative equality (with no requirement to kneel, as was usual for common folk), in addition to many other forms of special treatment.

Gentry families had a common interest in maintaining the prestige of their class; they made use of a range of strategies to support solidarity within the elite community, including arranged marriages to create family alliances. This is reflected in *Turbulent Stream* when the Gao patriarch attempts to solidify his family's ties to the Feng family by offering Mingfeng (and then Wan'er) to his old friend Feng Leshan as a concubine and by arranging for his grandson Juemin to marry a young lady from the Feng family.

The Gao patriarch believes himself justified in making marriage arrangements and other major life decisions for the junior members of the household because of the emphasis in the Confucian texts on the responsibility elders have to guide their dependents. In *Spring* and *Autumn*, Ba Jin frequently has the conservative scholar Zhou Botao cite lines from the *Analects* and other Confucian texts to impress on his own children their obligation to respect and obey him. Zhou Botao directs his son to write practice exam essays on the importance of filial behavior.[7] This aspect of the officially sanctioned Confucian texts helped gentry families maintain discipline. The legal system in place in Qing times also backed up the authority of household heads, making it a serious offense to disobey one's parents or grandparents. The death penalty could be imposed if a child struck a parent.[8]

Even after the abolition of the exam system in 1905—part of the Qing dynasty's reforms of its governing institutions in response to repeated military defeats—Chengdu's patriarchal gentry families continued to see themselves as the best and brightest in the community. A brief attempt to establish constitutional government with elected assemblies between 1908 and 1913 limited the electorate to people who paid a fairly substantial level of taxes, which meant, in essence, that only the gentry could vote. In Chengdu, men from gentry families participated with enthusiasm in this democratic experiment. Few of them, if any, wanted to see significant transformation of the social order, however. One of the most prevalent slogans in Sichuan in the early twentieth century, more popular than the call for a democratic republic, was "Sichuan for the Sichuanese."[9] For Chengdu's gentry, the decline of the central control of the Qing held out the promise that they, as the city's natural local leaders, would be able to play more prominent roles in the governance of their province and city. They would have been well satisfied if it had been possible simply to take the reins of government out of the hands of what they considered the incompetent Qing court and the haughty officials it had assigned to Chengdu.[10]

Very briefly in 1911 it seemed that the gentry would get their wish. A series of decisions by the Qing government, including the nationalization of the railroad company that had originally been financed by provincial taxes, enraged people across Sichuan, who responded by forming militias and cutting Chengdu off from communication with the central government. After a series of revolutionary uprisings, other provinces began to declare independence. With no hope of military support from troops outside Sichuan, the Qing governor-general negotiated a deal with the gentry leaders of the new Sichuan Provincial Assembly. Among its provisions was a promise by the gentry to protect the lives and property not only of all the Qing officials in the province but also of the hundreds of Qing military families known as Bannermen (*qiren*) who lived in the city's garrison—an extensive walled area in the west part of the city. In exchange for this pledge of safety, the Banner troops laid down their arms and Qing officials turned the provincial government and its treasury over to the Provincial Assembly. But the unrest in the lead-up to the Qing abdication opened the door for some powerful political rivals to the cultured and conservative gentry leaders—younger men who had made their names as leaders of the militias and rebellious military units that fought against loyal Qing troops and in the fall of 1911 surrounded and besieged Chengdu.

About a week after the last Qing governor-general of Sichuan Province handed power over to Provincial Assembly leaders, a military coup overthrew the new government. Many of the Provincial Assembly leaders fled for their lives as the treasury was ransacked. Gentry homes across the city were looted in a night of chaos and terror on December 8, 1911. A prominent military official, a Sichuan native who had joined the anti-Qing revolution, stepped in to restore order, becoming the first in a long series of strongman military governors of the province who were only nominally loyal to the central government of the newly established Republic of China.

The militarists themselves usually came from gentry families, although many of them grew up in small towns or villages, not in the big cities.[11] While ruling Chengdu, most of them tried to show respect to and win the support of the cultured leaders of the city's gentry community. Even after the Provincial Assembly was disbanded in 1913, the gentry continued to be seen as community leaders. As military governors came and went with the fortunes of the almost continuous civil wars in the three decades after 1911, a group of prominent scholars, learned in the Confucian canon, emerged as the city's unofficial spokesmen. People called them the "five elders and seven sages." Their history offers us a window into the world of the Gao patriarch and his friends in *Turbulent Stream*.

Five Elders and Seven Sages: Chengdu's Post-1911 Cultural Sphere

Ba Jin's grandfather, Li Yong, was not one of the five elders and seven sages, but he probably had met them all. And, actually, there were not necessarily just twelve of them. The term "five elders and seven sages" was more poetic than precise; it was an allusion to two popular subjects of Chengdu's storytellers: the Daoist gods of the five directions and the "seven sages of the bamboo grove." Both references conjured up images of wise figures who were not officials and yet could do good in the world. Thus, the term was used, beginning about 1917, as shorthand for a group of distinguished scholars who acted as intermediaries between the militarists controlling Chengdu and the people of the city.[12] They believed that their Confucian learning and degree-holder status obliged them to take on the role of protectors of the common people. The militarists found it useful to appear to be guided by these community elders and therefore did not often challenge their cultural authority. This relationship between "warlords," as the militarists were beginning to be called in the early 1920s, and the old-style scholar-gentry appeared to the more radical young men like Ba Jin to be unsavory collusion.[13] Such relationships no doubt increased Ba Jin's disgust for what he considered the hypocrisy of Confucian scholars.

In this attitude, however, he was unusual. The contempt for classical learning and the Confucian canon expressed in *Turbulent Stream* was not at all common in Chengdu in the 1910s and 1920s. In the decades right before the 1911 Revolution, Chengdu had experienced a flowering of classical scholarship that continued to shape the cultural sphere all the way up to the victory of the Communists in 1949. Ba Jin left Chengdu as a very young man, so he did not have a chance to enter that sphere. Had he stayed, it is likely that he would have found himself pulled into the cultural world surrounding the five elders and seven sages. That happened, for example, to the novelist Li Jieren, who also spent several years in France and, like Ba Jin, was interested in progressive ideologies. After Li Jieren returned to Chengdu in 1924, he was recruited to teach at Chengdu University, where some of the elders and sages also taught, and became good friends with several of them. Li Jieren's depiction of gentry characters in his Chengdu novels makes them seem much more like conflicted human beings than Ba Jin's gentry characters in *Turbulent Stream*.[14]

Ba Jin's novels give the impression that Chengdu's Confucian scholars, like the fictional characters Feng Leshan and Zhou Botao, were reactionaries—stubbornly clinging to a set of outdated beliefs and rituals so as to maintain their own authority within their families and communities. If we take a look at the careers of the most prominent of Chengdu's five elders and seven sages and some of the people they interacted with, Ba Jin's image of Chengdu's scholar-gentry crumbles. Even the most conservative of Chengdu's literati was far more complex and interesting than Ba Jin's creations Feng Leshan and Zhou Botao.

Liu Yubo, one of the elders and sages, has already been mentioned in Chapter One, in the context of the discussion of concubines, as an example of a Chengdu man in his late fifties who took a teenaged girl as concubine in the 1920s. In the Chengdu of Ba Jin's youth, however, he was far more famous as a teacher, as an accomplished poet and painter of pictures of orchids, as a holder of a high-level degree in the civil service exams, and as the direct descendent of the renowned Confucian scholar Liu Zhitang. The Liu family was among the two or three most eminent families in Chengdu in the decades around the turn of the twentieth century. They produced generations of outstanding scholars at the Huaixuan Academy, founded in 1813 by Liu Zhitang at his residence near the city's South Gate. The academy emphasized broad learning, extending beyond the Confucian canon to Buddhist and especially Daoist texts. More than a hundred Huaixuan students earned the two highest degrees in the civil service exam.[15] In chapter 11 of *Family*, the Gao patriarch gives his grandson Juehui a copy of a (real) book by Liu Zhitang called *A Manual for the Instruction of Filial Piety and Warning against Carnality*. Juehui tears the book to shreds after skimming through it and finding such stock "Confucian" sayings as "If a lord orders his subject to die, not to die would be disloyal; if a father orders his son to die, not to die would be unfilial."[16]

Huaixuan began to be eclipsed as Chengdu's elite academy in the 1870s, when the Qing court sent Zhang Zhidong to Sichuan to serve as provincial education commissioner. Zhang, one of the three or four most powerful officials in China in the early twentieth century, was completely loyal to the dynasty but open to new ideas as long as he deemed them compatible with Chinese cultural traditions. His position on change is summed up in the phrase "Chinese learning constitutes the essence; Western learning provides practical applications," an idea historians have abbreviated as *ti-yong* ("essence-application"). In practice, for Zhang Zhidong and many likeminded members of the elite, *ti-yong* meant continuing to base education on Chinese classics and history and selecting officials primarily for their understanding of the Confucian canon but, at the same time, encouraging the development of industry, the broadening of education to include knowledge from Japan and Europe, and the adoption of useful new technologies, particularly Western military technology.[17]

Zhang Zhidong arrived in Chengdu in 1874 and soon persuaded the Sichuan governor-general to make use of a surcharge on the land tax to found a new provincial academy. This school, the Zunjing (Respect the Classics) Academy, was intended to re-energize classical studies in Sichuan. In that it was a great success, but not exactly in the way Zhang had foreseen. Liao Ping, one of its most influential alumni, came to adopt the radical position that Confucian texts should be read not as history but as guides to the contemporary world. His writings inspired the scholar-activist Kang Youwei as he in turn promoted the idea that Confucius was not at all as conservative as later scholars had depicted him—he had understood the need for cultural change as human society evolved. If Confucius had been alive in the nineteenth century, Kang and his followers argued, he would not have objected to China's adoption of Western-style constitutional government or to changes in women's roles and the organization of family life.[18] Ba Jin's teacher Wu Yu, whom we have already encountered, was also a Zunjing Academy student and studied alongside Liao Ping. But, whereas Liao, like Kang Youwei and Zhang Zhidong, continued to think Confucian texts should be at the core of education, Wu Yu used his formidable training in the classics to attack orthodox Confucian learning in the years after the 1911 Revolution. Wu Yu believed that scholars should study Western legal traditions, which he considered superior in many ways to the Confucian canon.

Wu Yu is not counted among the elders and sages, although he was the classmate of many of them and the nephew of Liu Yubo (Wu Yu's mother was a member of the Liu family and, like Liu Yubo, a grandchild of Liu Zhitang). He was too much of a political incendiary to play the role of a wise elder. He challenged conventional gentry values of filial conduct directly in 1910 by distributing a broadside entitled "One Family's Bitter Story" around Chengdu. In it, he accused his own father of immoral and profligate behavior and of indirectly causing the death of Wu Yu's only son, an infant who had fallen ill when Wu Yu was forced out of the ancestral home in 1893. Members of Chengdu's elite were scandalized, especially when rumors spread that, just before the thirty-eight-year-old Wu Yu published the broadside, he had given his father a severe beating. The Qing provincial governor-general responded to the clamor to punish Wu Yu by issuing an order for his arrest, but Wu was able to flee Chengdu and hide out, with the help of sympathetic friends. Everyone in Chengdu's elite community knew that Wu Yu's father was not an upright person; still, such a public challenge to the central Confucian idea that elders deserve respect was unacceptable to almost all of them.[19]

In 1919, Wu Yu taught at the school that Ba Jin attended, the Foreign Languages School. There can be no doubt that Ba Jin and his classmates were thoroughly familiar with the scandal of Wu Yu's attack on his own father. It may well be that the example of Wu Yu's rejection of filial piety inspired Ba Jin's depiction of Gao Juehui and Gao Juemin standing up to their grandfather and uncles in *Turbulent Stream*. Ba Jin himself seems not to have behaved that way in his own family—at any rate until he blackened his elders' reputations by publishing *Family*. Wu Yu's personal history can also be related to *Turbulent Stream* via the character of the evil and hypocritical Feng Leshan, described in Ba Jin's fiction as the head of Chengdu's Confucian Society. It is hard not to see Feng Leshan as a caricature of Wu Yu's classmate and nemesis Xu Zixiu, yet another of the elders and sages.

Xu Zixiu, like Wu Yu, studied at the Zunjing Academy. He earned a prestigious *juren* ("elevated scholar") degree in the civil service examinations but was disgusted when the Qing court executed six scholar-officials for treason in 1898 during an abortive reform movement launched by Kang Youwei and the Guangxu emperor. After the executions, according to his biographer, Xu refused to take part in the examinations or serve in the Qing government.[20] Nevertheless, in 1910, when Wu Yu's fight with his father occurred, Xu Zixiu was head of the Sichuan Educational Association, a quasi-governmental advisory body made up of local gentry. In that capacity, he took the lead in the movement to have Wu Yu arrested for attacking his father.

After the 1911 Revolution, Xu Zixiu continued to be a leader in the educational community, where he was the most prominent advocate of classical studies of the traditional variety, and he did his best to keep Wu Yu from gaining a teaching position in Chengdu. During the early years of the Republic, there was a nationwide movement to promote Confucianism as a state religion.[21] Xu Zixiu supported this movement. In 1916 he raised funds to build a shrine to six Song-dynasty Confucian thinkers from Sichuan, whose works had helped constitute the old imperial-era orthodoxy. The building included a library and reading room, where he lectured on the classics to outstanding students sent from various high schools in the city. In 1920, a few years before Ba Jin left Chengdu, Xu Zixiu founded the Dacheng Association, a society that has a fictional counterpart in Feng Leshan's Confucian Society. Dacheng, or "Great Culmination," was one of Confucius's honorary titles; the main building in Confucian temples across China is called the Dacheng Hall. Under Xu Zixiu, the association promoted respect for Confucius in many ways. For example, it persuaded military leaders to protect a local temple to Confucius from demolition. It also opened its own academy to train students in the classics.[22]

Xu Zixiu wrote textbooks for the use of students enrolled in the Dacheng Association's academy, and it is possible that Ba Jin borrowed from them when he was writing the scenes in *Autumn* in which Zhou Botao assigns examination essays to his son. Xu Zixiu's textbooks represent Chinese history in a decidedly traditionalist way, rejecting the new interpretations that many of his Zunjing classmates and Kang Youwei had begun to introduce. In a speech at the opening ceremony of the Dacheng Middle School in 1923, Xu Zixiu had the following to say about the purpose of the school and the state of contemporary China:

> There is one main goal of this school, and three main hopes for it. What is the one main goal? It is to expound the great teachings of Confucius. What are the three main hopes? They are to remake society within twenty years, to remake the nation within forty years, and to remake the world in eighty years. To achieve this greatest hope, of course there are methods. The methods are two. We must remake our own hearts and minds and we must remake the work we engage in. Why must these things be remade? Because the society that surrounds us is full of evil—it is as debased as the worst eras in four thousand years of history. Why is it so evil? It is because those who are in charge of education in our country are either ignorant of true learning or foolish and insane. Students are either immoral enemies of the Confucian Way or radical firebrands who are disrespectful of their superiors. At some schools in Beijing,

they have even gone so far as to publicly support such ideologies as wife sharing, Communism, attacking fathers, and overthrowing filial piety. In short, they want to turn people into animals. Not even Huang Chao [leader of a rebellion at the end of the Tang dynasty] or Li Zicheng [leader of a rebellion at the end of the Ming dynasty] was capable of such evil![23]

As with many generations of scholars preceding him, Xu Zixiu believed that the key to ethical behavior could be found in the Confucian classics and in the study of Chinese history. His dissatisfaction with the new intellectual currents of the times stemmed from his fear that soon no one might know or care about the cultural legacy he thought so valuable. In this speech, he made use of some of the new vocabulary and concepts being popularized in the May Fourth era, such as "ideology" (*zhuyi*). It seems probable that he used this term ironically and disdainfully, although it is hard to judge without seeing his expression as he said it.

One way in which Xu Zixiu seems quite different from his fictional counterparts Feng Leshan and the Gao patriarch—if not from the pedantic and rigid Zhou Botao—is his lack of interest in poetry and the more sensual pleasures of Chengdu gentry life. From all accounts, Xu was an austere person, totally devoted to classical scholarship and moral instruction. When he established the Dacheng Academy in the early 1920s, he moved into its dormitory so that he could demonstrate proper conduct to his students throughout the day. Two of his most famous students became serious and sober leaders of the Nationalist Party: Zhang Qun, who served as governor of Sichuan during World War II, and Dai Jitao, who helped Chiang Kai-shek formulate his Confucian-inspired New Life movement, launched in 1934, with its emphasis on upright, clean living (see Chapter Seven for more on the activities of these two in Chengdu in the early 1920s). Among Chengdu's gentry, Xu Zixiu was unusually strict in his emphasis on constant study. Most of the other elders and sages, and their more radical colleague Wu Yu as well, were enthusiastic participants in the cultural activities that Ba Jin has the elder Gao men engage in.

The centrality of poetry to Chengdu culture in Ba Jin's youth can be seen clearly enough in his novels—the patriarch and his sons collect scrolls inscribed with poetry and the younger generation plays games in which they match each others' poetic lines with lines of their own, many of which allude to poems from the Tang or Song dynasties, the two golden eras of Chinese poetry. Over the course of the 1920s, short stories and novels began to edge out poetry as the most fashionable genres. For the "elders and sages" generation, though, poetry was much more satisfying. There was a social aspect to poetry that helped unite elite communities. A skillful poet could show off his learning through allusion and also pay tribute to friends and make subtle references to contemporary issues.[24] Wu Yu was very proud of the book of poetry, *Autumn Waters* (*Qiushuiji*), that he published in 1914. His diary from that year is filled with the names of friends to whom he presented copies, in Chengdu, other parts of China, and Japan.

Also in 1914, the head of Chengdu's Chamber of Commerce, book merchant Fan Kongzhou, founded a literary supplement, *Amusing Accounts* (*Yuxianlu*; Figure 2.2), for a major Chengdu newspaper.[25] The initial issue proclaimed that its intent was not only to amuse. Given the unsettled state of the world, it noted, direct criticism of contemporary society and politics was too dangerous. Sly commentary and humor might succeed in opening people's eyes to the truth more effectively than serious essays. And, it added, people always needed opportunities to laugh and be merry. Two thousand copies of the first edition were distributed, and the bimonthly publication continued to be very popular until the authorities shut down its parent newspaper in 1918 (Fan Kongzhou had been assassinated the year before; see Chapter Five). Many among Chengdu's elite, including some of the elders and sages, contributed poems, plays, and stories to it. Wu Yu and his wife both published in it, as did the young writer Li Jieren. When men like the Gao patriarch and Feng Leshan met to chat, most probably they would have talked over the contents of the latest issue of *Amusing Accounts* and similar publications. It was as absorbing for the older generation as the new journals coming out of eastern China, like *New Youth*, were for Ba Jin or his fictional counterpart, Gao Juehui.

Amusing Accounts frequently reported on the lively local opera scene. In *Turbulent Stream*, Ba Jin's treatment of Sichuan opera and its enthusiasts is dismissive—none of his young protagonists enjoy it, finding it noisy, gaudy, and superficial. They prefer the new spoken drama, such as the production of *Treasure Island* Juehui's school is staging. Unlike the spoken drama, which at this time in China was performed mostly by amateur actors like the young gentry in Ba Jin's stories, Sichuan opera was performed primarily by professional troupes of actors who had entered the profession as apprentices when very young. Stories in these dramas came from Chinese history and folktales and covered a wide range of material, from accounts of famous warriors to

Figure 2.2 A cover of *Amusing Accounts (Yuxianlu)*. *Yuxianlu*, issue 17, March 16, 1915.

tragic love affairs to Buddhist parables. Costumes were elaborate, and actors wore vivid face paint. Drums and gongs accompanied the singing and choreography, with its martial arts moves. Operas were performed on temporary stages at temple festivals, in guildhalls, and on special occasions in private residences, as in *Turbulent Stream*.

Well before the 1920s rise of the spoken drama, some among the Chinese elite had criticized older forms of Chinese theater, such as Sichuan opera, as frivolous and vulgar. Love stories, in particular, were said to corrupt the morals of the young by celebrating the emotional and sexual desires of individuals over higher values like hard work and family harmony. Opera troupes tried to get around this sort of criticism by staging stories of passionate lovers that ended in tragedy and remorse, so the production could be presented as a moral lesson but still enable the audience to enjoy a romantic fantasy.

Women were generally prohibited from performing in opera, leading to the custom of training boys to specialize in women's roles—"boy actresses," in the words of historian Andrea Goldman.[26] In Chapter Four, we will look at this phenomenon and Zhang Bixiu, the actor supported by the fourth son of the Gao patriarch in *Turbulent Stream*. Many gentry writers celebrated the beauty and talent of these female impersonators in poems and essays. To others, though, this was further sign of the degradation of the art form.

The reputation for vulgarity and lewdness attached to Sichuan opera in the early twentieth century concerned some gentry leaders enough that they founded an association to promote opera reform. One of the elders and sages, Zhao Xi, played a central role in this organization in the 1910s and 1920s, and others (even the abstemious Xu Zixiu) were active in it. Their goal was to save the genre from the harm caused both by those who vulgarized it and by those who condemned it for being vulgar. Their method was to write new, morally irreproachable scripts and promote performances of these reformed operas in the new public theaters that were being built in the first decade of the twentieth century. The opera reform leaders thought that, purged of content that was sexually charged or that dwelt on ghosts and other supernatural phenomena, Sichuan opera could educate the common people while entertaining them in an uplifting way. They also wanted to preserve the traditional singing styles, colorful costumes, and music, which were almost universally enjoyed in early twentieth-century Chengdu.[27] Advocates of older cultural forms, as much as they valued heritage, were not necessarily satisfied with the status quo: the debate over the content of opera provides an example of the dynamism within cultural spheres relatively untouched by new currents of thought.

Most of the Chengdu gentry, even the opera reformers, were not particularly prudish. In its first year of publication, *Amusing Accounts* ran many stories comparing the charms of the city's most famous courtesans and female impersonators, without stirring up calls for it to be shut down. Poetry, opera, painting, calligraphy, delicious food and drink, and other forms of beauty, valued for their artistry and good taste, formed an important part of elite life during Ba Jin's youth—a part that he personally did not appreciate. Ba Jin considered such cultural enjoyments to be hypocritical in light of the suffering he saw in the world and the gentry's professed belief in Confucian morality. Whereas some Confucian thinkers viewed beauty as closely linked to morality, Ba Jin believed that many of the arts supported by Chengdu's gentry were frivolous and diverted people from their moral duty. But, again, his views on this were unusual in Chengdu. Ironically, the disgust with which Ba Jin regarded many aspects of Chengdu elite culture seems to mirror in some respects the beliefs of such orthodox scholars as Xu Zixiu, a point we shall return to below.

Liu Yubo, grandson of the Huaixuan Academy's founder and uncle of the radical Wu Yu, is much more representative than Ba Jin of the elite men of Chengdu, most of whom continued to respect Confucian learning but also enjoyed other intellectual and sensual pleasures. These men, like the Gao patriarch, had no notion that their lifestyle was out of date. They continued to write poetry, drink wine while gazing at the moon, and take concubines. At the same time, however, they certainly welcomed many aspects of the new culture emerging in China, such as the periodical press, electric lights, and educational institutions like Chengdu University.

The aura of wisdom and culture that surrounded Liu Yubo and others among the elders and sages, in spite of what Ba Jin considered their hypocrisy, lasted into the 1940s, well after the publication of *Family*. Lin Zhiyuan, the son of one of Liu Yubo's students, recalled meeting Liu during the war with Japan in 1943, when to avoid air raids he had moved to a small town outside Chengdu's East Gate. Liu Yubo did not interact much with his new neighbors, but he made a point of visiting his students who lived in town, taking turns composing and reciting poetry with them. Lin's father asked him to share the secret of the Liu family's Huaixuan Academy exercises for

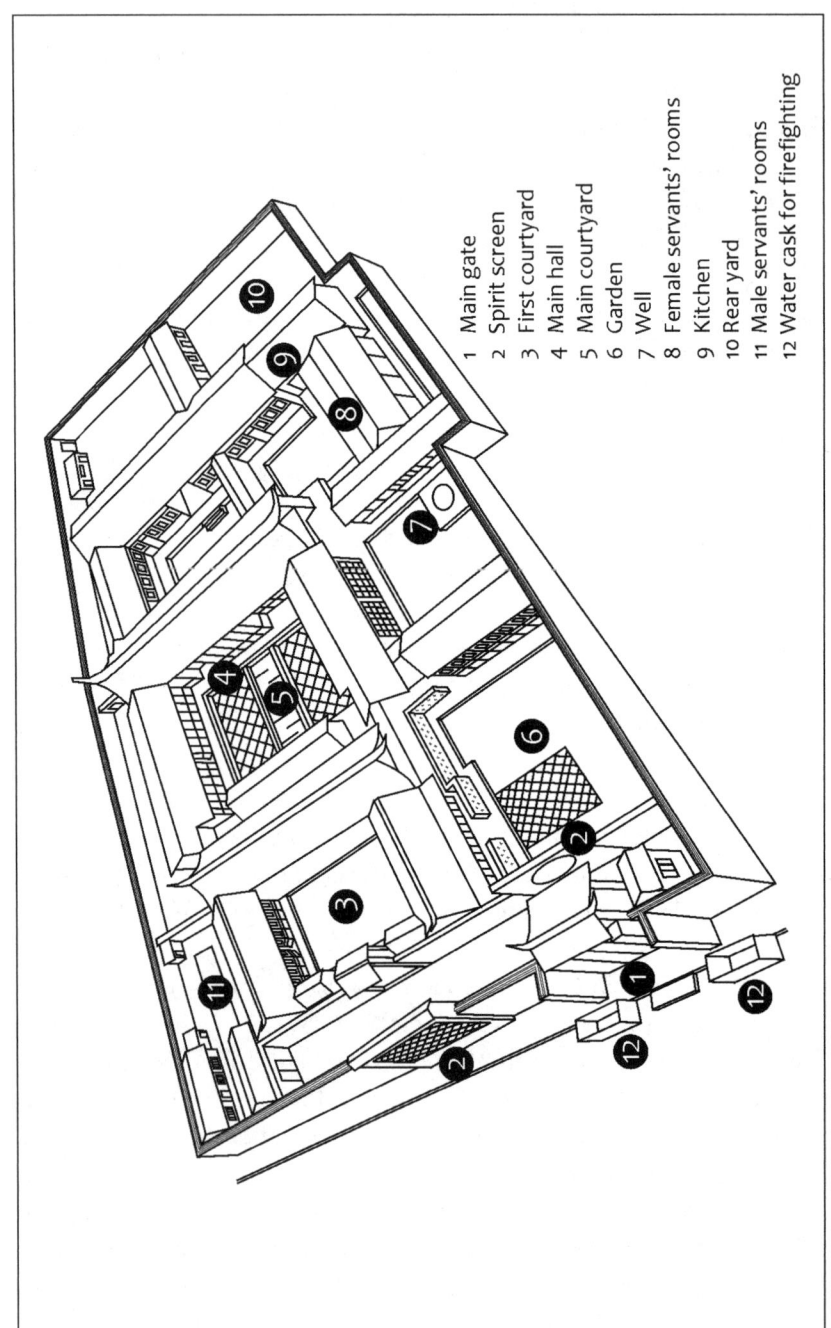

Figure 2.3 Diagram of Ba Jin's childhood home. Drawing by Debbie Newell. Based on a drawing by Zhang Yaotang dated November 1984.

regulating the body (old-style East Asian academies often included as part of their curriculum physical practices akin to yoga, including seated meditation and regulated breathing). According to Lin's father, who told the story often afterwards, Liu Yubo responded: "Actually, the true 'Liu Family' teachings were never transmitted to me; but, in my opinion, the best form of exercise is to practice sincerity and benevolence to the utmost. You seek movement [physical exercises] from a position of quietude; I seek quietude while in the midst of action."[28] This response, which blends a Confucian emphasis on moral righteousness with an awareness and acceptance of Buddhist- and Daoist-influenced bodily practices, was characteristic of the accommodating worldview of most of the elders and sages. Lin Zhiyuan respectfully describes how Liu Yubo carefully prepared himself to write characters to be inscribed on a temple gate; even after concentrated effort, he was dissatisfied and crumpled up the paper, only to return several days later and complete the assignment. People like Lin's father, and Lin himself, continued to find that approach to art and life inspiring and worthy of study.

The Gao Residence and the City from the Perspective of the Patriarch

The Gao family residence plays a central role in *Turbulent Stream*. At the beginning of the trilogy, we see its gate with the auspicious and optimistic couplet: "Benevolent rulers, happy family; long life, good harvests." In a scene set at the celebration of the New Year, the Gao patriarch happily surveys his whole family as they sit down to a meal together in the central courtyard's largest hall—four generations together, including Juexin's young son Hai'er—after having paid their respects to the Gao ancestors in a solemn ritual. At the end of *Autumn*, the sale of the family residence is the death blow to the Gao family—the patriarch's dream of family harmony and prosperity is buried. His grandson Juemin does not lament, having lost all belief in the dream. Gao Juexin, though, perhaps representing the trilogy's readers as well as himself, mourns the loss of his childhood home and the disintegration of the family itself.

Since the residence is so central to the story, Ba Jin discussed it to some extent in essays about *Turbulent Stream*. It is based on his family's house in the northeast section of Chengdu, with some modifications (Figure 2.3 shows Ba Jin's childhood home). The imposing main gate is just like his family's. Just inside it was a small building where the gateman lived and managed the family's interactions with the life of the street. Beyond that stood a "spirit screen," a tall masonry wall. According to fengshui principles, the spirit screen kept evil influences from entering the residence.[29] An adjacent open area offered room for visitors to alight from their sedan chairs, with housing for male servants nearby. Then, visitors would walk through an interior gate into a courtyard with a large hall at the far end, where the family had its banquets. Passing through that hall, they would see a large central building across another spacious paved courtyard adorned with trees and flowers in planters. Ba Jin's grandfather lived with his concubine in the main part of this central building, which also housed the family altar. His sons and daughters-in-law and their children lived in rooms on the sides and in another set of buildings around a courtyard behind the main building. The female servants lived in small rooms at the rear of the walled residence, near the kitchen. Ba Jin estimated that close to a hundred people lived in the compound when he was young, half of them Li family members and half of them servants.[30]

In *Turbulent Stream*, the Gao residence has a large attached garden, with a grove of wintersweet trees where Juehui and Mingfeng speak of their love, a lake on which the young people go boating (and in which Mingfeng drowns herself), and pavilions where drinking parties are held. This garden did not exist at Ba Jin's childhood home, which had two modestly sized gardens with a few trees, a well, and a small pond that his grandfather ordered filled up after Ba Jin fell into it once. As most Chinese readers of *Turbulent Stream* immediately realize, the fictional Gao family garden is much like the Grand View Garden, constructed in the novel *Dream of the Red Chamber* in honor of a young lady in the Jia family who becomes the consort of the emperor. Jia Baoyu, the hero of *Dream*, lives an idyllic life in the garden with his female cousins for a time.

Ba Jin probably found the idea of this special garden refuge, where young people of both sexes talk and play together, very useful because of its familiarity to Chinese readers. But, unlike cities in the Yangzi delta, Chengdu was not particularly noted for its gardens. The 1909 Chengdu encyclopedia lists only three private family gardens inside the city walls.[31] Liu Yubo's family home, located near the South Gate where now Chengdu's most famous hotel (the Jinjiang) stands, was probably the largest residence in the city, but it did not have an elaborate garden. After Liu Yubo's grandfather moved there in the early nineteenth century, the number of courtyards and residential buildings steadily grew to accommodate the expanding family, filling up all the available space.

Many of the city's temples and some guildhalls, though, had nicely landscaped gardens and courtyards. These too were important parts of the elite social world. In the last years of the Qing dynasty, a large piece of land at the southern end of the Banner garrison was made into a public park, which was named Shaocheng Park because of its location in the Shaocheng ("smaller city"), the common name for the Banner garrison. The park was enormously popular among the people of Chengdu, especially after the walls that separated the Shaocheng from the larger city were torn down in the early years of the Republic after 1911. It is still the most important park in Chengdu, having been renamed "People's Park" after 1949. From its founding it was a favorite spot for a wide range of Chengdu people to gather in teahouses and pass the time with friends.[32] It was also well suited for political demonstrations and other forms of civic activism. A monument to the activists who protested the Qing attempt to nationalize Sichuan's railroad was set up there shortly after the 1911 Revolution.

Before 1911, the Shaocheng garrison area was much more sparsely populated than the rest of the walled city of Chengdu; no one was allowed to move in there, since it was a military garrison, and the families of Banner troops who lived there were for the most part relatively poor and not able to support many dependents. In the fall of 1911, these Banner families feared they would be slaughtered by the anti-Qing forces besieging the city; that fate actually befell many of the Bannermen in other urban garrisons around China.[33] In Chengdu, some gentry leaders offered to move into the garrison during the crisis, in order to reassure and protect its residents. Xu Zixiu and his family were among them.[34]

When the situation calmed down after the founding of the Republic, many Banner families who had previously identified themselves proudly as Manchu or Mongol began to downplay their Banner background and represent themselves as Sichuan natives—easy enough for those who spoke Mandarin with a Sichuan accent after many generations in the Chengdu garrison. Some of them, though, thought it would be safer to sell the land they controlled in the Shaocheng and move to another part of the city or leave Chengdu entirely. Large amounts of property in the former garrison area therefore came on the market beginning in 1912. That year, Ba Jin's teacher Wu Yu took advantage of the opportunity to buy a residence in the Shaocheng. His diary entries on this occasion reflect the pride he felt in his house and give us a strong sense of the importance of their family residences to Chengdu's elite men.

Wu Yu had been paying 90 yuan a year to rent a house for himself and his family in Chengdu since he had parted ways with his father in the mid-1890s. Evidence from Fu Chongju's 1909 Chengdu encyclopedia suggests that the house he would have been able to rent for that much money would have been quite small. A large furnished residence, according to Fu, went for as much as 30 yuan a month, and the landlord often required that his tenant employ an approved gateman, so that the latter could keep an eye on the landlord's furniture.[35] In 1912 Wu Yu negotiated a deal with a Manchu Bannerman to buy a property for 500 yuan, getting the approval of a committee that had been set up to oversee the financial interests of the Banner community in the wake of the 1911 Revolution. He borrowed 300 yuan of the purchase price from friends. The seller tried to raise the price after the deal had been struck, but Wu Yu was able to make use of intermediaries to satisfy the seller with what amounted to a tip at the time the title was transferred. He noted in his diary on February 11, 1912, that someone told him that foreigners were trying to buy up land in the Shaocheng but that the military government had forbidden it; still, on March 5 he reported that authorities in the Shaocheng told him that more than ninety properties had already been sold there and that prices were rising quickly.[36]

For the next few months, Wu Yu set down many details about his house restoration in his diary. He invited a noted scholar to compose and write out a couplet to affix on either side of his main gate; he had the gate refurbished, and he added many bamboo plants to the garden. He had workers rebuild a crumbling room near the gate to serve as a guest room for his tenants when they came from the countryside to Chengdu to bring him his share of the rice they grew. Most importantly, though, he fitted out a beautiful study for himself and a smaller one for his wife.

The contemporary Chengdu writer Ran Yunfei published a book on what can be learned about Chengdu from Wu Yu's diaries, and he points out that for scholar-gentry such as Wu Yu, owning a home provided a real sense of security in a turbulent era of rapid political change. Wu Yu's study gave him a peaceful environment for reading and writing, well away from the rooms his unruly daughters occupied. He paid no taxes on the property, although he was obligated to make small payments to the local police regularly, sometimes to equip a street militia that patrolled for thieves and protected the neighborhood against soldiers and bandits during times when Sichuan's militarists were fighting near the city. Wu Yu was so happy with his house that he celebrated the anniversary of its purchase for several years afterward and, even after he stopped doing that, continued to congratulate himself periodically on his foresight in seizing the opportunity to buy it.[37]

Wu Yu frequently urged himself in his diary to stay home and study, in order to expand his knowledge, keep out of trouble, and save money. But he was unable to resist the attraction of Chengdu's social scene. Ran Yunfei made a count of the number of restaurants Wu Yu and his friends patronized over the several decades covered in his diaries—forty-one are mentioned by name.[38] He also spent time at the new opera theaters built in the first decade of the twentieth century and at teahouses that had a much longer history.[39] It was the privilege and custom of patriarchs of gentry families to patronize the most elegant gathering places the city had to offer, as well as to welcome each other to their own tastefully appointed homes.

Ba Jin, however, never became the patriarch of a Chengdu family. In 1923, when he was nineteen, he left the city, along with his elder brother Li Yaolin (the model for Gao Juemin), to go to school in eastern China. By the time he returned for the first time at age thirty-seven in 1941, his uncles had sold the Chengdu house he grew up in to a military officer. The old front gate had been torn down during a 1924 road widening campaign and soldiers were stationed all around, so Ba Jin just walked by, reflecting on the happy and sad times of his youth. After 1949, the residence was assigned by the new Communist government to the theatrical corps of the People's Liberation Army (PLA) unit headquartered in Chengdu, which built a dormitory for its members on the site, tearing down the existing buildings to make room. When Ba Jin traveled to Chengdu in 1960, everything he had remembered was gone, although visitors these days can see an old double-mouthed well that stood down the street from the old homestead.[40] Reflecting on the twentieth-century history of the site, it is tempting to imagine the ghost of Ba Jin's grandfather—and the fictional Gao patriarch—trying to understand the revolutionary songs and dances being rehearsed by the PLA performers in the space where once Sichuan opera had delighted its gentry audience.

Schools and Hospitals:
Gentry Attitudes toward Foreign Influence in Chengdu

Mention has already been made of the 1905 abolition of the civil service examinations. Among Qing officials, that had been a controversial decision, made possible only because the exam system was to be replaced immediately by an extensive new school system. The new schools, it was hoped, would achieve the same ends of cultivating and identifying talent to serve the state, but with an updated curriculum that included foreign languages, science, mathematics, and world history in addition to Chinese history and classical texts. Many public and private schools were indeed established in the first decade of the twentieth century, including some for girls. These were part of a broader transformation in institutional life in early Chinese cities that was explicitly linked to foreign cultures—the new school system was modeled on the Japanese system that thirty years earlier had itself been modeled on European and American schools. The new police force, discussed in Chapter One, was inspired in the same way. And Western medicine also made inroads into Chengdu with the establishment of several hospitals in the first decade of the twentieth century.

The foreign origin of all of these institutions might have stood in the way of their success if Chengdu's gentry had been as conservative as Ba Jin depicts them to be in *Turbulent Stream*.[41] Education and medicine were closely linked to the self-conception of the Chinese elite. In the 1890s, Sichuan had been virtually closed off to the outside world; the few Europeans who visited it reported considerable hostility among the people there, especially the gentry. In 1895, a small medical clinic set up in Chengdu by Canadian missionaries was burned down by an angry mob. Ten years later, though, the situation had changed completely. Foreigners and their ideas had become popular among the gentry.[42] The great majority of Chengdu's elite community believed, though, that they could "domesticate" foreign products and ideas to make Chengdu life even better, without radically changing it.[43]

What caused such a change in attitude in the ten years between 1895 and 1905? In part, it was a result of the Qing court's 1901 decision, forced on it by the occupation of Beijing in the wake of the Boxer uprising, to launch a series of Western-influenced reforms as the Japanese had done in the 1870s. Suddenly men who knew something of Japan, Europe, and the United States were in demand in the government. Provincial leaders needed them to help set up the new police and local assemblies. This led thousands of young (and not so young) Chinese men to go to Japan to get the credentials needed to take advantage of these new opportunities. Travel allowed them to experience life in the rapidly changing cities of Japan and colonial Asia, including British Hong Kong and the foreign concessions in Shanghai. In the minds of many among Chengdu's elite, foreigners were transformed from a threat to a source of valuable new knowledge that could help China become richer, stronger, and better able to protect itself and its core culture (the *ti* of *ti-yong*).

Ba Jin's uncles studied in Japan in the early twentieth century, as did both Xu Zixiu and Wu Yu. Many in Chengdu's elite community supported the efforts of foreigners to establish schools in Chengdu. Robert Service, the dynamic American missionary who set up Chengdu's YMCA in 1907, made friends widely in the city, which helped him acquire a piece of land for the YMCA right in the center of town after the 1911 Revolution.[44] Meanwhile, in 1910 another group of missionaries, mostly Canadian, established the West China Union University on what had been agricultural fields and gravesites to the south of the walled city. Moving the gravesites provoked some discontent, but with the help of prominent city leaders, the Canadians pushed ahead and set up a beautifully designed Western-style campus. Its multistory brick buildings were all topped with Chinese-style curved tile roofs.[45] The 1988 television miniseries of *Turbulent Stream* begins with a scene in which the actor playing Gao Juexin accepts his high school diploma and descends the steps of one of the well-preserved West China Union University buildings, although Juexin did not study there in the novel.

As much as they welcomed foreign innovations in Chengdu in the first two decades of the twentieth century, hardly any of Chengdu's elite were much interested in the Christianity of the missionaries. In Chengdu, the YMCA was popular among youth from gentry families, who went there for English lessons, sports, films, and lectures. Very few, though, became Christians. Wu Yu sent two of his daughters to a Protestant mission-run school and approved of the moral lessons it taught them. The eldest ran off with a married man after she left school, however, and the school refused to allow her younger sisters to enroll. His second-eldest daughter wrote him to say that the school was bad anyway and advised him to send her sisters to the French Catholic girls' school, where "they will not be required to be religious."[46] He did just that. Wu Yu himself, like most other elite men, found the Buddhist sutras and commentaries on them more interesting to read than the Bible. Buddhist thought, including Tibetan Buddhism, experienced a strong revival among the wealthy population in Chengdu in the 1910s and 1920s.

The West China Union University made a mark for itself by establishing the first educational program in dental medicine in China. As in other parts of China, the missionaries introduced Western-style dentistry and medicine in Chengdu in the hope of making themselves welcome in the community and therefore able to spread the Christian message more effectively. French Catholic priests and doctors established a hospital in the northern part of town, and Methodist missionaries built their own not far from Ba Jin's family home in 1905, adding a women's hospital later. In *Turbulent Stream*, the conservative elders are suspicious of Western medicine. As Gao Juexin's cousin Zhou Hui lies ill in *Spring*, Juexin urges her husband to take her to the French hospital for treatment. Her husband delays until she is too close to death to be saved, but her death at the hospital confirms his belief that Western medicine is useless.

No doubt there were some people in Chengdu in the 1910s who believed, like Zhou Hui's husband, that foreign doctors were not to be trusted. But many among the Chengdu elite welcomed this new alternative in medical care. When Ba Jin's older sister fell ill with tuberculosis, his mother sought out a Western doctor, a woman, and became friends with her, even though the girl died not long afterward.[47] Ba Jin was allowed to keep the Bible given to him by the doctor.

The Western doctors in Chengdu certainly drew a sharp line between the medical sciences that they practiced and the customary medical lore of most Chengdu doctors.[48] Members of the Chengdu elite also distinguished between the two traditions but tended to accept them both as valid and appropriate for different circumstances. Ran Yunfei points out that Wu Yu never consulted Western physicians on his own account, but he did allow his wife to be seen by a Western doctor in Chengdu; his daughter sought out a German doctor when she was studying in Beijing in the early 1920s.

Acceptance of Western medicine did not require that Chengdu's gentry reject the Chinese practices they had known all their lives. Before the new hospitals were built, a broad range of medical practitioners operated in Chengdu. At the elite end, some accomplished scholars devoted years to the study of Chinese medical texts, including the *Yellow Emperor's Inner Classic* and the many medical treatises of the Ming and early Qing periods. Some of them, such as the novelist Li Jieren's father, had inherited formulas for herbal remedies from their ancestors. These doctors generally made house calls to diagnose illnesses by checking the pulse and observing the patient's appearance. Herbal treatment might be supplemented with acupuncture or moxibustion (burning small amounts of herbs on the patient's skin).[49]

People who could not afford a gentleman-doctor could visit a pharmacy and seek treatment there or consult medical practitioners who set up small shops or just simple stalls in market areas. Such doctors could set a broken leg or remove a rotten tooth, in addition to prescribing herbal remedies. Surgery on internal organs was not part of the Chinese medical tradition; medical missionaries from Europe and North America introduced it to Chengdu at the beginning of the twentieth century. Childbirth was generally handled by midwives, and, just as in other parts of the world before the twentieth century, complications often led to the death of the mother.[50] Near the end of *Family*, the young wife Ruijue's death in childbirth is implicitly attributed to her banishment to an isolated house outside the city walls during the mourning period for the dead patriarch, but such events were common enough, even in the comfort of the luxurious homes of the elite.

In the novel, Ruijue's death is connected to the perspective on illness and the afterlife that Ba Jin attributes to the Gao patriarch's concubine, Miss Chen. She believes that evil spirits played a role in the death of her husband/master and that, if Ruijue gives birth in the family residence while the newly dead body is lying there, his corpse and his ghost will suffer. The "blood glow" from the birth will cause his body to seep blood, she says. As discussed in Chapter One, the line separating medical and religious practices such as exorcisms could be fuzzy in early twentieth-century Chengdu. Unfortunately, historical sources that might help us understand the "blood-glow" phenomenon and how widely people believed in it are not available to us. One of the foremost scholars of the history of childbirth in Ming and Qing China, Yi-Li Wu, does not mention this phenomenon in her detailed book on the topic. In an essay on *Family*, though, Ba Jin writes that his own sister-in-law did have to move out of the family residence when she was in the final stages of pregnancy around the time Ba Jin's grandfather died. Unlike Ruijue, she did not die in childbirth.[51]

There is evidence that members of Chengdu's elite were much concerned about the quality of medical practice in the first decades of the twentieth century. Fu Chongju, the editor of the 1909 Chengdu encyclopedia, befriended the Canadian doctors and helped them set up a branch of the Red Cross in town. In his encyclopedia, he railed against quacks and called on the practice of medicine to be more tightly regulated to ensure that doctors did not harm their patients. He even complained about the bad handwriting of most Chinese medical practitioners, claiming that the pharmacists often made up the wrong prescriptions because they could not read doctors' scrawl. His anger at those in the medical field seems understandable, given his personal experience. Four of his children and a niece died of illness over the ten years before his encyclopedia was published in 1909. Western doctors had seen two of them, to no avail, leading him to bemoan the limited powers of all doctors. But he believed the average Chinese medicine practitioner was less to be trusted than the Western doctors in Chengdu.[52]

A late Qing provincial official instituted a formal licensing examination for doctors in the last years of the dynasty, and Fu Chongju included the names of those who passed the exam in his encyclopedia. The government seems to have tested candidates only on their knowledge of medical texts, without requiring them to demonstrate their ability to diagnose and treat actual patients. And the effort was abandoned after the 1911 Revolution. Meanwhile, the foreign-run hospitals became increasingly popular. In the 1920s, the city government established clinics to offer inoculations and other simple treatments to the masses of city dwellers. Still, before the Communist takeover in 1949, most people could not afford to consult a trained doctor of Western medicine, and many preferred the treatment provided by traditional practitioners.

Family Rituals

Turbulent Stream is full of descriptions of the ceremonies that take place in the Gao household and among their relatives—such as weddings, funerals, and ancestor worship—as well as accounts of the everyday etiquette that family members follow when they meet each other. There is a particularly rich scene in *Spring* in which Ba Jin meticulously describes a visit by the Zhou family to their Gao relatives, including who speaks, when different people stand up, what sort of expressions people maintain on their faces, etc. After some five pages of polite chitchat between guests and hosts, those assembled move into the garden:

> Naturally, Old Madam Zhou went first, with Qixia [one of the Gao family slave girls] supporting her. Her two sons' wives followed her. The married ladies of the Gao family came next. Behind them, Zhou Hui and Zhou Yun followed, with Gao Shuying and the other Gao girl cousins. Cuihuan [another slave girl] followed Gao Shuzhen, and behind her were Qian'er, Chunlan, Zhang Sao, He Sao, and the third branch's maid Tang Sao. At the very end came Juexin, holding [his son] Haichen's hand, and walking with Zhou Mei.[53]

Ba Jin includes this sort of detail to emphasize how much of the Gao family life was governed by family ritual that established everyone's relationship to everyone else—to whom they had to defer and who had to defer to them. Family rituals and etiquette often seem oppressive in *Turbulent Stream*.

How should we understand the importance that the Gao patriarch's generation placed on family ritual? Historian Richard Smith explains that, in Confucian societies, ritual was the process by which "harmony based on hierarchical difference" was achieved. Family rituals were intended to unify the family by fitting each member of it into his or her place, based on generation and gender, as well as other attributes such as scholarly achievement. Worship of the ancestors, for example, occurred in a set pattern, with the senior generation offering respect first, followed by younger generations and then finally by the household servants. Smith describes the many ritual handbooks that circulated during the nineteenth century, helping gentry families ensure that their family rituals conformed to the patterns considered orthodox by the Qing dynasty's leading scholars and officials. In addition, he lists some of the many popular proverbs about the importance of proper ritual conduct, including, for example: "With propriety one can travel throughout the world; without propriety it is difficult to go forward an inch."[54] Many families had formal "clan rules," composed by a revered elder and intended to guide the behavior of younger generations in perpetuity.[55] Ba Jin's own Li family does not seem to have had such a written document, but the rules were nevertheless clearly imparted to the Li children as they grew up. In his memoir Ba Jin recalled that the first time he remembered his normally loving mother beating him was when he was six or seven and he tried to get out of making a formal prostration—kowtow—to pay respect to his grandfather on the old man's birthday.[56]

Smith also points out that for much of Chinese history, the rituals of family and state were seen as tightly connected to the actions of the cosmos. Correct performance of rituals—by everyone from the emperor to a young boy on his grandfather's birthday—contributed to harmony in human society and in the cosmos itself. Neglect of proper rituals—particularly by the emperor, but even by his lowliest subjects—both caused and was a sign of trouble in the world. This was the justification for punishing some forms of misconduct between relatives very harshly. In 1996 the popular Sichuan history magazine *Longmenzhen* (a Chengdu term meaning something like "shooting the breeze") published an article about the gruesome death penalty—being quartered by water buffalo—meted out to a small child in a Sichuan county in 1916. The seven-year-old boy had accidentally caused the death of his grandmother when she fell and hit her head while trying to stop him from eating food prepared for a family ritual. Since the area northeast of Chongqing in which the accident occurred had been suffering from drought and warfare, the county magistrate accepted the demands of some in the community that the boy's unfilial behavior be punished in a highly visible and dramatic way, so as to restore harmony and prosperity. This is an extreme example and possibly apocryphal, but it illustrates how family ritual could be related in people's minds to the fate of entire communities.[57]

For the more rationalistic Confucian scholars, including such Chengdu luminaries as Xu Zixiu, ritual served to keep human beings focused on the "Path" or "Way" (*Dao*) of moral behavior of the sage. When sagely behavior was common, families would be well ordered, the nation prosperous, and the world at peace. Proper behavior was enough, and no special intervention by supernatural forces could make up for violations of proper behavior.

The Gao patriarch seems to represent this rationalist school of Confucian thought, since he is annoyed when his concubine, Miss Chen, brings an exorcist into the family residence to frighten away evil spirits that she thinks are making him ill. Most people in Chengdu in the early twentieth century, though, combined a respect for Confucian family rituals with an acceptance of the Buddhist concept of karma—the idea that one's behavior in this life would influence future lives for good or for ill. To these was usually added a firm belief in the existence of supernatural powers that intervened in everyday life: causing illness, helping businesses flourish, ensuring the birth of a boy, and so on.

The sociologist Richard Madsen, borrowing a term from religious studies scholar Charles Taylor, calls this sort of belief system characteristic of "embedded religion": "The world of embedded religion is 'enchanted,' filled with good and bad spirits. Religious practices are used to call upon the good and control the bad, as much for the sake of the material health and prosperity of oneself and one's community as for any otherworldly salvation."[58]

For men like the Gao patriarch, family rituals were aimed at achieving harmony in human society by cultivating the morality of family members and teaching them how they should relate to each other, including their ancestors. But many of the Confucian principles that underlay family rituals, such as filial respect for elders, could also be appealed to in support of rituals to create harmony in the spirit world surrounding the family. In *Family*, Juehui thwarts the exorcist called to banish evil spirits during the patriarch's illness, and the concubine Miss Chen says that Juehui is unfilial—he must want his grandfather to die. Juehui appeals to the more orthodox Confucian beliefs of his uncle Keming, asking him why he tolerates her talk of evil spirits. Ashamed, Keming withdraws, implicitly acknowledging that he was only going along with Miss Chen because he himself was afraid of being accused of a lack of filiality.[59]

The literary critic Rey Chow argues that Ba Jin's treatment of such family rituals and practices as the formal mourning for the Gao patriarch springs from the assumption that these rituals are stale remnants of a dying culture, empty of meaning for any of the participants. Ba Jin presents them, she writes, as "something of an exotic ethnographic find, whereupon an age-old custom receives the spotlight not for the significance it carries in its conventional context but rather for a displaced kind of effect—that of an absurd spectacle seen with fresh eyes."[60] Clearly the generation of the uncles and aunts in the trilogy only go through the motions of family rituals, and Ba Jin does ridicule the behavior of the women mourning at the patriarch's funeral. He also makes it plain that the aunts support Miss Chen's determination to remove the pregnant Ruijue from the household not because they believe in "the curse of the blood glow" but because it gives them a chance to seem to be upright and respectful daughters-in-law. At the same time, they are also happy to bring pain and trouble to Juexin and his brothers, whom they see as insufficiently respectful to them.

Rey Chow is right to call critical attention to Ba Jin's treatment of many family rituals and customary beliefs as "absurd spectacles" and "premodern barbarity." He misrepresents the Chengdu of his youth by suggesting that only those whose power depends on such practices and beliefs (the patriarch) or the uneducated (concubines and slave girls) considered them meaningful. But, Ba Jin is not consistent in this message. The jarring scene of hypocritical ritual mourning for the patriarch in *Family* that Rey Chow analyzes can be compared to another death scene later in the trilogy: Juexin's long struggle in *Autumn* to see that her young cousin Zhou Hui is given a proper burial by her cruel husband's family (so that her ghost—and her living grandmother—can be at ease). This struggle is viewed as valuable and even heroic, both by the narrator and by Juexin's more iconoclastic siblings and cousins.

It is possible and perhaps more fair to view Ba Jin not as an ethnographer of an exotic dying culture but as a representative of a branch of Chinese moral thought that extends as far back as Confucius himself and that criticized the formulaic practice of rites as sometimes worse than no rites at all.[61] Juexin is terribly pained that his sorrow at the loss of his cousin Hui cannot be expressed appropriately at her grave, because she has been denied one. But when real respect and love is not present, as with the Gao women's relationship with the patriarch, rituals designed to allow respect and love to be suitably expressed must fail. The writer Lin Yutang made this point in regard to Chinese rituals of mourning in 1936. His comment appeared in an essay in which he claimed—in his caustic, tongue-in-cheek way—to be analyzing Chinese humor in comparative perspective:

> I have studied this Chinese type of humour very carefully, and found a formula for it. That formula is the greatest care for form as such, coupled with the greatest contempt for it in actual life. Chinese humour is a result of Chinese formalism. When there is such an insistence on artificial form, everybody is bound to see its hollowness and take it humourously. On the other hand, in a civilization where there is a closer harmony between forms and sentiments, it is more possible for people to take the forms more seriously. A western funeral can be a serious affair, because the difference between form and sentiment is smaller. Not so with the Chinese funeral. So many farcical elements of mere form have entered into it, that everybody must take it just as light comedy. For instance, when you compel a daughter-in-law to weep at the coffin after a signal, break out into a loud wail, count ten, and ask her to stop, you can't expect either the daughter-in-law or the master of ceremony to treat it as anything but a joke. Of course, the daughter-in-law turns round in the next minute to smile at her baby.[62]

Confucian-influenced critics of formalistic Confucian-inspired ritual, such as Lin Yutang and—I would argue—Ba Jin, generally were even less tolerant of the sort of "superstition" practiced by an exorcist than they were of rituals of mourning with no real mourners.[63] In this, Ba Jin probably resembled the stern Xu Zixiu more than he did his religiously ecumenical teacher, Wu Yu.

Richard Smith points to one more significant aspect of ritual that gave it value in Chinese culture—its aesthetic qualities.[64] As we discussed above, gentlemen like the Gao patriarch devoted much time and money to cultural pursuits such as poetry and appreciation of the theater. Family rituals certainly had a poetic and theatrical quality and, when done well, really could stir the emotions. Ba Jin seems to have felt that. The mourning scene, in his depiction of it, is bad theater. By contrast, the New Year's feast near the beginning of *Family* is described as a truly emotional and joyous occasion, where the ceremony of four generations sharing a meal reflects an all-too-brief moment of harmony within the Gao family compound. This is what people like the Gao patriarch worked and lived for. This is what they feared would be lost if young radicals like Ba Jin turned their backs on their families and rejected the wisdom of the past.

CHAPTER THREE

Juexin's City

The Chengdu Economy

In this chapter, we follow Gao Juexin out of his family compound into the world of trade and commerce to see how people like him experienced the city—where he worked, how the production and distribution of goods were organized and financed, and how the world of work and business was changing in the first few decades of the twentieth century. Near the end, we will bring Juexin back home and consider how families like his were affected by economic and political developments in the first decades of the twentieth century. Even as mechanized industry, electricity, and new fashions in dress and construction changed Chengdu's commercial life, workers and merchants alike suffered from the uncertainty and destruction that resulted from almost constant warfare between rival militarists. In stressing the timelessness of the Gao family drama, Ba Jin glosses over important transformations in economic life and their impact on city and family.

While the powerful hand of the patriarch still keeps the Gao family in line, money matters are not often brought into the open in *Family*.

Clearly, at some point in the past the old man had built up a substantial fortune.¹ The patriarch prefers to talk about morality rather than money and does not dwell on matters of income and expenditure. After his death, the speed with which his sons divide up the family property suggests that, despite their Confucian studies, material interests have always been uppermost in their minds. In vain does eldest grandson Gao Juexin try to get them to follow the patriarch's wishes and maintain the family home and family unity.

Juexin is the central character in the *Turbulent Stream* trilogy as a whole because of his key role in the Gao family: he is the eldest son of the eldest son of the Gao patriarch. Because his own father is dead, Juexin must take on heavy responsibilities managing the extended family at a very young age. His submission to the will of his grandfather and his uncles and aunts causes him to sacrifice his personal ambitions and hurt those he loves. His beloved female cousins die in unhappy arranged marriages he does not try to prevent, and his younger brothers are contemptuous of him for failing to take charge of his own life and defy his elders. His youngest brother, Juehui, who is the main protagonist of *Family*, can escape to a new life in Shanghai at the end of that book. Juexin, though, must stay and handle various family crises throughout all three novels, even though he is probably no more than twenty-five years old at the end of the trilogy.

The dilemmas Juexin faces because of his position in the family—being torn between the dictates of the conservative patriarch and his wish to support his iconoclastic brothers and cousins, his childhood sweetheart Mei, and his loving wife Ruijue—are shown clearly in the trilogy. They are Ba Jin's central concern. The position of men like Juexin in the wider world of the city is not explored at all in the novels, however. Since his grandfather decides that Juexin should begin working after he finishes at the top of his high school class (instead of going abroad to study, as Juexin's uncles had done and he himself had hoped to do), his story provided an opportunity for Ba Jin to explore the world of business and labor. He chose not to: he wanted to focus on the psychological drama of the family and attack the values and behavior of the older generation. But the work world of the real-life model for Juexin provides a starting point for examination of the Chengdu economy at the time.

Juexin and the Commercial Arcade: Economic Development

The position that Juexin's grandfather secures for him is quite a specific one. It is the identical job held by Ba Jin's eldest brother, Li Yaomei, when Ba Jin was growing up. Ba Jin writes in his memoirs that their father obtained for his brother the position in the management office of Chengdu's commercial arcade, where he earned twenty-four silver dollars a month, a respectable but by no means large salary for a well-educated man at the time.[2]

In *Autumn*, Ba Jin provided a true-to-life description of the commercial arcade, showing how it looked as Juexin left at the end of his workday: long boards have been installed vertically across the fronts of the shops to shut them up, the sound of mahjong tiles being pushed around on a table can be heard from inside some of the closed shops, and from others come the sounds of musical instruments and Sichuan opera singing. Presumably the shop employees and apprentices are whiling away their time before they pull out their bedding and go to sleep on the shop floors. A large electric light shines on the deserted arcade entryway, outside of which snack shops are packed with happy customers.[3]

The commercial arcade was built in the first decade of the twentieth century as the centerpiece of a new downtown core in Chengdu. In those years, the Qing court and provincial governments had begun trying to emulate the Japanese government's earlier policies to encourage economic development, primarily in order to defend China from exploitation by foreign powers.[4] This emphasis on economic development was encapsulated by the slogan "industry to save the nation" (*shiye jiuguo*). In the decade before the 1911 Revolution, Sichuan's economic development commissioner worked with prominent local men—merchants and others with money to invest—to form a chamber of commerce and launch initiatives such as an experimental silk production facility and the arcade. Many of these projects were inspired by similar developments in Japan, which Qing officials and their staffs visited and studied. Beginning in 1906, the provincial government organized an annual industrial promotion fair, with prizes for those who created ingenious new products or successfully copied advanced foreign technology. The arcade was intended to become a more permanent showcase for provincial products. Prizewinners from the industrial fair were given the right to set up shop there.[5]

The arcade building was constructed by a stock company formed by a group of prominent men, with official encouragement. Illustrating the contemporary fear of foreign economic invasion, the company's bylaws stated that stock could not be sold to foreigners or to people with foreign partners. Construction on the site, a former salt warehouse and shop, was finished in the spring of 1909. The two-story wooden arcade stretched between two major streets in the heart of Chengdu. There was room for more than 150 shops, teahouses, and restaurants inside. Chengdu's first electric lights, powered by an imported German generator, were installed in the arcade. At the front (south) and back (north) entrances space was provided for sedan-chair bearers to wait while their employers walked through the shops. The south entrance featured columns with botanical capitals in the ancient Egyptian revival style popular in China and other parts of the world in the early twentieth century. Probably no one involved in the arcade construction in Chengdu had built anything like it before, but some of them may have seen such buildings during travels in eastern China, Hong Kong, and Japan.

By 1910, the shops in the arcade brought in more than 460,000 ounces of silver annually, over ten times the cost of building the arcade. Li Daojiang, a cousin of Ba Jin's father, invested in the arcade and took part in stockholders' meetings to discuss issues such as rent and repairs. It was no doubt due to his role in the project that Ba Jin's brother Li Yaomei was able to get a job in the management office. Family connections were important in the Chengdu economy in the early twentieth century, even if no direct family ties to the employer existed. Anyone seeking a position or signing a contract had to have a guarantor vouch for him or her (just as in the slave girl contract discussed in Chapter One). The guarantor could be held accountable if the person he vouched for failed to live up to the contract or did something illegal. As a result, it was easier and cheaper for someone from a respectable family to find a guarantor.[6]

To judge from *Turbulent Stream*, Ba Jin may not have had much understanding of how his older brother earned his pay. In the trilogy, Gao Juexin has an office in the arcade in which his brothers lounge around reading magazines, and he frequently makes use of an abacus to add up sums, since the boys hear the sound of clicking abacus beads as they read. On occasion, their aunts and other relatives stop by to seek Juexin's advice in making purchases of silk fabric and other goods. These relatives assume that Juexin is familiar with the business of all of the tenants of the arcade. Probably he (and Ba Jin's brother) performed such management functions as keeping account of rents, drawing up leases, and hiring and supervising maintenance contractors.

In December 1917, the commercial arcade burned down, but it was quickly rebuilt and a smaller arcade was constructed on each side. In 1924, right after Ba Jin left Chengdu, a particularly ambitious military governor named Yang Sen decided to construct a similar project on a grander scale—a whole commercial street called Chunxi Road, modeled on Shanghai's bustling Nanjing Road, with its department stores and trams.[7] The project was located just to the south of the arcade on the site of an extensive provincial office compound that had been rented out after the fall of the Qing. With the commercial arcade and Chunxi Road, that part of the city became the most popular entertainment district and shopping destination for luxury goods, including foreign and east-China imports. The arcade and Chunxi Road became the face of modern Chengdu.

As a symbol of modernity, though, Chunxi Road might be thought somewhat inappropriate, if not misleading. First, Chunxi Road was dedicated to commerce above all, not industry, despite industry's position at the heart of the rhetoric of economic patriotism in the early twentieth century. Second, even before the arcade and Chunxi Road were built, Chengdu already had a thriving commercial culture. The fact is that Chengdu had long been a very wealthy town. In the 1910s and early 1920s, many of the city's streets were lined with shops that did good business. Meyrick Hewlett, British consul general in Chengdu from 1916 to 1922, offered this description of the city:

> When I was there no wheeled traffic, not even a rickshaw, was allowed inside the city [wheels—particularly those of the heavy wooden Sichuan wheelbarrows—dug ruts into the street surfaces]. The mode of conveyance was by sedan-chair, and the chair coolies of Sichuan were famous. The main streets of the city were stone-paved, wide and flanked by shops on either side completely open to the road. As the shops displayed their shop-signs on large boards of scarlet or black with gold Chinese characters on them, the effect in the main streets was of passing through a long arcade of Oriental beauty. This effect was heightened in summer when the streets were sheltered by straw mats on huge erections of bamboo poles to protect them from the sun. Unpaved side streets run in parallels connecting the main streets, and in these most of the residences of the wealthy residents of Chengdu were located. Silk was in profusion, Sichuan silk being deservedly famous. There were streets with shops selling nothing but furs, brass shops,

copper shops, medicine shops with rare native medicines of every sort, curio shops, jade, amber, silversmiths, priceless embroideries—a paradise for the lover of beautiful things.[8]

There certainly were many poor people in Chengdu in the 1920s and 1930s, those who eked out a living as peddlers or transport workers, prostitutes or beggars. We will discuss what can be known about their lives in Chapter Four. But many people lived fairly comfortably in the city, and some were wealthy. For them, the arcade and Chunxi Road became associated with the new culture emerging in eastern China not so much because of what they could buy there but because the space seemed new. Wider roads for rickshaws and pedestrians, shops and restaurants on two levels, theaters and elegant teahouses located among the shops, and—above all—electric lights projected a modern image.

From the point of view of Ba Jin's grandfather, placing a grandson in a position as manager of the arcade made a lot of sense. He and his sons had trained for careers in the civil service, but the collapse of the Qing and subsequent political turmoil lessened the prestige and security of a government job. Those who were well off in Chengdu considered the arcade a positive civic contribution to the city's development. Its prominence and association with the ideology of economic progress must also have made it seem a relatively safe investment in troubled times. In *Autumn,* Juexin urges his brother Juemin to enroll in a school that trains post office personnel, another job associated with the forces of progress. When Ba Jin was young, the Chinese post office was one of a very few stable national bureaucracies. The famous Irish administrator Sir Robert Hart set up the post office on behalf of the Qing dynasty in the 1870s. Even after the collapse of the Qing, foreigners headed the Chinese postal service, and its twenty-five thousand well-paid Chinese employees all had to know English. The postal service's prestige and its importance to the foreign powers active in China tended to protect it from the whims of local authorities, so it offered attractive employment for educated youth.[9] A few other such modern professions were emerging in Chengdu in the early twentieth century, including police officer. Ba Jin's uncles, like the Gao uncles in *Turbulent Stream,* set up a law office in Chengdu, but it isn't clear that they did much business—relatively low-status customary legal advisers probably still handled most legal documents.[10] In short, career options for educated men who did not want to teach or serve on the staff of a militarist were relatively scarce in Chengdu when Ba Jin was young.

Mapping the City of Workers, Merchants, and Managers

How were most Chengdu people employed when Ba Jin was growing up? Population censuses can help to some extent to answer that question. Censuses were not new in twentieth-century China. They had been a basic technique of governance since the founding of the first empire, the Qin, in 221 BCE. By the last decade of the Qing in the early twentieth century, though, new approaches to public administration pioneered in Western Europe began to affect how and what information was collected in Chinese communities. More and more social surveys were published in books and magazines, giving anyone who could read access to quantitative information about their hometowns. Chengdu novelist Li Jieren clearly took advantage of such sources as he wrote his stories about city people; Ba Jin, however, based the accounts of Chengdu in *Turbulent Stream* pretty much entirely on his memories of his childhood and stories he heard from others.

Social surveys of Chengdu were carried out occasionally in the first few decades of the twentieth century, first by the police force established in the years before 1911 and later by social science departments in schools and universities. Surveys and other materials on society and the economy reveal that Chengdu was a very busy, if not industrious, city. The service sector, in particular, was large. The census of 1909, conducted by police authorities, included data on population and urban occupations, displayed in Table 3.1. A 1910 police report listed a total of 4,771 people under the category of sedan-chair bearers, rickshaw pullers, and porters in the five police precincts in Chengdu.[11] In the absence of mechanized transport, many men in Chengdu supported themselves by carrying other people and goods around the city and beyond.

The 1909 census noted that there were six factories in Chengdu, in addition to all of the government offices, schools, hotels, and service workers such as rubbish collectors and water-pipe purveyors (the latter owned water pipes and rented them to patrons of teahouses who wanted to smoke some tobacco as they drank their tea and chatted). The six factories included the large arsenal and mint that had been built by the provincial government in the 1870s with equipment imported from Europe. Most of the others were also government enterprises, including a paper mill outside the East Gate that produced high-quality paper for government reports and for sale to

Table 3.1 Frequency of occupations or places of employment in the service sector reported by Chengdu residents in the 1909 census

Occupation or place of employment	Frequency
Water-pipe purveyors	931
Rubbish collectors	900
Chinese medicine doctors	624
Water carriers	589
Wineshops/restaurants	558
Teahouses	518
Porters	380
Schools	324
Hotels	320
Licensed prostitutes	311
Temples*	263
Government offices and agencies	140
Housing agents	70
Pawnshops	50
Moneychangers	49
Employment agents	47
Midwives	41
Christian churches	17
Western medicine doctors	15

*Buddhist and Daoist temples, but probably also mosques: the census recorded 2,615 Muslims.
Note: The census recorded the city's population as 323,972.
Source: Data from: "Xuantong yuannian Shengcheng jingqu dyiyci diaocha hukou yilanbiao" [Chart of the first statistical report of the first year of Xuantong (1909) on the population of the police districts of the provincial capital], file 308, Zhao Erxun records, First Historical Archives, Beijing.

the public.[12] Altogether, these new factories probably employed fewer than five hundred men. This census gives no figures for the many small, family-run shops of weavers, tailors, leather workers, carpenters, ironmongers, and manufacturers of face powder and other beauty products.

The reason that the police census paid attention to service workers and not to the manufacturing trades in 1909 has to do with the mission of the new police. Service workers who operated in public spaces or, like doctors, were seen as critical to community safety and security, fell into the sphere of police work. Public sanitation and morality formed vital parts of the police mission in the early years of the twentieth century.[13]

In Chengdu when Ba Jin was young, each type of manufacturing and commercial service was regulated by its own guild. Guild leaders, chosen from among the established families in that trade, mediated disputes and set standards for pricing and other aspects of business. They also represented their trade in negotiations with local officials.[14] In 1905 the Chamber of Commerce was established, made up of representatives from the major guilds, and it became the main voice of the commercial interests in the city. When the provincial or city government tried to impose taxes or issued new regulations that affected commerce, the chamber would negotiate and sometimes protest. Unlike the police administration, though, the leaders of the Chamber of Commerce did not publish detailed statistics about its members. From their point of view, it was best for officials not to have too clear a picture of the resources at their command.

Over the course of the 1920s, the terminology of business in Chengdu changed in line with changes occurring in eastern China, as China's officials and businessmen continued to borrow new concepts and vocabulary from abroad. Guilds (*hang*) were renamed trade associations (*gonghui*). But their functions do not seem to have changed much. They still created a sense of unity among the members of a trade by meeting together, setting standards for prices and trade practices, overseeing group rituals, and disciplining misbehaving tradesmen. In 1927, a local newspaper reported that a carpentry foreman was punished for an infraction against trade rules; to make up for the infraction, the carpenters' trade association ordered him to repair the temple dedicated to their guild's patron saint—Lu Ban, a famous builder who lived at the time of Confucius. When the guilty party refused to do the work, the assembled carpenters tied him up and paraded him through the Chengdu streets to shame him.[15]

By the time Ba Jin left Chengdu in 1923, there was still little mechanized industry there. Shanghai's modernizing manufacturing sector, in contrast, included new textile mills that had begun to attract large numbers of migrants, especially young women.[16] Chengdu had a well-developed silk industry, but the complicated looms used for weaving silk (and cotton) cloth were powered by the weaver him- or herself. The most elaborate patterns required looms operated by two people. The cost of transporting machine-produced cloth from eastern China to Chengdu meant most people still could only afford local handwoven material until well after the power looms themselves came west during the war with Japan after 1937.

George Hubbard, an American geographer who visited Chengdu in 1920, was impressed by the productivity of the city's handicraft sector and published this record of it:

> While all the city, even the busiest business streets, is a residential section, and no place is without its children, chickens, and pigs playing in the streets, yet in some parts, these last-named elements predominate. Side streets off the main streets, or connecting two main business thoroughfares, will have few or no shops. Here homes alone fill the streets and come to the front. In every home something is manufactured for sale. Women wind cotton, yarn, thread, or silk; they embroider, weave, sew, make toys, incense sticks, flowers, or funerary money. Men make mats, tubs, buckets, baskets, or feather dusters, weave cloth, mats, or embroider scrolls or banners, shape iron, brass, or silver tools or trinkets, or work with the women on the projects they have in hand. Children down to six or eight years old often help at something—reeling yarn, sorting feathers, smoothing wood, mixing or grinding incense powder, or any other little thing their unskilled hands can do.[17]

The goods produced were either peddled by a family member along the street or sold to a store.

Although detailed statistics on businesses and workers in Chengdu in the 1910s and 1920s are lacking, we can get some sense of that world from particular commercial transactions about which details were recorded. We are fortunate to have records of some construction projects in the city in the years of Ba Jin's youth. The diary of Wu Yu, Ba Jin's teacher, helps us see how tradesmen were hired. In July 1922, for example, Wu Yu negotiated with carpenter Liao Nanting to reconstruct the main entryway to his west Chengdu residence, described in Chapter Two. Liao came to the site and the two men inspected the other gates that already existed along Wu Yu's street. According to Wu Yu, they were all laughable: "Sichuan cement masters' idea of Western style." Wu Yu told Liao that he wanted a gate modeled on the main entry of the Methodist girls' school on Shaanxi Street in the center of town. Happily for Wu Yu, Master Liao claimed to have already completed several similar gates for other customers, and the price, 470 silver dollars for a gate and three small rooms near it, was acceptable. They signed a contract stating that the work must be completed within a month. When the main beam over the gate was installed in August, Wu Yu presented a gift of pork and wine to the workers, which he noted was customary.[18]

The YMCA sent Americans to establish a branch of that organization in Chengdu early in the twentieth century, and they also left records of the process of constructing their buildings that reveal how work was organized in the city. According to a September 1926 report from YMCA secretary George C. Helde, the plans for what became the Y's main building, near Chunxi Road, were drawn up at YMCA headquarters in Shanghai in summer 1925. No Chengdu general contractor was judged capable of taking charge of the building, since none had experience with large Western-style buildings or sufficient capital to fund the construction under the standard terms of payment upon completion. So Helde made arrangements for the different parts of the construction himself:

> Contracts were made for brick all of which had to be made; lumber, much of which was still back in the mountains; and lime, which had to be burned and brought in on wheelbarrows from a point four days away. A mason foreman and three carpenter foremen were secured, and prices made with them for so much a square for masonry, plaster, lathing, and floors, each door and window to cost how much, and so on ad infinitum.

The large stone pillars for the front of the building were brought from a quarry twenty miles away. With its wooden packing frame, each pillar weighed two tons, and thirty-two porters were needed to carry each into the city. In the middle of construction, in fall 1925, Yang Sen, the military governor in power, was driven out of Chengdu, rice prices rose, and the agreements with the tradesmen all had to be revised. Fortunately for Helde, the YMCA's shipment of glass, electrical fixtures, and porcelain tubs from Shanghai made it upriver from Chongqing in the midst of scattered fighting. Finally, the building was completed in April 1926. Leaders in Chengdu's business community joined officials from the military government and prominent gentry at the grand opening ceremony for a building that still stands in the heart of the city.[19]

From the accounts of Wu Yu's gate and the YMCA headquarters, we learn that foremen—called "labor heads," or *gongtou* in Chinese—served as the chief organizers of labor in the construction trades, and that was true in many service industries as well. It is also clear that Chengdu's labor foremen were receptive to innovations, including adopting Western building styles. How they recruited and disciplined their laborers is harder to get at. Helde paid them a set amount per unit of construction, an amount that covered the price of materials and labor and the foremen's profits. The foremen managed all aspects of the job, leaving no written evidence behind to help us understand work dynamics.

In 1924, the students in an economics class at the Friends Middle School in Chengdu (run by Quaker missionaries) carried out a survey that reveals a little more about the lives of manual laborers at the time. They interviewed 330 men, including skilled and unskilled laborers, who worked on the campus of the West China Union University (Figure 3.1), which had been founded by Christian missionaries—mostly Canadian—in 1910. Among the 330 workers, 313 were between the ages of fifteen and fifty (3 were younger, 14 were older); 53 percent of them were unmarried, many of the married men had no children, and only 6 of them had children in school; 59 of the workers could write and 189 were completely illiterate. Slightly more than half of the workers came not from the Chengdu area but from other parts of Sichuan. Skilled workers reported earning less than 22,000 copper cash a month (the equivalent of about six and a half silver dollars at the time, or

Figure 3.1 Construction crew on the campus of West China Union University, 1920s. Courtesy of the Beech family.

about a quarter of Gao Juexin's salary as a manager at the commercial arcade), and unskilled workers earned about 13,200. Skilled workers reported the following monthly expenditures:

Accommodations:	700 cash
Food:	13,500 cash
Clothing:	1,200 cash
Tea and tobacco:	1,500 cash
Incense and other religious offerings:	750 cash
Total:	17,650 cash

This study concluded that skilled laborers with no family to support only managed to save 3,800 copper cash per month, about 17 percent of their wages. Those with dependents—and all unskilled workers—probably had no savings at all.[20]

This study also found that 34 of the 330 workers were apprentices. Their modest wages were given to their masters, who housed, fed, and clothed them. The practice of apprenticing boys to learn a trade makes a brief appearance in the *Turbulent Stream* trilogy: in *Autumn*, Gao Juemin joins a radical student organization, following the example of his younger brother Juehui. One of Juemin's friends, a student named Zhang Huiru, believes that to really understand society, he and his classmates need to experience the hardship of workers' lives. He therefore apprentices himself to a tailor. When Juemin and he get together, Juemin marvels at his work smock, so different from the long gowns of scholars and the military-style uniforms of students. They also compare their hands—the bookish Juemin's hands are soft and smooth, while Zhang Huiru's are rough and pocked with needle marks.[21] After this one scene, however, Ba Jin does not give us any more details of Zhang's experiences learning a trade.

Ba Jin based the character of Zhang Huiru on his friend Wu Xianyou, who left school and entered into just such an apprenticeship. But Wu Xianyou did not end up becoming a tailor. Instead, he soon accepted a job teaching at his alma mater, West China Union University.[22] It is not too surprising that the storyline of Zhang Huiru as an apprentice is very thin in the trilogy. There was a wide social gap between manual laborers and educated men in the Chengdu of Ba Jin's youth. It would have been very difficult for young men such as Ba Jin and his friends to defy and (from their elders' perspectives) humiliate their families by going into a trade. And the trades also had their own cultures, which would have been a challenge for young gentlemen to navigate. Apprentices were expected, for example, to join their masters' families in praying every day to the god of wealth at small altars installed in every shop.[23]

Still, Ba Jin knew something about the lives of tradesmen and apprentices from his encounters with them when they came to his family's house to work. In 1936 he published an essay about a carpenter named Chen who had repaired some of the woodwork in the Li family compound two decades earlier. Ba Jin took such an interest in the work that his family told him they would apprentice him to Chen. When the young Ba Jin shared the news with Chen, the carpenter shook his head and said they were just joking: "Wealthy young men study books so they can be officials; poor boys study carpentry." Chen also impressed on Ba Jin the dangers that manual laborers faced. Chen's father had died from a fall on the job. Later on, Ba Jin writes, Chen's shop was looted during street fighting in 1917, and eventually he went to work in the shop of a former apprentice. Ultimately, he shared his father's fate: a servant in Ba Jin's family heard that Chen had died after falling off a roof at a building site.[24]

The apprentice system for boys was similar in many ways to the contracting of slave girls that we examined in Chapter One. The master and the boy's family entered into a formal agreement. The master agreed to train the boy in a trade and take care of his living expenses for a certain number of years. In exchange, the boy worked for the master. As with slave girls, an apprentice was regarded as part of the master's household. He could be ordered to do all sorts of tasks not directly related to his trade. Discipline of apprentices could also be harsh. However, because of differences in gender roles in society and marriage, the master's authority over an apprentice was not as all-encompassing as in the case of slave girls. When their apprenticeships were over, boys were free to set up in business for themselves. Their master did not arrange their marriages. As the West China Union University survey suggests, many male workers were not able to marry until they had managed to save up enough money to show they were able to support a wife (see Chapter Four for more on this point).

Apprentices appear in newspaper reports occasionally. This case from 1915 suggests that boys could be apprenticed to masters of very modest means:

> A merchant by the name of Bai on Xiyu Street sells small amounts of rice for a living. He remarried several years ago after the death of his first wife. His new wife, who is in her twenties, is a simple woman who never argued

with her husband. Yesterday, Bai scooped rice from the barrel into his basket; when he returned at night, he measured the rice in the barrel and determined that five scoops were missing. He suspected his wife of stealing and selling it. He shouted at her and then hit her. The neighbors all heard the beating taking place. The next morning, the apprentice suddenly announced that his master's wife had died in the night. Neighborhood children crowded around the house and saw blood on the body; they informed the police.[25]

This anecdote offers a glimpse into what was the most common sort of household in Chengdu in the early twentieth century—a family headed by a small-scale merchant or artisan with an apprentice and family members to help run the business, living in a crowded street where all the neighbors know everything about everyone else.

Besides newspapers, another source of information on business and economics in the Chengdu of Ba Jin's youth are more recent publications: memoirs and local histories. After the establishment of the PRC in 1949, the Communist government funded the publication of local periodicals called "Materials on Culture and History." At first, these tended to feature articles about the history of the Communist Party and its involvement in such activities as labor strikes and uprisings. Later on, beginning in the late 1980s, after China's economy was opened to the world and cities were competing to attract outside investors, these publications and new popular history magazines began to focus on colorful local customs and even to celebrate successful local businesses that had previously been ignored or criticized for exploiting workers.

An example of the older-style article on the history of labor and the Communist Party may be found in the twenty-sixth issue of Sichuan Province's *Selected Materials on Culture and History*. A Communist labor organizer, Gao Sibo, writes of his efforts to encourage workers to strike for better working conditions in Chengdu in 1926 and 1927. He and his comrades set up a citywide union and invited workers in each trade to form a branch. They wanted to challenge the guild-style trade associations that already existed, which they viewed as dominated by bosses and foremen who oppressed the common laborers. By 1928, he reports, about 120 branches had formed and become affiliated with the citywide union. But their organization was crushed that spring, when the city's military governors decided to crack down on student and worker protests. Sichuan's militarists followed the example of

Chiang Kai-shek in eastern China, who began arresting Communists and the labor activists associated with them in spring 1927.[26]

As in most articles of this sort, details about the lives and views of the workers who participated in this short-lived labor movement are few. Gao Sibo does mention, however, that his Communist-led labor union competed for the loyalty of workers with two other, "yellow" unions set up by other political parties. The Communist union seems to have had some success at organizing weavers, but their meeting to discuss labor demands was infiltrated by "thugs" from the other unions who started a brawl. Right before their union was crushed, the weavers took their struggle directly to two of the merchant bosses whom they accused of keeping wages low. The workers paraded the two bosses through the streets. Gao does not reveal how this event ultimately played out and whether it was related to the crackdown on the Communist union. The politics of labor activism in Chengdu in the 1920s is murky, but it is clear that there was considerable tension that erupted periodically into demonstrations and violence.

A more recent account of labor conditions in Chengdu in the 1920s, which does not focus on conflict, appears in a 1996 article in the magazine *Longmenzhen* by Ye Chunkai on the pre-1949 coffin industry. Writing in a way that suggests he was thoroughly familiar with the business, Ye explains that some twenty coffin shops were located outside the East Gate, where logs could easily be brought upstream from the mountainous areas to the southwest.[27] The logs were laid out in a lumberyard to dry and then sawed into boards. Each shop employed three to five carpenters and two or three apprentices. The young, strong carpenters were paid according to how many coffins they finished (in other words, by piecework); older ones received a daily wage and helped the shop's owner with the business side of the trade. Ye Chunkai notes that apprentices generally served for three years, but masters could kick out those who were lazy or did not learn their trade quickly enough.

Shopkeepers stacked coffins in front of the workshops, which were kept closed; owners came out to talk with customers and look over the samples. Cheap coffins, made of thin boards with gaps between them, were purchased by philanthropic societies and used for unclaimed corpses of the poor or soldiers left behind by retreating armies. The most expensive coffins might cost more than 1,000 silver dollars—almost four times the annual salary of Gao Juexin. Customers would examine the wood to make sure of the quality and then have the finished coffin lacquered or painted. According to Ye Chunkai, the cheapest paint was made from a mixture of pig blood and lime and gave off a strange smell. The Gao family in *Turbulent Stream* certainly would have bought a fine lacquered one for the patriarch (in fact, heads of households often picked out their own coffins and had them stored until they were needed). Ye Chunkai reports that some Chengdu families ordered red coffins with sparkling ground porcelain mixed into the lacquer for elders who had lived very long and prosperous lives. Wu Yu, who hated his father, paid only eighty yuan for his father's coffin in 1913, at a time when he was making a salary of about a hundred yuan a month, in addition to his income from rents.[28]

Ye Chunkai's account of the coffin trade does not mention any change over time in the nature of the business until the late 1930s, when the war with Japan resulted in a flood of migrants from eastern China into Sichuan. Then a Chongqing company that sold elaborately decorated coffins and also rented out funeral clothes (formerly a separate trade in Chengdu) moved to town and lured customers from the old-style shops. A dozen years later, after the PRC was established, cremation was mandated; the old coffin shops quickly disappeared.

Compared to coffins, Chengdu's market in clothing shifted more, following trends that affected the whole nation, as we can see in an essay in *Longmenzhen* by someone writing under the pseudonym Lao Zu (old foot-soldier). Lao Zu gives us a picture of commercial life along Fuxing Street, near the commercial arcade, a street that was widened at the time Chunxi Road was built. A famous restaurant named Café of the Bamboo Grove was located there, along with a fortune-teller popular with military officers. The buildings were made of wood with narrow storefronts, most of which were occupied by men's hat shops. Lao Zu notes that generally the apprentices and members of the family fabricated the hats on the second floor above the shop; the kitchen and living space occupied the first floor behind the shop. The older men served customers; the older women cooked and did other household chores. The shops were clean and simple, with wooden plaques on each wall, carved with such sayings as "Honest and trustworthy" and "Good products at reasonable prices." Men chose hats to match their social status. Wealthy merchants and officials wore Western-style hats with brims. Customers who wanted to seem cosmopolitan wore "Luzon hats" (likely similar to Panama hats). Most men, though, wore the brimless, bowl-like skullcaps known as "melon rind hats," if they wore a hat at all.[29] Manual laborers generally wrapped pieces of white cloth around their heads.[30]

Lao Zu tells us that the most popular shop on Fuxing Street was named Victory. During the New Year's festival and other holidays Victory Hats was packed with city people, as well as peddlers who bought the hats and sold them at country markets. He notes that, about 1930, in order to compete with the stores on Chunxi Road, Victory Hats installed glass windows and mirrors and hired young women as salespeople. He himself accompanied an older cousin to buy a hat shortly after this transformation, but when the saleslady smilingly asked him what he wanted, he left the shop in embarrassment.

Changes in clothing styles could be rapid, spurred by the popular magazines that flourished in the early decades of the twentieth century. Antonia Finnane's study of Chinese clothing over the twentieth century shows how fashion was linked to politics—people bought new styles of clothing to indicate allegiance to republican ideals after the 1911 Revolution or, as Lao Zu noted, to show that they were cosmopolitan.[31] Like the craftsmen who built Wu Yu's Western-style gate, Chengdu's tailors, cobblers, and hat makers were willing and able to work from new patterns and models. Some older people grumbled at the transformations in people's personal appearance in the decades after 1911, but not many. In *Turbulent Stream*, Gao Juehui always seems to wear a short jacket and pants, a style associated with the new schools, whereas his older brothers wear the more traditional long gowns of the scholar-official and merchant class. But, although his choice of clothing clearly helps to identify Juehui as someone who is rejecting the past, it never becomes an issue in his family relations—unlike his cousin Qin's decision to bob her hair.

The Chengdu market had an appetite for many of the new products being introduced to the world in the early decades of the twentieth century, including phonographs, bicycles, and fountain pens, which slowly began to supplement writing brushes—but never replaced them entirely. As Frank Dikötter shows in his study of the material culture of that period, across China new commodities "rapidly became part of the texture of everyday life."[32] Many of the new products could not be made in Chengdu in Ba Jin's youth, but merchants brought in what they could, since they knew the city's wealthy would be interested. Boatmen and porters were kept busy on the rivers and roads connecting Chengdu to eastern China, as well as within the city itself, moving goods and people around and trying to avoid getting caught in the frequent outbreaks of civil war.

Farmer-Tenants: Chengdu's Agricultural Economy

Gao Juexin's job in the commercial arcade paid a modest salary. A much more important source of income for his family was the rent they received from property they owned, both in the countryside and in the city. Interviews in the 1930s with well-off families in Shanghai and Beijing (then called Beiping) indicate that in each case about half of them owned land that they rented out.[33] We do not have such statistics for Chengdu, but the figure was probably comparable and perhaps even higher, given the relative lack of investment outlets in unindustrialized Chengdu. Property in the city itself usually was rented to shopkeepers. As we saw in the discussion of Wu Yu's purchase of a house in Chapter Two, Chengdu had a lively real estate market when Ba Jin was young, and it was possible to rent or buy land and buildings all across the city. A building like that of Victory Hats on Fuxing Street, described above, was likely to be owned by a wealthy family and rented to the shopkeepers.

The rural land owned by the Gao family, on the other hand, was leased to farmers. At various points in the trilogy, the Gao tenants and the rent they pay are mentioned. In *Spring*, an agent for the Gao family, Liu Sheng, travels outside the city to collect rent. Because of the number of bandits reported in the area, he decides to stay in an inn in a county seat and sends messages to the tenants to come to him. None of them dares venture out on the road, and Liu Sheng returns to Chengdu empty-handed.[34] The growing difficulty of collecting rent on their rural land is one of the reasons that Juexin's fourth and fifth uncles give in *Autumn* for why the family residence should be sold and the proceeds divided up among the branches of the family.

The wealth of Chengdu in the 1910s and 1920s really did depend to a great extent on agricultural surplus that accumulated in the hands of absentee landlords and trickled down to the people who supplied the food, fabrics, furniture, and other goods they consumed. Chengdu is located in the middle of rich farmland in the Sichuan basin—an ancient inland sea. Abundant water from the Tibetan plateau to the west is channeled through a network of streams that provide excellent irrigation. And, until recent decades when processed chemical fertilizers arrived on the scene, night soil— human waste that has been allowed to heat up and ferment in order to kill bacteria—was sold to farmers to help bring up their yields.

On the basis of surveys done in the late 1930s, Richard Gunde has estimated that in the early years after the 1911 Revolution about half of all farmers in counties around Chengdu owned no land and rented from others. Another 15 percent owned a small amount of land and rented additional fields. The other 35 percent included those who had enough land of their own to support their families, and landlords who rented out some or all of their land.[35] Relations between landlords and tenants probably varied quite a bit. Wu Yu's family had been prominent landlords in Xinfan County, north of Chengdu, for several generations, and their tenants may have been members of less well-off branches of the family. Ba Jin's family's wealth was built up largely in his grandfather's time, and his agents probably worked out agreements with the tenants of the previous landowners.

Wu Yu received quite a bit of agricultural land in the 1890s when his father agreed to a division of the family's assets after Wu Yu's mother died and his father remarried. As a child, Wu Yu himself had spent time in the family home in Xinfan County, but as an adult he preferred to live in Chengdu. As we saw in Chapter Two, he was particularly fond of the house he bought in 1912 for himself and his wife and children. When he had the gate rebuilt on his Chengdu home, he instructed the masons and carpenters to build small rooms next to it. These were for the male servants, but also to accommodate his rural tenants when they came to Chengdu to pay their rent. In his diary he reports chatting with them about people and events in his hometown. It is clear that, although his social status was higher than theirs, he treated them with courtesy. He even took pleasure in his encounters with them. In the fall of 1915, a tenant by the name of Diao Hongsheng came to the city to report that a fire had destroyed his house and pigpen. Wu Yu granted him money to build a new house, although on a smaller scale than the one that had burned.[36] We might speculate that, among Wu Yu's tenants, only the favored were given the task of traveling to the big city to deliver the rent to Wu Yu. In reference to them, he uses the word for tenant (*dian*), but it seems probable that some among his tenants acted as his agents in relation to other tenants. In the early 1920s, when he was teaching at Peking University, Wu Yu's third wife wrote to him to let him know that she and one of his daughters had traveled to Xinfan to pay their respects at the ancestral cemetery and collect the rent.[37]

As with industry, agricultural techniques did not change much in Sichuan in the first half of the twentieth century. Farmers continued to maintain irrigation channels that allowed them to flood rice paddies and grow two crops a year. They continued to harvest fruits and vegetables—and raise chickens and pigs—to sell in periodic markets in county towns.[38] Some families fed mulberry leaves to silkworms and sold the cocoons the silkworms produced—or reels of silk threads spun from the unraveled cocoons—to merchants in Chengdu. Tobacco, hemp, and tung oil trees were other important commercial crops in parts of Sichuan in the early twentieth century.

In some parts of the province, farmers were encouraged—even pressured—to grow opium poppies, since opium yielded high profits for the landlords and helped Sichuan militarists buy guns and ammunition in eastern China. This crop had been grown in Sichuan since at least the early nineteenth century, but the area devoted to it increased substantially in the decades after 1911.[39] The effects of increased opium production and consumption on Sichuan's economy in the 1920s and 1930s are not well understood. Historian Frank Dikötter has argued that the negative impact of opium on China as a whole has been greatly exaggerated, but many historians believe that investment in opium production and consumption in the decades after 1911 made farming more risky, impoverished the Chinese countryside, and undermined the health of many opium users, in addition to funneling funds into the hands of militarists and the criminal gangs associated with them.[40]

As with the variety of crops grown, land ownership patterns changed in Sichuan beginning in the mid-1920s. Gentry landlords, both those based in rural communities and those who lived in the cities, sold much of their land to newly prominent military figures. At the end of *Autumn*, the Gaos sell the family home in Chengdu to a military officer. Ba Jin's Li family did that too, and they also likely sold much of their rural land to military officers and people connected to them. Liu Wencai, of Dayi County west of Chengdu, became one of Sichuan's wealthiest landlords in the 1920s and 1930s. His connections to two of Sichuan's most powerful militarists—his brother Liu Wenhui and Liu Xiang, their cousin, once removed—helped him amass hundreds of acres of land and dozens of residential and commercial buildings. After the Communist victory in 1949, Liu Wencai's main family residence was turned into a landlord museum, which hundreds of thousands of children toured to learn about the horrors of the "old society." In the changed political circumstances after the death of Chairman Mao in 1976, Liu Wencai's reputation has improved substantially—local historians now declare that he contributed a great deal to charity and did not actually torture his tenants to death as claimed by the exhibitions in the landlord museum.[41]

The conscription of soldiers and laborers for the many armies that formed in Sichuan in the decades after 1911, discussed in Chapter Five, must also have had a significant, although unquantifiable, economic impact in the areas around Chengdu.

Aside from agricultural products, another important commodity was "harvested" in Sichuan in the early twentieth century—salt. *Turbulent Stream* does not mention the importance of salt to Chengdu's economy, but many people in the city of Ba Jin's youth made money from it. Madeleine Zelin's study of the Sichuan salt industry explains how salt wells were drilled deep into the ground in southern Sichuan. The water in the salt brine that was brought up was boiled away, leaving the dried salt to be packaged for sale across the province and beyond. Natural gas to fuel the fires was also obtained from local wells (as a former inland sea, the Sichuan basin has a good supply of buried, gas-producing organic matter, as well as salt deposits).

The production and sale of salt had been closely regulated by the Qing government, which relied on it for a substantial part of its revenue. Private merchants who produced salt had to be sure to be on good terms with officials in the provincial government in Chengdu. Their guild was active in the city. In 1911, the government monopoly collapsed. Attempts by the central and provincial governments to revive it foundered as the province fragmented politically. In the 1920s and 1930s, local militarists controlled much of the revenue from salt sales via special relationships with salt merchants who served as tax farmers. Despite this, Chengdu continued to be significant to salt merchants, both as home to many customers and as a key political and financial center.[42]

Warfare and the Economy

Zelin's detailed study of the Sichuan salt merchants shows how much the economy of the region suffered from the almost-continuous warfare between 1911 and 1950. Most obviously, businessmen and anyone else with visible property found themselves pressured by militarists to hand much of it over to pay the troops and buy weaponry. Zelin remarks on how the initial enthusiasm of the salt merchants to develop new chemical and pharmaceutical industries in the first few years after the 1911 Revolution seeped away as funds that might have been invested in such ventures were confiscated.[43] Sichuan's economy continued to be dominated largely by agricultural production and handicrafts, perhaps helping insulate it somewhat from the effects of the Great Depression, which slowed Shanghai's factories in the early 1930s.[44]

The most successful Sichuan company in the 1920s and 1930s was the Minsheng Industrial Company, based near the Yangzi River outside of Chongqing. Its founder, Lu Zuofu, whose career is examined in Chapter Seven, cooperated closely with Liu Xiang, the dominant military figure in that region. The Minsheng Industrial Company diversified beyond managing shipping into industry, but on a relatively modest scale. Mechanized industry on a large scale arrived quite suddenly in Sichuan beginning in 1938, when whole factories were moved from the war zone in eastern China to Sichuan after it became the base from which the Chinese government resisted the Japanese until war's end in 1945.[45]

Political uncertainty and occasional warfare in the streets in Chengdu itself contributed to economic disruption. The shop of Ba Jin's friend, the carpenter Old Chen, was looted during such fighting. Wu Yu's decision to have his outer gate rebuilt in 1922 may have been related to the feeling of insecurity that pervaded the city in the decades after 1911. Ba Jin's fellow Chengdu novelist Li Jieren noted that, whereas Sichuan's various militarists were building themselves elaborate houses in the city, most ordinary people stopped investing heavily in residential construction because of the unrest. Instead of building a house that would stand for several generations, he claimed, people built so cheaply that a cat might do damage to the roof tiles by walking on them.[46]

Merchants and workers in the city felt the scourge of warfare in many ways. An incomplete list of the complaints raised in local papers between 1911 and 1935: confiscation of property for use as barracks, looting and damage to life and property during times when the city changed hands from one militarist to another, miscellaneous taxes and fees charged by authorities to support their armies, currency devaluation because of excessive production of coins, and travel hazards. In the summer of 1917, the president of Chengdu's Chamber of Commerce, Fan Kongzhou, was assassinated on the road between Chongqing and Chengdu. Fan Kongzhou, classically educated in the mid-nineteenth century, had thrown himself into economic ventures near the end of the Qing, taking charge of building the commercial arcade and setting up a modern printing facility that captured much of the market for printing in the city (including Wu Yu's 1914 book of poetry, *Autumn Waters*). He imported books and newspapers from eastern China and established his own newspaper, for which the young Li Jieren wrote.

His assassination has been attributed to his newspaper's open criticism of the militarists who presided over the April 1917 street fighting in Chengdu and his support for salt merchants who were protesting the imposition of new taxes by these same militarists.[47]

As Fan Kongzhou's story suggests, Chengdu's better-off businessmen often found good relations with the military authorities and the bureaucrats who served them to be the most effective strategy for surviving the militarization of the province. The story of how Chunxi Road was built in 1924 illustrates the connections between militarists and ambitious men in Chengdu's business community.[48] Building a broad, paved, commercial street appealed to military commander Yang Sen, who wanted to link his rule to modern culture and economic progress. He planned to use the new street to promote use of rickshaws and bicycles, and eventually automobiles and streetcars, in Chengdu. Indeed, five thousand rickshaws were introduced into the city the year after Chunxi Road was built.[49]

In building Chunxi Road, Yang Sen found an ally in Yu Fenggang. Yu came to Chengdu from Shanghai in 1916 as accountant for the branch office of Shanghai's Commercial Press. In the chaotic years 1916–1924, Yu Fenggang took advantage of his status as a neutral party and helped several rival militarists organize their finances and raise money in the city. Enriched by this activity, he left the press and opened several jewelry stores. One was close to the commercial arcade, next to a pharmacy owned by a translator employed in the French consulate. The pharmacy stood directly in the path of Yang Sen's planned road, but, according to Chengdu historian Jiang Mengbi, its owner refused to relinquish the site and Yang Sen was afraid to take on an adversary with the backing of the French consul. Yu Fenggang stepped in and offered his own land as an alternative route. In exchange, Yang Sen gave him the right to buy as much of the new streetfront property as he wanted.

Yu Fenggang did buy much of the land along the new road, giving Yang Sen's administration a sudden influx of cash. Yu then set up a construction and management company to develop it and rent out the buildings to Chengdu merchants. Given that Yu Fenggang was from Shanghai, it is not surprising that a 1924 photograph (Figure 3.2) of the newly built Chunxi Road closely resembles earlier photographs of Shanghai's Nanjing Road. Jiang Mengbi writes that Yu Fenggang jumped at the chance to develop Chunxi Road precisely because he had seen how much money Shanghai financier Silas Hardoon had made from speculating on Nanjing Road real estate.[50]

Figure 3.2 Chengdu's Chunxi Road commercial zone shortly after construction in 1924. Courtesy of the Mullett family.

Yu Fenggang's tenants included branches of Shanghai bookstores, photography studios, and shops selling watches, jewelry, and eyeglasses. A famous Beijing pharmacy set up a branch there. And several prominent local firms moved their businesses there or set up new branches. In 1929, Yu and a group of investors built a theater on the south segment and induced over a hundred Beijing opera performers to come to Chengdu from Shanghai. The Chunxi Great Dance Stage was the first Chengdu venue for regular performances of Beijing (rather than Sichuan) opera. In the 1930s, at least thirteen banks and six newspapers funded by Sichuan militarists established offices on Chunxi Road. (It is still the commercial heart of the city today, the central part of a huge pedestrian mall—much like Shanghai's Nanjing Road has become.)

The example of the building of Chunxi Road inspired other attempts to develop different parts of the city after 1924, including the part of the city where Ba Jin grew up, in the northeast corner. The neighborhoods in the northeast had gone into decline after 1911 for several reasons. The construction in the early years of the Republic of a new city gate along the east wall, just south of a large open space used as a military parade ground during the Qing, laid the area open to incursions by the many disbanded soldiers and bandits who made periodic, profitable forays into the city. And, as we saw in Chapter Two, on the other side of town, the old Qing-era Banner garrison (Shaocheng) had been opened up for residential development. The western district quickly became the most desirable neighborhood in the city.[51]

Facing the threat that their northeastern sector might become an insecure backwater, some neighborhood leaders in that area banded together to try to avert decline. In 1933 a group of fifty neighborhood residents—including a dozen militia heads and neighborhood watch leaders—sent a petition to the city and provincial governments to adopt a plan they had devised for development of the East Parade Ground (Figure 3.3), which in

Figure 3.3 Aerial view of Chengdu, 1934. The East Parade Ground is the bare patch of ground at the top center of the image, which was taken from over the former Banner garrison looking east. The large rectangular area in the lower half of the photograph is the Imperial city. Ba Jin's childhood residence was near the upper left corner of the image. Photograph by Wulf-Diether Graf zu Castell, a famous German pioneer of aviation. Wulf-Diether Graf zu Castell, *Chinaflug* (Berlin: Atlantis-Verlag, 1938), p. 157. Reprinted by permission of Gabriele Gräfin zu Castell.

Qing times had been used for army exercises.⁵² (At that point, Ba Jin's family home had already been sold, so it is unlikely that any of his relatives were involved in this effort.) This urban initiative suggests that years of warfare and strife had not completely suppressed entrepreneurial energies in the city. The details of the proposal show that its supporters had closely followed the development of the other districts of Chengdu, such as the Shaocheng area and Chunxi Road. The development plan included a park, a public hall, and a tract of land to be sold to individual builders to pay for the other features.

The original petition adopted the language of city management that had been brought into Chengdu with the establishment of the police force in 1903 and a municipal government in 1921. The old East Parade Ground, the petitioners argued, was an important relic of Chengdu's history, and the creation of a park would help preserve this historical artifact, in addition to protecting public health. "As the nation becomes more civilized, the cities become more prosperous, and public places of recreation and entertainment increase," they noted, while pointing out that parks already existed in every other district in the city. Local students would benefit from the park, which would be provided with a library and newspaper reading room in addition to the teahouses and restaurants that would help pay for maintenance. Finally, the neighborhood leaders brought up the problem of crime in their quiet neighborhoods. The park project would encourage the development of commerce in the area, they argued, which would bring more people to the deserted streets of the northeast. For added security, they proposed that the authorities station troops next to the park. The neighborhood leaders waited two months for an answer from the city, and in May of 1933 sent another, more urgent petition that stated bluntly, "The sooner the park is built, the sooner this area will develop, and the sooner the people will be able to live in peace."

On June 17, the provincial construction bureau and city government reported that they had surveyed the area of the East Parade Ground and found it suitable for the development, since the only thing occupying it at the time was a brick factory. Unfortunately for the neighborhood residents, though, the city government decided to use the profits from the sale of the land primarily for the restoration of a temple near Shaocheng Park, which was to be turned into a public meeting hall. Still, the East Parade Ground park was judged an excellent project, and the city commended the neighborhood leaders for their plans. There is, however, no record that the park was ever built.

This fragment of a story suggests that many people in Chengdu sought the support of the military leaders who ran the city government for their own projects, using the language of economic development that had become accepted among China's political leaders. In the case of the 1933 development plan, however, neighborhood leaders succeeded merely in drawing the attention of city authorities to a resource that they could use to further their own ends.

Juexin's Social Network and the Urban Community

In *Turbulent Stream*, Juexin serves as his family's connection to the commercial world. In *Family*, he accompanies his aunt to buy cloth to be made into a dress. In *Autumn*, he does the same for his fourth uncle and Zhang Bixiu, the female impersonator his uncle patronizes. In the latter case, the narrator reports that they spent more than one hundred silver dollars on material, an amount equivalent to several months of Juexin's salary; the shop promises to send the material to Zhang Bixiu and the bill to Juexin. Some time later, Manager Zhu of the silk store looks in on Juexin in his office and apologizes for being out when Juexin was making his purchases. He complains to Juexin about the levies the city's authorities are imposing on shops to pave the roads.[53] Later on in the story, the commercial arcade burns down (as it actually did in 1917 and again in 1933), destroying the value of the family's shares in it, including some that his aunts have asked Juexin to buy on their behalf. They demand that he cover their losses out of his own resources, which he feels compelled to do. A local bank lends him the needed sum, because they know him and he has a good reputation. But, in despair over the demands his family makes on him, he quits his job.[54]

This description of Juexin's role as the financial agent for the family probably came from Ba Jin's memory of his talks with his older brother Li Yaomei, who visited him in Shanghai in 1930, and possibly also from letters he received from Li Yaomei. The pressure on Li Yaomei to manage the financial affairs of the extended Li family by making use of his personal connections to the city's merchants seems to have been intense. By 1930, Li Yaomei had resigned his position in the commercial arcade and sold much of his land. He used the proceeds to invest in various ventures. In an essay explaining how he wrote *Autumn*, Ba Jin mentions that Li Yaomei experienced a period of mental illness, during which he tore up and threw away all of the banknotes he possessed. Shortly afterward, just as the first chapters of *Family* began to appear in a Shanghai newspaper, he killed himself.[55]

Ba Jin originally intended to have Juexin commit suicide at the end of *Autumn*, just as his older brother had done in real life. Because so many of his fans wrote to him pleading for a hopeful story, Ba Jin changed Juexin's fate. Near the end of *Autumn*, Juexin and his uncles sell their commonly owned farmland and family compound, despite Juexin's qualms about violating his late grandfather's wishes that the family continue to live in it forever. Ba Jin based the details of the family division on his own family's experience. The amount received for house and land, 82,000 silver dollars, is divided among the branches of the family. Juexin's branch, responsible for carrying on the rituals of ancestor worship, receives twice as much as the other three branches.[56] As mentioned in Chapter One, Juexin marries the slave girl Cuihuan and moves with her and his stepmother to a small house of their own.

The idea of the small (nuclear) family gained popularity in China during the decades of the 1920s, as a generation of young people like Ba Jin struggled to free themselves of family constraints in a time of rapid social, economic, and political change. It is important to recognize, though, that family connections continued to play a vital role in the Chengdu economy throughout the decades following the 1911 Revolution. Outside merchants such as Yu Fenggang could be very successful in the city, but only if they connected themselves closely to the dominant militarists. Members of Chengdu's older elite families kept a wary distance from the militarists and continued to rely on their own family networks, even if they ceased living together in one large family compound. The disintegration of the Gao family in *Turbulent Stream*, reflecting as it does the dissolution of Ba Jin's own family, is a tragedy from the point of view of Juexin, who tries to maintain the family's reputation and therefore its economic stability. The lack of family cohesion had consequences graver than an unhappy home life—it could lead to bankruptcy and all the miseries that came with poverty.

CHAPTER FOUR

Sedan-Chair Bearers, Beggars, Actors, and Prostitutes

The Worlds of the Urban Poor

The fictional Gao family is among the wealthiest in Chengdu, just as Ba Jin's family was when he was a child. But they only seem secure in their wealth in the early scenes in *Family*, such as at the New Year's celebration. As the trilogy progresses, the patriarch's nagging fear that the family will fall apart is realized. The theme of the rise and fall of families is a popular one in fiction about China, whether by Chinese or foreign authors. The most famous example is the eighteenth-century *Dream of the Red Chamber*, by Cao Xueqin, which depicts the downfall of the fabulously rich Jia family. We see it too in Pearl Buck's novel *The Good Earth*, published in 1931, the same year *Family* began to appear in print. Because of the family's importance as an economic unit, the collapse of family unity often carried the threat of impoverishment for most of its members.

In *Turbulent Stream*, poverty is linked to powerlessness and lack of family support. We have already examined the lives of slave girls in Chapter One. When the birth families of these girls could not raise them, they became dependent laborers for more fortunate families. Although the Gao family seems to clothe and feed their servants fairly well, the novels depict class differences in living standards, as when Ba Jin writes of the room near the back of the compound that the female servants share. The cramped space is dark and unheated. Even worse than these living conditions is the treatment given Qian'er, the slave girl who works for Fourth Uncle Ke'an and his wife, the bitter Madam Wang. Qian'er falls ill in *Autumn*, and, to spite members of the family who show sympathy for the girl, Madam Wang refuses to give her any treatment. When she dies, her body is rolled up in a mat to be sent to an unmarked pauper's grave.

Life was precarious for all, but especially for the poor and powerless, as Qian'er's fate symbolizes. This chapter takes a closer look at the images of poor people Ba Jin presents in the trilogy. It then explores how poverty was understood and explained in early twentieth-century China, and how that was changing. Did charitable giving and government social programs exist to help the poor? How effective were such programs and how did they evolve as more Chinese embraced reform? Finally, we consider what historical sources reveal about the nature of social class and social mobility in Chengdu in the May Fourth era. How did people become poor? What sort of housing was available for the poor? How easy was it for them to move around and outside the city in search of opportunities? This chapter and the one on soldiers that follows are attempts to fill wide gaps in Ba Jin's portrait of his hometown.

Images of "The Poor" in Turbulent Stream

In *Family*, scenes with poor people serve primarily as a way to illuminate the character of Gao Juehui, the idealistic young grandson of the patriarch. Juehui falls in love with the slave girl Mingfeng but abandons her when he realizes how large the status divide between them is. He doesn't approve of such status consciousness, however. In the opening scene, he and his brother Juemin are walking home from school through the snow. When their stepmother later asks them if they took sedan chairs, Juehui immediately denies it, prompting his eldest brother laughingly to call him a "humanitarian." The rest of the family sees Juehui's disapproval of sedan chairs as quixotic. He has no idea how chair bearers could support themselves if people stopped hiring them; he just refuses to exploit the labor of another human being in that way.

Juehui's confusion and frustration at social inequities come out even more clearly in a scene in chapter 13 of *Family* in which he discovers a beggar boy outside the gate of the Gao compound on New Year's eve. Juehui hears a sobbing sound and sees the boy shivering in rags. He thrusts money into the boy's hands and flees in distress, hearing a voice inside his head mocking him for thinking he can save the world—or even help the child by giving him a few coins.

The link between lack of family support and poverty is highlighted in the case of the character Chen Jianyun, a distant relative of the Gao family. Chen Jianyun's parents died when he was young, and he relies on family connections to find teaching jobs that earn him a meager living.[1] Years of struggle have weakened his body as well as his resolve. He is in love with his cousin Qin but knows he can never marry her—or any other young gentry lady—given his poor financial prospects and bad health. Jianyun stands as a warning to the young Gao boys, Juemin and Juehui, of what could happen to them if they defy their grandfather and uncles and are cast out of the family. In a scene in which eldest brother Juexin is informed of his arranged marriage in the 1956 film version of *Family*, Juexin's father tells him straight out that rejecting the marriage the patriarch has negotiated for him would ruin his life, since no one would hire him or have anything to do with a person so lacking in filial piety.

Opium is also linked to poverty in Ba Jin's writings. In chapter 14 of *Family*, there is a scene featuring a former Gao servant, Gao Sheng, who had been fired for stealing from the family to support his opium habit. Ba Jin later wrote that this had indeed happened to one of his friends among the male servants in the Li family household when he was a child.[2] In the scene in the novel, Ba Jin portrays the fired servant's point of view:

> Because his clothing was in rags he did not dare to enter the compound, so he had to lurk at the gate waiting for a servant who had worked with him to come out and recognize him. Then he would beg the servant to convey his message. He did not ask for much, only a few small coins, and as this was a time [New Year's eve] when the masters were happy he always attained his goal. As time went by, this became a custom. . . . [He sees Juemin and Juehui pass by and longs to talk with them, but is too ashamed.] He stood dumbly in the middle of the street and he allowed the

pitiless wind to assault his frail body, and though he was covered only by a ragged jacket he did not shrink from the wind. Loneliness, a loneliness he had never felt before gnawed at him. "It's a dream, it's only a dream," he croaked to himself as he wiped his misty eyes. He walked away, turning back for one last look at the two stone lions, who placidly accepted his loving gaze. He left; he walked off slowly and weakly. One hand clenched the donation he received from his old employers, and the other covered his chest. He walked on without any goal, without any plans as to how to spend the money in his hand.[3]

Poverty is represented as bad health, shame, despair, and lack of connection to other beings—the impassive response of the stone lions to Gao Sheng's appeal is probably better than what he receives from most people he encounters.

Turbulent Stream offers the life story of one other unfortunate character—Zhang Bixiu, a young actor specializing in women's roles who is the protégé and companion of Gao Ke'an, the fourth son of the patriarch. As we saw in Chapter Two, Ba Jin portrayed Sichuan opera actors and their patrons as debauched and out of touch with the times. Juehui is bored by the performances at his grandfather's birthday party, while his degenerate uncles and aunts are delighted with them. In the 1956 film version of *Family*, the evil Feng Leshan notices the girl Mingfeng for the first time during the birthday celebration, suggesting perhaps that the lascivious opera scenes have heightened his lust and his need for an object through which to satisfy it. Ba Jin's harsh verdict on the widely loved Sichuan opera tradition is not overturned in the later novels of the trilogy, but he does take a closer look at the plight of the actors, presenting Zhang Bixiu as a victim, rather than as a corrupt and evil person.

In *Autumn*, Zhang Bixiu tells Gao Juexin that he was born into a wealthy and educated Chengdu family. His father died when he was still young, however, and his uncle arranged for him to be kidnapped and taken far away (as in Robert Louis Stevenson's novel *Kidnapped*, with which Ba Jin was no doubt familiar). The kidnappers sold him to a theatrical troupe, which forced him to learn how to play the role of the young female lead in Sichuan operas and to become a coquette on and off the stage. It was common for the young actors who played these roles to become intimate with older male opera patrons, hence his eventual relationship with Juexin's uncle, Gao Ke'an. When Juexin asks him why, as a grown man, he does not demand justice from his family, Zhang Bixiu bitterly explains that it would be impossible for his family to acknowledge a relative who had entered into such a shameful profession. Besides, shortly after Zhang Bixiu's uncle had arranged for him to be kidnapped, his mother had fallen ill and died, and all her assets had been taken over by the uncle. Even if a law court would accept a case filed by so disreputable a person as an actor, his uncle would be sure to bribe the authorities to get the verdict he wanted.[4]

Zhang Bixiu's good looks and acting talent and the charming manners beaten into him as a boy ensure that he is not hungry or destitute. Gao Ke'an seems genuinely fond of him, and he will be able to support himself as long as he can captivate opera audiences. His life is similar to that of Monday, the mistress of Fifth Uncle Gao Keding: illness, old age, and the changeable tastes of the Chengdu elite loom as the major threats to their precarious livelihoods.

Changing Attitudes toward Poverty

Before the twentieth century, a wide range of beliefs about the causes of poverty and wealth circulated in China. Theoretically at least, Confucian scholars devalued riches, stressing that one's goal in life should be to seek wisdom and serve humanity. There was no requirement, however, for the Confucian sage to take a vow of poverty. Gentry patriarchs firmly believed there was virtue in providing for and properly educating one's family, which required money. Building on Mencius's conviction that all humans have the capacity to learn, Confucian gentry tended to believe that what distinguished successful men, in terms of career advancement and material wealth, was their own willingness to accept discipline and work hard.

Philosophers also believed that broader forces, in addition to personal conduct, shaped human lives—that one's ability to prosper through discipline and hard work was limited by the age into which one was born. History moved in cycles of growth and decline, a pattern mapped out in the *Classic of Changes* (*Yijing* or *I-Ching*), part of the Confucian canon. Fengshui, another popular set of beliefs and practices, added a geological element to the conception of the impersonal forces affecting people's fate. Specialists in fengshui ("wind-water," often translated as "geomancy") could interpret the patterns of a local landscape and detect how cosmic energy (*qi*) flowed through it. Those who could afford to would align their houses and gravesites so as to benefit from the flow and bring prosperity to the family.[5]

The Buddhist concepts of reincarnation and karma had been popular in China for many centuries and continued to shape some people's thinking about wealth and poverty. In a worldview influenced by these concepts, virtuous or evil conduct in one life will be repaid with prosperity or suffering in a subsequent life. As with the Confucian view, there is still a cause-and-effect relationship between good conduct and success in life, but it is a more flexible one, since it is not limited to one lifespan. That made it possible to explain why an apparently hardworking, virtuous person might still be poor or fall ill—bad karma from a previous incarnation influenced the life of the person's current incarnation. In Ba Jin's trilogy, this is how many of the women in the Gao family explain their bitter lives. Madam Zhou refers to "fate" (*ming*) when informing Mingfeng that she must become a concubine: fate was understood in karmic terms.

Other beliefs about poverty and suffering had no connection to a person's own conduct, whether in this life or the last. Capricious evil spirits could attack for no reason comprehensible to human understanding.[6] Exorcists and Daoist priests were hired to deal with such attacks: in *Family*, the patriarch's concubine, Miss Chen, invites an exorcist into the Gao home to try to drive out the spirits that she believes are causing the patriarch's illness. In this case, the exorcist fails, and Miss Chen blames Juehui, because he refused to cooperate with the ritual. Most of the rest of the family seem to accept the patriarch's death, as they do the many other cases of illness and death in the family over the course of the trilogy, as a tragic but common fact of life. For most in the Gao family, poverty, too, is either the result of personal failings, as with the fired servant Gao Sheng, or just bad fortune, as with the beggar child.

Ideas about wealth and poverty may also be found in official records of the Qing dynasty. The economic health of Chinese communities had long been a matter of much interest to officials in the imperial bureaucracy. The term *minsheng*, usually translated as the "people's livelihood," was an important measure of good government. Of course, people who were able to make a living were less likely to become bandits and more likely to pay the taxes that supported the bureaucracy. During famines, the government tried to lessen the burdens of poverty and hunger, often making grain available cheaply and waiving taxes. Many county magistrates organized soup kitchens in the cities as a safety net during the lean winter months. To promote education and industriousness, officials encouraged members of the gentry to set up clan schools at which poor kinsmen could learn to read and write. They also subsidized the publication of manuals on agricultural and handicraft production.[7]

Wealthy Chinese engaged in philanthropy that went beyond their own clans, particularly in the tumultuous nineteenth century, when Qing rule was increasingly ineffective. Elite men raised funds to establish homes for destitute widows and orphans and to provide burials for unclaimed corpses. These and other philanthropic actions were seen as ways to uphold family values, protect the community, and demonstrate the virtue of the donors.[8]

Historian Janet Chen has shown how Chinese conceptions of poverty began to shift as a result of the threat posed by powerful outsiders in the early twentieth century and growing exposure to European ideas. Poverty was linked to national vulnerability, and so the poor became the targets of reform efforts. Workhouses proliferated in the years before the 1911 Revolution, and Chen examines this history in Beijing and Shanghai.[9] Following examples from east China, Chengdu officials established two "beggar workhouses" outside the city gates in 1906. The police sent men caught begging on the streets to these workhouses, and according to reports to the central government in Beijing, some 1,500 men lived in the workhouses within a few months of their founding. The men were organized into teams and required to work as unskilled laborers. A publicly funded orphanage opened in 1907 with space for more than five hundred children, who also were expected to work. Some of the young boys were taught to play band instruments—drums, cymbals, Chinese bugles—and the band performed for hire at funerals and celebrations.[10] The orphanage continued to operate after the 1911 Revolution, with a reduced budget and smaller capacity.

Growing concern over social problems in nineteenth-century industrialized Western European cities contributed to the development of new social sciences that began to shape discourse on poverty all around the world. The American YMCA helped establish Chinese branches of the Y in many big cities, including Chengdu, where Robert Service served as secretary (his wife Grace's memoir offers a window into the lives of Americans in Chengdu between 1909 and 1920).[11] The YMCA's work in China was guided by principles developed by social workers and sociologists and emphasized literacy and vocational education. In Beijing, YMCA secretary Sidney Gamble carried out social surveys in an attempt to quantify the economic conditions within which ordinary Beijing people lived.[12] In Chengdu, the YMCA did not have the resources for this kind of work. Beginning in 1923, it helped launch a campaign to spread literacy in Chinese to more people in the city.[13] Before then, though, it was most famous for its English classes, sports fields, and movie nights. For the most part it served relatively well-off young men. Ba Jin took English lessons at the Chengdu YMCA.

Ba Jin's *Turbulent Stream* trilogy does not make the issue of poverty and its causes central to the plot. The sad plights of the slave girls and other vulnerable people add pathos to the story and contribute to its indictment of "the system." Most of all, though, in *Family* class differences exacerbate young Juehui's dissatisfaction with his family and community and sometimes with himself.

The Lower Classes in the Historical Record

Chengdu in the time of Ba Jin's youth was a sharply stratified society. The social order was by no means stable, though—both upward and downward mobility were common. Political unrest in the decades after the 1911 Revolution led to the rapid growth of armies across Sichuan. Young men who had attended the new military academies set up in the last ten years of Qing rule rose quickly to the top of the new political system. Others lost out, including the families in the Qing Banner garrison, whose government stipends and special privileges were taken away. Wu Yu notes in a diary entry for 1914 that two little Manchu children from the former garrison area were being offered for sale for a pitifully small sum.[14]

Families that were well established in their trades and crafts were most likely to be able to ride out the political waves, although unpredictable catastrophes struck many of them too. Periodic outbursts of warfare could be devastating to lives and property and made travel dangerous. Still, the population of the city slowly grew over the first decades of the twentieth century—from about 335,000 in 1910 to about 492,000 in 1936—suggesting that many people were attracted to the relative safety and economic opportunities Chengdu continued to offer.[15]

For Chengdu residents or immigrants with no family support to help them enter a trade, the options were limited. A large number of men found employment "selling their strength" (*maili*): carrying things and people.

Horses were rare in Chengdu, and, until rickshaws and bicycles became more common after 1924, the only wheeled vehicles were rugged wheelbarrows. Geographer George Hubbard estimated that, in 1920, 20–30 percent of Chengdu men earned their living as porters. Some carried the sedan chairs the wealthy used for travel. In a diary entry from June 1922, Wu Yu reported paying four porters 7,000 copper cash each to carry him and his luggage from the town of Leshan to Chengdu, a three-day journey.[16] Other men hauled water from the river to teahouses and private residences for drinking and washing. Hundreds of men made a living carrying buckets of human waste out of the city to the manure ditches where it would ferment and be sold to farmers in the region as fertilizer.[17]

Men and women with a small amount of capital or a source of credit (i.e., borrowing from friends and family or pawning possessions at one of the city's many pawnshops) could try to support themselves as peddlers, either spreading out their wares at the side of the streets near the city's marketplaces or going from door to door. Women specialized in the products that women used, such as needles, thread, and cosmetics. Male peddlers sold pots and dishes and all sorts of other household goods. Some of them carried around portable cooking equipment and sold snacks made to order. A small group of men bought up old official robes, insignia, and other artifacts from Qing times and brought them to the households of foreigners living in the city, who collected them as souvenirs of Old China.[18]

As noted in Chapter Three, many Chengdu residents were employed in relatively low-skill service professions, such as the men who hung around teahouses and cleaned customers' ears or who set up street-corner barber stalls. Well-off families hired men to put on mourning clothes and take part in funeral processions to show off the status of the deceased and the filial piety of their families. During the major New Year's holiday, teams of men traveled around town doing dragon and lion dances to entertain and bring good fortune to those who paid for them.

Ba Jin includes a scene with a dragon dance in chapter 18 of *Family*. Uncle Gao Keding hires a troupe of dancers to come into the family compound and make the long, colorful, bamboo-and-paper dragon move around the courtyard in intricate patterns. To add to the "fun," Keding and the Gao family sedan-chair bearers aim bamboo cannons loaded with gunpowder and copper coins at the dancers, who endure the horrific attack to show how tough they are. They are paid for their efforts, but leave nursing their wounds and harboring resentment at how they have been treated. Such scenes probably did occur in Ba Jin's youth. Dragon dances that featured more-or-less mock attacks on the dancers were still occurring in the 1940s in Sichuan, according to field research from a site near Chongqing.[19] Nothing of importance to the plot comes of this scene in *Family*. Its main function is once again to show the complacency of the older generations, happy to oppress anyone in a subordinate position, and the sense of injustice felt by the younger generation represented by Gao Juehui, who is disgusted at his uncle's treatment of the dancers.

One other aspect of that chapter of *Family* is interesting, though. Ba Jin uses it to explore the relationship between master and male servant, a theme that does not appear in much of the rest of the trilogy. Because the dragon dancers are late, Uncle Keding sends the sedan-chair bearer Gao Zhong out to find them. Gao Zhong returns to say they have decided not to come, and Keding takes out his frustration by cursing and criticizing Gao Zhong, who meekly takes the abuse, since he realizes protest is useless. After a troupe is finally induced to come, all the sedan-chair bearers join enthusiastically in the game of aiming the bamboo cannons at them. Ba Jin makes sure to show that Gao Keding is the worst offender, since he aims his cannon point-blank at the leader of the troupe. But the male servants seem to have learned how to behave from their masters; they enjoy abusing the dancers, seemingly, almost as much as Keding does.

The uncomfortable message of *Family*'s chapter 18 seems to be that inhumanity is not a quality exclusive to the upper classes—their servants can display it, too. Given the limitations of the sources, attitudes among the "common people" about social justice and morality are difficult to assess for any period of history, and that is certainly the case for early twentieth-century China. The little bits of evidence available to us are not enough to come to firm conclusions. Nevertheless, the topic is worth thinking about. As noted in Chapter One, Old Mrs. Ning, a penniless woman who worked as a servant in wealthy households in eastern China in the 1920s, believed that slave girls who were raised in such households never learned how to treat people respectfully. She herself had been raised in a family that, however poor, taught its children to behave properly. From Mrs. Ning's account, we might hypothesize that some families in the Chengdu of Ba Jin's youth believed that neither the masters nor the servants in wealthy families offered good models of moral conduct.

Chinese elite culture viewed professions as demeaning when their function was primarily for entertainment, and that included sex work, theater, dance, and musical performance. Until the eighteenth century, the Qing Code gave people in these lines of work special legal status that justified particularly harsh treatment if they were involved in crimes. They and their descendants were also barred from taking the civil service examinations.[20] Although by 1911 the laws had been changed and the civil service examinations abolished, such sentiments lingered. In his work on Chengdu, historian Di Wang shows how the city's early twentieth-century police regulations treated actors as unworthy of rights accorded to "normal" residents.[21] The descriptions of some types of characters in *Turbulent Stream* reflect the elite Chengdu view of them that Ba Jin absorbed growing up. Miss Chen, the patriarch's concubine, is described as a former courtesan (a woman trained in singing, dancing, and chatting with men and who often also made money by providing sexual services). She dresses gaudily, wears heavy makeup, and is vulgar, ignorant, and vindictive. Zhang Bixiu, the female impersonator, is more refined and, because he was forced into his role, more to be pitied than censured. As a former member of the elite, he himself is ashamed of what he does.

Were there people who, despite elite condemnation, actually considered work on the stage and in brothels normal and even rewarding (financially and otherwise) in early twentieth-century Chengdu? Or was such work the only available option short of begging for the many people who did it? Historians of pre-1949 Shanghai, who have studied that city's lively entertainment culture in considerable depth, agree that it is virtually impossible to see past the elite and popular representations of prostitutes and actors to understand how an ordinary prostitute or actor experienced life. Nevertheless, it is clear that a few fortunate and skillful women and men were able to build successful careers within this world.[22] Brothel owners frequently began as sex workers who were able to put aside savings over the years when they could earn the most. Famous actors could establish their own troupes and begin training disciples who would support them in old age. Catherine Vance Yeh points out that the development of a "star culture" in late nineteenth-century treaty-port Shanghai allowed some actors to demand huge fees for performances and even to marry into the elite.[23]

The history of the sort of phenomenon Yeh describes has not been as well studied in the case of Chengdu, and, judging from the scarcity of rags-to-riches stories about entertainers in the local popular history magazines, it was much less common than in Shanghai. Still, some Chengdu courtesans and actors did become celebrities. The magazine *Amusing Accounts*, popular among the less puritanical gentry (see Chapter Two), published lists of the most renowned performers, along with poems written in their honor. As with Miss Chen in *Turbulent Stream*, courtesans could become concubines and acquire legal standing in a family or, as with Ke'an's Monday, be set up as mistresses in separate houses. The careers of the great majority of sex workers and other entertainers, however, were probably short and not financially rewarding.

In the first years of the twentieth century, the new Qing police tried to extend supervisory authority over many aspects of social life in Chengdu, particularly activities that were not already managed by guilds reporting regularly to the government. They required acting troupes to register and obtain official approval of their scripts. They also created a "licensed zone" for brothels, such as had long existed in large Japanese cities. Before this, sex work had been carried on in Chengdu without official notice but with unofficial tolerance. After 1905, brothels were told to register and were confined, for the most part, to one part of town. The police chief ordered that signboards with the words "household under surveillance" should be put on every known brothel.[24] This system was criticized at the time as offering government recognition and protection for what some saw as an immoral profession. Partly in response, the government opened a reformatory (*jiliangsuo*) for sex workers. Police were instructed to send young girls discovered in brothels or on the street to the reformatory, where they were taught proper conduct and trained in housewifely duties. Men who wanted wives could apply to marry them.

After 1911, the licensed zone idea was abandoned. By then the police had become too dependent on the prostitution tax not to continue trying to force brothels to register and pay up. The reformatory, like the beggar workhouses and most of the other newly established institutions of the late Qing, continued to exist in name in the early Republic but slid into a period of decline. During most of Ba Jin's youth, government social services and private philanthropy operated at a minimal level—people were too caught up in dealing with political chaos and ongoing civil wars to address pressing economic and social issues. Shortly after Ba Jin left Chengdu in 1923, though, a new municipal government was established in the city, and its chairman turned the management of the reformatory and other late Qing "social welfare" institutions over to a committee of prominent gentry led by Yin Changling, a Chengdu native who had earned the highest degree in the Qing civil service examinations and served in official positions in Shaanxi Province before 1911.

The municipal leadership gave Yin Changling's new committee the modern bureaucratic name of Chengdu Municipal Commission for Relief and Rehabilitation Work (Chengdushi jiuxu shiye dongshihui). Along with his fellow elders and sages (see Chapter Two), Yin preferred to associate himself with the past. He and his committee chose to operate under the name of the Hall of Mercy (Cihuitang), a benevolent association that had been more or less active since its founding by Chengdu officials in the early eighteenth century.[25]

In 1928, the Hall of Mercy reported on the wide scope of its work. It managed an orphanage for infants, which provided stipends to wet nurses to care for the babies (almost all girls). It ran four charity schools in various parts of town where poor boys learned to read the Chinese classics. Boys who showed no talent for a literary education could transfer to the trade school that had evolved from the orphan workhouse founded in the late Qing. The city government allowed the Hall of Mercy to take over the match factory outside the East Gate that the provincial government had established during the last decade of Qing rule. The proceeds from the match factory helped fund the Hall's activities, and the factory itself provided work for the orphans in its charge. Yin reported that several dozen orphans were being trained to make paper with which to wrap the matchboxes. The label on the boxes featured a drawing of a child eating rice from a bowl, and as a result the matches came to be called "kiddie brand" (*wawapai*) matches. The Hall also organized a music school for young blind boys. These boys learned to play the hammered dulcimer and performed at private parties dressed in long gowns. Because the boys were blind, young ladies in wealthy households were permitted to gather around them to hear the music. As of 1928, forty such boys were receiving musical training at the Hall.[26] In *Autumn*, some of the young members of the Gao family and their cousins recall learning songs from the blind singers invited to their compounds to perform.[27]

Hall of Mercy staff, seeing themselves in the role of family elders, took responsibility for finding husbands for girls raised in the orphanage they ran, as well as for those taken off the streets into the reformatory. In a memoir, one of Yin Changling's friends recalls a case from the late 1930s of a young girl being forced into prostitution by her stepmother. The outraged neighbors took the girl to the Hall of Mercy; its staff eventually found a husband for her. When Yin Changling heard that the stepmother planned to attend the marriage ceremony and contest its legality, he invited the provincial governor to be a witness, intimidating the stepmother into backing down. This friend also claims that Yin's reputation was so high that no one dared mistreat the girls his Hall had raised and none were ever given away as concubines.[28]

The history of Chengdu's reformatory shows that the strict views of the Confucian elite on the question of female chastity were by no means universal in Ba Jin's youth. Plenty of men wanted to marry the women from the reformatory, even though they were not virginal. As the survey of West China Union University workers discussed in Chapter Three suggests, many poor men were unable to marry while they were young and some not at all. One reason was that there were fewer girls than boys in the city in the 1920s and 1930s. Population censuses generally undercounted girls, so we must treat them cautiously. Nevertheless, 1916 population statistics for Huayang and Chengdu counties (the two counties within which Chengdu city was located) give a total of about 800,000 males as opposed to 410,000 females.[29] In addition to undercounting of females, this disparity may be due to two factors: a greater likelihood that men would leave their villages in other parts of Sichuan Province to try to make a living in the big city, and greater mortality among girls and young women. Girls often were not fed as well as boys as they were growing up, and their illnesses were not dealt with as quickly. Young women also faced grave danger of death during childbirth.[30]

Another reason poor men found it hard to marry was because a family with a marriageable girl expected the groom or his family to give it presents as part of the engagement and wedding—what anthropologists call the bride price. The orphanage and reformatory operated by the Hall of Mercy offered some men a chance to take a wife without the bride price, and they seized it. Judging from records of inheritance disputes heard by the Chengdu courts in the 1930s, widow remarriage was common in that era and probably earlier, as well, in all but the wealthiest of families. The 1919 Chengdu police file that contains the slave girl contract discussed in Chapter One (see Figure 1.1) also has paperwork registering the second marriages of widows.[31]

The scarcity of young women meant that they were in demand—especially as wives, but also as servants and sex workers—so relatively few young women begged in Chengdu when Ba Jin was young. But men of all ages and older women frequently found themselves with no other recourse, particularly in winter, when food was more expensive and work was scarce. Many died of exposure on the streets in the harsher months. Some people made a regular living as beggars. Di Wang has examined Chengdu beggar lore that suggests that professional beggars were a common part of city life. Sometimes they shared their techniques with newcomers, as when one old beggar advised a younger man to carry a destitute old woman around on his back. People were much more likely to give to a young man forced to beg in order to support his "aged mother."[32]

In his discussion of beggars, Di Wang notes that crime of various types, including thievery and extortion, flourished on the streets of Chengdu in the first half of the twentieth century. Local commentators in the 1910s and early 1920s considered the police themselves corrupt, and constables and their officers probably profited from some of the illegal activity. As the formal government lost its effectiveness in the years after 1911, neighborhoods were increasingly ruled by gangs of men known as the "Gowned Brothers" (Paoge), who charged businesses protection fees and ran gambling houses and opium dens. We will examine their activities in more depth in Chapter Five, when we consider the impact of war on Chengdu.

Opium, Illness, Housing, Sanitation, and Mobility in the City

How serious a problem was opium in Chengdu when Ba Jin was young? Was addiction common? Did it lead to an increase in crime, as is suggested by the story of Gao Sheng, the thieving servant in *Family*, cited above? This is another set of questions that is difficult to answer based on our current knowledge. Local activists such as Fu Chongju, editor of the 1909 Chengdu encyclopedia, identified opium consumption as one of the great evils afflicting the city. At that time, the Qing government had launched a campaign to get users to register and force them to quit. Historians have judged that campaign relatively successful. Di Wang comments, though, that "opium consumption surged" in the years after 1911.[33] Most of the sources we have on opium use in the city are vague, however. Certainly there was a large traffic in opium in Chengdu when Ba Jin was young, and some of his relatives indulged, in addition to some of the servants. The house where Gao Ke'an keeps the actor Zhang Bixiu is described in *Autumn* as smelling of opium.[34] In her study of opium in Sichuan, Xiaoxiong Li compiles numerous anecdotes about addicts who impoverished their families and sold their children.[35] These stories, though, come from all over the province. At this point it is impossible to evaluate the impact of opium on Chengdu's economy and the welfare of its residents.[36]

Some Western observers did claim that porters who carried heavy loads around the Chengdu region tended to use opium regularly to dull their pain. Frequent use, they believed, undermined the health of these laborers. Aside from suffering from the physical effects of the drug, they spent money on opium that they might have spent on nutritious food. A British official stated in 1923 that, in Chengdu, "the city chair coolies get opium for 100 cash a whiff. All of their earnings, which amount to from 600 to 1,000 cash a day, are spent on opium after deducting 300 or 400 cash per day for food."[37] Such observers thought that opium shortened the lifespan of many Chinese men. Judging from the 1916 Sichuan provincial census, living long enough to enjoy one's sixtieth birthday, as the Gao patriarch did in *Family*, was uncommon. Only 14.3 percent of the male and 13.4 percent of the female population was older than 55.[38] Estimates for life expectancy at birth for China as a whole in 1950 were 39.3 for men and 42.3 for women.[39] It was most likely even lower than that in Chengdu in the 1910s and 1920s.

Among the causes of death listed in the 1916 census report, the most common were typhoid, measles, scarlet fever, dysentery, cholera, and other illnesses. The highest death rate was for children nine and younger. Even in a wealthy family such as Ba Jin's, where food was plentiful, many children fell ill and died. In *Spring*, Ba Jin movingly describes the death of Gao Juexin's young son Hai'er. Li Zhi, the son of Ba Jin's eldest brother, reports that the scene of Hai'er's death was taken directly from personal experience. Ba Jin had been very fond of his eldest nephew, Li Zhi's older brother Li Guoqing, born in 1918. In 1921, the boy died of meningitis, although his frantic parents had summoned both Chinese and French doctors to treat him.[40]

The prevalence of disease and illness in Chengdu as Ba Jin was growing up was one of the core causes of poverty: so many people in the city depended on the strength of their bodies to earn a living; so few were able to build up savings to tide them over a period of sickness. Illness spread quickly in the crowded city. As we saw in Chapter Two, elite families walled their spacious compounds off from the urban crowds. Rental housing was available across a broad price range. On streets with shops, the shopkeeper's household, including apprentices, generally lived onsite. An extra room might be rented out. Compounds built in the "courtyard style" (described in Chapter Two) by well-off families might be sold and then each individual room rented separately to one or more families. This type of housing was known in Chengdu as a "mixed courtyard" (*zayuan*). In *Turbulent Stream*, Qin and her widowed mother, Mrs. Zhang, live in such a courtyard, together with Mrs. Zhang's widowed mother-in-law. The inhabitants of the other rooms of the compound are also mostly widows, with a few servants to care for them. Qin's grandmother spends much of her time in a Buddhist nunnery, where religious training and lodging could be obtained in exchange for donations.[41] The vast majority of city residents were unable to afford to rent a room in a mixed courtyard. They shared space with others and spent much of their time outdoors, including in markets, temples, courtyards, and the streets. The least well off slept on the riverbanks or under the eaves of temples, even in the winter.[42]

Many single male workers, who made a little money but wanted to spend as little as possible on housing, spent nights in what people in Chengdu called "chicken feather inns" (*jimaodian*), many located near the city gates (Figure 4.1). George Hubbard, who seems to have inspected some of these in 1920, described how a laborer would pass the time at such an inn:

> When he comes to an inn, he takes a washing-down as any beast of burden would. Then, with his same dirty, sweaty clothes on, he eats his plain, coarse supper of rice, vegetables, and bits of pork; then he smokes a pipe or two and "turns in." A whole squad of them sleep in a row on the floor with a little straw and some old *pukais* [*pugai*, quilted cotton bedding], or perhaps a half-dozen of them in as many board bunks in one small closed room.[43]

Such cramped conditions and rudimentary sanitation allowed disease to spread quickly through the city.

Although Ba Jin did not mention this subject in the *Turbulent Stream* trilogy, sanitation was a concern of the new police and city government in the first few decades of the twentieth century—particularly the management of human waste. Families such as Ba Jin's, who lived in compounds by them-

Figure 4.1 One of Chengdu's gates, circa 1920s. Photograph by Dr. Roy C. Spooner. Courtesy of the Spooner family.

selves or in mixed courtyards, generally had servants to empty chamber pots and deliver the contents to night soil carriers who made regular rounds. In poorer parts of town, public toilets constituted a business opportunity. Most streets featured one or more public toilets managed by night soil collectors. The profit came from selling the waste to night soil merchants outside the gates.[44]

Before the establishment of the new police in 1903, these public toilets generally were simple ditches surrounded by bamboo mats. The police soon issued regulations requiring that they be built according to a higher standard and offer separate facilities for men and women. Oil lamps provided a bit of light in the evenings and early mornings. In 1918, the police started collecting a tax from operators of such toilets to pay for street cleaning. In 1930, the city government tried to double the taxes on teahouses, hotels, and toilet operators to pay for construction of public toilet buildings that would meet newly issued national sanitary regulations. The association of fertilizer merchants protested, and the petition it sent to the city government at that time has been preserved in the archives. It includes a brief history of the business in Chengdu, explaining its importance to area farmers and claiming that, despite a long history of tax increases that made it hard to make any profit, several hundred families were supported by the labor of the night soil workers.[45]

Social mobility was related closely to physical mobility in the Chengdu of Ba Jin's youth. People who were able to move about physically could take advantage of opportunities to better their lot that might not have been available in the immediate neighborhood. That helps explain why a slave girl like Mingfeng is so helpless. She can never escape the supervision of her masters and mistresses. As was the case in the Gao compound, the people who oversaw Chengdu society tried to restrict mobility within the city and between it and the surrounding countryside. During the decades after 1911, street militia patrolled residential areas to deter thieves and set up street barriers at night to limit access to many neighborhoods. The great city walls funneled travelers from outside the city through one of seven gates (three built in the decade after 1911), which also were closed and guarded at night. During the day, people were free to come and go through the streets and gates as they pleased, but the police and military guards might stop anyone who seemed suspicious—a runaway apprentice, perhaps, or a kidnapper with young girls to sell.

The productivity of the agricultural land around Chengdu and the absence of mechanized transport meant that many men could easily find employment carrying produce and people around the Chengdu plain. This mobile population helped spread news about conditions throughout the province and beyond and connected Chengdu people to the villages and towns around them. In the turbulent decades after 1911, though, those mobile men were always in danger of being conscripted as soldiers or porters for the many armies that contested control of the province. A healthy young man who did not want a soldier's life was safest in the city working for a wealthy family that could protect him or in a profession that had a powerful guild. But, still, the armies were growing rapidly when Ba Jin was a young man, and it is to them, and to the students who were their fiercest critics, that we now turn.

CHAPTER FIVE

Students, Soldiers, and Warlords

Protest and Warfare in the City

Much of the tension in the *Turbulent Stream* trilogy arises from two sources: the psychological battles of will between the younger and older generations and the despair of the powerless, especially young women. But *Family* also includes an episode of street warfare: the Gao household quakes in terror as the bullets fly and rapacious soldiers are expected to break down the gate at any moment. Conflict between soldiers and students occurs throughout the trilogy, and in one scene in *Family* Gao Juehui and his friends march through town and demonstrate at the office of the military governor, demanding that he discipline his troops and make reparations for the damage they cause.

These episodes reflect a reality Ba Jin did not find it necessary to explain: Chengdu experienced multiple waves of political protests and invasions by rival militaries beginning in 1911. Ba Jin's early life coincided with what many historians call China's "warlord era." After the Qing collapse, a "Republic of China" was established in 1912, but the internationally recognized central government of the Republic—based first in Beijing (1912–1927) and then in

Nanjing (1927–1937)—found it difficult to extend its authority far beyond the eastern cities. The first president, Yuan Shikai, had gained his reputation by updating the Qing armed forces, following the Meiji Japanese model, during the dynasty's last decade. After 1911, his political network consisted largely of the young officers trained in military academies he set up. When he died in 1916, some of these officers seized political power in the provinces and began battling each other to expand their bases. The capital area and the central government itself changed hands several times in the late 1910s and early 1920s. Many journalists and political activists considered these developments a betrayal of the ideals of the Republic. They began to refer to military governors as "warlords" (*junfa*), a pejorative label. In Sichuan, control over the province was contested by a number of such militarists between 1916 and 1935, and the province was to a large extent cut off from the politics of eastern China.[1]

This chapter examines the history of warfare in the Chengdu area in the decades after the collapse of the Qing and then analyzes the effects of the militarization of the province on life and politics in Chengdu in the period in which Ba Jin's *Turbulent Stream* is set. The May Fourth movement was fueled throughout China by anger at political instability and the warfare that was both its cause and effect. The relationship between military officers and civilian activists was complicated, however. Though soldiers and their officers did clash frequently with students in the years around 1920, the military governors tried to win the support of both the older literati elite (the elders and sages discussed in Chapter Two) and talented younger men like Ba Jin. A few young men disdained the militarists and would have nothing to do with them, but many accepted official positions. After the wave of patriotic feeling inspired by the Revolution of 1911 had passed, few urban youth wanted to join the military; for the most part, officers and soldiers came from small towns and villages. This helps explain why Ba Jin's depiction of soldiers in *Turbulent Stream* is so one-dimensional—he knew little of the lives of soldiers and made no attempt to empathize with them.

Why Was There So Much Warfare in the Chengdu Area in the 1910s, '20s, and '30s?

Historians in China have published detailed studies of the complicated history of civil war in Sichuan between 1912 and 1935. Five thick volumes in the series Historical Materials on Sichuan Warlords appeared in the 1980s, filled with analysis of the alliances and betrayals and fighting between 1911 and 1934. Texts of hundreds of orders and telegrams issued by various military commanders in those years appear in these volumes.[2] Many battles were fought in Sichuan in the three decades after 1911—the Shanghai-based Chinese magazine *Eastern Miscellany* published an essay in 1932 that was semi-facetiously titled "The 467th Sichuan War."[3] All of this swirling political and military activity is reflected only faintly in Ba Jin's novels, as part of the oppressive atmosphere that stifles the hopes of the young members of the Gao family.

The seeds of the decades of civil war were planted in the years before 1911, when the new military academies began graduating officers. These young men, mostly in their twenties in the first decade of the Republic, were ambitious as well as nationalistic. Their instructors had impressed upon them the dangers China faced from the imperialist powers. Many a young man wanted, like Yuan Shikai himself, to emulate George Washington and lead the country to a strong and independent future.[4] But ambitions were not contained within a stable political framework. These would-be heroes in Sichuan and elsewhere allowed their hopes for the nation to be subsumed by their desire for control over the sources of wealth (and therefore power) in the regions around them. The result in Sichuan was twenty years of intermittent battles that stunted the provincial economy, encouraged banditry, replaced bureaucratic government with gang rule, and isolated Sichuan from the rest of China, giving it a reputation as a backward and savage land. Ba Jin's portrait of a benighted and reactionary Chengdu in *Turbulent Stream* was made plausible to his readers in eastern China by the many reports they heard about the fighting in Sichuan.

Table 5.1 lists some of the dominant political and military figures in Sichuan between 1915 and 1924, the years when Ba Jin observed warlord government close up. They were appointed to their positions by several different central regimes, in some cases simply in recognition of their de facto control, as fleeting as it usually was.

Although the seven-year-old Ba Jin was probably not exposed to it, Chengdu did experience some violence during the 1911 Revolution. In the fall of that year, troops of the last Qing governor-general fired on a crowd protesting his arrest of some prominent gentry leaders, killing several dozen people. Shortly afterward, the city was besieged by militias from the surrounding area. In November, the province declared independence. When

Table 5.1 Political and military commanders in Sichuan, 1915–1924

Dates	Names	Titles
December 1915 to June 1916	Chen Yi 陳宧	Military and civil governor (都督巡按使 *dudu xun'anshi*)
July 1916	Cai E 蔡鍔	Military and civil governor (督軍省長 *dujun shengzhang*)
August 1916 to July 1917	Luo Peijin 羅佩金 Dai Kan 戴戡	Military governor (都軍 *dujun*) Civil governor (省長 *shengzhang*)
August 1917 to February 1918	Liu Cunhou 劉存厚 Zhang Lan 張瀾	Military governor (*dujun*) Civil governor (*shengzhang*)
March 1918 to July 1920	Xiong Kewu 熊克武 Yang Shukan 楊庶堪	Military governor (*dujun*) Civil governor (*shengzhang*)
July 1920 to September 1920	Lü Chao 呂超 Yang Shukan 楊庶堪	Commander of the Sichuan Armies (川軍總司令 *Chuanjun zongsiling*) Civil governor (*shengzhang*)
September 1920 to November 1920	Xiong Kewu	Military governor (*dujun*)
December 1920 to March 1921	Liu Cunhou	Military governor (*dujun*)
July 1921 to June 1922	Liu Xiang 劉湘 (based in Chongqing) Liu Chengxun 劉成勳 (based in Chengdu)	Commander of the Sichuan Armies and civil governor (*Chuanjun zongsiling, shengzhang*) Commander of the Third Sichuan Army
July 1922 to February 1924 (in temporary exile from Chengdu in summer 1923)	Liu Chengxun	Commander of the Sichuan Armies (*Chuanjun zongsiling*); chair of the Sichuan Provincial Constitution Preparation Committee (四川省憲籌備處主任 *Sichuan shengxian choubeichu zhuren*); civil governor (*shengzhang*)
May 1924 to August 1925	Yang Sen 楊森	Supervisor of Sichuan Military Reorganization (督理四川軍務善後事宜 *duli Sichuan junwu shanhou shiyi*)

Source: This list, by no means complete, was compiled from the chronology in Zhou, *Minguo Chuanshi jiyao*, and from a list included in Sichuansheng wenshiguan, *Sichuan junfa shiliao*, vol. 3, 585–600. The commanders' titles changed frequently.

the new government, headed by local gentry, failed to pay the soldiers who had helped the militias overthrow Qing rule, the troops rioted, looting shops and homes throughout the city. Order was quickly restored, and the Sichuan native who put down the rioting became the first of many generals over the next two decades to claim the title of military governor. In early 1912, the province became part of the Republic of China.[5] The first years of the Republic were generally peaceful in Chengdu, but in 1917, when Ba Jin was twelve years old, warfare destroyed much of the city.

The 1917 fighting was connected to an uprising against President Yuan Shikai. Yuan did not share the republican ideals of Sun Yat-sen, the most famous revolutionary leader of the late Qing. But Yuan had been selected as president of the Republic in 1912 because he controlled the Qing armies and the revolutionaries thought it wise to make a deal with him to avoid a lengthy civil war. In 1913, when Sun Yat-sen's supporters seemed poised to win a national election, Yuan banned political parties and forced Sun into exile. In the fall of 1915, Yuan Shikai announced that he intended to revive the old imperial system, with himself as emperor, as a way to reestablish clear authority in a divided country. Many provincial leaders protested this decision, so Yuan tried to shore up his power by placing trusted allies into critical positions across the country. He sent Chen Yi to Sichuan, because Chen had served as director of the Sichuan Military Academy in the late Qing period and knew all the Sichuan officers.[6]

Meanwhile, however, Cai E, whose base was in Yunnan Province to the south of Sichuan, launched an uprising against Yuan Shikai.[7] Cai E marched his troops, mostly from Yunnan and Guizhou provinces, north to wealthy Sichuan in the spring of 1916. Chen Yi tried to retain his position by declaring Sichuan's independence from Yuan's government, but soon fled in the face of Cai's advance. Yuan Shikai died in June 1916, and his successor appointed Cai E as Sichuan governor. When Cai left Chengdu after a month to seek medical treatment in Japan, two of his officers, Luo Peijin from Yunnan and Dai Kan from Guizhou, replaced him as head of Sichuan's military and civil affairs, respectively. There was friction between the two, and Sichuan officers who had taken part in the anti-Yuan war were unhappy that forces from neighboring provinces were still occupying Sichuan. Fighting among the troops from the three provinces broke out in Chengdu twice, in April (Figure 5.1) and again in July of 1917. Thousands of people were

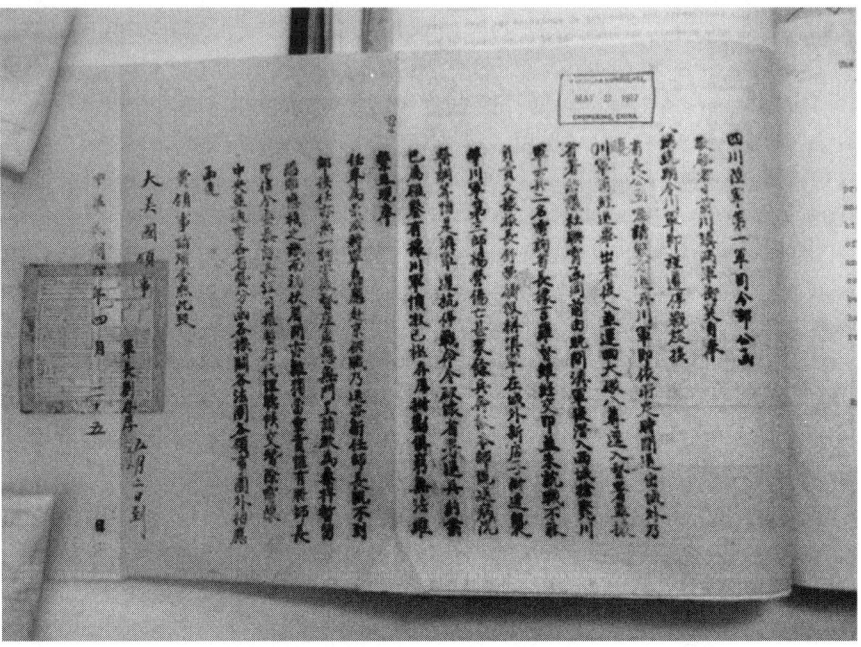

Figure 5.1 Message from Liu Cunhou to the US consulate in Chongqing (dated April 25, 1917), describing the Chengdu battles of Sichuan and Yunnan troops. US State Department, Records of Foreign Service Posts, US consular records, Chungking, official correspondence 84.800-811.9.

killed and whole sections of the city were burned by retreating troops. This experience of warfare in the streets had a deep impact on Ba Jin and many others in Chengdu, and it is reflected in scenes in *Turbulent Stream*.

One way to get a sense of the nature of the battles over Chengdu in Ba Jin's youth is to look at the careers of the men who ruled as military governors in the city during those years. Even as a teenager, Ba Jin would have been familiar with their names and actions. For the purposes of *Turbulent Stream*, however, he summed them up in two hazy characters: the unnamed "Commander" who is running the city at the beginning of *Family* and "General Zhang," whose troops oust the Commander in the middle chapters of *Family*. These two characters were probably based on the careers of four real people who battled for control over Chengdu between 1917 and 1923: Liu Cunhou, Xiong Kewu, Liu Chengxun, and Liu Wenhui. Brief biographies of them offer a window into military politics in Sichuan in that turbulent time.

STUDENTS, SOLDIERS, AND WARLORDS   137

Liu Cunhou, born into a Sichuan salt merchant family in 1885, entered the newly established Sichuan Military Preparatory Academy in Chengdu in 1903 and then studied infantry science in Japan for a year in 1907–1908. His classmates in Japan included several who became prominent militarists in other parts of China in the 1920s and 1930s: Yan Xishan, Sun Chuanfang, and Tang Jiyao. After he returned to China, he went to work as an instructor in the Yunnan Provincial Military Academy, where he met Cai E and was recruited into Sun Yat-sen's Revolutionary Alliance. During the uprising against the Qing in the fall of 1911, Liu led troops to Sichuan to support the rebels there. He was appointed head of one of the Sichuan armies in 1912 and helped suppress several early uprisings against Yuan Shikai's government, including one led by Xiong Kewu. In December 1915, however, he joined the armies seeking to overthrow Yuan Shikai after Yuan had declared his intention to become emperor.

Xiong Kewu (Figure 5.2), like Liu Cunhou born in 1885, was also raised in Sichuan.[8] His father had a modest medical practice in a small town south of Chengdu. In 1904, Xiong Kewu and a friend traveled to Japan and

Figure 5.2 Xiong Kewu (*center rear*) at the wedding of one of his officers in 1923. Elly Widler, *Six Months Prisoner of the Szechwan Military* (Shanghai: China Press, 1924).

enrolled in a military academy. Xiong joined the Revolutionary Alliance while in Japan and was sent by that organization back to Sichuan in 1906 to recruit members, particularly among military officers. He helped organize several armed uprisings in Sichuan before 1911; all were quickly suppressed. In the spring of 1911, he participated in another, more famous, failed Revolutionary Alliance uprising in Guangzhou. That fall, when provinces began declaring independence from the Qing state, Xiong Kewu returned to Sichuan and helped organize the new military government in Chongqing. He led troops in opposition to Yuan Shikai in 1913 and was defeated by Liu Cunhou. In 1915, however, Xiong Kewu and Liu Cunhou became allies in that year's anti-Yuan war. In 1921, Xiong Kewu teamed up with Liu Chengxun to drive Liu Cunhou out of Chengdu. Of all the Sichuan militarists, Xiong was the most engaged with east China politics, which drew him away from Sichuan. As a leading figure in the Nationalist Party, he took part in its factional infighting and was imprisoned by Chiang Kai-shek for joining an attack on Chiang in 1926 in Guangzhou.

Liu Chengxun was born in 1883 in a village near Chengdu, where his father sold paper and candles for a living. Like Liu Cunhou, Liu Chengxun attended the Sichuan Military Preparatory Academy in Chengdu, but he did not study in Japan or join the Revolutionary Alliance. At the time of the 1911 Revolution, he was stationed with the Qing army in northeast China (Manchuria). He returned to Sichuan early in 1912 and served as an officer in the force sent by the new Republic to exert control over Tibet. When war broke out among the victorious anti–Yuan Shikai forces in 1917, Liu Chengxun shifted alliances frequently and tried to keep his own troops out of the battles. For a while, his success at this allowed him to occupy Chengdu while most of the other military leaders were contesting control over south Sichuan in 1922 and 1923. In those years, as part of a short-lived movement to create a federal system in China, a Provincial Assembly based in Chengdu declared Sichuan's autonomy, sponsored the drafting of a new provincial constitution, and appointed Liu Chengxun as governor.[9] Rival militarists promptly marched on Chengdu to challenge Liu Chengxun's claims to rule the province. The fighting between these troops and Liu Chengxun's on the outskirts of Chengdu in March and April of 1923 probably inspired the battle scenes in chapter 20 of *Family*.[10] By the summer of 1923, the federalist movement in China had collapsed, Liu Wenhui had driven Liu Chengxun from Chengdu, and Ba Jin had left Chengdu for Shanghai.

Liu Wenhui was a member of a family of landholders in Dayi County to the southwest of Chengdu. A decade younger than the other three militarists whose stories we have outlined, he belongs to what Robert Kapp has called the second generation of Sichuan warlords. These younger men came of age when the province was already at war and therefore had less exposure to the world beyond Sichuan.[11] Liu Wenhui was a dominant general in the Chengdu area until his defeat by his cousin Liu Xiang in 1932. After that, Liu Wenhui moved his troops to the far western area of Sichuan, where the Nationalist government eventually created the new province of Xikang.[12] As noted in Chapter Three, Liu Wenhui's brother Liu Wencai was among Sichuan's wealthiest landholders in the 1930s and 1940s, controlling many acres in their home county of Dayi.

Three aspects of the careers of Liu Cunhou, Xiong Kewu, Liu Chengxun, and Liu Wenhui are particularly relevant to understanding the politics of Chengdu in the period in which *Turbulent Stream* is set. First, all four men tried to present themselves as the best hope for Sichuan unification, which was the stated goal of all the Sichuan militarists. As part of this effort, all maintained lines of communication with both of the regimes in eastern China that claimed the right to rule the Republic of China after Yuan Shikai's death—the "Beiyang" government (called that because it was headed by officers from Yuan Shikai's Beiyang Army) in Beijing and the government that Sun Yat-sen's Nationalist Party set up in Guangzhou in 1921. Because each of the four militarists wanted to seem to the eastern powers to be a legitimate provincial leader, they all borrowed much of the rhetoric and administrative policies of the Beiyang and Nationalist Party leaders, who also borrowed from each other. Liu Cunhou and Xiong Kewu, having joined the Revolutionary Alliance, knew how to speak in the revolutionary terms of the Nationalists. Both they and the others, though, also kept an eye on political events in Beijing and followed the Beiyang government's lead in certain respects. Thus, in 1922, Liu Chengxun set up a new city government structure for Chengdu, which the Beiyang government had done in Beijing in 1917 and the Nationalist government had done in Guangzhou in 1921. This willingness to adopt what were seen as progressive measures from eastern China was critical in attracting some support locally, particularly from among Chengdu men who had studied in Beijing or abroad and wanted to introduce new policies in Sichuan and/or to bring about a social revolution there.

Second, none of the four—the three Lius and Xiong—was ever secure enough in power to devote much attention to civil matters such as economic development, education, policing, and other public services. They needed money to pay and equip their soldiers, but they had little time to create conditions that would increase economic surpluses in the province. Instead, as discussed in Chapter Three, they bargained with and threatened wealthy merchants and landholders to raise money. Thus, their relations with urban communities such as Chengdu's were tense. On the surface, the heads of merchant guilds praised and flattered military governors, but only for the purpose of minimizing the militarists' financial demands. Meanwhile, despite the progressive rhetoric of the militarists, civil administration went into a decline.

Third, the militarists' need for quick cash and for weapons meant that southeastern Sichuan, centered on the Yangzi port of Chongqing, became much more important strategically than western Sichuan, centered on Chengdu. Although both Liu Cunhou and Xiong Kewu had occupied Chengdu in the years after 1916, both eventually led their armies to the Chongqing area to try to control south Sichuan's salt wells and opium fields and, most importantly, the Yangzi river trade. Liu Chengxun and Liu Wenhui were pushed out of the Chengdu area in 1924 by the more powerful army of Yang Sen, which had gathered strength in southeastern Sichuan. Beginning in the mid-1920s, the dominant militarist in Sichuan was Liu Wenhui's cousin, Liu Xiang, who ruled from Chongqing.

And so, in short, after 1916 Ba Jin saw his hometown decline rapidly in significance as an economic and political center. Control over the city passed frequently from one military leader to another. Although these leaders usually claimed to be progressive, the pressures of constant fighting led them to squeeze resources out of the city and antagonize the local population and the local elite. Their armies were usually not well disciplined. When one army supplanted another, the damage to the city could be heavy. The worst example of this occurred in April and July of 1917, but similar clashes threatened Chengdu almost every year in the 1920s, including in 1923, just after the new federalist provincial constitution had been drafted.[13] In 1932, another incident of fighting, this time between Liu Xiang and his cousin Liu Wenhui, again destroyed many houses and many lives in Chengdu.

Warfare's Effects on the City

The sense of terror that Ba Jin evokes in chapter 20 of *Family*, when he describes the Gao elders hiding out in the garden as Juexin stands alone in the great hall to defend their home against expected looters, well reflects what we can learn about street warfare from numerous eyewitness accounts of the 1917 battles in Chengdu. A detailed essay written in the 1970s by Huang Juegao, who in 1917 was a twenty-three-year-old cavalry officer in Liu Cunhou's army, reports that the Yunnan troops of Luo Peijin were divided between the East Parade Ground at the edge of the city and the "imperial city" in the city center, where in Qing times the governor-general had presided over the civil service examinations. In the years before and after 1911, schools and the provincial mint had been built within this great walled rectangle in the heart of the city (see Figure 3.3). In 1916 the Yunnan forces established themselves there. The Sichuan troops of Liu Cunhou were based in the North Parade Ground and outside the North Gate. The Guizhou troops of Dai Kan occupied the arsenal outside the East Gate.

A loyal son of Sichuan, Huang Juegao attributes tensions among the armies to the arrogance of Yunnan troops, who, he says, sent patrols of soldiers through the streets, headed by a soldier carrying a placard with a big character for "command" written on it. All other soldiers and police they encountered were required to make a formal salute. Huang writes that Yunnan soldiers beat up many on-duty police officers for failing to salute properly and stole property from merchants.[14] Fighting broke out in the middle of April 1917, according to Huang, when Luo Peijin felt threatened by a company of the Sichuan troops. He devised a plan to review them on the East Parade Ground—near Ba Jin's family's home—and have his soldiers disarm them. The disbanded soldiers, half-naked, then started running amuck in town, until another Sichuan unit gave them knives and urged them to attack Yunnan troops, who were easy to identify by the red trim on their uniforms (the Sichuan army uniforms were all grey). Civilians joined in the attack.

The Yunnan army fought back. From their base in the East Parade Ground, the Yunnan troops captured more than 1,200 Sichuan soldiers, policemen, and civilians, executed them, and threw the bodies off the city wall into the river running along it.[15] Other units of the Sichuan army then attacked the Yunnan forces. Dai Kan, leader of the Guizhou forces in the city, declared neutrality and called on the two sides to treat the city's main business district as a neutral zone. Liu Cunhou brought his artillery into the city, set it up on the city wall by the West Parade Ground, and began pounding Luo Peijin's headquarters in the old imperial city with shells. Luo then acknowledged defeat and, under a ceasefire negotiated by Dai Kan, the Yunnan troops left the city a week after the fighting had begun, departing via the new East Gate, just south of the East Parade Ground.

Huang Juegao attributes the second outbreak of fighting in 1917, between the Guizhou and Sichuan forces in July, to Dai Kan's ambitions and suspicions. That month in Beijing, a military leader had attempted to revive the Qing, putting the ten-year-old deposed Qing emperor Puyi back on the throne he had surrendered in 1912. Hoping Liu Cunhou would support the imperial government, Puyi's advisers had the emperor appoint Liu as Sichuan governor. When the appointment was made public, Dai Kan accused Liu Cunhou of treason against the Republic. His troops attacked Liu's troops in Chengdu on July 5, 1917. Dai Kan concentrated his troops in the imperial city and sent messages to Luo Peijin, south of Chengdu, to return to the city to defeat Liu Cunhou.

Liu Cunhou once more bombarded the imperial city, but with less success—shells hit residences outside the imperial city and killed scores of noncombatants. The tough Guizhou troops used spears to repel the Sichuan troops who tried to scale the walls of the imperial city. Eventually, they began to run out of food and made a break out of the imperial city, but the Sichuan troops pushed them back. While retreating, though, they set fires in the neighborhood south of the imperial city, burning down hundreds of houses. The Sichuan army then decided to blow a hole in the imperial city wall using a coffin full of dynamite, which they stuck into a tunnel dug partway under the wall. The huge explosion blasted a ten-foot gap in the wall, and the army rushed in, only to be cut down immediately by Guizhou troops who had detected that a tunnel was being dug there. Sichuan troops strung banners around the city promising a reward of 50,000 yuan for capturing Dai Kan alive and 25,000 yuan for bringing his head to Liu Cunhou. Finally, the remnants of the Guizhou army requested permission to withdraw from the city. It was granted, but instead of retreating, the Guizhou troops occupied the South Gate and began setting fires and attacking the Sichuan troops with swords and spears. Beaten back into the imperial city, the Guizhou troops eventually capitulated, and the few survivors left Chengdu.

Huang Juegao and his comrades were assigned the task of cleaning up the imperial city; he said they were all sickened by the stench of rotting corpses.

The death and destruction of 1917 touched every family in Chengdu. As noted in Chapter Three, the former head of the Chengdu Chamber of Commerce, Fan Kongzhou, director of the biggest publishing company in the city, was assassinated in June after he traveled to Chongqing to plead with central government representatives to try to stop the fighting.[16] A servant of one of Ba Jin's neighbors was shot and died in front of Ba Jin's family's gate as Ba Jin himself watched. Many people suffered from diseases that could not be treated during the fighting. Ba Jin's father died of diphtheria during an outbreak following the April 1917 battle.[17] Ba Jin's teacher, Wu Yu, lost his beloved wife, Zeng Lan, to an illness she contracted while trying to recover from the stress of being forced from her home in both April and July of 1917. In July, the family had sought refuge in the Confucian Temple, and Wu Yu had taken the opportunity to reflect on the harm Confucian thought was still causing China.[18] During the spring and summer of 1917 temples and schools in the city were jam-packed with panicked refugees trying to avoid being killed in the crossfire between the West Parade Ground and the imperial city.

The damage to the city and its residents produced widespread anger and disgust. Wu Yu's feelings about the militarists were so strong that he later turned down Liu Wenhui's commission to compose a celebratory ode for Liu's mother's birthday, even though Liu had sent him a present of 2,000 yuan with the request.[19] Chengdu's newspapers soon began popularizing the expression "warlord" (*junfa*) and derogatory terms for soldiers, such as *qiu ba* (丘八), made by pronouncing both the upper and lower parts of the standard character meaning "soldier" (兵 *bing*).[20] A literature that mocked militarists sprang up in the city, championed above all by a merchant named Liu Shiliang, whose business was destroyed in the fighting of 1917. He became famous in the 1920s as a writer and publisher of satirical doggerel that condemned all of Sichuan's would-be unifiers.[21]

Rebuilding began immediately but was hampered by skyrocketing prices for wood and other materials. The *West China Missionary News*, published by the Methodist church in Chengdu, reported that lack of maintenance had led to the failure of the dam at Dujiangyan, west of Chengdu, with the result that water flowing off the Tibetan plateau in the Min River had followed different channels, drying up the branch of the river that circled Chengdu.

Logs could not be floated down from the mountains to the city. An estimated seventeen thousand Chengdu families were homeless in July 1917.[22] The generators that produced electricity for lighting, purchased from a German company in 1909, were destroyed in 1917, and the system was not completely restored until 1923.[23] Because the Guizhou troops had used kerosene to set fire to neighborhoods in the heart of town, police in Chengdu and other Sichuan cities restricted the sale of kerosene in later years, limiting its use in heating and causing the Standard Oil Company to ask the US consul in Chongqing to lodge a protest with the provincial government in Chengdu.[24] The instability and financial distress lingered. Wounded soldiers gathered in the city seeking pay, and shops were regularly looted in the years after 1917.[25]

The effect of the fighting on the reputations of Sichuan and Chengdu elsewhere in China was also significant. These sank to their lowest levels after the "Two Liu" (Liu Xiang and Liu Wenhui) war of 1932, which coincided with the publication of *Family*. People all over China could compare the newspaper accounts of the 1932 street fighting in Chengdu with *Family*'s descriptions of similar battles inspired by the 1917 and 1923 fighting. But well before *Family* had appeared to cement Chengdu's image as a dark and oppressive city, the barbarity of the 1917 fighting was noted. In June 1917, the president of the Republic personally donated 20,000 yuan and ordered the central government treasury to send 100,000 yuan to Chengdu to provide relief for the people who had suffered during the street battles in April.[26] Whether or not these funds ever made it into the hands of needy people in Chengdu is not known. The frequent fighting made travel dangerous and increased Sichuan's isolation from eastern China.[27]

In addition to damaging people, property, and the provincial reputation, the warfare in the early Republic changed the sociopolitical order in Chengdu in two important ways. First, the periodic crises during which the city changed hands from one militarist to another created a need for suitable mediators to handle negotiations between the sides so as to limit the harm to the city.[28] The two groups that emerged to take charge of this—without much success in 1917, but more effectively later—were the gentry leaders we discussed in Chapter Two (the elders and sages) and the most prominent foreign residents of the city. The foreign community in Chengdu was small, numbering not many more than one hundred people in 1917. There were British, French, and Japanese consulates (the American consulate was in Chongqing), in addition to the West China Union University, the YMCA, foreign-run hospitals, and churches. The foreigners' access to outside sources of money (which they sometimes lent to the militarists) and power (the threat of calling in the intervention of the central Chinese government or their own home governments) and their claims to neutrality gave them opportunities to attempt mediation among the combatants. Meyrick Hewlett, the British consul general in Chengdu from 1916 to 1922, was particularly active in 1917. He negotiated with all sides in the conflict and gave cigarettes to the Yunnan troops to bribe them to leave the neighborhood of the consulate. In his memoirs, he claims that his grateful neighbors gave him a silk banner praising him for saving their lives and property.[29] Hewlett, however, opposed the involvement of other foreigners in Chinese politics. He wrote a stern letter to the US consul in Chongqing after the fighting was over, complaining that YMCA secretary Robert Service had interfered with his negotiations and given encouragement to Liu Cunhou.[30] During the tense period in spring 1923 when Liu Chengxun was in danger of being driven out of Chengdu, Liu Chengxun's chief of staff asked Joseph Beech, president of the West China Union University, if Liu and he could take refuge on campus; Beech suggested instead that they check into the Canadian hospital.[31]

As noted in Chapter Two, the militarists usually treated Chengdu's five elders and seven sages with respect, leading radicals like Ba Jin to see these traditional authorities as collaborators with the warlords. Many other Chengdu residents, though, were grateful to the old gentry leaders for trying to rein in the militarists. The feeling was initially the same toward the foreigners. Those who knew Robert Service and Consul General Hewlett urged them to step in to save the city in 1917 and in later years. But gradually more and more people in Chengdu began to identify foreigners as a source of the problem—their compatriots in Europe and the United States sold weapons to the warlords and profited from the constant civil wars.[32] Anti-imperialist sentiment began to spread in the wake of the May Fourth incident of 1919. But, as we will see when we examine the May Fourth movement in Chapter Seven, it had no major impact on the foreign community in Chengdu until 1926, well after Ba Jin had left the city.

Gentry elders and foreigners played a prominent role in managing military crises in Chengdu, but they had little to do with the everyday life of most of its people. During the years of warlord strife when Ba Jin was young, the lack of a stable administration to handle public business meant that the Chengdu community began to regulate itself with little regard to formal institutions of government. Although every militarist who controlled Chengdu supported, to some extent, the city's police force and allowed it to raise funds from taxes on hotels and brothels, street militias organized by local residents patrolled the neighborhoods. Disputes were often taken to teahouses for resolution, rather than to the formal courts. The public school system stagnated; most people learned to read in small private schools with one teacher and a handful of students.[33]

The decay of formal institutions in Chengdu after 1916 encouraged the growth of a different type of association through which power was exercised to manage social life. Historians and other observers have referred to it using several terms, including "secret society," "gang," and "brotherhood association." People in Chengdu when Ba Jin was young called it the "Gowned Brothers" (Paoge).[34] The origins of the Gowned Brothers are murky. The organizations certainly existed in the late Qing period, although they were illegal. Men formed lodges and held initiation ceremonies, as did the Masons in the Western world, pledging to support each other as brothers. Histories produced after 1911 by admirers state that they formed largely to oppose the Manchu rulers of the Qing, whom they considered to be illegitimate foreign conquerors. There is little evidence, though, to support this claim. Still, Gowned Brother lodges played a supportive role in the 1911 Revolution in Sichuan, which earned them a patriotic reputation in the early years of the Republic.

The numbers of Gowned Brother lodges and members expanded considerably in the period of civil war in Sichuan between 1916 and 1949, primarily for two reasons. First, Sichuan militarists such as Liu Wenhui and Liu Xiang patronized lodges to tap into local networks for support across the province. And, second, the lodges came to constitute the basis for managing local affairs, both in villages and in urban neighborhoods, in the absence of effective state institutions. There were lodges in every part of Chengdu by the 1920s. Their leaders were prominent merchants or tradesmen who oversaw the induction of new members, collected dues, supervised militias that patrolled their neighborhoods, and acted as local liaisons to police and military authorities, many of whom formed their own lodges.

Wealthy gentry families such as Ba Jin's generally did not participate in Gowned Brother activities, and Ba Jin does not mention them in *Turbulent Stream*. Ba Jin's elders, though, probably knew who the local chiefs were, and the prevalence of Gowned Brother lodges played a role in shaping social interactions in Chengdu in the 1920s. Gowned Brother culture embraced gambling, opium, and prostitution, and its rise had a significant impact on gender politics in Chengdu, a topic we address in Chapter Six. The Gowned-Brother mode of governance—characterized by in-group intimacy, hierarchy, and appeal to Chinese traditions of knight-errantry—put it at odds with the sort of democratic values that people like Ba Jin espoused, a topic to be examined in Chapter Seven. As products of the troubled years of militarist competition in Sichuan, the Gowned Brothers became a central feature of life in Chengdu during Ba Jin's youth.

Warlords and Students: A Conflicted Relationship

In eastern China in the 1920s, some militarists associated themselves closely with emerging political parties that espoused attractive ideologies. Chiang Kai-shek, who studied military strategy and practice in Japan between 1907 and 1911, championed Sun Yat-sen's Three Principles of the People and became the leader of the Nationalist Party after Sun's death in 1925. Zhu De, who was born in Sichuan and attended military school in neighboring Yunnan Province before 1911, threw in his lot with the Communist Party after its split with the Nationalists in 1927, becoming its most famous general. Most of the militarists who fought over Sichuan, though, did not emphasize their ideological leanings. It may be that they did not see the significance of ideology as a way to rally supporters. But they may also have been trying to keep their options open as they negotiated with the eastern militarists.

Some of Sichuan's rulers in the May Fourth era did encourage student activism. Xiong Kewu and Yang Shukan, who were both members of the Nationalist Party and governed Chengdu together for a time, supported students who attempted to confiscate Japanese goods from Chengdu merchants in December 1919. After a brawl broke out between some four hundred students and three hundred merchants in front of the offices of the Chamber of Commerce, the students damaged the building and paraded twenty-eight merchants through the streets as traitors. Yang Shukan, who was serving as civil governor at the time, made a speech that expressed sympathy for the merchants but also refused to punish any of the student demonstrators (see Chapter Seven for more detail on this incident).[35]

In Chapter Two we saw that not all of Chengdu's young people in the early 1920s shared Ba Jin's hatred of the city's old gentry culture. Likewise, not all educated youth despised all of the various militarists who aimed to rule Sichuan in the 1910s and 1920s. Usually, Chengdu's young people tried to appeal to the militarists to address the issues that most concerned them: the lack of public funding for education and aggressive behavior by soldiers in the city. This relation between students and military governors is reflected in chapters 9–11 of *Family*, in which Ba Jin describes soldiers forcing their way into a student performance, smashing up the theater, and beating students who try to resist them. Gao Juehui and his friends march to the Commander's office to demand redress. Eventually, the Commander

> made two announcements to mollify the students and he had his adjutant write a letter conveying his apologies to the United Students Association and guaranteeing the students' safety in the future. Thereupon the newspapers published orders from the Garrison Command forbidding soldiers to attack students. According to rumor they even arrested two soldiers who confessed to instigating the brawl, and gave them heavy sentences.[36]

This incident reflects real historical clashes between students and soldiers in Chengdu in 1920 and 1922, well documented in the local archives. In November 1920, soldiers interrupted a ball game near Shaocheng Park and students protested, leading to a fight. The park manager sent a report on this clash to the police (Figure 5.3). The students went on strike when their concerns were not addressed to their satisfaction. Liu Cunhou's staff mediated and the strike ended, but then, just as in *Family*, soldiers forced their way into a student performance and beat those who resisted. After this incident, the outraged students formed a student union and protested at Liu Cunhou's headquarters, as in Ba Jin's account.[37] In June 1922 Chengdu students demonstrated at the Provincial Assembly to protest Liu Chengxun's refusal to release the educational budget collected from the tax on pork. During that demonstration, soldiers killed three student protesters, and all Chengdu's schools again went on strike. Eventually, gentry mediators negotiated a settlement.[38]

As presented in *Family*, the students' actions constitute a sort of moral opposition to militarist rule fueled by the new spirit of the May Fourth movement. On the other hand, the student protests in Chengdu in the early 1920s can also be interpreted as following a well-established pattern of rela-

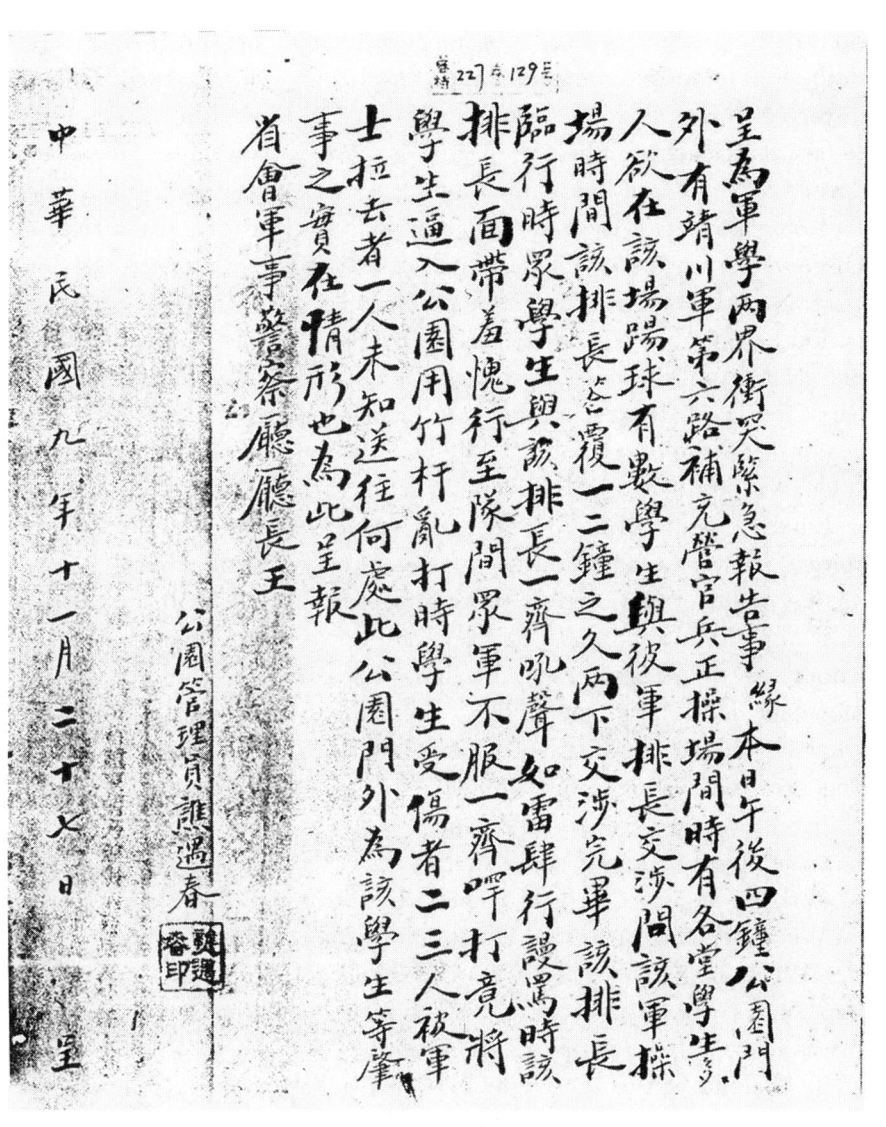

Figure 5.3 Report to the chief of Chengdu military police by the manager of Shaocheng Park on a clash between students and soldiers on November 27, 1920. Chengdu Municipal Archives, fond 93-6, file 227.

tions between scholars outside of the government and scholar-bureaucrats inside it. The most famous example of such a protest in modern Chinese history occurred in 1895, when hundreds of scholars who had gathered to take the palace examination in Beijing signed a petition to the emperor drafted by Kang Youwei: the petition criticized Qing officers and officials for losing a war with Japan and appealed to the emperor for major reforms. Of course, much about Chinese politics had changed between 1895 and 1923. Nevertheless, scholars of Chinese student activism in the republican period have pointed out that students benefited in their interaction with politicians from a widespread recognition of their high cultural status, in part a legacy of Confucian exam culture and in part because of their association with "modern learning." Officials often preferred to negotiate with students rather than to merely dismiss or arrest them.[39]

Educated youth of Ba Jin's generation sometimes made use of this high cultural status to establish themselves as external critics of militarist governments—working as journalists, professors, or novelists. Others tried to steer clear of politics. Still others, though, went to work for militarists, many of whom actively recruited them. Ba Jin's contemporaries who accepted employment in militarist governments in Chengdu are generally not as well known as he, but there were many. A young man by the name of Sun Shaojing, somewhat older than Ba Jin, helped his teacher Wu Yu and classmate Li Jieren edit a progressive newspaper in 1919 and then went to Japan and Germany to study urban administration.[40] He returned to Sichuan in 1923 to work for the new Chengdu municipal government. Sun Shaojing called on Wu Yu regularly for advice about municipal regulations and to talk politics. When unknown assailants murdered Sun in Chengdu in 1927, Wu Yu wrote in his diary of his shock and dismay, vowing to keep out of politics and live as a hermit to avoid dying as Sun had.[41]

By the end of the 1920s, the Nationalist Party under Generalissimo Chiang Kai-shek had succeeded in establishing a new internationally recognized government in Nanjing, and all the Sichuan militarists had expressed support for it and its ideology, Sun Yat-sen's Three Principles of the People. The dilemma of whether or not to work with any particular militarist-official did not disappear, but the choice to work with the government probably did not seem as difficult as at the height of the warlord infighting in the early 1920s.

Soldiers in Sichuan's Warlord Armies

By 1919, the number of soldiers in Sichuan was reported to be three hundred thousand, up from fifty-three thousand at the time of the 1911 Revolution.⁴² Who were these men? Why did they agree to take up arms in what often must have seemed like senseless battles between scheming militarists? Were they as arrogant and violent toward Chengdu's residents as Ba Jin suggests in *Turbulent Stream*? Unfortunately, the historical record does not provide much evidence with which to answer these questions.⁴³

Ordinary soldiers appear in archival records, but almost always as nameless miscreants. Detailed records from Sichuan military units, if they ever existed, are not available, unlike the archives of the Chengdu police and city government. One of the most common sorts of reports concerning soldiers in police files are accounts of soldiers attacking police and preventing them from carrying out their work. In 1922, for example, Chengdu's police bureau sent a report to Liu Chengxun stating that police constables had told some soldiers to stop bathing nude in the river along the city wall. The soldiers then beat up the constables and followed them to their police station, where they destroyed the furniture and stole three swords and three leather belts. Liu Chengxun ordered a thorough investigation and strict punishment of those responsible.⁴⁴ Police files are also full of petitions from people and organizations whose property was damaged or stolen by unidentified soldiers. There seems little doubt that soldiers turned loose in Sichuan's cities caused much havoc and damage in the 1910s and 1920s. This was particularly true during times of transition, when one set of troops replaced another. Then, soldiers tended to desert and hide out wherever they could in the city.⁴⁵ During such times, able-bodied men faced a serious risk of being forced to accompany the departing troops as "coolies": porters who carried military supplies from one base to another. During one such transfer of power in 1917 in Chongqing, the US consulate outfitted all of its workers with special armbands that were stamped with a military order forbidding them to be harassed or impressed for forced labor.⁴⁶

Were many soldiers themselves forced into joining the armies of Sichuan's militarists? Perhaps sometimes, but most signed on voluntarily. Historian Diana Lary writes that, unlike the frequent impressment of coolies, press-ganging of soldiers was rare in republican China because it produced unreliable troops who had to be guarded constantly. Most recruits, she argues, were younger sons of poor farm families who had few other ways to support themselves and found a life of hard rural labor too monotonous to bear.[47] Perhaps some of them had heard about the cases in which a common foot soldier had advanced through the ranks to become a commander. The most famous example of this was Feng Yuxiang, the so-called "Christian general" whose base was in north China. But most new recruits probably joined up for the prospect of food and pay and the possible new opportunities that mobility might bring.

The richest account we have of a 1920s soldier in Sichuan is contained in a story Li Jieren published in one of China's most widely read magazines, *Eastern Miscellany*, in 1927, several years after he had had returned to Chengdu from studying literature in France.[48] The story is presented as a "chronicle of the life of Big Uncle Soldier Chen Zhenwu," and the narrator claims to have compiled the account based on a detailed interview with the soldier when they met accidentally at a country inn. The story is clearly fictional.[49] However, it is also evident that Li Jieren intended it to reflect the reality of a soldier's life in Sichuan in the mid-1920s. Unlike Ba Jin, who wanted *Turbulent Stream* to be an indictment of the oppressive aspects of Chengdu culture, Li Jieren wrote fiction that we might characterize as sociological—his stories depict the whole range of Chengdu society realistically and sympathetically. In lieu of detailed historical information on common soldiers in Chengdu in the 1910s and 1920s, Li Jieren's fictional representation offers a valuable perspective with which to end this chapter on warfare in the city.

Big Uncle Soldier Chen Zhenwu, in Li Jieren's account, begins life as simply Third Son of the Chen Family (Chen Laosan). During his twenty-third year, a drought dries up the farmland in his village and, because all the farmers had been forced by local authorities to grow opium, they have no stored grain to carry them through the subsequent famine. Rather than stay at home and watch his widowed mother and young sisters starve, Chen sets off for Chengdu to find work. As he is resting in a teahouse, he sees a recruitment poster for the army occupying Chengdu and decides to enlist. His new commanding officer tells him that his given name, Third Son, is too common and gives him a better sounding one: Zhenwu, "stirring up martial feeling."

As a soldier, Chen Zhenwu is very naïve at first, but he is older than most of his fellow recruits, whose average age is about fifteen. The officers prefer younger soldiers, the narrator notes, because they are easier to discipline and more likely to charge enthusiastically into battle than older men. Chen Zhenwu soon falls in with some more experienced soldiers who teach him how to benefit from the "tiger skin" that is his military uniform. Chen starts to enjoy being treated with deference by the fearful city dwellers—he is called by the respectful title of "mister" for the first time in his life. Soon, he and his comrades are running a protection racket: rice merchants pay them off in exchange for being allowed to keep some of the grain Chen and his gang are sent to requisition on behalf of their brigade. They molest a woman carrying her child down a lonely street. They blackmail a wealthy family indulging in mahjong despite an official ban on gambling. Although the city walls are plastered over with edicts ordering soldiers not to misbehave, Chen Zhenwu and his buddies find the available opportunities too tempting to pass up.

Chen Zhenwu gradually becomes accustomed to casual violence. The military commander in Chengdu (clearly modeled on Yang Sen), playing mahjong with his many wives at his official residence, hears a disturbance on the street and goes himself to investigate. A gambling session involving Chen and his friends has led to a brawl. The brawlers are not identified, but the commander's bodyguard captures a carpenter and a sedan-chair bearer who happen to be in the area. Although they deny any involvement in the affair, the commander pulls out a pistol and shoots them dead as an example to anyone who might be tempted to gamble and brawl in future.

Eventually, the commander is ousted from Chengdu by another militarist (which Li Jieren witnessed happening to Yang Sen in 1925). Chen Zhenwu and his comrades are forced to march out of the city, along with press-ganged coolies. During the next few months, he witnesses the execution of deserters, helps devastate a village his company is ordered to occupy, rapes the female villagers, and joins in the looting of a defeated city. Finally, during a siege on a county town, the officer in charge of his unit switches allegiance to the enemy of his former commander and orders Chen Zhenwu's company to attack their former allies. Chen takes advantage of the chaos during this battle and slips away with his loot, thinking he will become a peddler in Chengdu. His plans are thwarted, however, when the innkeeper in a small town on the road to Chengdu summons the local militia as Chen settles in for the night at the inn. The militia head accuses him of being an army deserter and threatens to turn him in for what he knows is certain execution. Resigned to the inevitable, Chen Zhenwu buys his release by turning over his ill-gotten gains to the militia. He then tells his sad story to the narrator, who is also staying at the inn. "What will you do now?" the narrator asks. "Go back to being a soldier" is the answer. No amount of persuasion to follow some better path shakes this resolution. Chen Zhenwu merely replies that, from his point of view and given the sorry state of the world as he sees it, there is no better option—his food and clothing are paid for, he has plenty of opportunities to make money, and, although he has to take some abuse from his officers, he can, after all, lord it over civilians.

Li Jieren's imaginative account of the transformation of a simple country boy into a calculating opportunist with a gun and few scruples fills a gap in our historical knowledge—and in Ba Jin's picture of life in Chengdu—in a plausible way. The soldiers who fight with students and threaten the property and lives of the Gao family in *Turbulent Stream* are nameless and one-dimensional, but their actual counterparts in historical Chengdu, like Third Son Chen, certainly had their own names and personal stories, hardly ever recalled by novelists or historians.

CHAPTER SIX

Qin

Chengdu and the "New Woman"

Young women in China in the 1930s and 1940s loved Ba Jin's *Turbulent Stream*. Ba Jin himself met his future wife after she wrote him a fan letter in 1936, one of many he received from schoolgirls around the country. *Family* features a strong, smart, sympathetic female character—Qin, the Gao patriarch's granddaughter (daughter of his daughter, called in Chinese the equivalent of "outer granddaughter"). Because of the enthusiastic response to *Family* among female readers, Ba Jin chose Gao Shuying, the eldest surviving granddaughter of the patriarch, as the main character in *Spring*, the second novel of his trilogy. Qin, Shuying, and the other young ladies in the Gao family face pressure to accept their elders' decisions about their lives, including arranged marriages to men they haven't met. While trying—for the most part—to please their parents, they also aim to take advantage of new opportunities emerging for women in the early 1920s. But, as Ba Jin's readers knew, challenging customs was not easy—and could even be dangerous. Many young women in China in the 1930s looked to Ba Jin's fictional

155

"New Women" (*xin nüxing*), as such unconventional girls as Qin came to be called, for guidance and moral support.[1]

Qin's story is as poignant as that of the slave girl Mingfeng. Her predicament is expressed in particularly vivid terms in a scene in chapter 22 of *Family*, when the realities of the seemingly endless provincial warfare challenge her visions of her future. Facing the possibility of rape during an impending street battle, she begins to weep helplessly, "mourning the loss of her illusions."

> She had worked for years to build those beautiful dreams. She had struggled, she had fought, she had toiled, and finally she had made a little progress. In the face of this terror that progress seemed futile, as society attacked her from a new direction. In an instant everything she had spent ten years working for was destroyed. Ibsen said, "Try to be a human being," but what use were these ringing words now? She cried not only because she was frightened, but because she saw her own true face. Until now she had really believed that she was a brave woman, and she had been told so by others as well. Only now did she see what a weak girl she really was. She too could do nothing but wait, like a sheep or a swine about to be slaughtered. She had no strength to resist.[2]

As Qin's wretched reflections suggest, the chronic warfare in Sichuan shaped the environment in which young people challenged family rules and social customs. This chapter explores the status of women in gentry families in early twentieth-century Chengdu and how it was changing during the turbulent late 1910s and early 1920s, when Qin's real-life counterparts lived.

As we examine elite women's lives after the 1911 Revolution, we need to be especially aware of how writers in the 1920s and 1930s, including Ba Jin, produced a discourse about the oppression of women in what they called "traditional," or "Confucian," or "feudal" China. Many intellectuals active in those decades believed they were witnessing the birth of a democratic and progressive New China that would soon replace what they thought of as stagnant and corrupt Old China. They tended to homogenize, simplify, and condemn many aspects of Chinese history, but most especially women's status in Chinese society.[3] A stereotype was created: "the traditional Chinese woman" was said to be submissive, illiterate, isolated in the home, and concerned only with rearing children and caring for elders. Above all, as historian Dorothy Ko has argued, "the bound foot remains a shorthand for all that was wrong with traditional China."[4] Chinese cultural critics were assisted in their distortions of Chinese history by other interested observers, including Christian missionaries from the United States and Europe, who highlighted aspects of Chinese life that seemed to them barbaric and in need of Christian influence.[5] Scholars such as Ko and Susan Mann have called into question common perceptions of Chinese women that took root in the 1920s, and we will draw on their work and others', as well as evidence from Chengdu, to look beyond the stereotypes that writers like Ba Jin sometimes employed.

Nevertheless, an examination of the social conditions facing Chengdu girls who—like Qin—responded to a new discourse of women's equality and tried to take on new social roles in the early 1920s makes us aware of the real challenges they faced. A combination of militarism and a culturally conservative backlash against it proved dangerous to women who dared defy conventions and to men who associated with them.

Elite Women's Upbringing and Education

One of Qin's greatest hopes in *Turbulent Stream* is that she will be allowed to attend the school where her cousins Gao Juemin and Gao Juehui study, the Foreign Languages School. The young people frequently discuss the probability that boys' schools will begin accepting female students. At one point, they decide it is likely to happen: the militarist who has taken control of the city wants to send several of his young wives to college and so he is promoting the idea of coeducation.

This part of the trilogy is clearly based on fact. Until 1924, when General Yang Sen pushed the city's higher-level schools to accept girl students, academic institutions in Chengdu were segregated by sex. Girls' schools were almost all the equivalent of elementary schools. Hu Lanqi, a Chengdu native who became famous during the 1930s and was a few years older than Ba Jin, writes in her memoir that in 1905 she entered Chengdu's first private girls' school, run by a young widow who had herself learned to read from a neighbor. Just as in the boys' schools at the time, the students paid their respects to Confucius—bowing every morning to his portrait—and memorized the *Three-Character Classic*, a simple text that presented moral lessons along with a basic vocabulary.[6]

In the years before and after the 1911 Revolution, the foreign missionaries and some prominent Chinese members of the community set up both elementary and high schools for girls.[7] Ba Jin's teacher Wu Yu sent his daughters to the American Methodist high school and the French Catholic high school. Most elite women in Chengdu in Ba Jin's time, however, were educated at home. Ba Jin's accounts of how girls in the Gao family were taught seem to come directly from his memory of his sisters' and cousins' educations. In chapter 11 of *Family*, Ruijue, the wife of eldest brother Gao Juexin, recalls writing poetry with her sister when they were children and learning to raise silkworms from her mother. Ba Jin's own mother taught her children poetry and silkworm culture.[8]

In the Qing period, hired tutors often taught girls in elite families to read, and parents and older siblings sometimes taught girls to paint and write poetry.[9] A small number of women achieved recognition as outstanding poets and artists over the centuries. Everyone in Chengdu knew about Xue Tao, a Tang-dynasty courtesan patronized by Sichuan governors and renowned for her poetry and her papermaking skills. The well where she supposedly drew water for papermaking has been a local landmark for hundreds of years.[10] But as gender expectations shifted in the centuries following the collapse of the Tang in 907 CE, elite women gradually receded from public life. By Qing times, accomplished poetesses, such as the ladies of the Zhang family of Changzhou in east China, shared their literary work only within their families, for the most part. They gained fame primarily when their sons and grandsons wrote lovingly about them and published their poems in tribute volumes.[11]

As discussed in Chapter Two, the centrality of poetry to elite life in Ba Jin's Chengdu is clear, both for men and women. Ba Jin's grandmother wrote poems, as did many of his cousins, and his novels touch on this, including a scene in chapter 13 of *Family* when girls and boys in the Gao family play a drinking game that requires them to recite lines from poems. But poetry is not the only subject of the Gao girls' education, as Ba Jin shows in a scene in which Gao Shuzhen, the daughter of the patriarch's fifth son, recites her lessons. Gao Juehui hears Shuzhen repeating lines from the *Four Books for Women*: "When happy do not laugh aloud, when angry do not raise your voice. Sit without showing your knees, walk without swinging your skirt." Elementary literary texts for girls instructed them to be obedient, to control their bodies strictly, and to repress their emotions. Older girls read stories that stressed self-sacrifice. In his memoirs, Ba Jin recalled finding an illustrated copy of the book *Lives of Virtuous Women* (*Lienüzhuan*) in his eldest sister's room when he was five or six; in all of the pictures, beautiful women were suffering:

> Such terrible pictures! I did not understand them and asked my sisters. They told me that the book was about models of female virtue and that all young women were supposed to read about them and emulate them. I still did not understand. I asked my mother and she explained to me: that is a widow—she is cutting off her hand because a strange man has touched it; that is an imperial concubine—the palace caught fire but since she is forbidden to walk out without an escort she allowed herself to be burned to death in the flames, and so on.[12]

In the early twentieth century, newspaperman Fu Chongju began to publish the *Popular Pictorial* (*Tongsu huabao*), borrowing many of the artistic techniques used by the illustrators of the old editions of *Lives of Virtuous Women* to warn against various types of misconduct. In one example (Figure 6.1), a woman from a town near Chengdu who claimed to have supernatural powers and involved her young niece and nephew in her nefarious doings is struck down by lightning in divine retribution.

Such texts as the *Lives of Virtuous Women* were commonly used in women's education in the early twentieth century, just as the Christian Bible had been in early American education. How seriously they were taken, however, is an open question.[13] Hu Lanqi recalled that, as a young girl, she was inspired instead by a very different kind of story about a person who sacrificed herself for a very different cause: Qiu Jin, a woman from an elite family who left her husband and children to study in Japan in 1904. While in Japan, Qiu Jin joined a revolutionary group and plotted to overthrow the Qing dynasty by assassinating officials. Returning to China to carry out her plans, she was captured and executed in 1907. Qiu Jin became famous after the 1911 Revolution, when she was declared a martyr.[14] Hu Lanqi heard about Qiu Jin not from a textbook but from women in her neighborhood, who most likely were passing on stories that arrived in Chengdu from east China via newspapers and letters and spread through the city's teahouses, where men would sit and chat for hours and then bring the gossip home to their families.[15]

Ba Jin does not mention Qiu Jin in *Turbulent Stream*, but he refers to other models of strong women. In the quotation from *Family* discussed above, Qin bitterly remembers Ibsen's line "Try to be a human being." This is a reference to the Norwegian playwright Henrik Ibsen's *A Doll's House* (first performed in Denmark in 1879), which was hugely popular in China after it was translated

Figure 6.1 Image published in *Popular Pictorial* (*Tongsu huabao*) in 1912, showing a woman who had claimed supernatural powers being struck by lightning. *Tongsu huabao* (Chengdu), issue 3, 1912.

into Chinese in 1918. At the play's conclusion, its heroine, Nora, walks out of her materially comfortable but oppressive family life into an unknown world of struggle, where she hopes to gain self-knowledge and emotional fulfillment. By the time Ba Jin wrote *Family* (with its rather similar ending), *A Doll's House* had become a central text in the Chinese debate about women's place in society.[16] An even more important female exemplar for the young Ba Jin was the real-life Russian revolutionary Sofia Perovskaia. Perovskaia helped to assassinate Czar Alexander II in 1881 as part of an attempt to overthrow the Russian political order; she was hanged as a result. Ba Jin's biographer Olga Lang observed that Ba Jin's fictional heroines show a clear resemblance to the nineteenth-century Russian populists and anarchists. In *Turbulent Stream*, Qin and Shuying claim Perovskaia as their ideal of a politically engaged woman.[17]

Perovskaia's life had been fictionalized in 1902 in a popular novel published in Shanghai called *The Heroine from Eastern Europe* (*Dong Ou nü haojie*).[18] While in Paris in 1927, Ba Jin wrote a biography of her in Chinese, but he probably had not heard of her before he went to eastern China in 1923.[19] It seems even less likely that any young women in Chengdu would have known anything about Sofia Perovskaia in 1920. Nevertheless, the political and literary journals that came to Chengdu from east China in the years before and after 1911 did begin to introduce young people there to prominent female activists, such as Chinese suffragist Tang Qunying, American anarchist Emma Goldman, and Japanese feminist poet Yosano Akiko.[20] The influence of the global women's movement of the time is visible in Chengdu events. During the Railroad Protection movement that preceded the 1911 Revolution in Chengdu, a group formed to represent the "women's sphere" (*nüjie*) in the protests against the Qing court's nationalization of the Chengdu-Hankou railroad.[21]

In the late 1910s and early 1920s, new conceptions of women's education and roles in society entered Chengdu in a steady stream via the new journals, as well as through missionaries, returned students like the writer Li Jieren (who moved back to Chengdu in 1924 after four years in France), and sojourners from Shanghai and other parts of east China. Still, it would be an exaggeration to say that a feminist movement existed in Chengdu in the 1920s. Like Shuying in *Spring*, women who wanted freedom from established social norms were more likely to leave town, if they could, than to stay and try to change expectations for women. We will examine the reasons for this in later sections of this chapter.

Was Footbinding Still Prevalent in 1920s Chengdu?

The bound foot has become the most powerful symbol of the oppression of women in Chinese history, and, like most early twentieth-century Chinese writers, Ba Jin included bound feet in his stories. The practice of footbinding appears in *Turbulent Stream* in the context of the story of Gao Shuzhen, the daughter of the patriarch's fifth son. In chapter 14 of *Family*, Shuzhen struggles to play the Chinese version of hackysack with her cousins. Gao Juehui watches her small feet in their dainty red embroidered slippers:

> In his eyes these bound feet were the equivalent of the bullet scars on the walls by the city gates, and they called up a painful memory. The sobs that had been caused by binding Shuzhen's feet came to him again across the years. Now she was standing before him, still with those feet which were so seductive to some, still with those bound feet that had been created from her agony and her tears. Now she was laughing happily without a thought of them, and her face showed no signs of the anguish.[22]

In *Family*'s chapter 19, Shuzhen recalls the beatings she received from her mother as she resisted the binding cloths, which had been wrapped around her feet, bending the bones. She also recalls how her mother made fun of Gao Juexin's wife, Ruijue, whose feet had not been bound, and promised Shuzhen that she would be praised for her small feet. Instead, she is mocked by her cousins for being behind the times.

Footbinding such as Ba Jin describes in *Family* had been common in the nineteenth century among Chengdu's elite, as well as elsewhere across China. Historian Dorothy Ko notes that the practice varied regionally, and that its prevalence and meaning in Chinese culture changed considerably over the centuries. Some saw it as a way to enhance women's beauty, both for the dainty feet themselves and for the sway it caused in their walk. Some considered it a way to show that their daughters were obedient and not liable to run wild. Historians have pointed to footbinding as a type of conspicuous consumption—a way to show that a family did not need its daughters to do heavy labor and could buy slave girls to help them inside the household. Others argue that bound feet kept girls firmly under the control of their families, which profited from their weaving and needlework. The practice may also have spread in part as a sign of cultural resistance to the seventeenth-century Manchu conquest, since Manchu women did not bind their feet. As bound feet gradually became accepted, for some or all of these reasons, as a normal feature of most women's lives in the Qing period, women took pride in being able to bind their daughters feet well and especially in making the shoes that showed off their embroidery skills. In the nineteenth century, having shapely bound feet was considered essential for girls to be able to marry within Chengdu's elite community of gentry and well-off merchants.[23]

Footbinding, which had always had opponents in China, came under sustained attack in the late nineteenth century by Christian missionaries and Chinese activists. By the 1930s, when Ba Jin wrote *Turbulent Stream*, the "cultural prestige" identified with footbinding had been "extinguished," to borrow Ko's words, and the practice was almost universally condemned, at least among the elite.[24] Ba Jin's *Turbulent Stream* is therefore typical in its treatment of footbinding as an unmitigated tragedy in the passages cited above. In remarks on how he wrote *Family*, Ba Jin mentioned that Shuzhen was not modeled on any of his female cousins—none of them had bound feet.[25] Of course, his mother and aunts most certainly did have bound feet, but he does not have anything to say about that in his memoirs, nor do the older generations of women in *Turbulent Stream* seem bothered by their bound feet. Ba Jin's restriction of the footbinding theme to the sad case of Shuzhen—whose unhappy life ends in *Autumn* with her suicide in the family's well—supports Ko's argument that activists such as Ba Jin were not interested in how women understood footbinding. They used the practice simply as a symbol of the oppressiveness of traditional culture. This is underscored in *Autumn*: Ba Jin has Qin say that "in foreign countries, a woman is also a human being. In China, she is just a plaything."[26]

Footbinding seems to have declined substantially in Chengdu during the last decade of Qing rule. Fu Chongju, who published his Chengdu encyclopedia in 1909, attributed this to the Natural Foot Society (Tianjiaohui) set up in 1902 by Mrs. Archibald Little, wife of a British merchant, and Dr. Retta Kilborn, a Canadian medical missionary.[27] The society received the support of wives and daughters of prominent Chengdu officials and gentry, who attended lectures the society presented in the Dai family's Dianthus Garden on Green Dragon Street, near where Ba Jin grew up. A photograph of the gathered ladies was paired with an "anti-footbinding song" (a simply worded rhyming exhortation designed to be chanted), and tens of thousands of copies of this broadsheet were printed and distributed in the Chengdu region, according to Fu Chongju. In 1903, the Sichuan governor-general issued a proclamation urging parents not to bind their daughters' feet. Girls' schools barred girls with bound feet from admission. Although it is difficult to imagine how he got his information, Fu Chongju estimated that 30–40 percent of the girls of the age for footbinding had not had them bound in the few years before 1909. That group would have included Hu Lanqi and most of Ba Jin's female cousins. He also noted—something he would have been able to discover much more easily—that shoe stores were doing a good business selling shoes for bound feet that had been unbound.[28]

In the years around 1920, when *Turbulent Stream* is set, few girls in Chengdu were having their feet bound, although the practice had not died out completely. In 1918 the Chengdu police issued the following order: "The evil practice of footbinding has long been forbidden, but still some low class (*xialiu*) people continue the practice. This should stop. Violators will be punished."[29] Footbinding continued in rural areas into the 1940s. As surveys conducted by anthropologist Hill Gates indicate, its prevalence in the Sichuan countryside varied quite a bit and dropped gradually overall in the 1920s and 1930s.[30]

Love and Marriage and Childbirth

Arranged marriages are among the greatest sources of anxiety for all the young people in *Turbulent Stream*. None of the marriages of the older generations appears to be happy. The worst is the marriage of Fifth Uncle Keding and his wife, Madam Shen. Keding seduces (or is seduced by) Madam Shen's slave girl Xi'er, sets up another woman as a mistress (a courtesan known as Monday) in a separate residence across town, and berates his wife for failing to give birth to a son. Madam Shen constantly nags and finds ways to vent her ill humor on the servants and on Gao Juexin and his siblings. The unhappy couple mistreat their daughter, Shuzhen, to the point that she jumps into the family well.[31] The arranged marriages of the younger generation are also mostly horrendous. Gao Juexin's childhood sweetheart Mei is married into a family that abuses her. When her husband dies, she becomes a forlorn young widow, returning to live with her mother and slowly dying of what appears to be tuberculosis (she spits blood). In *Family*, Gao Juehui asks older brother Juexin why Mei cannot marry someone else. Juexin replies bitterly that social norms among the gentry, which Mei herself fully absorbed during her upbringing, demand that a widow be chaste.[32] In *Spring* and *Autumn*, respectively, the Gaos' cousins Zhou Hui (a girl) and Zhou Mei (a boy) are each made to marry very unsuitable people and, apparently as a consequence, die shortly afterwards. Gao Juexin's marriage to Li Ruijue is the only arranged marriage in the trilogy that seems happy, but it is haunted by Juexin's sadness about his failure to marry Mei and save her from her awful fate.

When Ba Jin was growing up, gentry elders did indeed claim the responsibility of finding mates for their young people—including, as we saw in Chapter One, for the slave girls they had purchased. Marriage was not considered primarily a personal matter—a daughter-in-law's most important role was to extend the family line by providing a male heir. Like the Gao patriarch, elders in gentry families considered themselves much better qualified to judge which young people could form suitable unions that would benefit both families. Passionate love between husband and wife was not considered necessary or even desirable, but mutual respect and affection were generally expected to develop as the young couple had children and shared in family life (Figure 6.2).[33]

The problem of arranged marriages was a common subject in the debates about Chinese culture and social life during the May Fourth era. One of the first essays that future Communist leader Mao Zedong published was a 1919 attack on arranged marriages in which he wrote about a girl, Miss Zhao, who committed suicide as she was carried in her wedding sedan chair to meet her groom for the first time.[34] Many, many similar essays appeared in those years. Historian Susan Glosser has shown that, in a survey of over six hundred young men in the Shanghai area in 1920, almost all disapproved of arranged marriages unless the young people consented. Most believed parental approval of marriage partners was important and indeed necessary, but, perhaps in order to shift the decision-making to a time when they would be better able to counter their parents' ideas, most thought marriage should not occur until men were in their mid-twenties. Among the respondents who were already married or engaged, however, fewer than 10 percent had had any role in choosing their wives. Fewer than 25 percent of the married men in the survey had even known their wives before becoming engaged to them.[35]

We do not have any similar survey results from Chengdu, so it is impossible to gauge attitudes about arranged marriage during the May Fourth

Figure 6.2 A young married couple in Chengdu in the 1920s. Courtesy of He Xingqiong.

period there. One factor that might have influenced them is suggested in *Turbulent Stream*: the frequency of marriages among cousins in Chengdu. The many children who live in the Gao family compound in *Turbulent Stream* are all descended from the patriarch through the male line—the sons and daughters of his sons. Therefore, they all share the Gao surname. They cannot marry each other, according to Chinese custom. But members of the Gao family can and do marry first cousins with different family names. By the end of the trilogy, Gao Juemin is engaged to another of the patriarch's grandchildren: his cousin Qin, daughter of his father's sister. His eldest brother, Gao Juexin, had wanted to marry Mei, the daughter of his mother's sister. According to the story, only a disagreement between the two sisters prevented the marriage. Once again, we don't know how often such cousin marriages actually occurred, but contemporaries of Ba Jin have said that it was common.[36] Wealthy families like Ba Jin's liked to ally themselves with other elite families, and so intermarriage among a small number of families might go on generation after generation, leading to closer and closer ties among families and more and more cousins. And, like Juexin and Mei, young cousins of the opposite sex were able to visit in each other's families. In the absence of coeducational schooling, this provided a rare opportunity for boys and girls to get to know each other as they were growing up. Cross-cousin marriages, as anthropologists call them, may have mitigated some of the anxiety associated with marriage to complete strangers.

The relatively small circles in which Chengdu gentry moved and married is illustrated in the personal history of Wu Yu and his wife, Zeng Lan. Wu Yu, one of the most vocal enemies of patriarchal families in the May Fourth era, loved and cherished Zeng Lan, although their families arranged the marriage without their involvement. In this case, the families lived next door to each other and were very close. Wu Yu's grandmother took a liking to the young Zeng Lan and pushed for the engagement. They married in 1891 when Zeng Lan was fifteen and Wu Yu was nineteen. Wu Yu encouraged Zeng Lan to read widely and to hone her writing skills. She gained fame locally as a calligrapher and helped found two women's journals in Chengdu after 1911. Before her death in 1917 she sent essays and a play she wrote on the subject of women's rights to *New Youth* and other publications in eastern China.[37]

Hu Lanqi, born in 1901, was fifteen years younger than Zeng Lan. In her case, her mother arranged for her to marry into a family that Hu Lanqi's family had helped financially at a critical time. According to Hu Lanqi's memoirs, her mother thought this family would treat her well, since her own family had come to their aid in the past and they were now well off. She was introduced to her future groom before the wedding and did not find him at all suitable—too much like a merchant, with no interest in intellectual matters. She considered resisting the marriage, but, because her mother and some of her siblings had fallen ill and died shortly before, she went through with the wedding so as not to cause her father difficulties and grieve her grandmother.

The marriage ceremony was performed in the customary way in Chengdu in the fall of 1920: "On that day, I rode in a red sedan chair carried by eight men, crying my eyes out. What sort of wedding was this? It seemed just like going to a funeral." If we can trust Hu Lanqi's memoirs, written in the 1990s, to accurately reflect her thoughts in 1920, it seems that it was not out of the question for a Chengdu girl in the May Fourth era to resist an arranged marriage, as Gao Shuying does in *Spring*. Hu Lanqi's actions of a few years later lend credence to her account of her feelings at the time of her marriage: in 1922 she abandoned her husband, renounced the marriage, and took a job at a school in southern Sichuan run by the Communist Yun Daiying.[38]

Hu Lanqi's behavior was considered extremely scandalous in Sichuan, and she did not return to Chengdu for many years. After marriage, gentry women were supposed to live quietly with their husbands' families, have children, help manage their households, and pay respects to their husbands' elders. The 1920 survey of young men in eastern China cited above indicates that a majority of them approved of married sons continuing to live in their parents' homes. Most wanted to do this, themselves, and to take care of their parents.[39] Zeng Lan, Wu Yu's wife, did not live with her parents-in-law, since Wu Yu and his father had had a violent falling out. But she did manage the household that she and Wu Yu maintained in Chengdu and looked after the upbringing of their many daughters. After her only son died and it seemed possible that she would not have another, she helped Wu Yu acquire concubines in an attempt to provide him with the son he longed for. Wu Yu's love for her was probably related as much to her "traditional" devotion to his comfort and needs as it was to her "modern" ability to write essays advocating women's rights.

The daughters of the union of Wu Yu and Zeng Lan, unlike their mother, aspired wholeheartedly to the New Woman ideal of the independent female who would not be confined to her husband's family home.[40] With Wu Yu's help, the two eldest surviving daughters moved to Beijing to study in 1920. Wu Yu frequently chastised them for taking more interest in their social lives than in their books. One went to Europe to take part in a work-study program and had an affair with a Chinese poet she met on the boat, even though she was headed to join her fiancé, whom she had chosen herself and who had helped pay for her trip. Her younger sister went to California with a married man. A Chengdu newspaper reported on this elopement in the summer of 1920, leading to a debate over the propriety of "free love" (*ziyou lianai*).

Public sentiment in Chengdu seems to have condemned it, and not only the Chinese community. The Methodist girls' school, which Wu Yu's two eldest daughters had attended, informed him that, in view of his elder daughters' actions and to protect its reputation as a moral institution, it could not accept his younger daughters. Although Wu Yu often berated his daughters for being flighty, this attack on them by their old school enraged him. "Who says they have done anything wrong," he demanded in his diary.[41]

The May Fourth critique of arranged marriages was accompanied by conversations about sexuality as well as free love. Charlotte Furth, who has analyzed the history of Chinese medical views about sex, points out that sexual fantasies and premarital sex were considered by many pre-twentieth-century medical practitioners to be harmful to a person's health.[42] These views came under explicit scrutiny in the May Fourth period, as activists and essayists debated the social benefits and costs of chastity as well as the nature of the human body.[43] A significant thread in the discourse on sexuality concerned eugenics. Margaret Sanger—an American promoter of birth control—visited China for a few weeks in April 1922 and, despite not knowing anyone at first, was soon giving talks before large, mostly male audiences in cities in east China. She found they were not much interested in her ideas about women's liberation from endless childbirth but were anxious to improve the quality of China's citizenry and strengthen the nation.[44] People in Chengdu in the early 1920s would have been able to read about Sanger's speeches and other views on female sexuality in the newspapers, but there are no signs that many considered these pressing issues at the time.

Death due to childbirth features in *Turbulent Stream*—the most significant example being that of Ruijue, who is forced by the Gao elders to leave the family residence in the final stages of pregnancy so that the birth does not interfere with the transmigration of the soul of the dead patriarch. She dies shortly after giving birth, as her husband Juexin struggles to break down the door to her room, which custom dictated that he not enter during the delivery.[45] Earlier in the story, we learn that Ruijue's older sister also died in childbirth. Such tragedies were frequent in Chengdu in Ba Jin's youth. In September 1922, for example, Wu Yu received news that the wife of one of his friends had become ill after giving birth. He wrote this in his diary: "It recalled to my mind the ten times Xiangzu [Zeng Lan] gave birth—one boy and nine girls. I can't imagine how much pain she experienced. I suppose she was fortunate to live as long as forty-two years. Daoxiu

[Wu Yu's second wife] fell ill after giving birth and quickly died. For the rest of my days I no longer want to witness any childbirth, whether of a boy or a girl."[46] Seven years later, his second eldest daughter died in childbirth at the age of twenty-eight.[47]

Western medical practitioners tended to point to poor sanitation and misguided folk beliefs when explaining what they considered a shockingly high death rate for women in childbirth. William Reginald Morse, a physician who served on the faculty of Chengdu's West China Union University between 1914 and 1938, gave the following description of a scene he witnessed in the city: "I was called to a case of child-bed fever—the woman was very ill indeed—the treatment consisted in burning incense to the spirits, and in beating gongs to expel evil spirits, and a woman was stationed by the bed waving a sword to drive away the spirits causing the disease."[48] That a foreign doctor was called in suggests that Chengdu families were open to new approaches to the problem. Even so, for elite young women in early twentieth-century Chengdu, marriage was usually followed by a long series of pregnancies, which carried considerable risk. Contraceptive practices were part of Chinese medical tradition, but they have left little trace in the historical record in Chengdu. As we have seen, Hu Lanqi entered an arranged marriage at nineteen. After leaving her first husband two years later, she married a man she chose herself in the mid-1920s, but she never had any children. Her memoir does not reveal whether her childlessness was by choice or not.

The Fight over Women and Public Space

Over the course of Ba Jin's trilogy, the topic of women's place in public life becomes increasingly significant. In *Family*, Qin longs to attend her male cousins' school, but she is not allowed to have any contact with men outside of the family home. All of the unmarried ladies travel in closed sedan chairs when they leave the residence. In *Spring*, Qin and her female cousins visit the public Shaocheng Park. As noted previously, this was a real park in Chengdu that opened before 1911 and quickly became a center of public life. During their visit to the park, though, they find themselves being ogled by soldiers and male students. They are taken aback when their fifth uncle, Keding, arrives in the park with Monday, his mistress. Obviously he did not expect to meet them there. In *Autumn*, a female friend of Qin complains that, although it is the twelfth year of the Republic of China and four years after the May Fourth protests (that is, 1923), she is still harassed when she goes outside her home and criticized when she receives letters from male friends.[49]

When Ba Jin was young, Chengdu families aiming to be respectable—as the gentry defined respectability—kept their women out of the public eye. The case of Hu Lanqi's teacher offers a good example. According to Hu Lanqi, Teacher Cao's mother died shortly after giving birth. Her father was a successful carpenter who adored his only child and, while she was young, took her to his worksites and teahouses every day. At the teahouses she memorized the tales of professional storytellers who performed there. When she got to be twelve or thirteen, however, it was time to shave the front of her head and grow the rest of her hair long, arranged in the style customary for unmarried young ladies. At that point, respectable girls could no longer go out in public, so she stayed home alone. Her father allowed her, however, to spend part of her day tending to a sickly neighbor, who taught her to read, write, paint, and play chess (*weiqi* or, in Japanese, *go*). At seventeen she was married to a carpenter, but her husband died shortly afterward. Although her neighbors encouraged her to remarry (which would not have been the case for a widow in a gentry family), she decided to return to her father's home and support him. And so, Hu Lanqi wrote, with the encouragement of her neighbors she opened Chengdu's first girls' school.[50] Teacher Cao's story is unusual: a tradesman's daughter managed to become literate and even open a school that gentry girls attended. Her school was acceptable to Hu Lanqi's parents in part, no doubt, because as a young lady Teacher Cao had been kept indoors as gentry girls were and seems to have absorbed gentry notions of propriety, such as that widows should not remarry.

Women who did not—or could not afford to—care about gentry values were certainly visible in Chengdu's public life. Women maintained stalls in the marketplaces. Married women bought food and other necessities of life there for their families or their employers' families. In the city's crowded neighborhoods, the lack of interior lighting meant that women did their sewing and washing in their doorways or courtyards with neighbor women.[51] So it was certainly not the case that women were never seen in public. But they were relatively scarce. Archibald Little visited Chengdu before the collapse of the Qing and was able to tour the Shaocheng garrison area (which he and other foreigners called the "Tartar City"). He noted that the "women from the Tartar City, moving about with uncramped feet and rosy faces, give a variety wanting in the Chinese City, as do the Lamas and Man-tse aborigines who visit Chêng-tu [Chengdu] in the winter season."⁵²

In Qing times and in the first decade of the Republic, gentry women—and particularly unmarried girls—rarely appeared in public in Chengdu except at a few special times and places. According to some accounts, there was a local custom of ladies strolling atop the city walls on a particular day in spring. Gentry women were able to visit Buddhist and Daoist temples at certain times to take part in religious services. On festival days, historian Di Wang notes, "the boundaries of gender as well as of social class were loosened" to allow more public mixing.⁵³ Hu Lanqi recalled that Teacher Cao took her female students to watch the biannual city god parade outside the North Gate one year when she was a child.

Participation in public life was even rarer than public appearance. Gentry women's involvement in the arena of public debate got a boost in 1911, when a few women gave public addresses in Chengdu during rallies to protest the Qing government's nationalization of the Chengdu-Hankou railroad; students of girls' schools attended some of these with their teachers. Hu Lanqi remembered a female teacher named Sun Yougen delivering a speech at an assembly at the railroad company's headquarters. What struck the ten-year-old Hu Lanqi most was Sun's hair, cut short in what she called the "Napoleon" style.⁵⁴ After the establishment of the Republic in 1912, gentry women seem not to have continued to play a public political role. In the fall of 1916, after the death of President Yuan Shikai, the Sichuan Provincial Assembly convened in Chengdu for the first time since Yuan had disbanded all provincial assemblies in 1913. A female reporter for the newly established *Women's World* (*Nüjiebao*) requested permission to cover its sessions, but she was turned down. Fan Kongzhou, head of the Chengdu Chamber of Commerce and a publisher himself, intervened on her behalf, and she was allowed to attend. But she had to sit behind a curtain.⁵⁵

During the decade of the 1910s, various local laws tried to set limits on the mixing of men and women in public places. For instance, the several new theaters that were built in Chengdu, modeled on those in eastern China, had balconies to accommodate women, but the police bureau still thought it necessary to publish rules that banned pointing from the balcony or having presents or food delivered to the men below (a complementary rule prohibited men from sending presents to women in the balcony—both seemingly designed to prevent the theater from becoming a place for illicit lovers to communicate with each other).⁵⁶ In the case of Chengdu's annual spring flower festival, held on the grounds of a large Daoist temple complex, separate gates were set up for men and women to enter. The police informed Sichuan opera actors who attended the festival in their feminine dress and makeup that they could not use the women's gate.⁵⁷

The ogling and harassment that the Gao girls and their friends meet with when they go to the park and walk on the streets in *Turbulent Stream* reflects a real historical phenomenon that was evident between 1911 and the late 1920s. The women's movement that gained momentum in east China had its supporters in Chengdu, but a much stronger sociocultural development worked against them: the growth of the mafia-like Gowned Brothers associations and their rejection of much of the May Fourth agenda, including the New Woman ideal. Chapter Five has briefly discussed the Gowned Brothers in the context of the militarization of Sichuan after 1911. Their role in shaping the cultural atmosphere in the province is significant for the history of the women's movement in Chengdu in Ba Jin's youth, although Ba Jin did not touch on this in his trilogy.

In the eighteenth century, the Gowned Brothers had been a loose network of marginalized young men, including demobilized soldiers, who banded together to support themselves through gambling rackets and banditry. In the late nineteenth century, some west China communities organized their own Gowned Brother lodges with the aim of redirecting the energies of such semi-alienated men into tasks that the state was now less able to handle, such as keeping the peace and protecting the property of the local elite. A Gowned Brother ideology developed that was similar in many ways to the orthodox ideology of the Qing state, even though Qing law prohibited organizations like the Gowned Brothers. Loyalty, filial piety, and chaste behavior were celebrated in lodge rituals.

The political and military unrest of the early twentieth century led to the proliferation of Gowned Brother lodges across Sichuan, and the Revolution of 1911 brought them into Chengdu with the militias that converged on the provincial capital that fall. Soon, most neighborhoods had a lodge and Gowned Brother "helmsman" (*duobazi*, the term for lodge leader), who often worked in close association with the city's police force. Local strongmen who were not interested in gender equality and other May Fourth values thus were in a position to enforce their own ideas of proper behavior in the city. Female students, particularly those who tried to follow the fashions of eastern China and cut their hair short, found themselves in danger on Chengdu's streets. Both Wu Yu's and Hu Lanqi's parents sent their daughters to boarding schools in the decade after 1911, so they would not have to make a daily trip to campus along streets that could be hazardous.

Gowned Brother disapproval of New Women was fueled by the patriarchal ideology that had developed within the associations since the nineteenth century. It was also spurred by the perceived connections between New Women—in the form of female students—and the militarists. Militarists, Gowned Brother leaders, and female students were linked together in an odd triangular relationship in Chengdu when Ba Jin was young. Gowned Brother leaders were able to exercise power in their local areas because, as we saw in Chapter Five, the militarists were busy fighting each other. So the militarists depended on the Gowned Brothers to keep order. But the militarists were also viewed by many of the local men who made up the Gowned Brothers as rapacious outsiders intent on stirring up trouble. Many militarists had been influenced by the revolutionary ideas circulating in China during the early twentieth century and did try to change Chengdu's culture, often in clumsy and authoritarian ways.

The best but by no means only example of this is the Sichuan militarist Yang Sen, who marched into Chengdu in the spring of 1924 and ruled the city for about a year.[58] Yang Sen considered himself progressive, and so in Chengdu and in other cities he occupied he ordered women to unbind their feet and promoted women's involvement in physical exercise. He married multiple times but considered all his wives of equal status, not distinguishing between wife and concubine. As an advocate of women's education, he sent some of his wives to school and encouraged them to ride bicycles and take part in other sports. Hu Lanqi had gotten to know Yang Sen and his family when she lived in southern Sichuan in 1923 and, according to her, Yang Sen sent one of his wives to her with the message that Yang Sen would be happy to marry her too. She declined that offer, but, as noted in Chapter Two, she did tutor two of his wives who had been slave girls in the family before he married them.[59]

Yang Sen promoted his wives' involvement in civic affairs. When he controlled Chengdu, the centerpiece of his improvement plans for the city was the widening of streets so that rickshaws and eventually automobiles could navigate them. Yang Sen's fourth wife, Tian Hengqiu, became the head of the Ladies' Auxiliary of the Sichuan Branch of the National Road-Building Association and presided over its public meetings. Tian Hengqiu was the daughter of a prosperous merchant in the town of Langzhong, in northeastern Sichuan. Yang Sen had courted and married her while occupying that town in the early 1920s. In her inaugural speech for the Road Association Ladies' Auxiliary, she stated that gender equality had already become an accepted part of the political order, but that Sichuan's women were too accustomed to being dependent on others and shirked their responsibility to the nation. She called on them to join together in associations to improve society.[60] Some members of Chengdu's gentry may have accepted Tian Hengqiu's public role as a sign of progress, but many more found Yang Sen an abomination. His authoritarian style of rule, coupled with his unusual attitude toward gender relations, helped forge a connection in people's minds between militarists and unconventional women. Both of them could be seen as symbols and causes of declining morality and increasing disorder. The Gowned Brothers presented themselves as local heroes combating these evil outside influences.

Tension over issues of sexuality and gender was a powerful force in Chengdu in the May Fourth era. The experience of Shu Xincheng in Chengdu in 1924 illustrates how such issues could be exploited effectively in political struggles that, at their root, had little to do with cultural matters.[61] In the early 1920s, Shu Xincheng, a native of Hunan Province, was a well-known specialist in education who had taught at schools in Shanghai and Nanjing. Later in his career he gained fame as the chief editor of the renowned dictionary titled *Cihai* ("ocean of words"). In the fall of 1924, he accepted an invitation to teach at the Sichuan Teachers College, the best school in Chengdu. Yang Sen was still in command of the city then. In letters to his wife, subsequently published in Shanghai as a book, Shu Xincheng described the Chengdu campus as an old-fashioned sort of place with an inadequate library. Neither the teachers nor the majority of the students had much interest in the social and cultural debates going on in eastern China, and relations between teachers and students were formal and distant. Tension on campus was high, because—thanks to Yang Sen—female students had been admitted to the school for the first time that fall. The young men and women were in the process of trying to figure out how to behave toward each other. Men outnumbered women by 40 to 1, and the female students were the subjects of intense and often amorous interest on the part of the male students.

No female students enrolled in Shu Xincheng's class, but he came to know several of them through his acquaintance with the female teacher who was their adviser. When they discovered that he had a camera and was teaching some of their male classmates to take and develop photos, two of these students, Lin Jingxian and Liu Fang, asked him to teach them too. With the permission of the Lin household, where Liu Fang was also living, Shu Xincheng agreed to teach them. He showed them how to develop pictures in a darkroom and took them on a photography expedition to a public park. He also discussed contemporary social and cultural issues with Liu Fang, whom he considered one of the brightest students at the school.

Just as Shu Xincheng was getting to know these female students, a controversy broke out on campus concerning the wedding of a male teacher at the school and a female student. Although the couple had been engaged before the woman enrolled in the school, some students and teachers demanded that he be fired and she be expelled. Without, as he noted later, knowing anything about the political background of the dispute, Shu Xincheng jumped into the public debate over the issue and spoke on the need to reform the relationship between teacher and student and the importance of free choice in love. Shortly after this incident, Liu Fang's diary was stolen from her room and Shu Xincheng was accused of having improperly fraternized with girl students by taking her and Lin Jingxian out in public. He was also accused of having seduced Liu Fang, defying the moral values that ought to guide relations between teachers and students.

At first, Shu Xincheng refused to believe that the matter was serious; Liu Fang vigorously denied the charges and claimed her diary, if produced, would back her up.[62] Students with whom he was close convinced him it would be best to hide out for a time, however, and so he left campus and moved in with the writer Li Jieren, who had just returned to Chengdu from France. Although Shu Xincheng and Li Jieren had not met before Shu Xincheng arrived in Chengdu, both had long been members of the Young China Association and they had many friends in common. Shortly after moving to Li Jieren's house, Shu Xincheng was told that the school's teachers had demanded his arrest and that Yang Sen intended to send soldiers to take him into custody. He managed to escape over the wall into a neighbor's house while Li Jieren stayed behind to delay the soldiers. Deprived of their quarry, the soldiers arrested Li Jieren. He stayed in jail for ten days, and Shu Xincheng stayed in hiding until he was spirited out of the city two weeks later.

In an open letter to his former colleagues at the teachers college, written when he had arrived safely in Chongqing, Shu Xincheng addressed only the ostensible and public basis of his case: as he described it, he had dared to flout conventional standards of conduct by treating women as human beings rather than playthings. This claim sounds very much like Ba Jin's rhetoric in *Turbulent Stream*. Shu Xincheng's later reflections on the incident in his autobiography, however, which highlight different aspects of the case, show a subtle understanding of the place of cultural issues in the politics of the teachers college and, by extension, Chengdu at large. In this analysis, he saw resentment against him building up at the school from the day he arrived, a privileged outsider with the powerful advantage of a high salary and the air of a representative from China's future, with the leisure to enlighten the students who eagerly clustered around him. He judged that he exacerbated the resentment by accepting dozens of invitations to speak at local middle schools where he criticized many educational practices common in Sichuan. And when the teachers at the college stopped holding classes in the spring of 1925 in an undeclared strike to protest their arrears in pay, Shu Xincheng decided to go ahead with his teaching to fulfill his contract, since unlike them he was receiving his salary regularly.

Anger at these provocations, he reasoned, surged up in the hearts of his colleagues, and they were pleased to be presented—possibly by jealous classmates—with the case of the seduction of Liu Fang, which they used as a club to drive him out of the school. His colleagues had not originally been out for his blood, Shu Xincheng believed. They would have preferred that the incident end quietly with his and Liu Fang's expulsion from campus and subsequent removal from Chengdu. But when a group of students rallied around him and openly attacked the actions of the school's president, school authorities were "unable to get off the stage," and, to uphold discipline, they felt forced to harden their stance and seek help from a higher authority.

It is ironic that Yang Sen, who was also vulnerable to charges of subverting conventional sexual and gender norms, was called in to discipline Shu Xincheng. It may be that, feeling vulnerable himself, Yang Sen used the incident to enhance his reputation with the champions of "custom and morality" by directing harsh measures against someone who, as a stranger in town, was essentially defenseless. Although Shu Xincheng had a few old college friends in the city government, they refused to stand up for him. Wise Chengdu public figures no doubt did their best to avoid involvement in political conflicts that had been defined in the emotional language of sexual morality.

The explosive nature of the issue of women's role in public life in Chengdu resulted from the atmosphere of constant warfare and the rise of the culturally conservative Gowned Brothers. The fear Qin and the Gao girls feel when they challenge conventions in *Turbulent Stream* would by no means have seemed unreasonable to their real-life equivalents in Chengdu in the early 1920s. One reason Wu Yu's daughters and Hu Lanqi were able to act in ways that made them notorious in Chengdu was because they left the city.

New Professions for Women and the Question of Inheritance

In *Spring*, Qin tells her cousins that Feng Leshan, the hypocritical head of the Confucian Society, had lectured at her school and told the assembled female students that "lack of talent is a virtue in women." This famous phrase, which first appeared in print during the Ming dynasty, was the literary equivalent of bound feet—it was pervasive in the Qing dynasty and then in the early twentieth century became a symbol of the backwardness of Chinese attitudes toward women.[63] It is not clear whether Xu Zixiu, who was one of Ba Jin's real-life models for Feng Leshan (see Chapter Two), ever actually used the phrase, but it would not be surprising.

In the outline of Chinese history that Xu Zixiu prepared for his Dacheng Academy students in the early 1920s, he gave a two-character explanation for the fall of the Qing dynasty: 女禍 (*nühuo*), that is, a disaster caused by a woman or women. By this he meant that the Empress Dowager Cixi had involved herself in affairs of state and, by so doing, had destroyed the dynasty.[64] Orthodox Confucian scholars believed that women should not be involved in making government policy and considered emperors who were influenced by their wives and other female relatives to be bad rulers on that count alone.

The Empress Dowager Cixi kept her nephew, the Guangxu emperor, under house arrest after 1898 and took charge at the court in Beijing until her death in 1908. Her decision to execute six young officials who led the 1898 reform movement with Kang Youwei, two of whom were Sichuan natives, shocked and alienated Xu Zixiu and many others at the time, so it is not surprising that his textbook would invoke her in connection with the downfall of the imperial system. Still, the two-word answer "female disaster" to explain the fall of a dynasty, with no mention of the new democratic political ideals upon which the Republic was founded or the attacks on

China by the European imperialist powers, was a clear sign of the traditional thinking of the Dacheng Association and Xu Zixiu.

There was a long tradition in the Chinese dynastic histories of blaming women and their wiles (talents) for the corruption of emperors and courtiers. But in the early twentieth century, many cultural critics decided that China was weak in part because it had wasted the talents (productivity) of its women by binding their feet and restricting their education to household skills and poetry. Some even went so far as to accuse Chinese women of being lazy, an idea that Yang Sen's wife Tian Hengqiu drew upon in 1924 when she accused Sichuan's women of being too dependent on others.[65] In eastern Chinese cities, elite women began to be urged—and to encourage each other—to take up professions and earn a living outside of the home.

In the 1990s, historian Wang Zheng interviewed several women of Hu Lanqi's and Tian Hengqiu's generation who were able to make careers for themselves in Shanghai, including a banker, an attorney, and the head of the Chinese Christian Temperance movement. Wang argues that by the 1920s it was possible for a woman to take on a public role as the wife of a prominent man.[66] Tian Hengqiu, of course, is a Chengdu example, but there were many fewer such women in Chengdu than in Shanghai in those years. And Tian Hengqiu's role in Chengdu public life quickly ended when Yang Sen was driven out of the city in May of 1925. In Shanghai, some women became successful without relying on the stature of their husbands. Those who came to the city from other places told Wang Zheng that they doubted they would have been able to be as successful in their hometowns. This may have been less because Shanghai was more progressive than because they had removed themselves from the watchful gaze of their families.[67] Still, the fact that many activist women moved to Shanghai gave the city a different and more welcoming atmosphere than women found in other Chinese cities of the time.

During the debates over women's status in China in the 1920s, it was frequently pointed out that unless women had career options that would allow them to support themselves, they would never be able to emancipate themselves from their patriarchal families. For gentry girls, work in Shanghai's factories was not considered appropriate, although many girls from farm families worked in them. As in many other parts of the world, the teaching profession became a respectable way for women to make a salary in early twentieth-century China. Hu Lanqi's Teacher Cao was a pioneer in this regard in Chengdu, and the increasing number of girls' schools in the early years of the Republic created some demand for female teachers. In Shanghai, banks and department stores began employing women clerks in the 1920s. Retail jobs were not available to women in Chengdu until the 1930s. In 1922, a telephone company was established in Chengdu, and the next year it hired two dozen female operators.[68] But, all in all, professional jobs for women were scarce. And some still feared that the new ways of educating girls might actually harm women and the community in general. Wu Yu sent all of his many daughters to school. Nevertheless, in 1923 he remarked in his diary that "Chinese society is not like society in foreign countries. Even if a girl gets a good education, nobody will employ her. And the ones who go to school and don't get a good education are even worse off, with no understanding of how to be a good person and how to manage a household."[69]

Hostility toward women who held jobs in public life could take the form of rumors and character assassination. Hu Lanqi recalled that a Chengdu girls' school principal was attacked in this way in the 1910s. The woman's husband worked in the provincial education bureau. A story was spread that the wife had been a fortune-teller (a low-class occupation) as a girl and had discovered while telling his fortune that her future husband would rise to be a high official, so she seduced him.[70] When Wu Yu was living in Beijing in 1922 with his daughter and the previously married husband with whom she had eloped, someone sent them anonymous hate mail.[71] The influence of rumors on social behavior is one of the hardest topics for historians to address, given the nature of our sources. How many businesses and offices in Chengdu delayed hiring women because of social opposition to women taking roles outside the household? How many young women in Qin's generation would have sought careers—and been encouraged by their families to do so—if they had not feared gossip and harassment? We will never know, but there is some evidence to suggest this dynamic might have influenced women's decisions.

Aside from a career, another way for women—and men, of course—to achieve a degree of independence was through ownership of property. In *Turbulent Stream*, the patriarch's power is buttressed by cultural expectations such as filial piety, but it is grounded in his control over family resources. As with Ba Jin's real-life uncles, some of the patriarch's sons are described as having careers as officials in Qing times and as lawyers after 1911. It would be interesting to learn the details of how elite Chengdu families managed their finances—did Ba Jin's uncles give a percentage of their income to the family as a whole? Who decided how much spending money to give each member of the family? In *Autumn*, Gao Juexin discovers that his fifth uncle, Keding, has been selling land—acquired by the patriarch—without telling anyone else in the family. Juexin is upset, but his young sister Gao Shuhua snaps at him: "People who have strength of character don't rely on their ancestors to get through life."[72] Unfortunately the trilogy ends without revealing how Shuhua intends to support herself.

As an unmarried daughter, Shuhua would not have had a legal right to inherit family property, although the heads of the household—her uncles and Juexin as her eldest brother—would certainly have felt an obligation to arrange a good marriage for her. Historian Kathryn Bernhardt has studied how inheritance practices evolved in China over the past thousand years. She shows that during the Qing, widowed concubines, like the patriarch's Miss Chen, had a claim to family property as long as they remained chaste and had a male heir.[73] This explains why Miss Chen formally adopts one of the sons of Gao Ke'an in *Autumn* as the Gao family prepares to divide its property. Married daughters, such as Qin's mother, had no claim on an estate.

Wu Yu was interested in female inheritance, since he had property and no son. In 1929 he bought a copy of a local paper because he heard it included an article about the decision by Liao Ping, a prominent Chengdu scholar who had been Wu Yu's classmate, to designate his daughters as heirs to his estate.[74] Although Chinese law at the time had clearly stated rules for inheritance, it seems that in Chengdu there was some flexibility for heads of household to name their own heirs via wills. In Wu Yu's case, when he stopped trying to have a son in the 1920s, he adopted a brother's son as his heir, the legally approved course of action. The nephew was to inherit the bulk of his farmland in Xinfan County, but Wu Yu's third wife was given control over part of it, as well as his Chengdu property, while she lived. He stipulated that when she died the Chengdu residence and property would go to his unmarried ninth daughter (the youngest daughter of Zeng Lan) and the land set aside for his wife would go to his tenth daughter, who had been born to a concubine. But he added a provision that if his daughters rejected his instructions about the management of the property they would be disinherited and his property would be divided between the Chengdu Buddhist Association and Chengdu University. None of his estate was to go to his married daughters. In subsequent diary entries we learn that Wu Yu quarreled with his nephew and disinherited him.[75] Whether or not his youngest daughters managed to hang on to the property is not clear. A will like the one Wu Yu described in his diary seems likely to have faced a court challenge, but, if it did, the court records have not yet come to light.

Intergenerational Strains

The cast of characters of *Turbulent Stream* includes several generations of elite women. For the most part, the young, unmarried women feel that their environment is oppressive, and they are attracted to the new cultural ideals of gender equality. The older married women, including Gao Juexin's aunts and his wife, Ruijue, have their problems but respond either with resignation or by seeking petty advantages in the intra-family quarrels. Madam Zhou, the stepmother of Juehui, sums up their attitude in *Spring* when she hopes that in her next life she will be born a man.[76]

Throughout *Turbulent Stream* Ba Jin implies that older people in Chengdu were stuck in their ways and resistant to change. Negotiating between the generations ultimately seems impossible—driving Gao Juexin, especially, to the brink of despair. In the relationship between Qin and her mother, Ba Jin spells out the reasons he thinks intergenerational cooperation is impossible. Qin's mother, Mrs. Zhang, the daughter of the Gao patriarch, wants very much to support Qin's aspirations to education. But she realizes that Qin's more radical ideas, such as her plans to enroll in the Foreign Languages School as soon as it admits females and to cut her hair short, would reflect badly on herself, as Qin's mother, in the eyes of the Gao elders and their circle. Conventional respectability trumps all in the Gao family, and it pressures Mrs. Zhang to curb the behavior of Qin, just as Gao Juexin is expected to manage and subdue his younger brothers.

Again, Ba Jin's portrait of Chengdu life is too stark. Because short hair had become a powerful symbol of the New Woman, it attracted much negative attention in Chengdu and elsewhere in China.[77] But not every fashion or lifestyle choice had the same extreme significance in the cultural politics of the day. Despite the impression *Turbulent Stream* creates, fashions changed, and not only for the young people: older women also adopted new styles of dress and makeup in the early decades of the twentieth century. Hu Lanqi's mother benefited from the rising interest in fashion and new technologies. In the years right after the 1911 Revolution she took a class that the US-based Singer Sewing Machine Company offered through its agent in Chengdu, and she went on to set up her own sewing school using a Singer machine.[78] The scandalous nature of women's short hair did not last long even in Chengdu. By 1929, short hair had become fairly common and accepted—although, as this newspaper announcement from that year suggests, the greater freedom of women to appear in public was still viewed with disfavor by some: "The Pacific Ocean hair salon on Chunxi Road reports that many more women have been coming lately to have their hair cut. Since it is not good to have men and women mixing in public, Pacific Ocean has decided to open a ladies' salon across the street."[79] In Chengdu, culture was always changing, but at certain times cultural change became politicized. The New Woman, with her bobbed hair, came under attack in Chengdu at a time when warfare was destroying the economy and destabilizing lives. Later in the 1920s, the situation improved, but the economy still lagged behind that of eastern China, and career options for women grew slowly.

Although Chengdu was far from stagnant, *Family* and its sequels established Chengdu in the imaginations of the educated public in eastern China as a close-minded city of stifling conservatism, particularly deadly to young women. Hu Lanqi's life, as unusual as it was, shows us that that picture is oversimplified. In many ways, though, women who attempted to carve out new roles for themselves in Chengdu had a much more difficult time than their counterparts in other major cities, such as Shanghai, Guangzhou, and even Beijing—another city with a conservative reputation. There are multiple reasons for this, including the fact that these eastern cities became magnets that attracted many revolutionary youth away from interior cities like Chengdu.

CHAPTER SEVEN

Juehui

Revolution, Reform, and Development in Chengdu

Gao Juehui, the central character in *Family*, defies his grandfather by joining a group of like-minded young men and becoming a political activist. Although Ba Jin denied that Juehui was a literary self-portrait, scholars of *Turbulent Stream* have pointed out so many commonalities between Juehui and Ba Jin that *Family* is widely regarded as an autobiographical novel. Ba Jin, like Juehui, had two older brothers, many cousins, and a dictatorial grandfather, and he attended Chengdu's Foreign Languages School. Like Juehui, he demonstrated in Chengdu's streets in the wake of the 1919 May Fourth incident and wrote essays for a radical newspaper that was shut down by the authorities. Like Juehui at the end of *Family*, he left Sichuan in his late teens to go to eastern China out of frustration with his life in Chengdu and in search of solutions to the social problems that bothered him. Like Gao Juemin in *Spring* and *Autumn*, before he left Chengdu Ba Jin joined an underground political organization dedicated to the overthrow of China's militarist authorities.[1] In writing the lives of the two younger Gao brothers, Ba Jin was reflecting his own experiences and emotions.

The Gao brothers' political activism is a subplot in the *Turbulent Stream* trilogy—the main narrative concerns the collapse of the extended Gao family and the emancipation of some of its young people. But the political convictions of Juehui and Juemin, like Ba Jin's, are very much shaped by their experience of growing up in an authoritarian family. Feeling constrained by his family, Ba Jin fell in love with anarchism when he was a boy in Chengdu and continued to be inspired by it as an adult, even as he encountered other ways of thought, traveled abroad, and wrote his novels, short stories, and essays. In 1949, he accepted Communist rule and became a citizen of the PRC, celebrated as one of its leading literary figures, although also subject to criticism at times for his pre-1949 politics. Under Communist guidance he revised *Family* and his other novels to better suit the party's political and cultural agenda. In his revisions of *Family*, he simplified the writing style, removed the foreign words he had occasionally used (introducing foreign vocabulary in literature was considered cosmopolitan in the 1930s, but snobbish and unpatriotic in the 1950s), and, most importantly, made the students in *Turbulent Stream* more deeply committed revolutionaries while obscuring the anarchist inspirations of Gao Juehui's and Gao Juemin's political activism.[2] Anarchism was just one of many intellectual perspectives that combined in a volatile mixture of ideas during the 1920s in Chengdu.

This chapter examines the various revolutionary and reformist currents swirling around China during the May Fourth period. Many scholars have already produced excellent work on this topic, but they have concentrated on events and people in the big cities in eastern China.[3] There has also been a tendency to overemphasize the activities of the two major parties that have been rivals for power since the early 1920s—the Nationalists and the Communists. Until the Japanese invasion in 1937, the political stage in China was crowded with many different actors promoting many different approaches to political and cultural change.[4] Anarchism was one option, but, as we will see, others came to attract a greater number of activists over the course of the 1920s. In Chengdu, politics were strongly regional, and the two major parties struggled to maintain adherents in competition with other reform ideas and with Sichuan nativist sentiment. The aim of this chapter is to show how Chengdu's young people such as Ba Jin and his cousins and classmates, who did not have to spend all their waking hours in manual labor, became aware of new political visions and advocated social change.

After an overview of events connected to the May Fourth movement in Chengdu during 1919 and 1920, we examine how as a fifteen-year-old in western China in 1920 Ba Jin came to advocate anarchism, an ideology formed in nineteenth-century Europe. In *Turbulent Stream*, Ba Jin contrasted Juehui's and Juemin's anarchism-inspired activism with their older brother Juexin's more passive approach to conflict, also justified with reference to contemporary philosophical positions that can be identified. In addition to these, other currents of thought and social movements influenced people in Chengdu in the late 1910s and early 1920s, including nationalism, Communism, Christianity, and various programs for economic development. This last category of activism, represented by the Chinese term *jianshe* (often translated as "reconstruction" or just "construction"), had a wider and more long-lasting appeal to young men in Chengdu than the type of political agitation that Ba Jin extols in *Turbulent Stream*. Organized political parties were not as important in 1920s Chengdu as they were in eastern China; in Sichuan, many people were interested in social change, but, until the 1930s, few of them regarded participating in political parties as the best way to transform their province and locality. Rather, many Chengdu activists sought and found backers among the ruling militarists for particular approaches to developing Sichuan. Literacy, technological advances, and urban planning were promoted through social campaigns and other means, with the idea that they would lead to economic development—and, many hoped, to a more just society.

The history of a generation of educated young people is best studied via biography, as Jonathan Spence showed in *The Gate of Heavenly Peace*, his pioneering book on twentieth-century Chinese writers and revolutionaries. This chapter introduces a number of men who are not well known outside China and, in some cases, are not even well known these days in Chengdu. Their stories show how unusual Ba Jin was in his political convictions and actions and depict the range of approaches that young activists took to reforming, revolutionizing, and developing Chengdu.

The May Fourth Movement in Chengdu

The May Fourth movement began on May 4, 1919. On that day, some three thousand students marched in downtown Beijing to protest the Versailles Treaty that ended World War I. Although the Republic of China had entered that war on the victors' side in 1917, rights that defeated Germany held over territory in eastern China were not returned to the Chinese at the end of the war; instead Japan gained these rights as payback for supporting the war effort. The Chinese delegation to the Versailles conference protested the decision, but news soon leaked that the Chinese government itself had signed secret loan agreements with Japan that gave Japan substantial claims over the Chinese economy. This fact undercut the credibility of the Chinese delegation's arguments, and its protests were ignored by the European powers and by the American delegation, headed by President Woodrow Wilson. News of the Versailles settlement and the Chinese government's complicity in Japan's gains provoked fury in Beijing. The young activists who protested in May 1919 were angry not only at the imperialist European powers and Japan but also at the weak Chinese government and the military leaders who fought among themselves rather than for the country. The democratic ideals of the 1911 Revolution had been betrayed, they proclaimed.[5]

The events in Beijing in May 1919 marked the beginning of a new type of mass politics in China's cities. Protest marches, demonstrations, strikes, boycotts and destruction of Japanese goods, and pamphleteering became common. Student unions immediately arose to coordinate these activities. Within a few years, the Nationalist Party, the Communist Party, the Chinese Youth Party, and other, smaller parties formed (or, in the case of the Nationalists, reorganized) to try to harness and direct the political activism that emerged in those years. What quickly came to be called the "May Fourth movement" expanded from an initial concern about national sovereignty to a full-scale cultural critique inspired in large part by the question of why the 1911 Revolution had failed to bring about democracy and prosperity in China. *New Youth* magazine, which pioneered this sort of cultural critique in 1915, was joined in the years after the May Fourth protests by dozens of other journals calling for cultural, social, economic, and political change to unite the Chinese people, liberate them from oppression, and build democracy.

As is reflected in *Turbulent Stream*, the May Fourth period in Chengdu also featured political demonstrations, the formation of student unions, strikes, anti-imperialist theater performances, pamphleteering, and a radicalization of young people.[6] Ba Jin was a witness to and a participant in many of these activities, which is why *Turbulent Stream* is arguably the most significant account of the May Fourth movement in all of Chinese fiction.

A critical factor in the spread of May Fourth ideas in Chengdu appears prominently in *Family*—the hyperactive publishing that went on in those years. As in eastern China, the years between 1918 and 1923 were relatively good for freedom of the press in Chengdu. After the devastating street fighting of the preceding year, Chengdu became more stable in 1918. In March 1918, the city was occupied by forces under General Xiong Kewu, a Sichuan native who had been an early supporter of Sun Yat-sen's revolutionary party. Yang Shukan, who became civil governor later that year, was also aligned with Sun Yat-sen. Both Xiong and Yang identified themselves as politically progressive and sympathetic to the goals of May Fourth activists.[7] While they ruled in Chengdu, many newspapers and journals were established in the city. The one that did the most to spread news about the May Fourth movement in eastern China was the *Sichuan Journal* (*Chuanbao*), edited by Li Jieren, the future novelist.[8]

Li Jieren (Figure 7.1, left) attended high school in Chengdu in the late Qing period and witnessed the 1911 Revolution unfold in the city. From 1913 to 1915 he worked for his uncle, a county magistrate who served in two Sichuan counties in those years. Li Jieren compiled statistics and drafted official documents. After his uncle resigned his post in the summer of 1915, Li Jieren returned to Chengdu. There he began writing short stories for *Amusing Accounts*, founded in 1914 by Fan Kongzhou, head of the Chamber of Commerce. As noted in Chapter Two, *Amusing Accounts* was a gossipy cultural journal that published poetry and opera reviews, essays, and short stories. Men in Ba Jin's grandfather's circle read it, as did Wu Yu, despite their very different views on Confucian propriety. The short stories Li Jieren contributed to *Amusing Accounts* drew on his experiences working in county government in the early years of the Republic, which had convinced him never to try for an official position. Li Jieren's satires on the corruption and misgovernment in Sichuan's counties proved popular and convinced Fan Kongzhou to appoint Li head writer for *Sichuan Masses* (*Sichuan qunbao*; Figure 7.1, right), a newspaper Fan launched late in 1915. After Fan Kong-

Figure 7.1 Li Jieren in 1920 (*left*) and *Sichuan Masses* (*right*). Courtesy of Li Jieren's granddaughter, Li Shihua.

zhou's assassination during the warfare of 1917, the authorities shut down *Sichuan Masses*. Li Jieren and his newspaper friends established the *Sichuan Journal* to succeed it, and Li Jieren served as editor and head writer until he left Chengdu early in 1920 to study in France.⁹

Among Li Jieren's high school friends, three had already left Chengdu in the early years of the Republic to pursue higher education and were based in Beijing, Shanghai, and Tokyo, respectively, in the late 1910s. These three served as the "foreign correspondents" for *Sichuan Journal* during the May Fourth movement. The Beijing correspondent, Wang Guangqi, sent telegrams and letters almost every day with news about the protests and demonstrations he witnessed during May 1919. *Sichuan Journal* published them, and Chengdu's May Fourth movement sprang up in response.[10] A leader of the Chengdu student association recalled that he and his classmates at the Sichuan Teachers College were eating breakfast when the issue of *Sichuan Journal* that broke the news about the May Fourth Beijing protests arrived. One student stood on a table and read Wang Guangqi's report aloud. The dining hall erupted with excited conversations, and it was decided that the student association would organize a demonstration for that day and telegraph its support to the Beijing students.[11]

After the initial Chengdu demonstration on May 7, the students' publicity efforts led a crowd of ten thousand to gather in Shaocheng Park on May 29. Some twenty thousand people joined in another demonstration on June 8.[12] In addition to urging the Chinese delegation in France to refuse to sign the Versailles Treaty, the protest leaders called for the convening of a citizen's assembly and a boycott of Japanese goods. The effort to organize a boycott continued for more than half a year. As noted in Chapter Five, in late December 1919, a student team inspecting shops on the Great East Street for Japanese goods came under attack by angry merchants. Each side summoned supporters, and a huge brawl ensued. Students came out in greater numbers, though, and they smashed up the headquarters of the Chamber of Commerce and took twenty-eight "traitorous" merchants into custody on the grounds of the imperial city. Governor Yang Shukan and the head of the provincial police bureau met with the angry students and promised to take care of those who had been injured. After having been paraded about the streets, the captured merchants were delivered up to the local court for criminal investigation, and the Chamber of Commerce distanced itself from them while decrying the students' destruction of property. Over the next few months, the student association succeeded in forcing the merchants to sell off their Japanese goods and pledge not to purchase more.[13] The Chengdu correspondent for Shanghai's English-language *North China Herald* claimed that the resulting deeply discounted sales would have an ironic effect: they would "scatter Japanese goods into nearly every house."[14] The conflict over boycotting Japanese goods died down after the spring of 1920, but demonstrations continued in the city throughout the 1920s over other issues, such as the lack of funding for schools.

During the tumultuous summer of 1919, Ba Jin was fourteen years old. The May Fourth debates and demonstrations that occurred in Chengdu gave him an early taste of politics and social action (Figure 7.2). At the time,

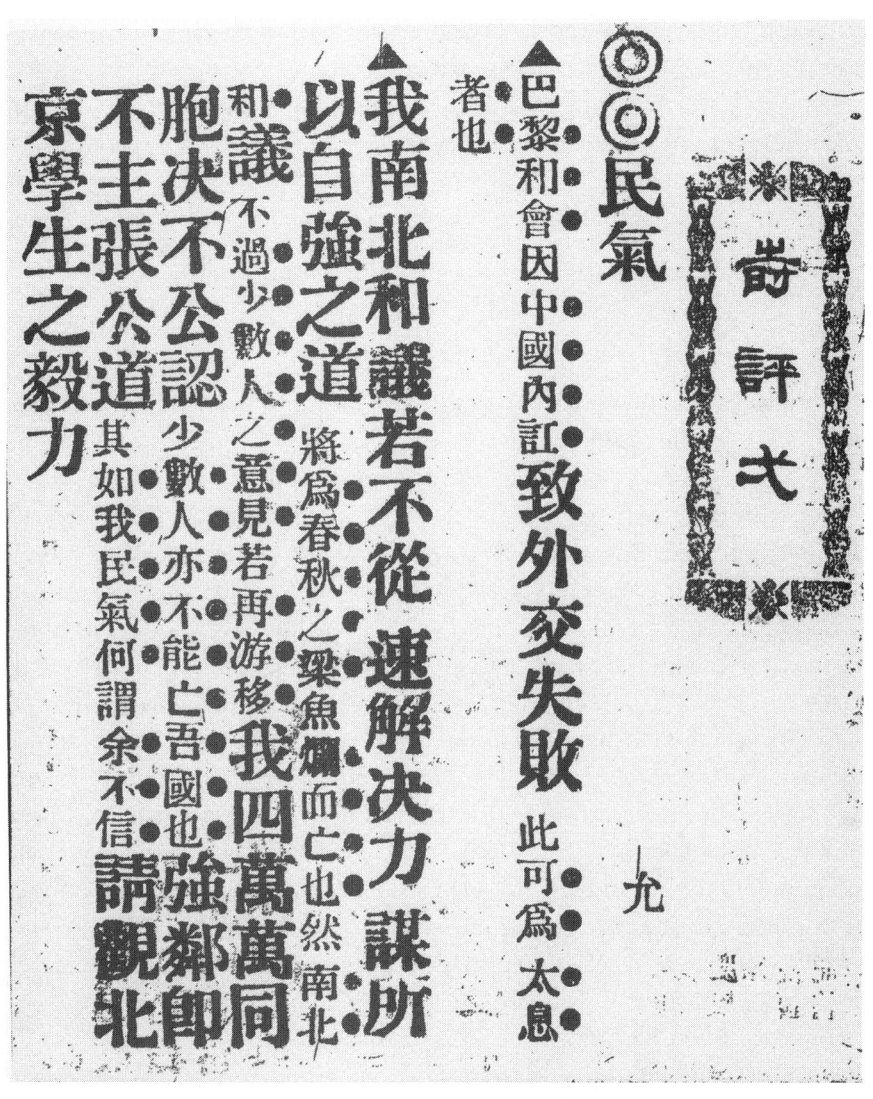

Figure 7.2 Editorial published in the *Citizens' Gazette* (*Guomin gongbao*) praising the patriotism of Beijing students who protested the Versailles Treaty on May 4, 1919. *Guomin gongbao* (Chengdu), May 19, 1919.

his health was poor, and it does not seem that he personally joined the protests that year. But he read the newspapers and political journals voraciously, along with his older brothers. By the end of 1920, he had discovered anarchism, and his subsequent activism and writing were guided by that philosophy. In the early 1920s, he joined street demonstrations and wrote political essays, just as Gao Juehui and Gao Juemin do in *Turbulent Stream*.

Ba Jin and Anarchism

Relying primarily on several memoirs that Ba Jin published in the 1930s, Ba Jin's biographer, Olga Lang, tells the story of how he became an anarchist. His memoirs can be supplemented somewhat by the memoirs of other young men from Sichuan who participated in the same anarchist groups that Ba Jin joined. But these additional sources do not change the picture much.[15] Through a careful comparison of Ba Jin's memoirs and the text of *Turbulent Stream*, Lang shows that Ba Jin incorporated his own early political experiences directly into his trilogy, particularly in sections of *Family* in which Gao Juehui writes editorials for a radical journal and sections of *Spring* in which Gao Juemin joins an underground political organization and disseminates revolutionary literature throughout Chengdu and Sichuan. Ba Jin joined just such a political organization in Chengdu in 1920, wrote editorials for its journal, and carried on clandestine correspondence with other radical groups. In his memoirs, Ba Jin makes it clear that the members of this organization identified themselves as anarchists. In the novels, the specific ideological inspiration for their revolutionary activities is not explicitly mentioned.

In 1920, when Ba Jin became an anarchist, anarchism stood at the peak of its popularity in China. By 1931, when he wrote *Family*, most anarchist groups in China had disbanded.[16] Anarchism was denounced (and suppressed) by the central authority of the day, the Nationalist government headed by Chiang Kai-shek. The Nationalists' major political opponent, the Communist Party, also rejected anarchism and criticized its advocates. So, although Ba Jin still considered himself an anarchist, it is not surprising that his references to anarchism in the 1930s editions of *Turbulent Stream* are subtle. In the 1950s revised versions, produced under Communist rule, they are even more fully obscured.

According to Ba Jin, the teachers who introduced him to anarchism were Peter Kropotkin and Emma Goldman. Kropotkin, a Russian philosopher and activist, inspired anarchists all over the world.[17] His 1880 essay *An Appeal to Youth* was directed primarily at educated young Russians, encouraging them to devote their lives to help the masses out of their misery by bringing about social change. In passionate language, he called on his readers to disregard their own comfort and put their talents at the service of the downtrodden. If a privileged young man were to observe the life of an ordinary worker seeking social justice, Kropotkin wrote that this is what he would see:

> His thoughts are constantly exercised in considering what should be done in order that life, instead of being a curse for three-fourths of mankind, may be a real enjoyment for all. He takes up the hardest problems of sociology and tries to solve them by his good sense, his spirit of observation, his hard experience. In order to come to an understanding with others as miserable as himself, he seeks to form groups, to organize. He forms societies, maintained with difficulty by small contributions; he tries to make terms with his fellows beyond the frontier; and he prepares the days when wars between peoples shall be impossible, far better than the frothy philanthropists who now potter with the fad of universal peace. In order to know what his brothers are doing, to have a closer connection with them, to elaborate his ideas and pass them around, he maintains—but at the price of what privations, what ceaseless efforts!—his working press. At length, when the hour has come, he rises, reddening the pavements and the barricades with his blood, he bounds forward to conquer those liberties which the rich and powerful will afterward know how to corrupt and to turn against him again.[18]

Why, Kropotkin asked, are not the privileged young men coming to the aid of this poor worker instead of helping to oppress him? And Ba Jin, like many other young men around the world, asked himself that same question. He read the essay in its Chinese translation, widely distributed in the decade of the 1910s, and had a strong reaction: he kept the pamphlet next to his bed and read it over and over, crying and laughing with joy, because it expressed just what he thought about the world with a clarity that he had not been able to achieve himself.[19]

Thus inspired, Ba Jin continued to search out guides to help him understand how to do good in the world. His first exposure to anarchism as an ideology (Kropotkin's *Appeal* had not mentioned anarchism by name) came through Emma Goldman, the American anarchist. In 1919, Ba Jin's eldest brother began buying copies of many of the journals being published in east China, including a complete set of the existing five volumes of *New Youth*. Ba Jin learned about Emma Goldman in *New Youth* and *Records of Freedom* (*Ziyoulu*), the journal of the Truth Society (Shishe), an anarchist organization founded in 1917 in Beijing. That journal published essays by Goldman in Chinese translation.[20] In them, she explained the goal of anarchism as "the freest possible expression of all the latent powers of an individual. . . . A free grouping of individuals for the purpose of producing real social wealth. . . . An order that will guarantee to every human being an access to and full enjoyment of the necessities of life, according to individual desires, tastes, and inclinations."[21] In 1923, after he left Chengdu to attend school in eastern China, Ba Jin began corresponding with Goldman. The two became long-distance friends and comrades.

Historian Arif Dirlik has shown the extent to which anarchism was promoted in Chinese political journals in the years around 1920—far more than other revolutionary ideologies, including Marxism. He summarizes the message Ba Jin would have received from writings of the time this way: China needed "a social revolution to remove authoritarian structures, and a cultural revolution to purge individuals of habits of authority and submission which had become second nature in a long history of living under coercion."[22] This message accorded well with an argument made by Wu Yu in an essay in *New Youth* that Ba Jin certainly read (Gao Juehui mentions it in *Family*). Wu Yu attacked the Chinese "family system" and its stress on filial piety because he believed it socialized people to be obedient and unable to stand up for themselves. Thus, he identified the patriarchal family as an important tool for despotic rulers—"a great factory to produce submissive people."[23] Ba Jin's depiction of his grandfather, uncles, and eldest brother—both in his memoirs and in the characters in *Turbulent Stream*—indicates that he agreed with Wu Yu. Anarchism helped animate Ba Jin's critique of the way gentry families worked to uphold the existing social and political order.

Ba Jin did not begin writing fiction shaped by anarchist ideas until he was a student in France in 1927 and 1928. Before his novels gained him fame in the early 1930s, he had devoted more time to writing essays promoting anarchism and translating important anarchist literature into Chinese. He also joined anarchist organizations. The first such group he heard about was based in Chongqing in eastern Sichuan. It published a manifesto in *Bi-weekly* (*Banyue*), a Chengdu journal, in the spring of 1921. Ba Jin found this manifesto so inspiring that he wrote to the editors of *Bi-weekly* for more information about the Chongqing group. Soon, he was writing editorials for *Bi-weekly* and hanging out with its editors, just as Juehui does in *Family*.[24] Together, Ba Jin and other *Bi-weekly* writers founded their own anarchist organization, the Equity Society (Junshe), modeled on the Chongqing group. The Equity Society is the real-life counterpart of the fictional political group that Gao Juehui and Gao Juemin join in *Turbulent Stream*.

Although the story of the Equity Society is told for the most part in *Spring* and *Autumn*, its publishing activities are mentioned in *Family*, since Juehui becomes caught up in writing essays and publishing critiques of the militarist government. Ba Jin wrote essays for *Bi-weekly* until the authorities shut it down in July 1921. The reason for the shutdown is exactly the same as that recounted in *Family*. *Bi-weekly* had published an editorial criticizing the police for forbidding young women to bob their hair. When police visited the *Bi-weekly* editorial office to confiscate the issue and order them to stop meddling in politics, the young activist-journalists refused to submit.[25] This experience is reflected in chapter 29 of *Family*, when a kindly police officer comes to tell Juehui and his friends to moderate their editorials. They refuse, and their paper is shut down. In 1922, Ba Jin and his friend Wu Xianyou (the model for *Turbulent Stream*'s Zhang Huiru, who apprentices himself to a tailor) launched another journal, the *Voice of the Common People* (*Pingmin zhi sheng*). In the trilogy, the corresponding fictional paper is called the *Benefit the Masses Weekly* (*Liqun zhoubao*).

In *Spring* and *Autumn*, Gao Juemin meets frequently with a small group of other Equity Society members. Their main activities are establishing secret communications with similar groups in other cities and producing and distributing their journal, pamphlets, and other literature.[26] They hand out revolutionary leaflets on May 1, International Workers' Day, and paste revolutionary posters on the walls near intersections, as Ba Jin had done in 1921— taking a servant along with him to help carry the supplies.[27] They also stage a play about Russia's Revolution of 1905 called *Before the Dawn*, which Ba Jin and his friends also performed in Chengdu in the early 1920s. According to Ba Jin's account in *Autumn*, two thousand copies of each issue of the Equity Society journal were distributed, and the periodical enrolled three hundred regular subscribers.[28] Altogether, there were seven or eight anarchist societies in Sichuan in the early 1920s; the biggest was the one in Chongqing, and its members had managed to buy their own printing press in Shanghai.

Ba Jin's experience as a political activist in Chengdu gave him an emotional haven from his life in the bickering Li household. Without the strong hand of his grandfather, who died in 1920, the extended family disintegrated rapidly. Surrounded by his friends and immersed in political debates and writing, Ba Jin realized a different vision of a social order, one that corresponded to his budding anarchist ideals. In chapter 29 of *Family*, the young people work together to establish a public reading room and a new newspaper after their old one is banned. Gao Juehui's reflections at the end of the party to celebrate their new venture sum up Ba Jin's conception of the good life:

> This gathering of a dozen young people was like a loving family. However, the members of this family were not brought together by blood relationship or shared property; what brought them together was a common goodwill, a common ideal. In this environment he felt only the communion of sincere minds, entirely removed from the shackles of profit and loss. He felt that there was not a single stranger, not a single lonely person. He loved everyone around him, and he was loved by them as well. He understood them, and they understood him. He trusted them, and they trusted him.[29]

Gao Juexin, Juehui's eldest brother, cannot share in this nonhierarchical, idyllic society. As the eldest male in his generation, he is responsible for the family and too emotionally embedded it to abandon it for an anarchist "communion of sincere minds." Ba Jin thought his own eldest brother—Li Yaomei (Figure 7.3)—was destroyed because of his commitment to the extended family, which ground him down with its injustices and strife. Li Yaomei committed suicide just as *Family* began to appear as a serial in Shanghai's *Eastern Times* in the spring of 1931.

In his memoirs, Ba Jin recalled that his eldest brother read the eastern China journals in the May Fourth years as enthusiastically as Ba Jin himself. But Li Yaomei admired Tolstoy more than he did Kropotkin and Emma Goldman. Leo Tolstoy, the great Russian novelist, was well known in China in the May Fourth period as a critic of individualistic, materialistic, industrial society and as a promoter of the values of agrarian life. Instead of violent resistance to the institutions of oppression, however, Tolstoy advocated nonresistance: social values could only be humanized through love.[30] According to Ba Jin, his elder brother also admired Liu Bannong, a poet and proponent of the reform of the Chinese written language to make it more accessible to people without an elite education. Liu Bannong published an essay in *New Youth* suggesting that political activists should not argue with

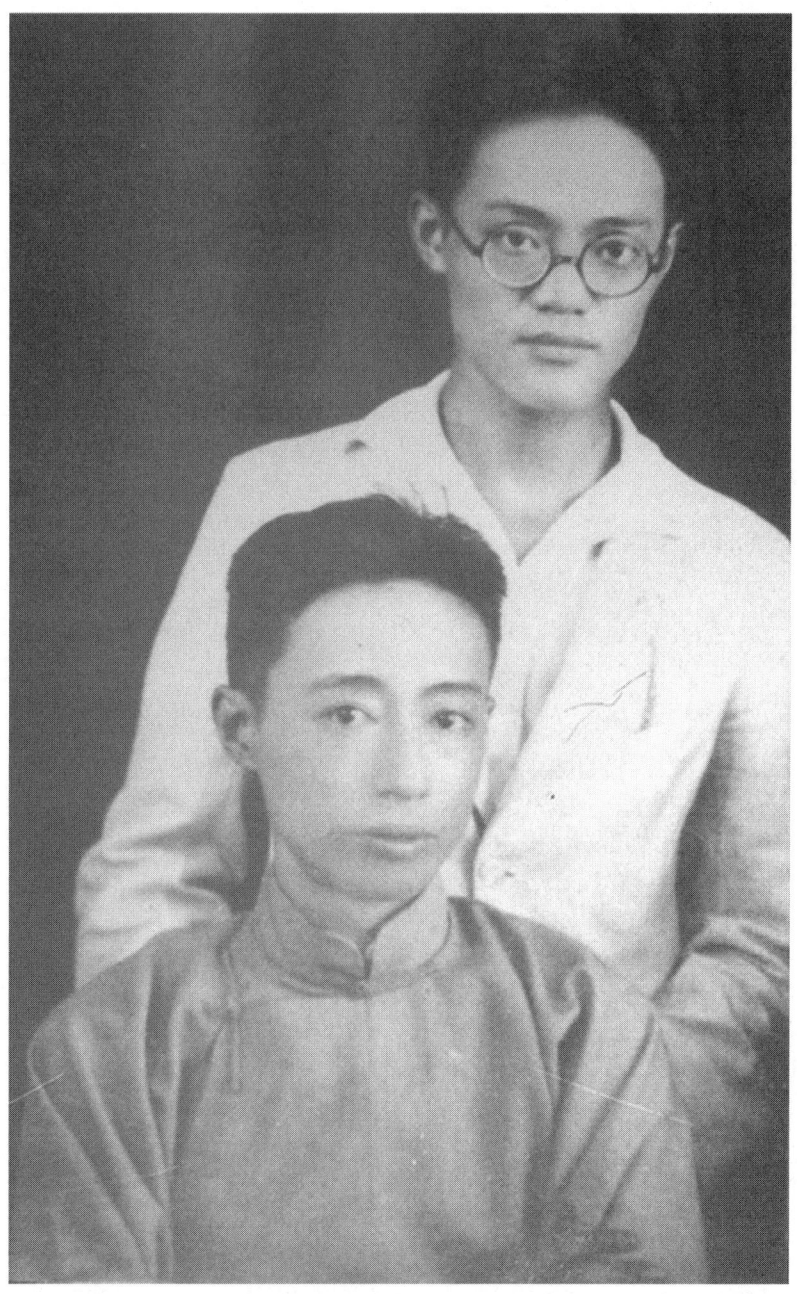

Figure 7.3 Ba Jin (*standing*) and his eldest brother, Li Yaomei (*seated*), in Shanghai in 1929. Courtesy of the Ba Jin Research Association.

their opponents. Instead, in an approach that Liu himself likened to Tolstoy's nonresistance and that a friend called Daoist, he said they could respond with a simple bow and feigned agreement. He titled his essay the "Philosophy of the Bow" (*Zuoyi zhuyi*). Liu Bannong did not actually practice this philosophy; he attacked writers of the day whom he considered too old-fashioned.[31] But Ba Jin wrote in his memoir that his eldest brother wore himself out trying to suppress his annoyance at the petty demands and criticisms that the senior members of the Li family directed his way.[32] Li Yaomei practiced the "philosophy of the bow" without the Daoist impassivity that would have made it a viable strategy.

Nationalists, Communists, and Sichuan Nativists

The Chinese anarchists, like anarchists everywhere, did not choose to organize tightly disciplined political parties. They believed in helping the masses to shake off their shackles via education and direct resistance to oppression, not by taking control of a state structure—which they thought would inevitably turn them into the oppressors. Political parties that did try to gain power over government institutions, though, came into being in the wake of the 1911 Revolution. Early in 1912, Wu Yu wrote a platform for the Progressive Politics Party (Zhengjindang), one of a handful of new political parties that had a brief existence in Chengdu.[33] In eastern China, Sun Yat-sen and his allies transformed their revolutionary organization into the Nationalist Party (Guomindang; GMD), and it quickly attracted followers. In 1913, Yuan Shikai banned political parties, but the Nationalist Party defied him and continued to grow.[34]

After the death of Yuan Shikai in 1916, regional commanders such as Sichuan's Xiong Kewu and Liu Chengxun (see Chapter Five) competed with each other to control territory and make a claim to national leadership. In 1921, the Nationalist Party struck up alliances with southern militarists and established a base in the city of Guangzhou. In that same year, a Chinese Communist Party (Gongchandang; CCP) was established in Shanghai by a small group of activists inspired by the 1917 Bolshevik Revolution that had created the Soviet Union. Between 1923 and 1927, the Nationalists and Communists worked together in a United Front with support from the Soviet-backed Communist International (Comintern). In 1926 their joint forces launched the Northern Expedition, an attempt to unify China militarily. The next year, Sun Yat-sen's successor as Nationalist leader, Chiang Kai-shek, expelled the Communists from the Nationalist Party (killing many of them) and established a new central government in the city of Nanjing, west of Shanghai.[35] Fighting between the Nationalist-controlled armies and the Communist-controlled armies escalated, continuing until the Japanese invasion of China in 1937, at which point the parties again cooperated to fight the external foe.

In the 1920s, Ba Jin criticized both the Nationalists and the Communists from the perspective of a committed anarchist. Some of his Chengdu contemporaries who had gone to eastern China, however, played leading roles in those two parties. And young men a few years older than Ba Jin, including Li Jieren's high school friend Zeng Qi, were the main organizers of a third party, the Chinese Youth Party (Qingnian dang). The Chinese Youth Party was founded in December 1923 by young Chinese men living in France, but it came to have some influence in Sichuan politics in the late 1920s. Like the Nationalist Party, it emphasized China's need to strengthen itself in order to resist imperialist interference. In the late 1920s and early 1930s, some of Sichuan's militarists preferred it to the Nationalist Party, which was dominated by easterners.[36]

In the early 1920s, before Ba Jin left Chengdu, he would have had opportunities to learn about the Nationalist Party from local supporters and from representatives sent to Chengdu by central party leaders. But the Nationalist Party in Sichuan, as in other parts of China at that time, was divided into factions that did not work together well. The head of the Sichuan provincial police bureau just after the May Fourth demonstrations in Chengdu—the man who had to deal with the brawl between students and merchants during the campaign to boycott Japanese goods in December 1919—was a Nationalist Party member named Zhang Qun, who as a young man had studied with Xu Zixiu, as noted in Chapter Two.[37] In the years before 1911, he was Chiang Kai-shek's classmate at a military academy in Japan and became acquainted with Sun Yat-sen. Because Zhang Qun was a native of the Chengdu region, Sun Yat-sen asked him to return there in 1919 to try to mediate between two feuding Nationalist Party leaders who were ostensibly in charge of the province—military commander Xiong Kewu and governor Yang Shukan. In deference to Sun Yat-sen, Xiong and Yang appointed Zhang Qun as Sichuan's provincial police commissioner, with direct control over Chengdu's police, even though Zhang Qun was only thirty. But Zhang's attempts to get Xiong and Yang to work together failed, and he left Sichuan in 1920. The political situation in Chengdu was too complicated for this young man to negotiate.[38]

If Zhang Qun had been in Chengdu one more year, perhaps the provincial police bureau would not have issued its ban on bobbed hair for women—and the *Bi-weekly* journal that Ba Jin wrote for would not have been shut down as a result. Cultural politics in Chengdu were very changeable. Even within the Nationalist Party, attitudes toward cultural issues varied so much among members that a change in personnel could mean a radical change in policy. And party loyalty, even among long-term Nationalist Party members, was quite flexible in the early 1920s. After leaving Chengdu, Zhang Qun went to work for General Feng Yuxiang, an on-again off-again ally of Sun Yat-sen. Zhang joined the Nationalist leadership again in the course of the Northern Expedition of 1926–1927.

Incidents in the careers of two other Sichuan natives who rose to prominence within the Nationalist and Communist Parties—Dai Jitao and Wu Yuzhang—also illustrate how difficult it was to organize politically in Sichuan in the early 1920s. Ba Jin does not mention these men in his memoirs, but he must have been aware of their activities between 1920 and 1923; Chengdu newspapers gave them extensive coverage.

Both Dai Jitao and Wu Yuzhang were introduced to Chinese party politics in Japan and eastern China and returned to Chengdu when Ba Jin was a teenager. Like Zhang Qun, Dai Jitao, born in a small town to the north of Chengdu in 1891, had been a student of Xu Zixiu in the early years of the twentieth century. He studied law in Japan as a teenager, and his Japanese language skills caught the attention of Sun Yat-sen in the early years of the Republic. Sun recruited Dai Jitao to be his secretary, and Dai gradually started to play an important role as a Nationalist Party theorist and publicist. In the 1930s and 1940s he was head of the Nationalist government's Examination Yuan, charged with assessing the quality of civil servants. In 1922, Sun Yat-sen sent Dai to Chengdu as an adviser to Liu Chengxun, just as he had sent Zhang Qun to Xiong Kewu and Yang Shukan.[39]

By 1922, many political activists had rallied around the idea of a federal political system for China. As with states in the United States, within such a federal system each Chinese province would have had considerable autonomy. Some political theorists believed a stable national government could best be built after provinces had become more stable and democratic, and so they called for adoption of provincial constitutions and local elections.[40] The idea of a federal republic also seemed more attractive to many of the regional rulers than a highly centralized political order. In Sichuan, Liu Chengxun and the Provincial Assembly that had been elected after Yuan Shikai's death invited Dai Jitao to write a constitution for the province that would organize provincial and local government and spell out the powers the province would retain in the envisioned federation of Chinese provinces.

Among the members of the constitution-drafting committee that Dai Jitao headed was Wu Yuzhang, who eventually became a senior leader in the Communist Party. Wu Yuzhang was born in southern Sichuan in 1878 and in the late Qing years attended the Zunjing Academy in Chengdu, where Wu Yu was also a student.[41] Like so many other young men at the time, he studied in Japan and joined Sun Yat-sen's Revolutionary Alliance in the years before 1911. In 1911, he participated in the revolution in Sichuan and then joined Sun Yat-sen in Nanjing to help set up the Republic of China. After Yuan Shikai cracked down on political parties in 1913, Wu Yuzhang went to France, where he became interested in socialism. Back in China in the May Fourth period, he followed the news of the Bolshevik victory in Russia with interest. In 1920 he accepted appointment as a high school teacher in Nanchong, a city in northern Sichuan.

The head of the Nanchong high school who hired Wu Yuzhang, Zhang Lan, held a status within Sichuan that was equivalent to that of the so-called elders and sages in Chengdu (introduced in Chapter Two). Zhang Lan had earned a degree under the old Qing examination system and in 1911 had been a top leader of the protest in Chengdu against the Qing court's nationalization of railroads. He was widely recognized as an important cultural and political figure and was elected a Sichuan delegate to the first National Assembly of the Republic of China in 1913. When Yuan Shikai disbanded the legislature that year, Zhang Lan returned to his hometown of Nanchong and began developing it into a sort of model town, following the example of east China's Nantong, hometown of the famous scholar and industrialist Zhang Jian.[42] Zhang Lan spent 1919 in Beijing and witnessed the May Fourth protests, which he supported. In 1920, he returned to Nanchong and recruited Wu Yuzhang to teach there.

Zhang Lan also hired Yuan Shiyao to teach at the Nanchong high school. Yuan Shiyao was one of Chengdu's first self-identified anarchists and, like

Ba Jin, a member of the Equity Society. In 1919 and 1920, he promoted the study of Esperanto, the anarchist-approved world language, in Chengdu. His friend Ba Jin became an enthusiastic student of Esperanto and later based the character of the political activist Fang Jishun in *Turbulent Stream* on Yuan Shiyao. Unlike Ba Jin, however, Yuan Shiyao turned from anarchism to Marxism. In late 1920, Yuan joined Chengdu's first Marxist study society, founded by Wang Youmu, the provost of the Sichuan Teachers College.[43] After Yuan Shiyao moved to Nanchong, he and Wu Yuzhang continued to study Marxism there, and their lectures on it helped recruit several future Communist leaders to the cause. Among them was Luo Ruiqing, who joined the Communist Party in 1928, took part in the Long March in 1934–1935, and become the PRC's first minister of public security.

Wu Yuzhang had become a well-known public figure in Chengdu in the early 1920s and joined the constitution-drafting committee headed by Dai Jitao, probably on Zhang Lan's recommendation. He pushed for the document to include provisions for workers to organize their own unions and laws that would protect workers' rights. Dai Jitao and his committee completed the draft constitution in the spring of 1923. But before it could be implemented, another round of fighting broke out among the Sichuan militarists. In the end, the document was utterly ignored. Dai Jitao spent some time with his elderly mother and then returned to eastern China at the end of 1923.[44]

Communist and Nationalist activists stepped up their efforts to build organizations in Sichuan after the collapse of the federal movement. Wu Yuzhang succeeded Wang Youmu as the provost of the Teachers College. In the beginning of 1924, he set up a Young Communist Brigade in Chengdu. The previous fall, Wang Youmu had established a separate organization—the Chengdu branch of the Socialist Youth League. It would appear that several competing Communist groups coexisted in the city. When the United Front between the Communists and Nationalists was made known, Wang Youmu joined the Nationalist Party and became the head of its local propaganda section. On May 1, 1924, Wang Youmu organized a memorial ceremony for Lenin in Shaocheng Park.[45] Although it seems that Yang Sen, the military governor, permitted the ceremony, he was suspicious of the intentions of the Communists. He attempted to bribe Wang Youmu to support him and tried to arrest Wu Yuzhang. Both men fled the city in the summer of 1924.[46]

At about the same time, the Chinese Youth Party also began to compete in the struggle for political influence in Chengdu. The Sichuan strategy of all three major parties—the Nationalists, the Communists, and the Chinese Youth Party—was to appeal to sympathetic militarists while spreading their message among teachers and students and among workers via labor associations. The visibility of this political contest among parties increased in the late 1920s, encouraged by Zhang Lan, who had moved back to Chengdu to serve as president of Sichuan Teachers College (1925–1927) and Chengdu University (1928–1931).[47] In January 1927, a great meeting was organized in Shaocheng Park to celebrate the successes of the Northern Expedition. Ba Jin's old friend Yuan Shiyao, who would shortly join the Communist Party, happened to be in the city and took the stage to rail against all militarists and call on the common people to rise up against them.[48] A few months later, representatives from the three major parties held a debate in front of a thousand people at Chengdu University. As historian Nagatomi Hirayama has pointed out, the militarists who ruled Chengdu and its region at that time were among the audience.[49] They may well have been trying to understand how to appeal more effectively to Chengdu's youth.

This period of political ferment ended in a burst of violence on February 16, 1928, when Chengdu's militarist leaders sent troops to surround the college and high school campuses and arrested more than a hundred campus leaders, including Yuan Shiyao, who had taken a job at the high school attached to the Sichuan Teachers College. Two days before, the new principal appointed to head the best public high school in town had been beaten to death by students upset by his ties to the militarists. The generals decided to crack down on all student activism by making an example of leftist teachers. Yuan Shiyao and thirteen other suspected Communists were tried in secret and executed by firing squad that day. In the wake of Chiang Kai-shek's purge of Communists in eastern China, which had begun in April 1927, Sichuan's militarists felt free to follow suit. The headquarters of the Communist Party in Sichuan was in Chongqing, and it was effectively shut down in 1927.[50]

After the crushing of the Communist Party in Sichuan, the Nationalist Party and the Chinese Youth Party continued to recruit members. Officially, all Sichuan's generals pledged loyalty to the Nationalist Party's government after 1928. But unofficially they ignored it. In the first half of the 1930s, Liu Xiang was the dominant military leader in the province. The central government recognized him as the governor of Sichuan. But his political operatives were more active in the Gowned Brother networks across the province than in formal political parties. As suggested in our discussion of the Gowned

Brothers in Chapter Five, militarists like Liu Xiang agreed that people from Sichuan should rule Sichuan. In attempting to control the province, Sichuan nativists found the Gowned Brothers to be more reliable and more effective allies than the political parties based in eastern China.

By the 1940s, Zhang Qun, Dai Jitao, and Wu Yuzhang were known throughout China as outstanding political leaders, administrators, and thinkers. If they ever reflected on their experience trying to promote political revolution in Chengdu in the early 1920s, however, they surely must have acknowledged defeat. The political parties of eastern China were not really welcomed in Ba Jin's hometown.

Social Campaigns and Development

The militarists who controlled Chengdu in the 1920s may have been Sichuan nativists, but they kept a close eye on developments in eastern China and in the wider world. They all desired, on the one hand, to seem up-to-date and attract the support of the younger generation and, on the other, to take advantage of opportunities to increase their revenue and their access to resources, including the most advanced weapons. So in some ways Chengdu was not as isolated and stuck in the old ways as it appears in *Turbulent Stream*. Frequent warfare kept the economy in a shaky condition, but the militarists did hire and otherwise encourage entrepreneurial young men who wanted to transform Sichuan society and culture. Many of these young reformers had professional networks and other associations that extended beyond China, and they found friends and supporters within the Euro-American community in Chengdu as well as among the militarists and their officers. The foreign community, though small, was in a position to exert considerable influence in the city. After a brief history of the foreign presence in Chengdu, we will examine the work of two prominent 1920s Chengdu reformers and their relations with foreigners and militarists: Chen Weixin of the YMCA and National Road-Building Association and Lu Zuofu, founder of the Minsheng Industrial Company.

Chengdu is in China's interior, but that does not mean that its population lacked diversity. Sichuan was a relatively sparsely populated frontier land during the first half of the Qing, and people moved there from many parts of China in search of land and other opportunities.[51] Gradually a Sichuan version of Mandarin developed, but some people also retained the versions of Chinese spoken in their former communities. Ba Jin's paternal ancestors were from Zhejiang in eastern China; by the time he was born, however, the family had been in Sichuan for five generations, and he spoke Mandarin with a Sichuan accent.

In addition to migrants from the east, Chengdu attracted Tibetans and Chinese Muslims from the west, although in small numbers. Tibetan traders brought medicinal products and metalwork to sell in Chengdu and bought cloth, tea, and other products there. Most did not stay in the city year-round, but some Tibetan lamas lived at Buddhist temples in the region. Chengdu did have a resident Muslim community whose members built more than a dozen mosques over the years. These were located, for the most part, between the "imperial city" in the middle of town and the Banner garrison (Shaocheng) in the west. During the Qing period, the Banner garrison housed Banner troops and their families, including Manchu, Mongol, and Han Bannermen. After 1911, much of the property there was sold off; the Shaocheng area, particularly in the south around Shaocheng Park, became the neighborhood of choice for the militarists and other people with disposable funds in the republican era. Of the Bannerman families that had lived there, most gradually merged with the wider Chengdu community so that few identified themselves as anything other than common citizens of the Republic by the May Fourth period.[52] Although Chengdu's Muslim community declined in the last decades of the Qing and first decades of the Republic, it was still several thousand strong in the 1920s; it included a number of military officers and well-known doctors.[53]

Tibetans, Muslims, Manchus, and Mongols do not appear at all in *Turbulent Stream*, although Ba Jin would have known of their presence in Chengdu as he was growing up. The Westerners in Chengdu are only a little more apparent in the trilogy, even though they played a significant role in local politics. In the early republican period, Europeans and Americans in Chengdu had considerable power in the city because of their relative wealth and the prestige associated with Western culture at the time. Perhaps as important, their nationality protected them from the provincial authorities. French, British, and German consular offices were set up in the city in the late Qing, and a US consulate was established at Chongqing. Diplomats intervened aggressively in any case in which their citizens claimed mistreatment. German citizens lost their protected status in 1917, when China joined the Allied cause in World War I; most Germans left Sichuan. There was a small Japanese community in Chengdu. Because of anger toward Japan in the wake of the Versailles Treaty, though, the Japanese government had less leverage within Chengdu than the Western governments. There was an informal Japanese consular office in the city after 1916, but Sichuan's military authorities refused to recognize it.

Most Euro-American residents of Chengdu in the May Fourth period were associated with church missions and schools, where their goal was to win people over to Christianity and spread aspects of their cultures. In the first half of the twentieth century, foreigners founded twenty schools in the city.[54] The most famous was West China Union University, established in 1910 by leaders of the various Protestant schools and churches in town. It grew slowly in terms of numbers of students, but its celebrated medical and dental schools quickly gained it the support of local notables. Its president in the 1920s, Dr. Joseph Beech, was an important figure in Chengdu. Ba Jin's friend Wu Xianyou, the model for *Turbulent Stream*'s Zhang Huiru, attended the high school attached to West China Union University. The campus of the Union University, designed by the British architect Fred Rowntree, featured a pagoda-like bell tower and large classroom buildings arranged across 120 acres of what had been fields and gravesites south of the walled city (see Figure 3.1).[55] Shu Xincheng, the visiting professor who ran afoul of Yang Sen in 1924 (see Chapter Six), described the beauty of the campus in letters to his wife and noted that ordinary Chengdu residents were barred from entering the gates.[56]

Americans provided the initial funding for a branch of the Young Men's Christian Association in Chengdu, and, as noted in Chapter Two, its first secretary, Robert Service, managed to secure a large lot in the heart of the city near the commercial arcade for the YMCA headquarters building and athletic field. In the May Fourth period, the YMCA served as a gathering place for young men, including Ba Jin, who wanted to learn English. The YMCA also showed American movies, organized athletic competitions, and hosted lectures on science and world affairs. Robert Service and his staff and successors (he left Chengdu in 1920) developed more or less close relations with all the contenders for power in Chengdu. In June 1920, the YMCA hosted a special event for Police Commissioner Zhang Qun and more than four hundred Chengdu police officers.[57] In this way, the YMCA was able to attract support for a number of social initiatives launched in the city in the early 1920s. Service and some other foreigners also believed that their relationships with the Sichuan militarists allowed them to protect the local community—Service, for example, negotiated with the adversaries in the 1917 fighting to try to arrange a truce and remove the troops from Chengdu. The French consul in Chengdu allowed militarists who were facing defeat in battle to retreat to the French hospital for "treatment," as a way to defuse tense situations and avoid additional violence.

Just like some of the militarists, the Americans, Canadians, and British in Chengdu used their privileged positions to support the efforts of young Chinese social activists. One such person Ba Jin surely would have known of and perhaps met was Chen Weixin, who in 1923 was a Chengdu representative for Shanghai's largest publisher, the Commercial Press. Chen Weixin had been born in Chengdu and was sent by the Chengdu YMCA for training in Shanghai in the early 1910s. During World War I, he was employed by the YMCA to work among Chinese laborers in France, where he was a colleague of Yan Yangchu (James Yen), who gained fame in the 1920s for his "rural reconstruction" work in eastern China's Ding County. During his time in France, Yan Yangchu had pioneered the "Mass Education movement" and its techniques for teaching illiterate adults one thousand of the most commonly used Chinese characters. Chen Weixin brought the Mass Education movement to Chengdu, along with many other ideas about how to reform society. He organized a branch of the Shanghai-based National Road-Building Association, which was dedicated to urban planning, and advised Liu Chengxun and Yang Sen to widen the city's streets, set up regulated vegetable markets, and fix the sewer system.[58] When Yang Sen controlled the city during 1924 and 1925, he followed much of Chen Weixin's advice, tearing up and widening street after street, which angered many of the city's merchants.[59]

Yang Sen justified his remaking of the city on the grounds that better transportation would promote economic development. As noted above, "construction" (*jianshe*) was a powerful idea in Chengdu in the 1920s, more attractive to many than the political visions that inspired Ba Jin. Trade schools proliferated in the city. Chen Yi, the foreign minister of the PRC in the 1960s, spent part of his youth in Chengdu. In 1915 he enrolled in the Sichuan Industrial College, located next to Shaocheng Park, to study textile manufacture. As a young Chengdu technical student, he wore a Western-style jacket and tie. (When he withdrew from the school in 1918 because his family could no longer afford tuition, he took an exam to enter a military academy set up by Xiong Kewu, but failed the math section of the test. Nonetheless, he went on to head the Communist New Fourth Army during the war with Japan.)[60]

A few Chinese intellectuals spoke out in the 1920s and 1930s against this widespread enthusiasm for development, arguing that the excessive desire for wealth would destroy what they considered core Chinese values of living within nature and striving above all to behave ethically toward all human beings. Many of them were inspired by the visit to China of the great Bengali poet Rabindranath Tagore, who told his audiences that Asian wisdom should not be sacrificed to Western materialism and technological progress.[61] But this strand of thinking was not popular in Chengdu or in China as a whole. In response to arguments of this sort, Ba Jin himself wrote the following in 1933, the same year *Family* first appeared in book form:

> I love cities, I love machines, I love what they call material civilization. They are alive, hot, fast, powerful. I know that cities contain much that is evil, that machines cause workers to suffer, and that material civilization only offers a small minority of wealthy and powerful people the means to enjoy luxuries. But this should be blamed on our perverse social system (and so we should transform it). Let those people who curse the cities, who curse the machines, who curse material civilization go comfort themselves with their "spiritual civilization." As for me, I say once again, I love cities, I love machines, I love material civilization.[62]

In the early 1920s, it would seem that most of the elite community in Chengdu welcomed the presence of Americans and Europeans in their city, in large part because of their association with modern technologies and other useful knowledge. Despite an anti-imperialist rally in September 1921, Chengdu YMCA secretary George Helde noted that a membership drive that year resulted in 1,250 new YMCA members in the city.[63] By the mid-1920s, however, a couple of incidents in other parts of China had cast a different light on foreigners' involvement in Chinese affairs. In 1925, Shanghai's International Settlement police shot and killed demonstrators protesting labor conditions at a Japanese-owned factory. This "May Thirtieth incident" led to anti-imperialist rallies across China, including Chengdu.[64] Foreign economic exploitation and arms sales began to be seen as among the causes of incessant civil war in China. In Chengdu, the height of the anti-foreigner movement occurred in the fall of 1926, after a British gunboat fired its cannon at the town of Wanxian, a Yangzi port city east of Chongqing, where Yang Sen had stationed himself after being forced from Chengdu in 1925. The bombardment came during an attempt by the British to free two steamships seized by Yang Sen in Wanxian on charges that a British gunboat had capsized several Chinese boats on the Yangzi, drowning their occupants. The British, on their side, claimed that nobody had drowned and that the gunboat had left port swiftly because Yang Sen had been trying to commandeer it to carry his troops upstream. More than six hundred people were reportedly killed in the bombardment of Wanxian. Several dozen British marines and Chinese soldiers also died in the fighting.[65]

News of the Wanxian tragedy traveled to Chengdu quickly, and protests against British imperialism rocked the city. At the West China Union University, President Joseph Beech called a meeting of the students and, striking his fist on a table, chastised those who were calling the British "barbarians." In response, the students gathered to discuss a strike, but, by a vote of 99 to 114, rejected that option. Still, it was reported that thirty to forty students decided to withdraw from the university. Protest organizers also encouraged (forced, in the view of the foreigners) the servants who worked on the campus and in the homes of the teachers to go on strike. Due to the turmoil, the West China Union University shut down from October 20 to November 8, 1926.[66] The university weathered the storm, however, and continued to attract students. (When the Japanese invasion in 1937 forced evacuation of colleges in eastern China, several—including Yenching University and China's most famous women's school, Ginling College—relocated for the war years to West China Union University's campus.)

Still, anti-imperialist sentiments among young Chinese continued to grow, and throughout the 1920s and 1930s the urge to outcompete foreigners economically was strong. The career of Lu Zuofu, a colleague and friend of Li Jieren, offers the best example of what the Communists came to call the "national bourgeoisie"—capitalists who were not subservient to foreigners and could be very patriotic. Lu Zuofu (Figure 7.4) grew up in a merchant family in a county town near Chongqing.[67] In 1908, at the age of fifteen, he walked the 150 miles between his hometown and Chengdu and, while supporting himself as a tutor, taught himself mathematics and English. After spending a year in Shanghai in 1914–1915, he returned to Chengdu to work as an editor for *Sichuan Masses*, the paper founded by Chengdu Chamber of Commerce head Fan Kongzhou. He and Li Jieren were coworkers at the

Figure 7.4 Lu Zuofu in the 1940s. Courtesy of the Minsheng Industrial (Group) Co., Ltd.

paper. In 1921, the militarist Yang Sen hired Lu Zuofu to oversee educational affairs in Luzhou, the Yangzi town where Yang was headquartered at that time. Lu Zuofu helped Yang Sen make a name for himself as a progressive militarist by vigorously promoting educational reforms. The centerpiece of his efforts was the South Sichuan Teachers College (Chuannan shifan xuexiao), where he recruited to the faculty a number of well-known leftist intellectuals, including the Communist Yun Daiying. Hu Lanqi, the Chengdu woman discussed in Chapter Six who divorced her husband, also found a teaching job at South Sichuan Teachers College during Yang Sen's occupation of Luzhou.

During a second trip to Shanghai, in 1922, Lu Zuofu began to take an interest in manufacturing as a way to employ men who might otherwise have no alternative but to become soldiers. In the spring of 1924, after Yang Sen had marched into Chengdu, he brought Lu Zuofu back to the city and gave him the go-ahead to work full-time to popularize knowledge of new technologies. At the same time that Chen Weixin was launching the Thousand Character Mass Education movement in Chengdu, Lu Zuofu was setting up the Popular Education Institute in Shaocheng Park (Figure 7.5). Much like the YMCA, the Popular Education Institute featured a public library, athletic fields and competitions, public lectures, and exhibitions on technology, sanitation, science, and history.[68] In all likelihood it was intended as a sort of "import substitution"—a completely indigenous alternative to the YMCA.

Yang Sen was ousted from Chengdu within a year, and Lu Zuofu returned to his home region around Chongqing. There he ended up working closely with Yang Sen's rival militarist, Liu Xiang, who gradually expanded his control over much of Sichuan before Chiang Kai-shek and the Nationalists arrived in the late 1930s in the context of the war with Japan. Beginning in 1926, Lu Zuofu's major achievement was to establish a Sichuan shipping company that could compete effectively with the Japanese and British companies that dominated the steamship business on the Yangzi: Nisshin Kisen Kaisha; Jardine, Matheson & Company; and Swire & Butterfield. Lu

Figure 7.5 Chengdu Popular Education Institute, circa 1924. Courtesy of the Minsheng Industrial (Group) Co., Ltd.

Zuofu's Minsheng Industrial Company—*minsheng*, or "the people's livelihood," was one of Sun Yat-sen's Three Principles of the People—was at the heart of a broad effort on his part to "reconstruct" Sichuan, including the sort of rural reconstruction work advocated by Yan Yangchu. With Liu Xiang's support, the Minsheng Industrial Company had a remarkable degree of success before the war with Japan, operating 45 steamships on the Yangzi and its tributaries by 1935.[69]

Lu Zuofu's friend Li Jieren, like Ba Jin, studied literature in France and hoped to become a successful writer upon his return to Chengdu in 1924. But he could not support himself at writing. Yang Sen invited him to work in his government, but Li Jieren refused. Although Lu Zuofu may have felt that Li Jieren disapproved of his own willingness to serve under Yang Sen, his position allowed him to do Li Jieren a good turn when Yang Sen's officers arrested Li Jieren for satirizing one of them in a newspaper he was editing. Lu Zuofu intervened to have Li Jieren released. A few years later, Lu Zuofu helped Li Jieren make plans for a paper factory that Li and other entrepreneurs founded. He also hired Li Jieren to manage the Minsheng Industrial Company's machine shop when the paper company struggled in the early 1930s (it revived during the war years of the late 1930s, when supplies of paper from eastern China were cut off). If Ba Jin had stayed in Chengdu, it is likely that, like Li Jieren, he would not have been able to support himself solely by his pen. Perhaps he, too, would have joined Lu Zuofu's efforts to change the social order in Chengdu via economic development and rural reconstruction.

As Olga Lang notes, Ba Jin devoted his entire life to writing, after a brief experience of political organizing in the 1920s. The practical work of social reform and revolution, with its frequent need to compromise with authority, was not something he chose to do. What did he think of such men as Lu Zuofu, who built a thriving business and tried to develop his home region economically as well as culturally? We don't know. Certainly he did not celebrate such men in his fiction. Ba Jin's worldview was unusual in 1930s China, however. As an anarchist, he believed that the way to bring about a better world was to make it possible for each individual to develop his or her talents in an environment of equality and cooperation. Ba Jin was not nationalistic. Rather than seeing Christianity as a tool of foreign imperialists, he appreciated its message of humility and service to humankind.[70] For him, service meant writing stories that would inspire young people and let them know they were not alone in their troubles, as his heroes had done for him. While in France in 1927, he wrote a letter of support to Bartolomeo Vanzetti, in jail in Massachusetts and about to be sentenced to death along with his coworker Nicola Sacco in what many anarchists worldwide considered a politically motivated frame-up. Like Emma Goldman, Vanzetti wrote back to Ba Jin. In his reply, Vanzetti encouraged Ba Jin "to live honestly, love people, and help them."[71]

For his compatriots in Chengdu, though, Ba Jin's (and Juehui's) choice to escape to eastern China and stay clear of political entanglements was not the only path to a meaningful life. The great majority of his classmates and relatives stayed in Chengdu and helped change it, most of them in small ways such as welcoming new technologies into their lives or sending their daughters to school. A few, such as Chen Weixin and Lu Zuofu, shaped the city more obviously—launching literacy campaigns and other social movements, founding companies, and redesigning the city according to new standards of urban planning. Although political operatives such as Wu Yuzhang and Dai Jitao found Chengdu unreceptive, for the most part, to the appeal of the established eastern parties, the city's politics were very fluid. Despite (and sometimes because of) the discontinuities in urban governance, local initiatives for reform and economic development changed the face of the city. Cultural debates flourished in Chengdu in the 1920s, and many urban experiments and improvements were actually implemented.

EPILOGUE

Family and City in China's Twentieth-Century Revolutions

Turbulent Stream is a portrait of a family and a city in the years between 1919 and 1923—the height of the cultural revolution known as the May Fourth movement. The patriarchal family is Ba Jin's focus, because he and others at the time saw it as a primary cause of China's problems. In their view, the old generation was clinging to its privileges and bending all to its will, crushing the spirit of the young people who were in touch with the great ideas circulating around the world. In Ba Jin's view, the family was the main obstacle to the younger generation struggling to narrow the gap between rich and poor, end the civil wars, and improve the status of women. The city in *Turbulent Stream* is mostly a dark and gloomy background, in which bullets shatter the night, students and soldiers clash, and poor beggars huddle waiting for handouts.

Turbulent Stream's critique of Chinese families attracted generations of young readers to the novels, and many of them strongly identified with its heroes, the young people of the Gao family. Like Juehui and Qin, they wanted to have control over their lives and play a part in changing China.

Some of them did, like Gao Juehui, escape their families by moving away from home. Some no doubt changed family dynamics from within by persuasion and resistance to established ways. And many were probably grateful that their own families were supportive and loving, unlike the Gao family of Ba Jin's novels.[1] Ba Jin's own rancorous family was not typical, even of all large, wealthy families. Although some felt threatened by the rise of the ideal of the New Woman and the revolutionary ideologies discussed in Chapters Six and Seven, most Chengdu families were not torn apart by New Women or revolutionaries—warfare and poverty were harder on Chinese families than either of these rare cultural figures.

However necessary in Ba Jin's eyes, reform of the "family system"—including the rejection of Confucian learning and values such as respect for elders—was by no means universally accepted as a top priority among activists in China in the decades of the 1920s and 1930s. Economic development and a national leadership that could resist foreign imperialism were goals that more people could unite around. One enticing path that promised to achieve these twin goals was urban development. Urban advocates of the day believed Chinese cities could and should become the main drivers of economic progress. Some argued that, in addition to making China strong, economic development would solve many of the problems of patriarchal families, by offering new opportunities that would lessen dependence on the family head.[2] This urban reform enthusiasm extended across China and, indeed, across much of the world in the early twentieth century. And so, although *Turbulent Stream*'s urban setting is murky and grim, in real life every Chinese city was the subject of ambitious reform schemes in the 1920s and 1930s. Chengdu was not at all different from Shanghai in this respect. Ba Jin's trilogy obscures this important fact.

Compared to transforming families and the "family system," reforming cities was actually simpler in many ways—the methods of achieving paved streets, smartly uniformed police, clean marketplaces, and even increased literacy were all much more straightforward and progress was more easily measurable. The relative difficulty of family reform is apparent if we consider the question of slave girls and concubines—the case of people like Mingfeng, with which this book began. Laws limiting or banning the purchase of slave girls and concubines had been included in new legal codes drafted in the late Qing and again in the republican period, but transactions of both types continued to be widespread through the 1940s. Occasionally, an essay or editorial would call for an end to the sale of women. But in general the issue was considered too intractable to address because the practices were so entrenched in the cities and because social disorder and widespread poverty in the countryside continued to pressure rural families to sell children they could not support. Family reformers focused instead on promoting the nuclear family, and no doubt many hoped the proliferation of small nuclear families in modern urban enclaves might eventually lead to a decline in the numbers of concubines and slave girls.

From the point of view of urban planners and administrators, on the other hand, the greatest threat to their main objective—urban productivity—was disorder. Slave girls had a well-defined and well-established place in urban families. Of far more concern to urban administrators in the republican era was the great mass of displaced vagrants driven to the cities by rural unrest and pulled by the promise of economic opportunity.[3] To the extent that "patriarchy" helped create places for slave girls in urban families—and thus a way for the rural poor to be accommodated in the cities in an orderly way—the new city managers were not interested in confronting it.

Commentators throughout the period argued that the liberation of girls could occur only after the Chinese economy had been transformed.[4] When it seized power in 1949, the Communist Party used new political and organizational tools to transform the Chinese economy and, at the same time, to change the social order radically. The old gentry culture was quickly abolished. Patriarchal households such as the one Ba Jin grew up in lost their status and property. Concubines and slave girls, like their masters and mistresses, entered a world in which everyone was expected to do productive labor—and those who did not accept the new order could expect to be "reeducated."[5] In this environment, Ba Jin's forceful indictment of the old order in *Turbulent Stream* was a useful tool for justifying a revolution in which "serving the masses" was supposed to replace "filial piety" as a core value. In *Turbulent Stream*, Shanghai symbolized freedom, but the new Communist vision for China condemned all existing Chinese cities—and especially Shanghai—as capitalists' playgrounds built with the blood and sweat of oppressed workers. In Mao's China, economic development certainly remained a key goal, but bourgeois, consumer-oriented cities were to be replaced by producer cities centered on large-scale, state-managed industrial units, in emulation of the Soviet model of urbanization. China's own history of urban change and creativity was not of interest to the new rulers of China. The early twentieth-century urban boosterism that is evident in Chengdu and other Chinese cities declined precipitously, as all attention was focused on social revolution and industrial production within the new "work unit."[6]

In the decades since Mao died in 1976, however, earlier Communist conceptions of families and cities have been—and are being—revised. First, Mao's successor Deng Xiaoping authorized the revival of China's coastal cities as centers of international trade and industry. Then, cities in the interior were encouraged to follow their example and get rich. Beginning in the 1990s, as China increasingly opened up to the world, the Communist Party began to reconsider its previous negative assessment of Confucian thought and values and to encourage people to take pride in Chinese culture.[7] Formerly, influenced by the discourse of the May Fourth movement, Chinese Communist leaders, like Ba Jin, had denounced many Chinese customs and values as "backward" and "feudal." These days, however, values such as filial piety and respect for book learning are viewed as positive traits of the Chinese people that are entirely compatible with socialism and modernity (two very flexible concepts that continue to carry a positive connotation in China). Confucian rituals are once again being performed in Confucius's hometown of Qufu, although the family rites that Ba Jin hated so much are mostly absent from Chengdu.

Chinese history is now commonly read in China as a record of achievements or as an entertaining drama, rather than above all as a story of feudal oppression and struggle leading step by painful step to the "Liberation" of 1949. Recent productions of *Turbulent Stream* and *Family* as television dramas downplay Ba Jin's critique of the "family system" and highlight the romantic elements of the plot, dressing the Gao family and servants in beautiful (idealized) clothing to appeal to the fashion sense of their consumer-focused audiences. Since its cultural critique is no longer relevant in today's very different Chinese society, the place of *Turbulent Stream* in Chinese culture is now similar to that of one of its inspirations—the eighteenth-century novel *Dream of the Red Chamber*.[8] Both are beloved classics of Chinese literature well suited for retelling in various media.

Nonetheless, Ba Jin's trilogy continues to influence the way that Chinese society in the May Fourth era is imagined. It remains the most powerful depiction of "the patriarchal family" and "the traditional Chinese city" in the first decades of the twentieth century. Ba Jin's own popularity as the writer of emotional bestsellers made him the most famous Chengdu native in China from the 1930s on, and therefore his view of the city and its elite families had an authority that no one else's could match. The Gao family has become the prototypical patriarchal gentry family. As a novelist, Ba Jin created powerful images that resonated with a large audience. He succeeded in representing a historical time in an emotional register that continues to appeal to readers, as do the sympathetic characters he created. From the point of view of a historian, his *Turbulent Stream* trilogy is an invaluable resource as a popular, vivid account of cultural tensions within Chinese communities in the 1920s and 1930s. But, as compelling fiction, *Turbulent Stream* necessarily simplifies history, particularly the multifaceted story of the transformation of Chinese cities in that era.

The preceding chapters chronicle the story of one city in a time of great instability and uncertainty. The case of Chengdu extends the gradually widening geographic scope of historical research on Chinese cities in the May Fourth/New Culture era and cities across the world in the turbulent 1920s, when global economic currents touched every region and arguments about the nature and value of cultural heritage intensified. Below the surface of intellectual debates and the transformation of elite society, the historical record reveals something of the experiences of people in other subsets of the Chengdu population during the tumultuous early decades of the twentieth century. My consideration of May Fourth–era Chengdu from multiple perspectives shows us that social change in that era was significant, but that the profound generational gaps we see in Ba Jin's *Turbulent Stream* by no means characterized Chengdu society as a whole. Family connections remained important to economic and cultural life in the city, in spite of some change in family organization attributable to the May Fourth era's attacks on patriarchy. The gentry continued to play a key civic role, even as political and military authority over Chengdu shifted repeatedly. Contrary to stereotype, Chengdu, and most of its elite, embraced foreign technology and certain new ideas readily, but new roles and greater independence for women in gentry families came unevenly; in contrast, poor women and slaves never achieved emancipation. Another constant, despite social mobility, was that rural youth (bartered, conscripted, or displaced) usually occupied the lowest rungs of urban society.

The characters and situations from Ba Jin's fiction help call attention to the social history of cities like Chengdu and explain how this urban history influenced the thinking of the revolutionary youth of Ba Jin's generation, leading many of them to abandon (or deemphasize) the focus on family reform and turn instead to urban development as a path to a better society. Because of its influence on the memory of May Fourth, *Turbulent Stream*, with its focus on the family as the central problem in Chinese society, obscures the extent to which many of Ba Jin's compatriots saw China's salvation in its cities and worked to develop them in the 1920s and 1930s.

Many of those who read *Turbulent Stream* over the years may not have realized that the story is set in Chengdu. Just as Ba Jin intended the Gao family to be a representation of a typical gentry family, he included only a few obvious clues as to the identity of the city in which the family resided because he wanted the setting to serve as a sort of Chinese "every town" in contrast to Shanghai. But, as I hope this book has shown, the autobiographical origins of the characters and stories ensure that Chengdu's rich history permeates Ba Jin's fiction.

APPENDIX I

Timeline of Chengdu's History and Ba Jin's Life

1813	Liu Zhitang founds the Huaixuan Academy in Chengdu.
1818	Ba Jin's ancestor Li Wenxi comes to Sichuan from eastern China.
1839–1842	Britain defeats the Qing and claims Hong Kong, extraterritorial privileges, and land in five coastal "treaty ports."
1850–1864	Taiping uprising and its suppression devastate the Yangzi valley and isolate Sichuan from the east.
1874	Zhang Zhidong becomes Sichuan education commissioner and founds the Zunjing Academy to promote Confucian scholarship.
1895	Japan defeats the Qing navy and army.
1898	Kang Youwei leads a reform movement in Beijing, with the support of the Guangxu emperor: Empress Dowager Cixi quickly shuts it down and orders the execution of six scholar-officials who supported it, including two from Sichuan, with close ties to the Chengdu elite.
1901	Foreign armies suppress Boxer uprising; New Policies reforms begin: new schools, army, police forces, and other institutions are created; Hu Lanqi born in Chengdu.
1902	Ba Jin's father, Li Daohe, takes a post in the Qing bureaucracy in Sichuan.
1903	Chengdu police force established; Li Daohe leaves office and travels to Beijing, seeking an audience with the emperor.
1904	Ba Jin born in Chengdu; British incursion in Tibet stirs nationalism in Sichuan.
1909	Ba Jin's father is appointed magistrate of Guangyuan; in Chengdu, Robert Service establishes the YMCA, a Sichuan provincial assembly forms, and the commercial arcade and Shaocheng Park open to the public.
1910	Ba Jin's future teacher Wu Yu publishes "One Family's Bitter Story," an attack on his father, and goes into hiding; West China Union University founded.

1911	The Railroad Protection movement in Sichuan leads to protests and an independence declaration; the Qing dynasty falls; a military coup installs the first of many military governors of Sichuan based in Chengdu.
1912	Foundation of the Chinese Republic under President Yuan Shikai; in Sichuan the Gowned Brothers begin a long period of expansion in numbers and in local influence.
1914	Ba Jin's mother dies.
1915	*New Youth*, the premier magazine of New Culture reform, begins publication in Shanghai.
1916	Yuan Shikai, president of the Republic, dies; regional militarists and political parties vie for power for the next two decades; Gowned Brother lodges become de facto local authorities in absence of a stable government in Sichuan.
1917	Street fighting between Sichuan forces and occupying Guizhou and Yunnan forces destroys much of Chengdu; Ba Jin's father and Wu Yu's wife both die of illness in the aftermath of the fighting.
1919	May Fourth incident occurs in Beijing, Chengdu people learn about it soon after; students demonstrate and organize boycotts of Japanese goods; Zhang Qun appointed head of the Sichuan provincial police; the Chengdu branch of the Young China Association is established.
1920	Young China Association member Li Jieren goes to France to study literature; Ba Jin reads Kropotkin's *An Appeal to Youth* and develops an interest in anarchism; his grandfather dies; soldiers and students clash in Shaocheng Park; Hu Lanqi enters into an arranged marriage after the death of her mother.
1921	Ba Jin contributes essays to *Bi-weekly* (a political journal published by his friends) and joins the Equity Society (an anarchist organization in Chengdu); Ba Jin's teacher Wu Yu moves to Beijing to teach at Peking University; the Chinese Communist Party is founded in Shanghai; soldiers clash with police and with students in Chengdu.
1922	Hu Lanqi abandons her husband and takes a teaching job in Luzhou, the base of the militarist Yang Sen; Dai Jitao and Wu Yuzhang serve on the drafting committee for Sichuan's provincial constitution during the movement to establish a federal system in China.
1923	Ba Jin and his second elder brother, Li Yaolin, depart Chengdu for eastern China; Nationalists and Communists establish a United Front against the Northern militarists; Chen Weixin promotes mass education and urban planning in Chengdu.
1924	General Yang Sen occupies Chengdu and begins a major renovation of the city, including the construction of the Chunxi Road commercial

	area; Wu Yu returns to Chengdu from Beijing; Li Jieren returns to Chengdu from France; both Wu Yu and Li Jieren are hired by Chengdu University, which begins to accept female students along with male students; Lu Zuofu establishes the Chengdu Popular Education Institute; the Chinese Youth Party is active in Chengdu.
1926	Wanxian incident stokes anti-imperialist feeling in Sichuan; Lu Zuofu founds the Minsheng Industrial Company; militarists and their associates own much of the land around Chengdu, having gradually bought out prior owners.
1927	Ba Jin studies in Paris; the United Front between the Communists and Nationalists collapses during the Northern Expedition; Chiang Kai-shek establishes a national government in Nanjing; Communists are forced out of cities into rural base areas.
1928	Ba Jin returns to Shanghai; militarists purge leftist teachers in Chengdu.
1931	*Family* is published as a serial; Ba Jin's eldest brother commits suicide.
1932	Chengdu is terrorized by street fighting between rival Chinese armies once again; Liu Xiang dominates Sichuan politics; a large section of Shanghai is destroyed in a Japanese attack.
1933	*Family* is published as a book.
1934–1935	The Nationalists encircle the Communist base area in Jiangxi, so the Communists undertake the Long March, eventually establishing a new base in Yan'an in northwest China.
1937	The Japanese invade north and east China and devastate Nanjing; Ba Jin continues to live in Shanghai's French Concession, free of Japanese control.
1938	*Spring* is published; the Nationalists retreat to Sichuan, establishing a temporary capital in Chongqing.
1940	*Autumn* is published; Ba Jin leaves Shanghai for southwest China, still controlled by the Nationalist government.
1941	Ba Jin visits Chengdu for the first time since leaving in 1923.
1942	Cao Yu directs a stage version of *Family* in Chongqing, the wartime Nationalist capital.
1944	Ba Jin marries Xiao Shan in Guiyang, Guangxi.
1945	War with Japan ends; Ba Jin returns to Shanghai.
1949	The People's Republic of China is founded; Ba Jin pledges his support to the new regime and serves in various literary posts.
1953	A revised version of *Family* is published in Shanghai; a Hong Kong film version of *Family* is produced.
1956	A Shanghai film version of *Family* is produced.

1966–1976	In the Cultural Revolution, Ba Jin's writings are banned, Ba Jin is accused of political mistakes and forced to undergo "reeducation," and his wife dies of untreated cancer.
1978	New editions of Ba Jin's novels begin to be published, including, in 1982, a graphic novel edition of *Turbulent Stream* (with a bilingual Chinese and English version published in 1995).
1988	A TV miniseries version of *Turbulent Stream* airs.
2005	Ba Jin dies in Shanghai.
2007	A TV miniseries version of *Family* airs.

APPENDIX 2

List of *Turbulent Stream* Characters, with Pinyin and Wade-Giles Romanizations

In this book, with the exception of Sun Yat-sen and Chiang Kai-shek, Chinese names of real and fictional people are spelled in standard pinyin romanization. The pinyin system is also used in the bilingual graphic-novel version of *Family* (Asiapac Books, 1995). Below, alternate forms of names for prominent characters in *Turbulent Stream* are provided. After the names as they appear in this book are the corresponding Chinese characters, the Wade-Giles equivalent spellings and other forms that are used in Sidney Shapiro's translation of *Family*, and approximate pronunciations of the names.

Pinyin	*Characters*	*Wade-Giles*	*Other names, relationships*	*Pronunciation*
Chen Jianyun	陳劍云	Ch'en Chien-yun	Poor relative/ family tutor	chun jee-en yooin
Chen Yitai (Miss Chen)	陳姨太	Ch'en I-t'ai	Mistress Chen; concubine	chun ee ty
Chunlan	春蘭	Ch'un-lan	Slave girl	chwun lahn
Cuihuan	翠環	Ts'ui-huan	Slave girl	tsway hwahn
Feng Leshan	馮樂山	Feng Lo-shan	Venerable Master Feng	fung luh shahn
Gao Juehui	高覺慧	Kao Chueh-hui	Third grandson	gow joo-eh hway
Gao Juemin	高覺民	Kao Chueh-min	Second grandson	gow joo-eh min
Gao Juexin	高覺新	Kao Chueh-hsin	Oldest grandson	gow joo-eh sheen
Gao Ke'an (Fourth Uncle)	高克安	Kao K'e-an	Fourth son	gow kuh ahn
Gao Keding (Fifth Uncle)	高克定	Kao K'e-ting	Fifth son	gow kuh ding
Gao Keming (Third Uncle)	高克明	Kao K'e-ming	Third son	gow kuh ming

225

226 APPENDIX 2

Pinyin	Characters	Wade-Giles	Other names, relationships	Pronunciation
Gao Laotaiye (Gao Patriarch)	高老太爺	Kao Lao T'ai-yeh	Venerable Master Kao	gow lau ty yeh
Gao Shuhua	高淑華	Kao Shu-hua	Third granddaughter	gow shoo hwa
Gao Shuying	高淑英	Kao Shu-ying	Second granddaughter	gow shoo ing
Gao Shuzhen	高淑楨	Kao Shu-chen	Fourth granddaughter	gow shoo jun
He Sao	何嫂	Ho Sao	Married female servant	huh sow
Li Ruijue	李瑞珏	Li Jui-chueh	Wife of Gao Juexin	lee ray joo-eh
Mei	梅	Mei	Former love of Gao Juexin	may
Mingfeng	鳴鳳	Ming-feng	Slave girl	ming fung
Qian'er	倩兒	Ch'ien-erh	Slave girl	chee-en ar
Qin	琴	Chin	Daughter's daughter	chin
Tang Sao	湯嫂	T'ang Sao	Married female servant	tahng sow
Wan'er	婉兒	Wan-erh	Slave girl	wahn ar
Xi'er	喜兒	Hsi-erh	Slave girl	shee ar
Zhang Bixiu	張碧秀	Chang Pi-hsiu	"Male actress"	jahng bee shee-o
Zhang Huiru	張惠如	Chang Hui-ju	Friend of Gao Juehui	jahng hway roo
Zhang Sao	張嫂	Chang Sao	Married female servant	jahng sow
Zhou Hui	周蕙	Chou Hui	Niece of Zhou Shi	joe hway
Zhou Mei	周枚	Chou Mei	Nephew of Zhou Shi	joe may
Zhou Shi (Madam Zhou)	周氏	Chou Shih	Madam Chou; eldest son's widow	joe sher

Notes

INTRODUCTION

1. The Chinese titles of *Family, Spring,* and *Autumn* are *Jia, Chun,* and *Qiu*. A complete synopsis of the trilogy appears in Mao, *Pa Chin,* chap. 4. Complete English translations of *Spring* and *Autumn* have not yet been published.
2. Ba Jin, "*Jia* chongyin houji," 610–11.
3. The Chinese term for these rituals and values is *lijiao*. The topic is treated in Chapter Two.
4. Stapleton, "Generational and Cultural Fissures." On the argument that multigenerational extended families created passivity and dependency in the young, see also Schwarcz, *Chinese Enlightenment,* 110–12.
5. On this point, see Fung, *Intellectual Foundations of Chinese Modernity,* chap. 1.
6. A recent critique of this old image of an oppressive, stagnant, and miserable pre-Communist China may be found in Dikötter, *Exotic Commodities.*
7. For example, see the critical statement issued by the Association of Black Women Historians, which ends: "The Association of Black Women Historians finds it unacceptable for either this book or this film to strip black women's lives of historical accuracy for the sake of entertainment." www.abwh.org/images/pdf/TheHelp-Statement.pdf (accessed August 20, 2015).
8. In a letter to Li Jieren's daughter Li Mei dated November 11, 1981, Ba Jin himself praised Li Jieren's fiction for bringing alive the Chengdu of his youth. Letter included in an exhibition in Chengdu's Li Jieren Memorial and Museum. On Li Jieren's novels of Chengdu, see Ng, *Lost Geopoetic Horizon.*
9. Lang's *Pa Chin* provides an excellent account of Ba Jin's life in English. Many biographies have appeared in Chinese. Among the most valuable are Chen, *Ren'ge de fazhan,* and Tan, *Zoujin Ba Jin de shijie.*
10. Ba Jin, "Guanyu *Jia*," 252–65.
11. Olga Lang comments on the theme of friendship in Ba Jin's work, noting its importance in Chinese literary history. Lang, *Pa Chin,* 65–67.
12. The influence of the Chinese literary tradition on Ba Jin's novel *Family* is the focus of Shaw, "Ba Jin's Dream." Lang, *Pa Chin,* chap. 10, analyzes the influence of European, especially Russian, literature on Ba Jin's writings.
13. See Chapter Seven for a discussion of the intellectual currents and institutions that influenced the young Ba Jin.

14. Shaw, "Changes in *The Family*," Fisac, "Rewriting Modern Chinese Literature," and Jin Hongyu, *Zhongguo xiandai changpian xiaoshuo*.
15. Ba Jin had already been attacked briefly in 1958, during the Anti-Rightist movement. See Mao, *Pa Chin*, 35–37.
16. On Ba Jin's call for a museum to the Cultural Revolution, see Schwarcz, *Place and Memory*, 205–6. Ba Jin's refusal to speak out in support of intellectuals and writers arrested for their involvement in the 1989 political protests in China is criticized by Liu Xiaobo, the 2010 Nobel Peace Prize laureate, in a 2005 essay written when Ba Jin died, "Ba Jin: The Limp White Flag."
17. Liu Jingzhi, "Zhang Ruifang, Sun Daolin, yu Ba Jin de *Jia*."
18. "Zhongguo xiandai wenxueguan lishi yan'ge," http://wxg.org.cn/gydh/lsyg/cjcs/2011-03-23/11966.shtml (accessed August 20, 2015).
19. Li Cunguang, Jia *dao du*. The Shanghai-based Ba Jin Research Association regularly organizes conferences and publishes scholarly work on Ba Jin. See http://bjwxg.cn/ (accessed August 29, 2015).

CHAPTER ONE

1. The similarities between Mingfeng and Qingwen, a major character in *Dream of the Red Chamber*, are discussed in Cheng, "*Hongloumeng* yu *Jia* zhong beiju renwu xingxiang bijiao—yi Qingwen he Mingfeng wei li." In an essay comparing female characters in *Family* and *Dream of the Red Chamber*, Sun Lianghao and Chen Jianwei note that when *Family* appeared readers immediately commented on similarities between the two novels. Ba Jin downplayed the influence, but most scholars judge it to have been significant. Sun and Chen, "Nüxing ziwo yishi de 'juexing' yu 'chenlun'"; see also Lang, *Pa Chin*, and Shaw, "Ba Jin's Dream."
2. When she translated her story "Jinsuoji" ("The Golden Cangue") into English, Eileen Chang used "slave girl" for *yatou*. In *Sex, Law, and Society*, Matthew Sommer translates *binü* as "unmarried female domestic slave." In Canton, *mui-jai* was the colloquial term for *binü*. In the entry on *mui-jai* in Drescher and Engerman's *Historical Guide to World Slavery* (292–93), Ching-Hwang Yen proposes the translation "young female domestic slaves."
3. Wei, Wu, and Lu, *Qingdai nubi zhidu*, 23–39.
4. Ibid., 166–79. See also Naquin and Rawski, *Chinese Society*, 118. Matthew Sommer offers an interesting analysis of the Yongzheng edicts in *Sex, Law, and Society*, 305–6, arguing that abolition of "mean" or "base" status was part of efforts to establish clear gender roles and norms of sexual conduct that did not vary by social class.
5. Wei, Wu, and Lu (*Qingdai nubi zhidu*, 41–42) describe a contract of this sort dated in the ninth year of the Yongzheng reign (1731). Other such documents from the late nineteenth and early twentieth centuries may be found in Jaschok, *Concubines and Bondservants*, 146–48, and in Hong, *Taiwan shehui shenghuo wenshu zhuanji*. James Watson points out that model contracts for the sale of children could be copied from household almanacs in the nineteenth and twentieth centuries. Watson, "Transactions in People," 234.
6. Wu Yu, *Wu Yu riji*, vol. 2, 318 (June 13, 1926); see also Ran, *Wu Yu he ta shenghuo de Minguo shidai*, 7. Ran Yunfei notes that Ba Jin's teacher Wu Yu also continued taking young women as concubines into his fifties and sixties. Ba Jin had left Chengdu by 1926 but probably heard of Liu's actions, and perhaps Wu's, in letters from his family.

7. Ransmeier, "No Other Choice," 286. Lisa Tran discusses the distinction between "members of the household" (*jiashu*) and "relatives" (*qinshu*) established by China's highest judicial court in the early 1930s. Tran, "Concubine in Republican China," 138.

8. Gates, *China's Motor*.

9. Anthropologist James Watson notes how varied the relationship between *mui-jai* and master/mistress could be in South China but judges it was thought of as a type of kinship (*mui-jai* were "second-class daughters"). Watson, "Transactions in People," 343.

10. Ba Jin, "Guanyu *Jia*," 596–600.

11. Waltner, *Getting an Heir*, 145–47.

12. Amy Tan's 1989 novel *The Joy Luck Club* includes a story of a child bride, Lindo Jong. For a comparison of Amy Tan's work with Ba Jin's *Family*, see Chu, *Assimilating Asians*, 160–65. Within Chinese literature, the most famous child bride is Xiaoxiao, protagonist of a 1930 short story set in rural Hunan. Shen Congwen, "Xiaoxiao," 97–110. The 1986 film version, *Girl from Hunan*, follows the original story closely.

13. Arthur Wolf and Hill Gates discuss the dynamics of and variance in the practice of "minor marriage" (bringing a future bride into the household as a child) in "Modeling Chinese Marriage Regimes."

14. Wei, Wu, and Lu (*Qingdai nubi zhidu*, 5–7) cite Fang Bao's comments about the rage for slave girls in eighteenth-century Suzhou.

15. Watson, "China," in Drescher and Engerman, *Historical Guide to World Slavery*, 151. The entry is a shortened, slightly altered version of Watson's earlier article; see Watson, "Transactions in People," 241–42.

16. Jaschok, *Concubines and Bondservants*, 97.

17. See, for example, Wei, Wu, and Lu, *Qingdai nubi zhidu*, 37–53

18. Jaschok, *Concubines and Bondservants*, 29, 45.

19. Pruitt, *Daughter of Han*, 66–72.

20. Su and Tao, "Xuantong yuannian jin'ge renkou maimai shiliao," 69.

21. Jaschok, *Concubines and Bondservants*, 90–91.

22. Watson, "Transactions in People," 229.

23. James Watson believes that, in early twentieth-century Hong Kong, most people knew the family origins of slave girls in their communities. Arrangements to transfer girls from one family to another were set up so that members of the selling and buying families did not meet, suggesting girls did not retain contact with parents after being sold. Watson, "Transactions in People," 235. Maria Jaschok (*Concubines and Bondservants*, chap. 1) relates the story of Moot Xiao-li, who became a wealthy concubine, then successfully traced and supported the birth family that had sold her.

24. Wei, Wu, and Lu, *Qingdai nubi zhidu*, 51–56. See Finnane, *Speaking of Yangzhou*, chap. 9, for more on long-distance trade in children in the early Qing.

25. Ransmeier, "No Other Choice," chap. 4.

26. Wen, "Muqian Zhongguo zhi nubi jiefang wenti."

27. Lim, *Sold for Silver*, 38–39.

28. Eastman, *Family, Fields, and Ancestors*, 26–27. See also the essays in Ropp, Zamperini, and Zurndorfer, *Passionate Women*.

29. Wei, Wu, and Lu, *Qingdai nubi zhidu*, 114.

30. Ibid., 118–19.

31. Pruitt, *Daughter of Han*, 82.

32. Sommer, *Sex, Law, and Society*, 49.

33. Jaschok, *Concubines and Bondservants*, 70–72.
34. Lim, *Sold for Silver*, 39–46.
35. Interview with Liu Bogu, Chengdu, September 2000.
36. Juemin refers to Wu Yu as Wu Youling. Youling was Wu's "style," a name used on formal, public occasions and usually chosen by the man himself as an adult.
37. Ran Yunfei discusses Wu Yu's purchases of slave girls and concubines in detail in *Wu Yu he ta shenghuo de Minguo shidai*, 3–19.
38. *Wu Yu riji*, vol. 1, 516 (entries for January 21 and 22, 1920). Wu Yu mentions renaming a newly arrived slave girl in the entry for February 26, 1919 (vol. 1, 450).
39. On the establishment of the new police system in Chengdu, see Stapleton, *Civilizing Chengdu*, chap. 3.
40. These documents are in several files in the First Historical Archives. See ibid., chap. 3, for a list.
41. Stapleton, "Age of 'Secret Societies'"; see also Wakeman, *Policing Shanghai*.
42. *Wu Yu riji*, vol. 1, 443, 511 (entries for January 17 and December 31, 1919).
43. Snow is rare in Chengdu now but was more common in Ba Jin's youth. Wu Yu noted that it snowed quite a bit at the lunar New Year in February 1919—at his house they piled snow in a vat to use as water later for boiling tea and making pickled vegetables. *Wu Yu riji*, vol. 1, 446 (entry for February 1, 1919).
44. Mingfeng is said to be sixteen *sui* in the novel. Chinese children in Ba Jin's time were reckoned to be one at birth; most people today would call her fifteen.
45. Fu, *Chengdu tonglan*, vol. 1, 392.
46. Wu Yu left no description of the actual market area where children were purchased, but Wu Tianming offers a striking cinematic picture of such a market, and a plausible representation, in his 1996 film *King of Masks* (*Bianlian*), set in Sichuan in the early 1930s.
47. Jaschok, "'Slave' Girls in Yunnan-Fu."
48. Service, *Golden Inches*, 57–59, 95.
49. Ibid., 70.
50. Pruitt, *Daughter of Han*, 146–47.
51. Li Jieren's *Dabo*, set in Chengdu in 1911, includes a scene in which a slave girl nods off while waiting for orders from her mistress, who is engaged in a late-night chat with her husband and nephew. The nephew demonstrates his Juehui-like political leanings by suggesting to his aunt that the girl be allowed to go to bed. *Dabo*, vol. 1, 162–65. The question of abolishing slave girl status is discussed by the characters in *Dabo* in vol. 3, 1540–41.
52. Pruitt, *Daughter of Han*, chap. 8–13.
53. Rubie Watson points to the similarity in the positions within households of *mui-jai* and concubines in "Wives, Concubines, and Maids."
54. A reproduction of the illustrated news report on this case appears in Stapleton, *Civilizing Chengdu*, 89.
55. Jaschok, *Concubines and Bondservants*, 25–34. The quotation is on p. 34.
56. Lisa Tran discusses popular perceptions of concubines and what can be learned about concubines via legal cases from the 1930s and 1940s in "Concubine in Republican China." See also Su, "New Women Old Mores."
57. Xie Bingying, *Woman Soldier's Own Story*, 40, 213.
58. Hu Lanqi, *Hu Lanqi huiyilu*, 58.
59. Pruitt, *Daughter of Han*, 108.

60. *Wushi*, known colloquially as *duangong*, are discussed in Sun, Jiang, and Chen, *Sichuan minsu daguan*, 360–62.
61. Deirdre Sabina Knight discusses how female characters invoke "fate" in much republican-era literature, touching briefly on Ba Jin's work, in her essay "Gendered Fate."
62. Stapleton, "Generational and Cultural Fissures," 131–48.
63. Fu, *Chengdu tonglan*, vol. 1, 110.
64. Ibid., 394.
65. A valuable source on popular religious beliefs in contemporary China is Overmyer and Chao, *Ethnography in China Today*. For Chengdu at the time of Ba Jin's youth, sources on popular religion are numerous but scattered; no good synthesis has appeared.
66. Su and Tao, "Xuantong yuannian jin'ge renkou maimai shiliao," 69.
67. This is my paraphrase of a memorial by Governor-General Zhou Fu included in ibid., 68.
68. The text of this edict, including the commission's memorial, may be found in ibid., 70–71. Marinus Meijer analyzes it in "Slavery at the End of the Ch'ing Dynasty."
69. Sinn, "Chinese Patriarchy and Women."
70. Hu Huaichen, "Jiefang binü yi." Translation from Ebrey, *Chinese Civilization*, 345–47.
71. Consular dispatches cited in Pedersen, "The Maternalist Moment."
72. Wen, "Muqian Zhongguo zhi nubi jiefang wenti."
73. Ibid.

CHAPTER TWO

1. Joseph Esherick and Mary Backus Rankin review scholarship on Chinese gentry and problems with that term in the introduction to their edited volume *Chinese Local Elites*.
2. See Elman, *Civil Examinations in Late Imperial China*. Henrietta Harrison describes one man's experience studying for and taking the exams in the late nineteenth century in *Man Awakened from Dreams*, chap. 2.
3. Those with no degree could also purchase official rank. For Sichuan examples in the post-Taiping years, see Zelin, "Fu-Rong Salt-Yard Elite."
4. Chen Sihe discusses Ba Jin's family history in *Ren'ge de fazhan*, 8–12. Ba Jin's own memoirs provide most of his evidence.
5. Li Cunguang, *Bainian Ba Jin*, 3–7, confirms Li Daohe's Guangyuan post but does not mention the forty *mu* of land.
6. This rough estimate is based on my reading of Wu Yu's diaries and other sources that provide a sense of the size of Chengdu's elite. Fu's *Chengdu tonglan*, vol. 1, 41–43, lists about ninety family shrines extant in 1909 in Chengdu and its suburbs; we cannot know how many were still being maintained by the families that built them. Ba Jin's family claimed a county in Zhejiang as its hometown and probably contributed to construction and maintenance of a Li family shrine there. If Ba Jin's ancestors had declared themselves Chengdu natives, they would have been ineligible for official positions in Sichuan; the Qing government forbade natives of a province to serve as officials there, to minimize favoritism and local loyalties.
7. Ba Jin, *Qiu*, 229.
8. Bodde and Morris, *Law in Imperial China*. Killing one's father was one of "ten abominations" deserving of the harshest punishment and no pardon; see Mühlhahn, *Criminal Justice in China*, 26.

9. In *Turbulent Stream*, Zhou Botao's son-in-law, Zheng Guoguang, writes an exam-style essay in classical Chinese in which he distinguishes between two of the armies fighting in Chengdu in 1917 on the grounds that one is led by a Sichuan man and one by a general from Guizhou. See *Qiu*, 214. In comments on this scene, Ba Jin claimed that one of his cousins had actually written such an essay; see "Tan *Chun*," 663.

10. Stapleton, *Civilizing Chengdu*, chaps. 4, 5.

11. Chapter Five examines the rise of militarists and how they and their troops affected Chengdu life during Ba Jin's youth. See also Kapp, *Szechwan and the Chinese Republic*.

12. See Stapleton, *Civilizing Chengdu*, 210–12.

13. Gao Juemin states this view strongly in *Qiu*, 108.

14. See particularly Li Jieren's *Dabo*, set in Chengdu during the 1911 Revolution. Li Jieren planned to write a novel about the New Culture movement in Chengdu but, alas, never did. Liu Yubo had been Li Jieren's teacher in 1909 and 1910; see Li Jieren's fond remembrance of Liu Yubo, in which he compared him (favorably, in some respects) to George Bernard Shaw, who was the same age as Liu. Li Jieren, "Jinghuai Liu Yubo xiansheng."

15. Sichuansheng difangzhi bianzuan weiyuanhui, *Sichuansheng zhi: renwu zhi*, 431–33.

16. The source of this line about loyalty and filiality is unclear; some attribute it to the Han philosopher Dong Zhongshu and some to a Yuan-dynasty play. Over the course of the Ming (1368–1644) and Qing (1644–1911) dynasties, it made its way into many texts on Confucian learning.

17. Bays, *China Enters the Twentieth Century*.

18. In *Confucian China and Its Modern Fate*, vol. 3, chap. 1, Joseph Levenson called Liao Ping a "small Confucianist" and, rather prematurely it seems at this point, "the last thinker of the last Confucian school." On Liao's ideas, see also Jensen, *Manufacturing Confucianism*, 177.

19. Stapleton, "Generational and Cultural Fissures," 131–48.

20. Wu Shaobo, "Xu Jiong."

21. Billioud and Thoraval, "Religious Dimension of Confucianism."

22. Wu Shaobo, "Xu Jiong," 282–83.

23. Xu Zixiu, "Dacheng Zhongxuexiao kaixue yanjiang."

24. Jon Kowallis shows that poetry in traditional styles remained popular among some elite communities through the 1930s. See his *Subtle Revolution*. On poetry in Chengdu in the late Qing, see Tan, *Shuzhong wenzhang guan tianxia*, 326–30.

25. On the history of *Amusing Accounts*, see Wang and Cheng, *Sichuan baokan jilan*, vol. 1, 62–63. The magazine is discussed in Jiang and Li, *Jindai Zhongguo chengshi yu dazhong wenhua*.

26. Goldman, *Opera and the City*.

27. Dai Deyuan, "Xiqu gailiang yu Sanqinghui." On late Qing opera reform in general, see Li Hsiao-t'i, *Qingmo de xiaceng shehui qimeng yundong*, chap. 5.

28. Lin Zhiyuan, "Liu Yulao shusan Zhonghechang yishi."

29. For an excellent introduction to Chinese residential architecture and fengshui principles, see Knapp and Lo, *House, Home, Family*.

30. Lang, *Pa Chin*, 7–8.

31. Fu, *Chengdu tonglan*, vol. 1, 24–25.

32. Di Wang analyzes the uses different classes of people made of Shaocheng Park in *Teahouse*; see especially 184–186. Shaocheng Park's history is discussed in Sichuansheng wenshiguan, *Chengdu chengfang guji kao*, 461–62.

33. Crossley, *Orphan Warriors*, 196–97.
34. Sichuansheng difangzhi bianzuan weiyuanhui, *Sichuansheng zhi: renwu zhi*, 470.
35. Fu, *Chengdu tonglan*, vol. 1, 303.
36. Wu Yu, *Wu Yu riji*, vol. 1. Entries for 1912 are on 22–80.
37. Ran, *Wu Yu he ta shenghuo de Minguo shidai*, 49–65.
38. Ibid., 23.
39. For a brief history of teahouses and the new opera venues, see Di Wang, *Street Culture*, 45–50. Wang's *Teahouse* offers a more extensive discussion of the history of teahouses in Chengdu.
40. Ba Jin, "Wo de laojia."
41. John Hersey's novel *The Call* tells the story of the introduction of Western ideas into Chengdu from the viewpoint of Westerners, whom he depicts as divided between liberal "social Gospel" activists and fundamentalists who thought only "that old time religion" was worth teaching the Chinese. In my view, *The Call* offers an inaccurate portrait of Chengdu, although the missionary debates Hersey describes likely did occur in other parts of China.
42. This rapid improvement in local attitudes toward Europeans and Americans in Chengdu is attested to by Canadian medical missionary Omar Kilborn, who lived in Chengdu for decades. Kilborn, "Historical Sketch."
43. The willingness of Chinese people to adopt and adapt foreign technologies between 1911 and 1949 is the major theme of Dikötter's *Exotic Commodities*, which includes examples of the appearance of new technologies in Chengdu, among other cities.
44. Service, *Golden Inches*. Reports from Robert Service covering his years at the Chengdu YMCA (1906–1921) are held in the Kautz Family YMCA Archives.
45. A fascinating collection of photographs and memoirs of Canadian missionaries in Chengdu is Canadian Old Photo Project Team, *Chengdu, Our Home*.
46. *Wu Yu riji*, vol. 1, 162–163 (December 27, 1914), and 541–42, 544, 552, 565–66 (June–November 1920). His daughter's advice is mentioned on p. 565.
47. According to Ba Jin's memoirs, the doctor his mother befriended was English (see Lang, *Pa Chi*, 23); it seems probable she was Canadian, since most medical missionaries in Chengdu at the time were. The doctor may have been Retta Kilborn, who practiced medicine in Chengdu from 1894 to 1933, working at the Methodist Hospital and at West China Union University.
48. John Service comments that, even as their infant daughter lay dying with no Western doctor to call, his parents never considered consulting a Chinese doctor. *Golden Inches*, 28n4.
49. Valuable scholarly English-language accounts of the history of Chinese medicine include Kuriyama, *Expressiveness of the Body*, and Unschuld, *Medicine in China*.
50. On medical practices relating to childbirth, see Yi-Li Wu, *Reproducing Women*.
51. Ba Jin, "Tan *Jia*."
52. Fu, *Chengdu tonglan*, vol. 1, 195–99.
53. Ba Jin, *Chun*, 96–105.
54. Smith, "Ritual in Ch'ing Culture," 287.
55. For an interesting example of such clan rules from the fifteenth century, see Ebrey, *Chinese Civilization*, chap. 54.
56. Ba Jin, *Autobiography of Ba Jin*, 33.
57. Huang Wenxuan, "Minguo wunian Quxian wuniu fenshi an." In support of the truth of this appalling story, Huang cites unidentified archival evidence and an interview

with a witness. He explains that firecrackers fixed to the tails of the water buffalo were set alight to scare them into running.

58. Madsen, "Secularism, Religious Change, Social Conflict," 252.
59. Mao makes this point in *Pa Chin*, 95–96.
60. Rey Chow, "Translator, Traitor," 566. See also Rey Chow, *Women and Chinese Modernity*, 150–54, for more analysis of Ba Jin's depictions of women.
61. Kai-wing Chow, *Rise of Confucian Ritualism*.
62. Lin Yutang, "Chinese Realism and Humour," 92.
63. For an interesting discussion of how the concept of "superstition" spread among educated youth in an early twentieth-century Chinese city, see Poon, *Negotiating Religion in Modern China*.
64. Smith, "Ritual in Ch'ing Culture," 290.

CHAPTER THREE

1. Gao Juehui reflects on his grandfather's rise from relative poverty in chapter 9 of *Family*.
2. Ba Jin, *Yi*, cited in Lang, *Pa Chin*, 34.
3. Ba Jin, *Qiu*, 365. Juexin's employment is also mentioned in Ba Jin, *Chun*, 255.
4. Zarrow, *China in War and Revolution*, provides a good overview of this period.
5. This description of the commercial arcade comes primarily from Chen and Jiang, "Chengdu quanyechang de bianqian." There is a good line drawing of the arcade in Wang, *Street Culture*, 114.
6. McElderry, "Doing Business with Strangers."
7. On Nanjing Road, see Cochran, *Inventing Nanjing Road*.
8. Hewlett, *Forty Years in China*, 89. Romanization of Chinese words in the quotation has been altered to conform to the pinyin system.
9. Juexin's hopes for Juemin may be found in *Qiu*, 271. Ba Jin himself was allowed to study English at the YMCA because his grandfather wanted him to have a career in the postal service. See Mao, *Pa Chin*, 18. On the Chinese postal service, see Xiaoqun Xu, *Chinese Professionals*, 35–36.
10. On the development of the legal profession in China, see Xiaoqun Xu, *Chinese Professionals*. On Chinese legal practitioners before the rise of the modern legal profession, see Macauley, *Social Power and Legal Culture*.
11. Sichuan jingwu gongsuo, *Xuantong ernian shangjie tongji shu*, 282. A copy of this document is in the Chengdu Municipal Archives (no. 5349). Rickshaws were introduced briefly to Chengdu in the last years of the Qing, but few streets were wide enough to accommodate them until military governor Yang Sen launched a street-widening campaign in 1924, when Chunxi Road was constructed.
12. The second volume of Fu's *Chengdu Tonglan* lists the products of this and other government factories and their prices.
13. On early twentieth-century police and sanitation, see Stapleton, *Civilizing Chengdu*, Strand, *Rickshaw Beijing*, and Rogaski, *Hygienic Modernity*.
14. On guilds, see Zelin, "Chinese Business Practice."
15. *Minshi ribao*, December 20, 1927.
16. Honig, *Sisters and Strangers*. On Sichuan's industry and economy in general in the early twentieth century, see Wright, "Distant Thunder."
17. Hubbard, "Geographic Setting of Chengtu," 125.

18. Wu Yu, *Wu Yu riji*, vol. 2, 44–47.
19. Helde, "Chengtu, China, Y.M.C.A. Buildings," Kautz Family YMCA Archives.
20. Gao, "Chengtu Campus Labor Conditions."
21. *Qiu*, 374–75.
22. Ba Jin, "Wo de jige xiansheng."
23. See the description of Chengdu shop life in Di Wang, *Street Culture*, 34–37. Han Suyin describes her ancestors' Chengdu tobacco shop and the role of apprentices in *Crippled Tree*, 37–41. By 1919 activists in eastern China were promoting a movement for educated Chinese youth to work and study in France, with the idea that their labor would help them identify with the needs of the working masses of China. On this movement, see Dirlik, *Anarchism in the Chinese Revolution*, 186–91, and Levine, *Found Generation*, chap. 1. In France in 1927–1928, Ba Jin studied French, attended meetings of an anarchist group, and wrote essays in his small apartment in Paris. See Lang, *Pa Chin*, chap. 6.
24. Ba Jin, "Mujiang Lao Chen."
25. *Xishu xinwen*, July 8, 1915.
26. Gao Sibo, "Chengdu 'er yiliu' can'an yu gongren douzheng." Much of the literature on labor history in China focuses on Shanghai. In addition to Honig, *Sisters and Strangers*, see Perry, *Shanghai on Strike*. On activism among service workers in 1920s Beijing, see Strand, *Rickshaw Beijing*.
27. Ye, "Jiefang qian Chengdu guancai pu yitiao jie."
28. *Wu Yu riji*, vol. 1, 114 (entry for December 6, 1913).
29. Lao Zu, "Fuxingjie yiwen."
30. Some say the white turban so common in the Sichuan countryside and among urban laborers was a tribute to Zhuge Liang, adviser to the king of Shu in the third century. See Crook et al., *Prosperity's Predicament*, 58. Zhuge Liang's clever strategies are a popular feature of the novel *Romance of the Three Kingdoms*; he is among Sichuan's most famous historical figures.
31. Finnane, *Changing Clothes in China*, chap. 4. See also Harrison, *Making of the Republican Citizen*, chap. 3.
32. Dikötter, *Exotic Commodities*, 1. Dikötter discusses the history of motion pictures in Chengdu in chapter 10.
33. Lang, *Chinese Family and Society*, 94.
34. *Chun*, 347–352.
35. Gunde, "Land Tax and Social Change."
36. Wu Yu's conversation with Diao may be found in *Wu Yu riji*, vol. 1, 217–18. Wu Yu lists the property he owns in Xinfan and who is farming it in *Wu Yu riji*, vol. 1, 107–8 (September 13, 1913). A detailed account of how tenant farmers dealt with agents of absentee landlords in one community in Fujian, in southeast China, in the 1930s is included in Yueh-hwa Lin, *Golden Wing*. Leaseholder Hwang Dunglin "would hasten from his store when the landlord's stewards came and entertain them in an urbane and careful manner" so as to impress them into treating him well (p. 14).
37. *Wu Yu riji*, vol. 2, 72 (December 15, 1922).
38. For detailed accounts of agriculture and marketing near Chongqing in southeast Sichuan in the first half of the twentieth century, see Crook et al., *Prosperity's Predicament*, chaps. 1 and 2.
39. Baumler, *Opium under the Republic*, chap. 5. On forced cultivation of opium, see Bianco, "Responses of Opium Growers."

40. Dikötter, Laamann, and Zhou, *Narcotic Culture*. A range of assessments of opium's impact on modern China may be found in Brook and Wakabayashi, *Opium Regimes*. For descriptions of how poppies were grown and opium was harvested in China in the early twentieth century, see Slack, *Opium, State, and Society*, 6–9.

41. The landlord museum was renamed the Liu Family Manor in the post-Mao era, and the exhibitions have changed. See Ho and Li, "Landlord Manor to Red Memorabilia," and Dai Jinhua, "Rewriting the Red Classics."

42. Zelin, *Merchants of Zigong*.

43. Ibid., 230, 244–56.

44. Tim Wright analyzes the effects of the Depression on Sichuan's economy in "Distant Thunder," 720–21. He shows that Sichuan's silk exports declined drastically but notes that they constituted a relatively small part of the provincial economy.

45. Howard, *Workers at War*.

46. Li Jieren, "Weicheng zhuiyi."

47. Xie Fang, "Fan Kongzhou."

48. The story of the building of Chunxi Road is outlined in Jiang Mengbi, "Chunxi Lu de youlai yu fazhan."

49. Helde, report from the Chengdu YMCA for 1925, Kautz Family YMCA Archives.

50. Hardoon's Nanjing Road investments are examined in Cochran, *Inventing Nanjing Road*, which includes photographs of Nanjing Road at various times.

51. Yang Bingde, *Zhongguo jindai chengshi yu jianzhu, 1840–1949*.

52. These petitions and related documents are preserved in the Chengdu Municipal Archives, fond 41, file 8880.

53. *Qiu*, 252–54.

54. Ibid., 510–20, 561.

55. Literary scholar Chen Sihe argues that Ba Jin shifted the focus of *Family* after getting news of his brother's suicide while writing installments of the story. At first, the two pairs of lovers, Juemin/Qin and Juehui/Mingfeng, were at the center of the story; afterward, Juexin and his struggles came to the fore. Chen, *Ren'ge de fazhan*, 144–45.

56. *Qiu*, 548–50.

CHAPTER FOUR

1. Chen Jianyun makes appearances throughout the trilogy; his background is explained most fully in Ba Jin, *Qiu*, 386.

2. Ba Jin, *Autobiography of Ba Jin*, 47.

3. Ba Jin, *Family*, chap. 14; translation by Craig Shaw.

4. *Qiu*, 494–95. Ba Jin based the Zhang Bixiu character on a real Chengdu actor named Li Fengqing, a friend of his uncle. See *Autobiography of Ba Jin*, 46. On pages 189–91 of *Qiu*, Zhang Bixiu tours the Gao compound with another actor friend of Gao Keding. Gao Ke'an calls Zhang Bixiu his "Yang Guifei" (the famous voluptuous consort of the Tang emperor Xuanzong). Wenqing Kang has analyzed Ba Jin's depiction of female impersonators in *Obsession*, 138–40.

5. Bruun, *Fengshui in China*.

6. Some such beliefs current in 1940s Sichuan are described in Crook et al., *Prosperity's Predicament*, chap. 7.

7. For an excellent discussion of Qing economic thought and officials' views on poverty, see Rowe, *Saving the World*, especially 300–303.

8. The authoritative study of philanthropy during the Ming and Qing dynasties is Leung, *Shishan yu jiaohua*. See also, Shue, "Quality of Mercy."
9. Janet Chen, *Guilty of Indigence*, chap. 1.
10. Stapleton, *Civilizing Chengdu*, 126–28.
11. Grace Service, *Golden Inches*.
12. Strand, *Rickshaw Beijing*, chap. 3. See also Janet Chen, *Guilty of Indigence*, 48–54.
13. The 1920s literacy campaigns were part of the Mass Education movement promoted by James Yen (Yan Yangchu), a YMCA leader who had attended high school in Chengdu. On the Chengdu campaign, see Chapter Seven. On the campaigns in general, see Hayford, *To the People*.
14. Ran, *Wu Yu he ta shenghuo de Minguo shidai*, 15. On the fate of garrison families, see also Di Wang, *Street Culture*, 172–73, 191.
15. Di Wang, *Street Culture*, 4; Li Shiping, *Sichuan renkou shi*, 209.
16. Wu Yu, *Wu Yu riji*, vol. 2, 44 (June 30, 1922).
17. Hubbard, "Geographic Setting of Chengtu," 128, 131.
18. Willmott, "Paradox of Gender."
19. Crook et al., *Prosperity's Predicament*, 158. British consul general Meyrick Hewlett wrote of his experience of a dragon dance in Chengdu between 1916 and 1922. Hewlett, *Forty Years in China*, 140.
20. Chü, *Law and Society in Imperial China*; Sommer, *Sex, Law, and Society*, 270–72.
21. Di Wang, *Street Culture*, 119.
22. Hershatter, *Dangerous Pleasures*, especially chaps. 1 and 6. See also Henriot, *Prostitution and Sexuality in Shanghai*.
23. Yeh, "Where Is the Center of Cultural Production?"
24. Stapleton, *Civilizing Chengdu*, chap. 4. In *Autumn*, when the slave girl Qian'er is gravely ill, Gao Juexin prevails on Gao Ke'an to send for a doctor. Ke'an's wife accuses her husband of taking too much interest in Qian'er, whom she calls a "little *jianshihu*" (household under surveillance; i.e., prostitute). Ba Jin, *Qiu*, 394.
25. Tao, "Yin Zhongxi yu Cihuitang."
26. *Chengdu Cihuitang tekan*, 25–26.
27. *Qiu*, 47. Blind musicians also feature in Ba Jin's *Garden of Repose*, 75–76.
28. Tao, "Yin Zhongxi yu Cihuitang," 116.
29. *Zhonghua minguo wuniandu Sichuan sheng neiwu tongji baogaoshu*.
30. On Chinese demographic history and the factors that shaped it, see Lee and Wang, *One Quarter of Humanity*, especially chap. 7. The high number of men in the two counties might also indicate that soldiers based there were included in the count.
31. The inheritance disputes from the 1930s are in the Chengdu local court records in the Chengdu Municipal Archives, fond 94, civil cases 1936–1941. The 1919 police files, also in the Chengdu Municipal Archives, are in fond 93, file 964.
32. Di Wang, *Street Culture*, 200–201.
33. Ibid., 305n33. See also Xiaoxiong Li, *Poppies and Politics*, chaps. 2 and 3.
34. *Qiu*, 490.
35. Xiaoxiong Li, *Poppies and Politics*, 134–37.
36. Xiong Zhuoyun, who was familiar with Chengdu's underworld, published a memoir that discusses opium dens, mainly in the 1930s and 1940s. See Xiong, "Fandong tongzhi shiqi de Chengdu jingcha." On the difficulties of assessing the extent of opium consumption in Chinese history and its implications, see Dikötter, Laamann, and Zhou, *Narcotic Culture*.

37. Foreign Office, *The Opium Trade, 1910–1941*, vol. 5, *1922–1926*, part 19, 3. Cited in Xiaoxiong Li, *Poppies and Politics*, 129.

38. *Zhonghua minguo wuniandu Sichuan sheng neiwu tongji baogaoshu*. These figures do not take into account people listed as "age unknown"; such persons amounted to 2.7 percent of the male and 1.9 percent of the female population.

39. Kinsella and He, *An Aging World*, 37.

40. Li Zhi, "Shuzhi qing."

41. Qin's home is described in chapter 15 of *Family*.

42. Di Wang, *Street Culture*, 198.

43. Hubbard, "Geographic Setting of Chengtu," 131–32.

44. Han Suyin describes public toilets in early twentieth-century Chengdu in *Crippled Tree*, 37–39.

45. Sichuan Provincial Archives, records of the secretariat, file 7557. On the introduction of the discourse and practices of hygiene and sanitation in eastern Chinese cities in the late nineteenth and early twentieth centuries, see Rogaski, *Hygienic Modernity*. She discusses public toilets on 176–77 and 209.

CHAPTER FIVE

1. Kapp, *Szechwan and the Chinese Republic*. On the "warlord era" in general, see McCord, *Power of the Gun*.

2. Sichuansheng wenshiguan, *Sichuan junfa shiliao*.

3. You Xin, "Di sibailiushiqi ci de Chuan zhan."

4. John Stuart Thompson, who was in China in 1911, remarked on the popularity of George Washington as a model at that time. See his *Revolutionizing China*, 210. Yuan Shikai was asked in 1913 if he thought of himself as a Napoleon; he denied it, declaring he wanted to be China's George Washington. See Xiong Yuezhi, "George Washington's Image in China and its Impact on the 1911 Revolution."

5. Stapleton, *Civilizing Chengdu*, chap. 5. A chronology of events related to the 1911 Revolution in Sichuan, compiled by Liang Yuwen and Cai Jisheng, may be found in *Xinhai Sichuan fenglei*, 307–23.

6. This is not the more famous Chen Yi who became foreign minister of the PRC in the 1960s; he was thirty years younger and had a different Chinese character for his given name. I mention that Chen Yi in Chapter Seven.

7. The history of the Yunnan army and its influence in Sichuan is told in Sutton, *Provincial Militarism*.

8. Zhou and Ma, *Xiong Kewu zhuan*.

9. Duara, *Rescuing History*, chap. 6. Xiong Kewu was a main promoter of this movement as was Chen Jiongming of Guangdong. The Sichuan Provincial Assembly hired Nationalist Party leader Dai Jitao—a former student of Xu Zixiu, one of Chengdu's elders and sages—to draft the provincial constitution, as I mention in Chapter Seven.

10. Joseph Beech, president of West China Union University, sent accounts of the 1923 fighting to the US consul in Chongqing. Letters dated April 7 and May 4, 1923, US consular records, Chungking, official correspondence 84.620-800. See also Zhou, *Minguo Chuanshi jiyao*, vol. 1, 293, and Zhang Huichang, "Yi, san, bianjun yu san, qi, ershiyi shi zhi zhan."

11. Kapp, *Szechwan and the Chinese Republic*, chap. 2.

12. Liu Wenhui dominated affairs in Xikang until 1949, when he shifted his allegiance to the Communists.

13. Zhou, *Minguo Chuanshi jiyao*, vol. 1, 293.

14. Huang Juegao, "Wo canjia Chuan Dian Qian junfa Chengdu hangzhan jianwen." Other eyewitness accounts may be found in Sichuansheng wenshiguan, *Sichuan junfa shiliao*, vol. 1, 138–51.

15. Huang Juegao, "Wo canjia Chuan Dian Qian junfa Chengdu hangzhan jianwen," 219. Huang cites a Red Cross report on cleanup after the fighting; it is excerpted in Sichuansheng wenshiguan, *Sichuan junfa shiliao*, vol. 1, 146–49.

16. Gu, "Jindai chubanjia Fan Kongzhou."

17. Ba Jin, *Yi*, cited in Lang, *Pa Chin*, 28.

18. Wu Yu, *Wu Yu riji*, vol. 1, 336–57 (August 21 to November 19, 1917).

19. Tang, "Wu Yu yanjiu," 98.

20. On the history of the term "warlord," see Waldron, "Warlord." *Qiu ba* echoes an expression meaning "bastard": *wang ba*, whose literal meaning is "turtle."

21. Zhong, *Liu Shiliang waizhuan*.

22. *West China Missionary News*, September 1917.

23. Wei Yingtao, *Sichuan jindaishi gao*, 755.

24. At the time, the Standard Oil Company of New York operated three retail kerosene stores in Chengdu and a large storage facility outside the walls. D. E. Kydd, manager of Standard Oil in Chengdu, reported in June 1918 that "90% of the people in [Chengdu] are using Native Oils, not because they prefer them but because there is no kerosene or very little on the market" due to restrictions on bringing it into the city. US consular records, Chungking, official correspondence 84.800-811.9. The letter is dated June 29, 1918.

25. See, for example, Hanson dispatch 137 to Reinsch, April 3, 1918, which describes looting in Chengdu on February 19, 1918. US consular records, Chungking, official correspondence 84.800-811.9.

26. Order from Li Yuanhong, dated May 17, 1917, cited in Zhou, *Minguo Chuanshi jiyao*, vol. 1, 183.

27. Reports from the early Republic in US consular files from Chongqing include a steady litany of cautions against travel to Sichuan because of the insecurity of roads and rivers.

28. David Strand discusses this phenomenon in regard to Beijing in *Rickshaw Beijing*, chap. 9.

29. Hewlett, *Forty Years in China*, 100–128.

30. Letter from Hewlett to US Consul G. C. Hanson dated July 24, 1917, and letter from Service to Hanson dated August 21, 1917, US National Archives, Record Group 84, Correspondence File, vols. 68 and 72.

31. Joseph Beech letter to the US consul, May 4 1923, US consular records, Chungking, official correspondence 84.711-800.

32. On foreign arms sales to Chinese militarists in the 1920s, see Chan, *Arming the Chinese*.

33. Hu Lanqi, for example, received such an education in the years after 1911. See Stapleton, "Hu Lanqi."

34. For a more extended discussion of the Gowned Brothers in Chengdu and the region, see Stapleton, "Age of 'Secret Societies.'" The Gowned Brothers were also called the Hanliu (Descendants of the Han) and Gelaohui (Society of Brothers and Elders). Cheng, "Collaboration or Suppression," analyzes newly emerging archival sources on this history.

35. Sokobin dispatch 99 to Tenney, January 8, 1920, US consular records, Chungking, official correspondence 84.620-810.5.

36. Ba Jin, *Family*, chap. 10; Craig Shaw translation.

37. Josselyn dispatch 133 to the Secretary of State, January 28, 1921, US consular records, Chungking, official correspondence 84.620-800. The clashes between Chengdu students and soldiers were reported in Shanghai's *North China Herald*; see Lang, *Pa Chin*, 61–62.

38. Zhou, *Minguo Chuanshi jiyao*, vol. 1, 280–81. Numerous petitions and police reports on these conflicts are available in the Chengdu Municipal Archives, fond 93, section 6, file 227.

39. Wasserstrom, *Student Protests*, especially chap. 2. Fabio Lanza writes that the post-1919 student associations differed from those of 1895 because they maintained a critical distance between themselves and the state. Lanza, *Behind the Gate*. In Chengdu, that critical spirit was not as evident as it was in Beijing, except in the case of a few people, such as Li Jieren.

40. Li Jieren lists Sun Shaojing among the founders of the Chengdu branch of the Young China Association in 1919 and writes that they were all between twenty-three and thirty-one years old. Li Jieren, "Huiyi Shaonian Zhongguo Xuehui Chengdu fenhui zhi suoyou chengli." See Chapter Seven for more on this organization.

41. *Wu Yu riji*, vol. 2, 360 (April 27, 1927).

42. Kapp, *Szechwan and the Chinese Republic*, 10.

43. On the question of sources for studying soldiers in the republican period, see the introduction to Lary, *Warlord Soldiers*.

44. Chengdu Municipal Archives, fond 93, section 6, file 192.

45. During the April 1917 fighting, Wu Yu's diary notes that patrols came regularly through his neighborhood, searching for runaway soldiers. *Wu Yu riji*, vol. 1, 301 (April 19, 1917).

46. Myers dispatch 55 to Reinsch, January 24, 1917, US consular records, Chungking, official correspondence 84.711.2-861.3. Appendix 6 of Lary's *Warlord Soldiers* includes an English translation of Sichuan writer Sha Ting's short story about press-ganged porters in Sichuan.

47. Lary, *Warlord Soldiers*, 16–19.

48. Li Jieren, "Bing dabo Chen Zhenwu de yuepu."

49. The influence of Lu Xun's "True Story of Ah Q" is evident, including in the preface, which explains the narrator's use of the word *yuepu* (monthly chronicle) as an alternative to the standard *nianpu* (yearly chronicle) in the title, just as Lu Xun explained his use of the term *zhengzhuan* (true story) in the Ah Q tale. Chen Zhenwu's first experience of groping a woman bears some similarity to Ah Q's encounter with the little Buddhist nun.

CHAPTER SIX

1. For a discussion of the idea of the New Woman, see Wang Zheng's introduction to *Women in the Chinese Enlightenment*. Literary scholar Jin Feng argues that Ba Jin depicted Qin as a failed revolutionary, since she is unable to break with her family, as Juehui does. Feng sees Qin as the flawed female foil to Ba Jin's male hero (whom she also views as flawed but, unlike Qin, able to overcome his weaknesses). Feng does not discuss Ba Jin's depiction of Gao Shuying in *Spring*, but Shuying is certainly not as powerful a character

as Qin. I suspect, though, that few readers have seen Qin as deficient in the way Feng suggests she is. See Feng, *New Woman*, chap. 4.

2. Translation by Craig Shaw.

3. Wang Zheng analyzes the development of the discourse of women's oppression in Chinese history in the introduction to *Women in the Chinese Enlightenment*. For a guide to the vast body of scholarship in English on women in twentieth-century China, see Hershatter, *Women in China's Long Twentieth Century*.

4. Ko, *Cinderella's Sisters*, 10.

5. Ho, "Women in Chinese History." Dikötter, Laamann, and Zhou examined this unknowing alliance between radical Chinese nationalists and Euro-American Christian missionaries in regard to the discourse surrounding opium addiction in *Narcotic Culture*.

6. Hu Lanqi, *Hu Lanqi huiyilu*, 5–6. The *Three-Character Classic* is discussed in Thomas Lee, *Education in Traditional China*, 460–61. Ba Jin also learned to read using the *Three-Character Classic* as well as a revised version that included facts on world geography. *Autobiography of Ba Jin*, 22.

7. Fu, *Chengdu tonglan*, vol. 1, 111.

8. *Autobiography of Ba Jin*, 12–13, 25–26.

9. Ba Jin, *Family*, chap. 11. The best account in English of Qing-era women's education is Mann, *Talented Women of the Zhang Family*. The family described in Mann's book was not from Chengdu but from the wealthier Jiangnan region of China around Shanghai.

10. Xue Tao's life is described in Lee and Wiles, *Biographical Dictionary of Chinese Women*, 520–25. The Xue Tao Well is mentioned as a local landmark in the 1909 Chengdu encyclopedia (Fu, *Chengdu tonglan*, vol. 1, 18) and became a prominent feature of Chengdu's Wangjianglou Park in recent decades.

11. Mann, *Talented Women of the Zhang Family*. For detailed accounts of the late imperial shift in gender ideals, see also Mann, *Precious Records*, and Sommer, *Sex, Law, and Society*.

12. Ba Jin, "Guanyu *Jia*"; this excerpt, translated by Olga Lang, is quoted in her *Pa Chin*, 16. *Lives of Virtuous Women*, written during the Han dynasty by Liu Xiang (79–8 BCE), was reprinted in many editions over the centuries. See Kinney, *Exemplary Women*.

13. Joan Judge examines the variety of images of model women available in late Qing China in *Precious Raft of History*.

14. On Qiu Jin's career, see Edwards, *Gender, Politics, and Democracy*, 61–64. A fuller account of Qiu Jin's life and posthumous fame may be found in Rankin, *Early Chinese Revolutionaries*.

15. The classic work on literacy and the spread of information through Chinese communities in the Qing (which remains relevant for the early twentieth century) is Johnson, "Communication, Class, and Consciousness." On teahouses and the spread of gossip in Chengdu, see Di Wang, *Teahouse*, chap. 8. In *Spring*, rumors about the bad character of Gao Shuying's potential fiancé travel into the Gao residence via the servants. Ba Jin, *Chun*, 5 and 33.

16. John Fitzgerald analyzes the controversy over the meaning of *A Doll's House* in *Awakening China*, 99–102. Taciana Fisac points out that 1950s editions of *Family* cut out references to more "frivolous" foreign literary works, such as Oscar Wilde's *Lady Windermere's Fan*, mentioned in the 1930s editions as popular among young members of the Gao

family. Additional references to Ibsen's work replaced them. Fisac, "Rewriting Modern Chinese Literature," 140.

17. Lang, *Pa Chin*, 237–245.

18. Hu Ying, *Tales of Translation*, chap. 3.

19. In *Autumn*, Gao Juehui is said to have written an article on female Russian revolutionaries while in Shanghai. Ba Jin, *Qiu*, 92.

20. On Tang Qunying, see Strand, *Unfinished Republic*, chap. 3; on Emma Goldman's essays in Chinese publications, see Dirlik, *Anarchism in the Chinese Revolution*, 220–21; on Yosano Akiko, see Wang Zheng, *Women in the Chinese Enlightenment*, 51–52.

21. Stapleton, *Civilizing Chengdu*, chap. 5; Hu Lanqi, *Hu Lanqi huiyilu*, 11.

22. Translation by Craig Shaw.

23. In addition to Ko's *Cinderella's Sisters*, see her *Every Step a Lotus*, which focuses on women's shoemaking but gives a concise introduction to the origins of footbinding and various explanations for its spread during the Qing.

24. Ko, *Cinderella's Sisters*, 14.

25. "Guanyu *Jia*."

26. *Qiu*, 35.

27. Fu Chongju mentions Mrs. Little and Mrs. Kilborn in his encyclopedia, *Chengdu tonglan*, vol. 1, 112. Retta's husband, Omar Kilborn, also a medical missionary, cited Chengdu's anti-footbinding movement in "Historical Sketch," 50–51. Hu Lanqi discusses the Natural Foot Society briefly, attributing its establishment to Luo Xuzhi, principal of a public high school for girls. Hu points out that in Hakka communities in eastern suburbs of Chengdu the women had never bound their feet. On Sichuan's Hakkas, see Han, *Crippled Tree*, 22–28, and Sun Xiaofen, *Sichuan de Kejiaren yu Kejia wenhua*.

28. Fu, *Chengdu tonglan*, vol. 1, 111–13. I have not located copies of the broadsheet Fu describes. Alicia Little founded the first Natural Foot Society in Shanghai in 1895 (using the word *zu* for foot, not *jiao*). See Ko, *Cinderella's Sisters*, 16. Little subsequently moved to Chongqing with her husband—who founded a steamship company to navigate the Yangzi River—and visited Chengdu occasionally. She describes her anti-footbinding campaign—including a meeting of the Chongqing branch of the Society in the late 1890s—in her *Intimate China*, chap. 7.

29. *Guomin gongbao*, April 2, 1918. Omar Kilborn, writing in 1916, remarked that the practice had declined since he arrived in Sichuan in 1891 but would take years to die out. He did not compare Chengdu to the rest of Sichuan, but Chengdu missionaries never raised the issue of footbinding in reports in the *West China Missionary News*. Kilborn, "Historical Sketch."

30. See the data from interviews with 3,300 Sichuan women with bound feet in Brown et al., "Marriage Mobility and Footbinding." Gates argues that footbinding was most prevalent in parts of Sichuan where spinning and weaving were important sources of income.

31. In *Autumn*, Madam Wang orders servants to sanitize the well in which Shuzhen committed suicide; Shuzhen's mother Madam Shen points out bitterly that porters bring drinking water in from the river. A young male cousin retorts that the servants use well water to cook the rice. *Qiu*, 481.

32. *Family*, chap. 15. In *Autumn*, the widow of the Gaos' cousin Zhou Mei weeps over her fate to remain a widow all her life, and Juexin thinks of the phrase "cannibalistic moral teachings" (*chiren de lijiao*), which, inspired by Lu Xun's story "A Madman's Diary,"

Wu Yu made famous in an essay in *New Youth*. *Qiu*, 525–26. Earlier in that novel, Qin advises Zhou Mei's sister Zhou Yun to read that essay by Wu Yu. *Qiu*, 35.

33. On Qing-era family ideals, see Mann, "Grooming a Daughter for Marriage."

34. Jerome Ch'en, *China and the West*, 385; Witke, "Mao Tse-tung, Women and Suicide." English translations of Mao's essay and many other May Fourth–era writings about women and family issues are available in Lan and Fong, *Women in Republican China*.

35. Glosser, *Chinese Visions of Family and State, 1915–1953*, 64–67.

36. See, for example, Hu Lanqi, *Hu Lanqi huiyilu*, 16.

37. Wang Lüping, *Sichuan jindai xinwen shi*, 335.

38. Stapleton, "Hu Lanqi."

39. Glosser, *Chinese Visions of Family and State, 1915–1953*, 62–63.

40. Margaret Kuo's *Intolerable Cruelty* examines how the legal system changed in China in the 1930s, giving women grounds on which to divorce and claim new rights within their marriages.

41. Wu Yu, *Wu Yu riji*, vol. 1, 541–42, 544, 552, 565–66 (June–September 1920). See also Gong, "Wang Guangqi yu Wu Rouying guanxi kao."

42. Furth, "From Birth to Birth."

43. Dikötter, *Sex, Culture, and Modernity*.

44. Ling Ma, "Negotiating Guilt." For a history of 1920s debates about women's sexuality, see Barlow, *Question of Women*, chap. 3.

45. On childbirth customs and practices in Chinese history, see Yi-Li Wu, *Reproducing Women*.

46. *Wu Yu riji*, vol. 2, 52 (September 12, 1922).

47. Ibid., 458 (July 6, 1929). This daughter was not living in Chengdu, and Wu Yu learned of her death through a letter from her husband.

48. Morse, *Three Crosses*, 48.

49. *Chun*, 177–190; *Qiu*, 378.

50. Hu Lanqi, *Hu Lanqi huiyilu*, 2–4.

51. Di Wang, *Street Culture*, 90.

52. Archibald Little, *Gleanings*, 166. Lamas are Tibetan Buddhist monks; "Man-tse aborigines" most likely refers to people now known as members of the Yi ethnic group.

53. Di Wang, *Street Culture*, 59, 91.

54. Hu Lanqi, *Hu Lanqi huiyilu*, 14–15.

55. Shao Ying, "Chubanjia Fan Kongzhou."

56. Wang Di, *Street Culture*, 181. A description of the women's balcony in a Chengdu theater appears in *Chun*, 369.

57. *Guomin gongbao*, March 14, 1917.

58. Although Ba Jin left Chengdu in 1923, he would have learned of Yang Sen's actions in Chengdu from newspaper accounts and letters from friends and family—Yang Sen's rule over Chengdu most likely influenced the plot of *Turbulent Stream*. I discuss Yang Sen's year of rule in Chengdu in detail in *Civilizing Chengdu*, chap. 7.

59. Stapleton, "Hu Lanqi."

60. *Guomin gongbao*, July 8, 1924.

61. My account of Shu Xincheng's Chengdu experience is based on two books he published: *Shuyou xinying*, which includes excerpts of letters he wrote to his wife at the time and statements he gave to Chongqing newspapers, and his autobiography, *Wo he jiaoyu*, chap. 10. The affair was reported on in detail by Chengdu's *Guomin gongbao* in

May 1925 and then discussed later that summer in the context of a debate over the idea of "tolerance" by scholars associated with the Beijing-based journal *Yusi*; see the issues numbered 34, 37, and 41.

62. Liu Fang also persuaded the student association from her home county, Meishan, to intervene on her behalf. See its public statement in *Guomin gongbao*, May 14, 1925.

63. On the debates about "talent" and women before the twentieth century, see Ho, "Cultivation of Female Talent."

64. *Dachenghui conglu*; on the Empress Dowager's career, see a book with a title that would surely infuriate Xu Zixiu: Jung Chang, *Empress Dowager Cixi: The Concubine Who Launched Modern China*.

65. The famous theorist Liang Qichao criticized Chinese women for not contributing to the nation's wealth. See Glosser, *Chinese Visions of Family and State*, 7.

66. Wang Zheng, *Women in the Chinese Enlightenment*, chap. 1. Another prominent Shanghai career woman born in 1900 is profiled in Natasha Chang's *Bound Feet and Western Dress*. The author's great-aunt Chang Yu-i served as vice president of the Shanghai Women's Bank after her husband, the famous poet Xu Zhimo, divorced her.

67. Wang Zheng, *Women and the Chinese Enlightenment*, 206.

68. *Guomin gongbao*, May 22, 1923.

69. *Wu Yu riji*, vol. 2, 77 (January 2, 1923).

70. Hu Lanqi, *Hu Lanqi huilu*, 10.

71. *Wu Yu riji*, vol. 2, 64 (November 11, 1922).

72. *Qiu*, 146–47. In contrast to *Turbulent Stream*, *Dream of the Red Chamber* is far more revealing about the finances of the family concerned; the Jia family funds are managed largely by the wife of Jia Lian, who is the equivalent of the Gao Juexin character in *Turbulent Stream*, that is, the eldest son of the eldest son of the patriarch.

73. Bernhardt, *Women and Property in China*, chap. 2.

74. *Wu Yu riji*, vol. 2, 454 (May 11, 1929).

75. Stapleton, "Generational and Cultural Fissures," 141.

76. *Chun*, 69.

77. Gilmartin, *Engendering the Chinese Revolution*, 99; Lung-kee Sun, "Politics of Hair." In *Turbulent Stream*, the issue of bobbed hair is featured most prominently in *Autumn*, when the anarchist society the young people join (Junshe) encourages its female members to cut their hair (*Qiu*, 267–69) and when Qin and Shuhua cut their hair (*Qiu*, 559).

78. Hu Lanqi, *Hu Lanqi huiyilu*, 16–17. On sewing and fashion in early twentieth-century China, see Finnane, *Changing Clothes in China*.

79. *Minshi ribao*, March 21, 1929.

CHAPTER SEVEN

1. Olga Lang notes that Ba Jin made Gao Juemin more politically active in *Spring* and *Autumn* to fill the gap left by the departure for Shanghai of Gao Juehui. She quotes Ba Jin's view that the Gao family "could not remain without a young man full of youthful energy.... Everything in the novel would be only gray." Lang, *Pa Chin*, 258. Ba Jin discusses Juemin's political activism in "Tan *Qiu*," 686–87.

2. Shaw, "Changes in *The Family*"; Fisac, "Rewriting Modern Chinese Literature"; Lang, *Pa Chin*, 265–75.

3. A review of literature on the May Fourth movement may be found in the intro-

duction to Chow et al., *Beyond the May Fourth Paradigm*. Three classic English-language studies are Tse-tsung Chow, *May Fourth Movement*, Yu-sheng Lin, *Crisis of Chinese Consciousness*, and Schwarcz, *Chinese Enlightenment*.

4. An excellent study of the politics of the 1920s and 1930s that does not overemphasize the Nationalist and Communist Parties is Fitzgerald, *Awakening China*.

5. For narrative accounts of the events in Beijing, see Spence, *Search for Modern China*, 293–94, 310–19, and Manela, *Wilsonian Moment*, chap. 9.

6. A detailed history of the May Fourth movement in Chengdu may be found in Deng et al., *Sichuan qingnian yundong shi gao*, part 1. Archival documents and other materials from the period have been reproduced in Zhonggong Sichuan shengwei dangshi gongzuo weiyuanhui, *Wusi yundong zai Sichuan*.

7. Zhongping Chen, "May Fourth and Provincial Warlords," especially p. 146.

8. *Sichuan Journal* issued its first edition July 1, 1918, according to a timeline of important events in Sichuan in that year published in its 1919 New Year's edition. This timeline includes the news that the commercial arcade had burned to the ground. "Sichuan yinianlai dashiji." In 1924 Shu Xincheng investigated the circulation of east China papers in Chengdu; he reports that about a hundred copies of Shanghai and Beijing newspapers sold in the city on a daily basis. *Shuyou xinying*, 163. It would usually have taken several weeks for eastern papers to arrive in Chengdu.

9. Li Shiwen, *Li Jieren de shengping he chuangzuo*, 11–13. Li Jieren's collected works were published in seventeen volumes in 2011 by Chengdu's Sichuan wenyi chubanshe.

10. On *Sichuan Journal*, see Wang Lüping, *Sichuan baokan wushinian jicheng*, 69. Wang Guangqi was a founder of the Young China Association in the wake of the May Fourth incident. Li Jieren set up a Chengdu branch of the society in the summer of 1919, which is how he came to be known to Shu Xincheng, whom Li Jieren saved from arrest in 1924 (see Chapter Six). Wang Guangqi spent the last decade and a half of his life in Europe, where he became a famous musicologist. On his life and thought, see Levine, *Found Generation*, 43–48 and 138–41.

11. Zhang Xiushu's memoirs, cited by Li Shiwen, in *Li Jieren de shengping he chuangzuo*, 13.

12. Zhongping Chen, "May Fourth and Provincial Warlords," citing reports in the Shanghai newspapers *Shenbao* and *Shibao*. The *Sichuan Journal*'s timeline of 1918 Sichuan events notes that Chengdu had been festooned with flags celebrating the end of World War I on November 14, 1918, so clearly the war was followed closely there. See "Sichuan yinianlai dashiji," 75.

13. Zhonggong Sichuan shengwei dangshi gongzuo weiyuanhui, *Wusi yundong zai Sichuan*, 215–33. In 1930s editions of *Family*, chapter 8 depicts people in Chengdu as indifferent or hostile to student activists trying to enforce a boycott of Japanese goods. That section was cut from 1950s versions.

14. *North China Herald*, February 14, 1920.

15. Lang discusses the origins of Ba Jin's anarchism in *Pa Chin*, chap. 2. My account of Ba Jin's political education in this chapter is indebted to her analysis. One source Lang did not use, but that corroborates her account, is Jiang Jun, "Lu Jianbo." Lu Jianbo, like Ba Jin, was born in 1904. He joined an anarchist group in Luzhou, east of Chongqing, and became Ba Jin's close friend and colleague during the mid-1920s in Shanghai.

16. On anarchism in China, see Dirlik, *Anarchism in the Chinese Revolution*, Zarrow, *Anarchism and Chinese Culture*, and Krebs, *Shifu*. All mention Ba Jin briefly.

17. On Kropotkin's life and ideas, see Krebs, *Shifu*, 20–23.
18. Translation by H. M. Hyndman (Chicago: Charles H. Kerr, 1899), Anarchist Archives, http://dwardmac.pitzer.edu/Anarchist_Archives/kropotkin/appealtoyoung.html.
19. Lang, *Pa Chin*, 45–46; Lang speculates (292–93n30) that Ba Jin's copy of *An Appeal to Youth* was a pamphlet produced in the 1910s in Guangzhou by the anarchist publishing house Minsheng (Voice of the People), based on a translation made by Li Shizeng in Paris before 1911. See Tan, *Zoujin Ba Jin de shijie*, 44–49.
20. Lang, *Pa Chin*, 293n45; on the Truth Society, see Dirlik, *Anarchism in the Chinese Revolution*, 173–74.
21. Lang, *Pa Chin*, 47; Lang quotes from a 1910 edition of Goldman's essays.
22. Dirlik, *Anarchism in the Chinese Revolution*, 28, 30.
23. Stapleton, "Generational and Cultural Fissures," 137.
24. Chen Sihe, *Ren'ge de fazhan*, 48–50. A history of *Bi-weekly* by Wu Xianyou, the real-life model for the character Zhang Huiru in *Turbulent Stream*, is included in Zhonggong Sichuan shengwei dangshi gongzuo weiyuanhui, *Wusi yundong zai Sichuan*, 678–80.
25. The story is told in memoirs by Wu Xianyou, excerpted in Zhonggong Sichuan shengwei dangshi gongzuo weiyuanhui, *Wusi yundong zai Sichuan*, 679. Wu Xianyou notes that a delay in closing *Bi-weekly* occurred because police confused the journal with a publication of the same name produced by a local high school and sent the order to stop publishing to the high school journal.
26. A letter Ba Jin wrote to one of his friends in the Equity Society in September of 1921 is quoted in Chen Sihe, *Ren'ge de fazhan*, 51–53. In it, Ba Jin reports on news from anarchist groups all over the country. It is clear he had a fairly extensive network of correspondents.
27. Olga Lang points out the irony of Ba Jin ordering a servant to accompany him on what he considered to be a risky mission to publicize International Workers' Day. Lang, *Pa Chin*, 64–65, 297n13.
28. For the publishing history of *Bi-weekly*, *Voice of the Common People*, and similar Chengdu journals, see Wang Lüping, *Sichuan baokan wushinian jicheng*. Wang was unable to provide distribution figures for many of the short-lived periodicals.
29. Translated by Craig Shaw.
30. On Tolstoy in China, see Widmer, "Qu Qiubai and Russian Literature." Mahatma Gandhi exchanged letters with Tolstoy in 1909–1910 as he was developing his strategies of passive resistance to British rule in India; Gandhi's *satyagraha* concept, however, was not widely known in China in the 1920s.
31. Liu Bannong's career at *New Youth* is discussed in Chen Pingyuan, *Touches of History*, chap. 2. For Liu Bannong's critique of "old fashioned" writers, see Hill, *Lin Shu, Inc.*, chap. 7.
32. Ba Jin, *Autobiography of Ba Jin*, 69–73.
33. Wu Yu, *Wu Yu riji*, vol. 1, 23–24. Wu Yu edited the party's newspaper, *Zhengjinbao*, until it folded after a month or two. The Progressive Politics Party combined with other local parties to form Sichuan's branch of the Gonghe (Republican) Party in 1912. See Wei Yingtao, *Sichuan jindaishi gao*, 743–45.
34. In Wade-Giles romanization, the party's name is spelled Kuomintang (KMT for short), still often seen in English. Biographies of the two predominant GMD leaders, Sun Yat-sen and Chiang Kai-shek, offer good accounts of the history of the party at the center: Bergère, *Sun Yat-sen*, and Taylor, *Generalissimo: Chiang Kai-shek*.

35. A good short account of the Comintern interaction with Chinese Nationalists and Communists and the 1927 split is provided in Spence, *To Change China*, chap. 7.

36. Hirayama, "Chinese Youth Party in Sichuan"; Levine, *Found Generation*, 179–84.

37. Zhang Qun is most famous for having been mayor of Shanghai in 1929–1930 and governor of Sichuan from 1940 to 1945 during the war with Japan. After the removal of Chiang Kai-shek's government to Taiwan in 1949, he continued to serve as a high-ranking official and played a prominent role in Taiwan politics almost until his death at age 101. Boorman and Howard, *Biographical Dictionary of Republican China*, vol. 1, 47–52.

38. Zhou Kaiqing, "Zhang Yuejun xiansheng yu Sichuan." According to reports in the *Guomin gongbao* (October 8, 1919, and July 27, 1920), Zhang Qun took up office as police commissioner in October 1919 and resigned in July 1920.

39. Zhang Liyuan, "Dai Jitao"; Boorman and Howard, *Biographical Dictionary of Republican China*, vol. 3, 200–205. On Sun Yat-sen's many appeals for support to various Sichuan militarists, the best source is Zhou, *Minguo Chuanshi jiyao*, vol. 1. Zhou's timeline of Sichuan history makes extensive use of GMD archives.

40. Duara, *Rescuing History*, chap. 6. On Sichuan's participation in the federalist movement, see Li Dajia, *Minguo chunian de liansheng zizhi yundong*, 84–87 and 118–19; Zhou and Ma, *Xiong Kewu zhuan*, 192–211.

41. Yang Shiyuan, "Wu Yuzhang." Wu Yuzhang's memoirs of the 1911 Revolution were published in English as *The Revolution of 1911: A Great Democratic Revolution of China*.

42. Despite sharing a surname, Zhang Lan and Zhang Jian were not related. On Nanchong's Zhang Lan, see Boorman and Howard, *Biographical Dictionary of Republican China*, vol. 1, 82–83. On Nantong's Zhang Jian, see Köll, *Cotton Mill to Business Empire*, and Qin Shao, *Culturing Modernity*.

43. Wang Shouxi, "Yuan Shiyao"; Deng, "Wang Youmu." Wu Xianyou recalled that Wang Youmu invited the anarchists who had written for *Bi-weekly* to a meeting in 1922 and tried to persuade them to abandon anarchism for Marxism: they debated through the night, but neither side persuaded the other. Wu does not mention whether Ba Jin was there. Zhonggong Sichuan shengwei dangshi gongzuo weiyuanhui, *Wusi zai Sichuan*, 680.

44. In the historiography of twentieth-century China, this Sichuan trip by Dai Jitao is most famous because of his attempt to commit suicide by jumping from his boat in the Yangzi River on the way to Sichuan; his miraculous rescue by a fisherman is said to have led him to Buddhism, from then on a lifelong interest. See Lu, *Re-Understanding Japan*, 146–48.

45. Deng, "Wang Youmu," 11–12.

46. In 1925 Wu Yuzhang joined the Communist Party in Beijing and renewed his membership in the Nationalist Party. When the United Front ended in 1927, he traveled to the Soviet Union, where he lived for ten years, teaching in the Communist University of the Toilers of the Far East. During the war with Japan, he headed most of the institutions of higher education in the Communist base area in Yan'an. After 1949 he became president of Beijing's Renmin University. Boorman and Howard, *Biographical Dictionary of Republican China*, vol. 3, 465–67.

47. Both Sichuan Teachers College and Chengdu University later merged into Sichuan University. See Sichuan daxue xiaoshi bianxiezu, *Sichuan daxue shi gao*.

48. Wang Shouxi, "Yuan Shiyao," 29.

49. Hirayama, "Chinese Youth Party in Sichuan," 223–24.

50. On politics in Chongqing in 1927, see Kapp, *Szechwan and the Chinese Republic*, 77–81.

51. Yingcong Dai, *Sichuan Frontier and Tibet*.

52. Liu Xianzhi, *Chengdu Man-Mengzu shilüe*, 38–40. Conducting research in Chengdu in 1990, I was fortunate to meet Liu Xianzhi, a member of a Mongol Banner family who grew up in Chengdu's garrison and witnessed the 1911 Revolution as a boy of ten.

53. The history of Chengdu's Muslim communities is discussed in issues of the *Chengdushi Yisilanjiao xiehui hexun*.

54. Ling, "Qingmo Minchu Chengdu Zhongwai xueshu wenhua jiaoliu."

55. Beech, "University Beginnings."

56. Shu, *Shuyou xinying*, 165–68.

57. *Guomin gongbao*, June 16, 1920. For more on the YMCA, see Stapleton, *Civilizing Chengdu*, 213–16. Chengdu YMCA secretaries' reports in the Kautz Family YMCA Archives describe their activities in detail.

58. Chen Weixin's urban construction proposals were published in *Guomin gongbao* in April and May 1924. The YMCA supported the Mass Education movement and helped stage a parade of 8,000 participants in literacy classes in 1924. A. J. Brace, Annual Report from the Chengdu YMCA for 1924, January 10, 1925, Kautz Family YMCA Archives.

59. Stapleton, *Civilizing Chengdu*, chap. 7.

60. Wang and Deng, "Qingnian Chen Yi zai Chengdu xunqiu 'gongye jiuguo' de fendou licheng."

61. Hay, *Asian Ideas of East and West*, 142–70. On the range of conservative thinking in 1920s China, see the essays in Furth, *Limits of Change*.

62. Ba Jin, "Haizhuqiao."

63. Earl Dome, Quarterly Report from the Chengdu YMCA, September 30, 1921, Kautz Family YMCA Archives.

64. The Chengdu correspondent of the *North China Herald* claimed in June 1926 that students had organized a three-day commemoration of the May Thirtieth incident on its first anniversary, when the body of a Sichuan man killed in the incident was returned for burial. He added, "It is reported that when the students approached [merchants and gentry] regarding an anti-foreign demonstration, the reply was that whatever foreigners might be in other parts, the foreigners of Chengtu were law-abiding, that they had harmed no one, that they had been a financial asset to the city, and that they would not countenance any movement directed against them." "Quiet May 30 at Chengdu," *North China Herald*, June 1, 1926.

65. Li Jianmin, "Minguo shiwunian Sichuan Wanxian can'an."

66. "Conditions in Chengtu," *North China Herald*, November 13, 1926. An account of how the mid-1920s anti-imperialist movement affected the Changsha campus of Yale-in-China may be found in Spence, *To Change China*, chap. 6.

67. On Lu Zuofu's career, see Liu Zhonglai, *Lu Zuofu*, and Zhang Jin, *Quanli chongtu yu bianqe*.

68. Liu Zhonglai, *Lu Zuofu*, 10–11.

69. Reinhardt, "Decolonisation."

70. Lang, *Pa Chin*, 207–14.

71. Ibid., 121–24; Chen Sihe, *Ren'ge de fazhan*, 99–105; Tan, *Zoujin Ba Jin de shijie*, 121–30.

EPILOGUE

1. Mae Franking, an American who married a Chinese classmate and joined his extended family in south China in the late 1910s, offers an interesting contrast to Ba Jin's views on Chinese families. She wrote that the family lived in perfect harmony (though the patriarch, her father-in-law, was frequently in the Philippines, managing his trading company). She enjoyed learning how to be a good Chinese daughter-in-law and playing the role as well as she could. Franking and Porter, *My Chinese Marriage*.

2. Glosser, *Chinese Visions of Family and State*, 34.

3. On the Nationalist government's policies on vagrancy, see Lipkin, *Useless to the State*, chaps. 2 and 3.

4. Wen, "Muqian Zhongguo zhi nubi jiefang wenti." This argument echoes the position of Hong Kong's elite Chinese community when anti-slavery activists in Britain protested against the sale of slave girls in the colony. See Sinn, "Chinese Patriarchy and Women," and Pedersen, "Maternalist Moment."

5. For recent work examining the transformation of a city (Tianjin) and rural areas around it in the Mao era, see Brown, *City Versus Countryside*, especially chap. 2.

6. An introduction to the history of Chinese cities during the PRC period may be found in Wu and Gaubatz, *Chinese City*, chap. 4.

7. Hammond and Richey, *The Sage Returns*.

8. For a guide to the historical context of *Dream of the Red Chamber*, see Schonebaum and Lu, *Approaches to Teaching* The Story of the Stone (Dream of the Red Chamber).

Glossary

Ba Jin (1904–2005)	巴金
binü	婢女
Chen Weixin (fl. 1920s)	陳維新
Chengdushi jiuxu shiye dongshihui	成都市救卹事業董事會
chiren de lijiao	吃人的禮教
Chun	春
Cihuitang	慈惠堂
Dai Jitao (1891–1949)	戴季陶
daiguren hu	代雇人戶
Fan Kongzhou (?–1917)	樊孔周
gouyin	勾引
Hanliu	漢流
Hu Lanqi (1901–1994)	胡蘭畦
Huang Juegao (1895–1988)	黃爵高
jia	家
jianshe	建設
jianshihu	監視戶
jiliangsuo	濟良所
junfa	軍閥
Li Jieren (1891–1962)	李劼人
Liu Bogu (dates unknown)	劉白谷
Liu Chengxun (1883–1944)	劉成勳
Liu Cunhou (1885–1960)	劉存厚
Liu Shiliang (1876–1939)	劉師亮
Liu Wencai (1887–1949)	劉文彩
Liu Wenhui (1894–1976)	劉文輝

Liu Xiang (1888–1938)	劉湘
Liu Yubo (1858–1949)	劉豫波
Lu Zuofu (1893–1952)	盧作孚
Minsheng Industrial Co.	民生實業公司
mui-jai (meizi)	妹子
Paoge	袍哥
Po Leung Kuk (Baoliangju)	保良局
Qiu	秋
Qun	群
ren fanzi	人販子
shenshi	紳士
shiye jiuguo	實業救國
Shu Xincheng (1893–1960)	舒新城
Sun Shaojing (?–1927)	孫少荊
ti-yong	體用
Wang Guangqi (1892–1936)	王光祈
Wang Youmu (1887–1924)	王右木
Wu Xianyou (1901–1962)	吳先忧
Wu Yu (1872–1949), also known as Wu Youling	吳虞　吳又陵
Wu Yuzhang (1878–1966)	吳玉章
Xiong Kewu (1885–1970)	熊克武
Xu Zixiu (1862–1936)	徐子休
xueguang	血光
Yang Sen (1884–1977)	楊森
Yang Shukan (1881–1942)	楊庶堪
Yin Changling (1868–1942)	尹昌齡
Yu Fenggang (fl. 1920s)	俞鳳崗
Yuan Shiyao (1897–1928)	袁詩堯
Zeng Lan (1875–1917)	曾蘭
Zhang Lan (1872–1955)	張瀾
Zhang Qun (1889–1990)	張群
ziyou lianai	自由戀愛

Works Cited

ARCHIVAL MATERIAL AND PERIODICALS

Chengdu Municipal Archives.
Chengdushi Yisilanjiao xiehui hexun [Newsletter of the Chengdu municipal Islam association], Chengdu.
Dachenghui conglu [Dacheng association recorder], Chengdu, 1922–1925.
Guomin gongbao [Citizens' gazette], Chengdu.
Kautz Family YMCA Archives, University of Minnesota. Reports from YMCA staff in Chengdu.
Minshi ribao [Gaze of the people], Chengdu.
North China Herald, Shanghai.
Sichuan Provincial Archives, records of the secretariat *Sichuansheng neiwuting*, Chengdu.
Tongsu huabao [Popular pictorial], Chengdu.
US consular records, Chungking, official correspondence, US National Archives.
Xishu xinwen [West Sichuan news], Chengdu.
Yusi [Threads of talk], Beijing.
Yuxianlu [Amusing accounts], Chengdu.
Zhao Erxun records, First Historical Archives, Beijing.

WORKS BY BA JIN, ENGLISH TRANSLATIONS

The Autobiography of Ba Jin. Translated by May-lee Chai. Indianapolis: University of Indianapolis Press, 2008.
Family. Translated by Sidney Shapiro. With an introduction by Olga Lang. Prospect Heights, IL: Waveland Press, 1989.
Family. Translated by Craig Shaw. Unpublished manuscript, 2013.
Garden of Repose. In *Selected Works of Ba Jin*, vol. 2. Beijing: Foreign Languages Press, 2005.

WORKS BY BA JIN, IN CHINESE

Chun [Spring]. Vol. 2 of *Ba Jin xuanji*. Chengdu: Sichuan renmin chubanshe, 1995.
"Guanyu *Jia*—gei wo de yige biaoge" [About *Family*—for one of my cousins]. In *Ba Jin sanwen*, edited by Lao Jiangxuan, 252–65. Hangzhou: Zhejiang wenyi chubanshe, 1999. First published in February 1937.

"Haizhuqiao" [Ocean pearl bridge]. In *Ba Jin sanwen jingbian*, edited by Zhejiang wenyi chubanshe, 234–36. Hangzhou: Zhejiang wenyi chubanshe, 1991. First published in Ba Jin, *Lütu suibi* [Random notes while traveling], Shanghai: Shenghuo shudian, 1934.

Jia [Family]. 10th edition. Shanghai: Kaiming shudian, 1938.

"*Jia* chongyin houji" [Postscript on the reprint edition of *Family*], dated August 9, 1977. In *Ba Jin sanwen jingbian*, edited by Zhejiang wenyi chubanshe, 610–11. Hangzhou: Zhejiang wenyi chubanshe, 1991.

"Mujiang Lao Chen" [Old Chen the carpenter]. In *Ba Jin sanwen jingbian*, edited by Zhejiang wenyi chubanshe, 43–46. Hangzhou: Zhejiang wenyi chubanshe, 1991. First published in Ba Jin, *Sheng zhi qianhui* [Life's repentance], Shanghai: Commercial Press, 1936.

Qiu [Autumn]. Vol. 3 of *Ba Jin xuanji*. Chengdu: Sichuan renmin chubanshe, 1995.

"*Tan Chun*" [Speaking of *Spring*]. In *Ba Jin sanwen jingbian*, edited by Zhejiang wenyi chubanshe, 657–71. Hangzhou: Zhejiang wenyi chubanshe, 1991. First published in 1958.

"*Tan Jia*" [Speaking of *Family*]. In *Ba Jin sanwen jingbian*, edited by Zhejiang wenyi chubanshe, 647–56. Hangzhou: Zhejiang wenyi chubanshe, 1991. First published in 1957.

"*Tan Qiu*" [Speaking of Autumn]. In *Ba Jin sanwen jingbian*, edited by Zhejiang wenyi chubanshe, 672–93. Hangzhou: Zhejiang wenyi chubanshe, 1991. First published in 1958.

"Wo de jige xiansheng" [Several of my teachers]. First published in *Duanjian* [Short conversations], Shanghai: Liangyou, 1937. http://www.tianyabook.com/xiandai/bajing/wodexiansheng.htm (accessed June 27, 2013).

"Wo de laojia" [My old home]. *Suixianglu*, no. 118 (February 6, 1984).

Yi [Memoirs]. Shanghai: Wenhua shenghuo, 1936.

OTHER WORKS

Barlow, Tani. *The Question of Women in Chinese Feminism*. Durham, NC: Duke University Press, 2004.

Baumler, Alan. *The Chinese and Opium under the Republic: Worse Than Floods and Wild Beasts*. Albany: State University of New York Press, 2007.

Bays, Daniel. *China Enters the Twentieth Century: Chang Chih-tung and the Issues of a New Age, 1895–1909*. Ann Arbor: University of Michigan Press, 1978.

Beech, J. "University Beginnings: A Story of the West China Union University." *Journal of the West China Border Research Society* 6 (1933): 91–104.

Bergère, Marie-Claire. *Sun Yat-sen*. Translated by Janet Lloyd. Stanford, CA: Stanford University Press, 2000.

Bernhardt, Kathryn. *Women and Property in China, 960–1949*. Stanford, CA: Stanford University Press, 1999.

Bianco, Lucien. "The Responses of Opium Growers to Eradication Campaigns and the Poppy Tax, 1907–1949." In *Opium Regimes*, edited by Brook and Wakabayashi, 292–320.

Billioud, Sébastien, and Joël Thoraval. "*Anshen Liming* or the Religious Dimension of Confucianism." *China Perspectives*, no. 3 (2008): 88–106.

Bodde, Derk, and Clarence Morris. *Law in Imperial China: Exemplified by 190 Ch'ing Dynasty Cases (translated from the Hsing-an Hui-lan), with Historical, Social and Juridical Commentaries*. Cambridge, MA: Harvard University Press, 1967.

Boorman, Howard L., and Richard C. Howard, eds. *Biographical Dictionary of Republican China*. New York: Columbia University Press, 1967.

Brook, Timothy, and Bob Tadashi Wakabayashi, eds. *Opium Regimes: China, Britain, and Japan, 1839–1952*. Berkeley: University of California Press, 2000.
Brown, Jeremy. *City Versus Countryside in Mao's China: Negotiating the Divide*. Cambridge: Cambridge University Press, 2014.
Brown, Melissa J., Laurel Bossen, Hill Gates, and Damian Satterthwaite-Phillips. "Marriage Mobility and Footbinding in Pre-1949 Rural China: A Reconsideration of Gender, Economics, and Meaning in Social Causation." *Journal of Asian Studies* 71, no. 4 (2012): 1035–67. doi:10.1017/S0021911812001271.
Bruun, Ole. *Fengshui in China: Geomantic Divination between State Orthodoxy and Popular Religion*. Honolulu: University of Hawai'i Press, 2003.
Canadian Old Photo Project Team, ed. *Chengdu, Our Home*. Chengdu: Sichuan chuban jituan and Sichuan wenyi chubanshe, 2012.
Cao Xueqin. *The Story of the Stone, or The Dream of the Red Chamber*. Translated by David Hawkes and John Minford. Five vols. New York: Penguin Classics, 1974–1986.
Chan, Anthony B. *Arming the Chinese: The Western Armaments Trade in Warlord China, 1920–1928*. Vancouver: University of British Columbia Press, 1982.
Chang, Eileen. "The Golden Cangue." In *Modern Chinese Stories and Novellas, 1919–1949*, edited by Joseph S. M. Lau, C. T. Hsia, and Leo Ou-fan Lee, 530–60. New York: Columbia University Press, 1981.
Chang, Jung. *Empress Dowager Cixi: The Concubine Who Launched Modern China*. New York: Knopf, 2013.
Chang, Pang-Mei Natasha. *Bound Feet and Western Dress*. New York: Doubleday, 1996.
Chen, Janet Y. *Guilty of Indigence: The Urban Poor in China, 1900–1953*. Princeton, NJ: Princeton University Press, 2012.
Ch'en, Jerome. *China and the West: A Study of Social and Cultural Changes*. Bloomington: Indiana University Press, 1979.
Chen Pingyuan. *Touches of History: An Entry into May Fourth China*. Translated by Michael Hockx. Leiden: Brill, 2011.
Chen Sihe. *Ren'ge de fazhan: Ba Jin zhuan* [Development of character: A biography of Ba Jin]. Taipei: Yeqiang chubanshe, 1991.
Chen, Zhongping. "The May Fourth Movement and Provincial Warlords: A Reexamination." *Modern China* 37, no. 2 (2011): 135–69.
Chen Zuxiang and Jiang Mengbi. "Chengdu quanyechang de bianqian" [The evolution of Chengdu's industrial promotion arcade]. *Jinjiang wenshi ziliao* 3 (February 1995): 144–58.
Cheng Qin. "*Hongloumeng* yu *Jia* zhong beiju renwu xingxiang bijiao—yi Qingwen he Mingfeng wei li" [A comparison of the images of tragic characters in *Dream of the Red Chamber* and *Family*—the case of Qingwen and Mingfeng]. *Duanpian xiaoshuo* 4 (August 2012): 24–25.
Cheng, Yi Meng. "Collaboration or Suppression: Guomindang Policy toward the Gelaohui in Wartime Chengdu and Chongqing, 1938–41." MSc thesis, University of Oxford, 2013.
Chengdu Cihuitang tekan [Special report of the Chengdu Hall of Benevolence]. Chengdu: Chengdu Cihuitang, 1928.
Chow, Kai-wing. *The Rise of Confucian Ritualism in Late Imperial China: Ethics, Classics, and Lineage Discourse*. Stanford, CA: Stanford University Press, 1994.

Chow, Kai-wing, Tze-ki Hon, Hung-yok Ip, and Don C. Price, eds. *Beyond the May Fourth Paradigm: In Search of Chinese Modernity*. Lanham, MD: Lexington Press, 2008.
———. Introduction to *Beyond the May Fourth Paradigm: In Search of Chinese Modernity*, edited by Kai-wing Chow et al., 1–26.
Chow, Rey. "Translator, Traitor; Translator, Mourner (or, Dreaming of Intercultural Equivalence)." *New Literary History* 39, no. 3 (2008): 565–80.
———. *Woman and Chinese Modernity: The Politics of Reading between East and West*. Minneapolis: University of Minnesota Press, 1991.
Chow, Tse-tsung. *The May Fourth Movement: Intellectual Revolution in Modern China*. Cambridge, MA: Harvard University Press, 1967.
Chu, Patricia P. *Assimilating Asians: Gendered Strategies of Authorship in Asian America*. Durham, NC: Duke University Press, 2000.
Chü, T'ung-Tsu. *Law and Society in Imperial China*. Paris: Mouton, 1961.
Cochran, Sherman, ed. *Inventing Nanjing Road: Commercial Culture in Shanghai, 1900–1945*. Ithaca, NY: Cornell East Asia Program, 1999.
Crook, Isabel Brown, and Christina Kelley Gilmartin with Yu Xiji. Compiled and edited by Gail Hershatter and Emily Honig. *Prosperity's Predicament: Identity, Reform, and Resistance in Rural Wartime China*. Lanham, MD: Rowman & Littlefield, 2013.
Crossley, Pamela Kyle. *Orphan Warriors: Three Manchu Generations and the End of the Qing World*. Princeton, NJ: Princeton University Press, 1990.
Dai Deyuan. "Xiqu gailiang yu Sanqinghui" [Opera reform and the Sanqing society]. *Sichuan xiju* 5 (1990): 39–42.
Dai Jinhua. "Rewriting the Red Classics." In *Rethinking Chinese Popular Culture: Cannibalizations of the Canon*, edited by Carlos Roja and Eileen Cheng-yin Chow, 151–78. New York: Routledge, 2009.
Dai, Yingcong. *The Sichuan Frontier and Tibet: Imperial Strategy in the Early Qing*. Seattle: University of Washington Press, 2009.
Deng Shouming. "Wang Youmu." In *Sichuan jinxiandai renwu zhuan*, edited by Ren Yimin, vol. 4, 8–12. Chengdu: Sichuan daxue chubanshe, 1987.
Deng Shouming, Zhang Jun, Yang Shun, and Liu Bangcheng. *Sichuan qingnian yundong shi gao* [Draft history of the youth movements in Sichuan]. Chengdu: Sichuan renmin chubanshe, 1990.
Dikötter, Frank. *Exotic Commodities: Modern Objects and Everyday Life in China*. New York: Columbia University Press, 2006.
———. *Sex, Culture, and Modernity in China: Medical Science and the Construction of Sexualities in the Early Republican Period*. Honolulu: University of Hawai'i Press, 1995.
Dikötter, Frank, Lars Laamann, and Zhou Xun. *Narcotic Culture: A History of Drugs in China*. Chicago: University of Chicago Press, 2004.
Dirlik, Arif. *Anarchism in the Chinese Revolution*. Berkeley: University of California Press, 1991.
Drescher, Seymour, and Stanley L. Engerman, eds. *A Historical Guide to World Slavery*. New York: Oxford University Press, 1998.
Duara, Prasenjit. *Rescuing History from the Nation: Questioning Narratives of Modern China*. Chicago: University of Chicago Press, 1996.
Eastman, Lloyd. *Family, Fields, and Ancestors: Constancy and Change in China's Social and Economic History, 1550–1949*. New York: Oxford University Press, 1988.

Ebrey, Patricia Buckley. *Chinese Civilization: A Sourcebook.* 2nd ed. New York: Free Press, 1993.
Edwards, Louise P. *Gender, Politics, and Democracy: Women's Suffrage in China.* Stanford, CA: Stanford University Press, 2008.
Elman, Benjamin A. *A Cultural History of Civil Examinations in Late Imperial China.* Berkeley: University of California Press, 2000.
Esherick, Joseph W., and Mary Backus Rankin, eds. *Chinese Local Elites and Patterns of Dominance.* Berkeley: University of California Press, 1990.
Feng, Jin. *The New Woman in Early Twentieth-Century Chinese Fiction.* West Lafayette, IN: Purdue University Press, 2004.
Finnane, Antonia. *Changing Clothes in China: Fashion, History, Nation.* New York: Columbia University Press, 2008.
———. *Speaking of Yangzhou: A Chinese City, 1550–1850.* Cambridge, MA: Harvard University Asia Center, 2004.
Fisac, Taciana. "'Anything at Variance with It Must Be Revised Accordingly': Rewriting Modern Chinese Literature during the 1950s." *China Journal*, no. 67 (January 2012): 131–48.
Fitzgerald, John. *Awakening China: Politics, Culture, and Class in the Nationalist Revolution.* Stanford, CA: Stanford University Press, 1996.
Franking, Mae M., and Katherine Anne Porter. *Mae Franking's "My Chinese Marriage": An Annotated Edition.* Edited by Holly Franking, with an introduction by Joan Givner. Austin: University of Texas Press, 1991.
Fu Chongju. *Chengdu tonglan* [Chengdu encyclopedia]. 2 vols. Chengdu: Bashu shushe, 1987. Originally published in 1909.
Fung, Edmund S. K. *The Intellectual Foundations of Chinese Modernity: Cultural and Political Thought in the Republican Era.* Cambridge: Cambridge University Press, 2010.
Furth, Charlotte, "From Birth to Birth: The Growing Body in Chinese Medicine." In *Chinese Views of Childhood*, edited by Anne Behnke Kinney, 157–92. Honolulu: University of Hawai'i Press, 1995.
———, ed. *The Limits of Change: Essays on Conservative Alternatives in Republican China.* Cambridge, MA: Harvard University Press, 1976.
Gao, C. C. "Chengtu Campus Labor Conditions." *Chinese Recorder*, August 1924, 543–44.
Gao Sibo. "Chengdu 'er yiliu' can'an yu gongren douzheng" [Chengdu's "February 16" massacre and workers' struggles]. *Sichuan wenshi ziliao xuanji* 26 (1982): 94–99.
Gates, Hill. *China's Motor: A Thousand Years of Petty Capitalism.* Ithaca, NY: Cornell University Press, 1996.
Gilmartin, Christina K. *Engendering the Chinese Revolution: Radical Women, Communist Politics, and Mass Movements in the 1920s.* Berkeley: University of California Press, 1995.
Glosser, Susan L. *Chinese Visions of Family and State, 1915–1953.* Berkeley: University of California Press, 2003.
Goldman, Andrea. *Opera and the City: The Politics of Culture in Beijing, 1770–1900.* Stanford, CA: Stanford University Press, 2012.
Gong Hong-yu. "Wang Guangqi yu Wu Ruoying guanxi kao" [A study of the relationship between Wang Guangqi and Wu Ruoying]. *Zhongyang yinyue xueyuan xuebao* 4 (2008): 49–56.
Gu Yuanzong. "Jindai chubanjia Fan Kongzhou" [Modern publisher Fan Kongzhou]. In *Chengdu lidai mingren*, 130–34. Chengdu: Chengdu wenguanhui, 1990.

Gunde, Richard. "Land Tax and Social Change in Sichuan, 1925–1935." *Modern China* 2, no. 1 (1976): 23–48.
Hammond, Kenneth J., and Jeffrey L. Richey, eds. *The Sage Returns: Confucian Revival in Contemporary China*. Albany: State University of New York Press, 2015.
Han Suyin. *The Crippled Tree*. New York: G.P. Putnam's Sons, 1965.
Harrison, Henrietta. *The Making of the Republican Citizen: Political Ceremonies and Symbols in China, 1911–1929*. New York: Oxford University Press, 2000.
———. *The Man Awakened from Dreams*. Stanford, CA: Stanford University Press, 2005.
Hay, Stephen. *Asian Ideas of East and West: Tagore and His Critics in Japan, China, and India*. Cambridge, MA: Harvard University Press, 1970.
Hayford, Charles W. *To the People: James Yen and Village China*. New York: Columbia University Press, 1990.
Henriot, Christian. *Prostitution and Sexuality in Shanghai: A Social History, 1849–1949*. Translated by Nöel Castelino. Cambridge: Cambridge University Press, 2001.
Hershatter, Gail. *Dangerous Pleasures: Prostitution and Modernity in Twentieth-Century Shanghai*. Berkeley: University of California Press, 1997.
———. *Women in China's Long Twentieth Century*. Berkeley: University of California Press and University of California Global, Area, and International Archives, 2007. http://escholarship.org/uc/item/12h450zf.
Hewlett, Meyrick. *Forty Years in China*. London: Macmillan, 1943.
Hill, Michael Gibbs. *Lin Shu, Inc.: Translation and the Making of Modern Chinese Culture*. Oxford: Oxford University Press, 2012.
Hirayama, Nagatomi. "Partifying Sichuan: The Chinese Youth Party in Sichuan, 1926–1937." *Frontiers of History in China* 8, no. 2 (June 2013): 223–58.
Ho, Clara Wing-chung. "The Cultivation of Female Talent: Views on Women's Education in China during the Early and High Qing Periods." *Journal of the Economic and Social History of the Orient* 38, no. 2 (1995): 191–223.
———. "Women in Chinese History." In *Demystifying China: New Understandings of Chinese History*, edited by Naomi Standen, 99–106. Lanham, MD: Rowman & Littlefield, 2013.
Ho, Denise Y., and Jie Li. "From Landlord Manor to Red Memorabilia: Reincarnations of a Chinese Museum Town." *Modern China* 41, no. 1 (2016): 3–37. doi:10.1177/0097700415591246.
Hong Liwan, ed. *Taiwan shehui shenghuo wenshu zhuanji* [Collected documents on social life in Taiwan]. Taipei: Taiwan History Institute, Academia Sinica, 2002.
Honig, Emily. *Sisters and Strangers: Women in the Shanghai Cotton Mills, 1919–1949*. Stanford, CA: Stanford University Press, 1992.
Howard, Joshua H. *Workers at War: Labor in China's Arsenals, 1937–1953*. Stanford, CA: Stanford University Press, 2004.
Hu Huaichen. "Jiefang binü yi" [A proposal to liberate slave girls]. *Funü zazhi* 6, no. 1 (January 5, 1920). Reprinted in Zhonghua quanguo funü lianhehui funü yundong lishi yanjiushi, ed., *Wusi shiqi funü wenti xuan*. Beijing: Sanlian chubanshe, 1981, 359–62. English translation published in Patricia Buckley Ebrey, *Chinese Civilization: A Sourcebook*. 2nd ed. New York: Free Press, 1993, 345–47.
Hu Lanqi. *Hu Lanqi huiyilu, 1901–1994* [Memoirs]. Chengdu: Sichuan renmin chubanshe, 1995.

Hu Ying. *Tales of Translation: Composing the New Woman in China, 1899–1918*. Stanford, CA: Stanford University Press, 2000.

Huang Juegao. "Wo canjia Chuan Dian Qian junfa Chengdu hangzhan jianwen" [What I saw and heard as a participant in Chengdu street battles of the Sichuan, Yunnan, and Guizhou warlords]. *Chengdu shi wenshi ziliao xuanji* 8 (April 1985): 215–24.

Huang Wenxuan. "Minguo wunian Quxian wuniu fenshi an" [The case of five oxen tearing apart a body in Qu County in 1916]. *Longmenzhen* 1 (1996): 30–36.

Hubbard, George D. "The Geographic Setting of Chengtu." *Bulletin of the Geographical Society of Philadelphia* 21, no. 4 (October 1923).

Jaschok, Maria. "Chinese 'Slave' Girls in Yunnan-Fu: Saving (Chinese) Womanhood and (Western) Souls, 1930–1991." In *Women and Chinese Patriarchy: Submission, Servitude, and Escape*, edited by Maria Jaschok and Suzanne Miers, 171–97. London: Zed, 1994.

———. *Concubines and Bondservants: A Social History*. London: Zed, 1988.

Jensen, Lionel M. *Manufacturing Confucianism: Chinese Tradition and Universal Civilization*. Durham, NC: Duke University Press, 1997.

Jiang Jin and Li Deying, eds. *Jindai Zhongguo chengshi yu dazhong wenhua* [Modern Chinese cities and mass culture]. Beijing: Xinxing chubanshe, 2008.

Jiang Jun. "Lu Jianbo xiansheng zaoniande wuzhengfu zhuyi xuanchuan huodong jishi" [An account of Mr. Lu Jianbo's anarchist activities in his youth]. In *Wuzhengfu zhuyi sixiang ziliao xuan*, edited by Ge Maochu, Jiang Jun, and Li Xingzhi, vol. 2, 1009–22. Beijing: Beijing daxue chubanshe, 1984.

Jiang Mengbi. "Chunxi lu de youlai yu fazhan" [Chunxi Road's genesis and development]. *Jinjiang wenshi ziliao* 1 (1991): 5–13.

Jin Hongyu. *Zhongguo xiandai changpian xiaoshuo mingzhu banben jiaoping* [Critical comparison of the editions of famous modern Chinese novels]. Beijing: Renmin wenxue chubanshe, 2004.

Johnson, David. "Communication, Class, and Consciousness in Late Imperial China." In *Popular Culture in Late Imperial China*, edited by David Johnson, Andrew J. Nathan, and Evelyn S. Rawski, 34–72. Berkeley: University of California Press, 1985.

Judge, Joan. *The Precious Raft of History: The Past, the West, and the Woman Question in China*. Stanford, CA: Stanford University Press, 2008.

Kang, Wenqing. *Obsession: Male Same-Sex Relations in China, 1900–1950*. Hong Kong: Hong Kong University Press, 2009.

Kapp, Robert A. *Szechwan and the Chinese Republic: Provincial Militarism and Central Power, 1911–1938*. New Haven, CT: Yale University Press, 1973.

Kilborn, O. L. "Historical Sketch." In *Our West China Mission*, 29–62. Toronto: Missionary Society of the Methodist Church, 1920.

Kinney, Anne Behnke, trans. *Exemplary Women of Early China: The Lienü zhuan of Liu Xiang*. New York: Columbia University Press, 2014.

Kinsella, Kevin, and Wan He. *An Aging World: 2008*. US Census Bureau, International Population Reports, P95/09-1. Washington, DC: US Government Printing Office, 2009. https://www.census.gov/prod/2009pubs/p95-09-1.pdf.

Knapp, Ronald G., and Kai-yin Lo, eds. *House, Home, Family: Living and Being Chinese*. Honolulu: University of Hawai'i Press, 2005.

Knight, Deirdre Sabina. "Gendered Fate." In *The Magnitude of "Ming": Command, Allotment, and Fate in Chinese Culture*, edited by Christopher Lupke, 272–90. Honolulu: University of Hawai'i Press, 2005.

Ko, Dorothy. *Cinderella's Sisters: A Revisionist History of Footbinding*. Berkeley: University of California Press, 2005.

———. *Every Step a Lotus: Shoes for Bound Feet*. Berkeley: University of California Press, 2001.

Köll, Elisabeth. *From Cotton Mill to Business Empire: The Emergence of Regional Enterprises in Modern China*. Cambridge, MA: Harvard University Asia Center, 2003.

Kowallis, Jon. *The Subtle Revolution: Poets of the "Old Schools" during Late Qing and Early Republican China*. Berkeley: Institute of East Asian Studies, University of California, 2006.

Krebs, Edward. *Shifu, Soul of Chinese Anarchism*. Lanham, MD: Rowman & Littlefield, 1998.

Kuo, Margaret. *Intolerable Cruelty: Marriage, Law, and Society in Early Twentieth-Century China*. Lanham, MD: Rowman & Littlefield, 2012.

Kuriyama, Shigehisa. *The Expressiveness of the Body and the Divergence of Greek and Chinese Medicine*. New York: Zone, 2002.

Lan, Hua R., and Vanessa L. Fong, eds. *Women in Republican China: A Sourcebook*. Armonk, NY: M.E. Sharpe, 1999.

Lang, Olga. *Chinese Family and Society*. New Haven, CT: Yale University Press, 1946.

———. *Pa Chin and His Writings: Chinese Youth between the Two Revolutions*. Cambridge, MA: Harvard University Press, 1967.

Lanza, Fabio. *Behind the Gate: Inventing Students in Beijing*. New York: Columbia University Press, 2010.

Lao Zu [pseud.]. "Fuxing jie yiwen" [Anecdotes about Fuxing Street]. *Longmenzhen* 1 (1977): 31–36.

Lary, Diana. *Warlord Soldiers: Chinese Common Soldiers, 1911–1937*. Cambridge: Cambridge University Press, 1985.

Lee, James Z., and Feng Wang. *One Quarter of Humanity: Malthusian Mythology and Chinese Realities, 1700–2000*. Cambridge, MA: Harvard University Press, 2001.

Lee, Lily Xiao Hong, and Sue Wiles, eds. *Biographical Dictionary of Chinese Women: Tang Through Ming, 618–1644*. Armonk, NY: M. E. Sharpe, 2014.

Lee, Thomas H. C. *Education in Traditional China: A History*. Leiden: Brill, 2000.

Leung, Angela K. C. *Shishan yu jiaohua: Ming-Qing de cishan zuzhi* [Doing good and civilizing society: Charitable associations in the Ming and Qing periods]. Taipei: Lianjing, 1997.

Levenson, Joseph R. *Confucian China and Its Modern Fate*, vol. 3. Berkeley: University of California Press, 1968.

Levine, Marilyn A. *The Found Generation: Chinese Communists in Europe during the Twenties*. Seattle: University of Washington Press, 1993.

Li Cunguang. *Bainian Ba Jin: shengping ji wenxue huodong shilüe* [Ba Jin at 100: Historical survey of his life and literary activities]. Beijing: Renmin wenxue chubanshe, 2003.

———. *Jia dao du* [Guide to reading *Family*]. Beijing: Zhonghua shuju, 2002.

Li Dajia. *Minguo chunian de liansheng zizhi yundong* [The federal self-government movement in the early Republic]. Taipei: Hongwenguan chubanshe, 1986.

Li Hsiao-t'i. *Qingmo de xiaceng shehui qimeng yundong, 1901–1911* [Lower-class enlightenment in the late Qing period]. Taipei: Institute of Modern History, Academia Sinica, 1992.

Li Jianmin. "Minguo shiwunian Sichuan Wanxian can'an" [The tragic Wanxian case of 1926]. *Zhongyang yanjiuyuan jindaishi yanjiusuo jikan* 19 (June 1990): 387–420.

Li Jieren. "Bing dabo Chen Zhenwu de yuepu" [The monthly chronicle of big uncle soldier Chen Zhenwu]. In *Li Jieren quanji*, vol. 6, 321–62. Chengdu: Sichuan wenyi chubanshe, 2011. First published in *Dongfang zazhi* 24, no. 3 (1927): 87–100, and no. 4 (1927): 83–94.

———. *Dabo* [The great wave]. 4 parts. In *Li Jieren xuanji*, vol. 2. Chengdu: Sichuan renmin chubanshe, 1980.

———. "Huiyi Shaonian Zhongguo Xuehui Chengdu fenhui zhi suoyou chengli" [Recalling the founding of the Chengdu branch of the Young China Association]. In *Li Jieren quanji*, vol. 7, 52–56. Chengdu: Sichuan wenyi chubanshe, 2011. Written in 1960 and first published in *Wusi shiqi de shetuan*, Shanghai: Sanlian, 1979.

———. "Jinghuai Liu Yubo xiansheng" [In respectful remembrance of Mr. Liu Yubo]. In *Li Jieren quanji*, vol. 7, 41–44. Chengdu: Sichuan wenyi chubanshe, 2011. First published in *Fengtu shizhi* 2, no. 6, 1949.

———. "Weicheng zhuiyi" [Memoir of a dangerous city]. In *Li Jieren xuanji*, vol. 5, 96–148. Chengdu: Sichuan renmin chubanshe, 1986. First published in *Xin Zhonghua* 5, nos. 1–6 (1937).

Li Shiping, *Sichuan renkou shi* [A demographic history of Sichuan]. Chengdu: Sichuan daxue chubanshe, 1987.

Li Shiwen. *Li Jieren de shengping he chuangzuo* [The life and works of Li Jieren]. Chengdu: Sichuansheng shehui kexueyuan chubanshe, 1986.

Li, Xiaoxiong. *Poppies and Politics in China: Sichuan Province, 1840s to 1940s*. Newark: University of Delaware Press, 2009.

Li Zhi. "Shuzhi qing: tan *Chun* zhong Hai'er de yuanxing" [Emotional bond between uncle and nephew: The model for the character Hai'er in *Spring*]. In Li Zhi, *Huigu*, 23–26. Chengdu: Sichuan renmin chubanshe, 1997.

Liang Yuwen and Cai Jisheng, "Xinhai Sichuan baolu yundong dashiji" [Timeline of important events in Sichuan's 1911 railroad protection movement]. In *Xinhai Sichuan fenglei*, edited by Chengdushi zhengxie wenshi ziliao weiyuanhui, 307–23. Chengdu: Chengdu chubanshe, 1991.

Lim, Janet. *Sold for Silver: An Autobiography*. Singapore: Oxford University Press, 1985.

Lin, Yueh-hwa. *The Golden Wing: A Sociological Study of Chinese Familism*. New York: Oxford University Press, 1947.

Lin, Yu-sheng. *Crisis of Chinese Consciousness: Radical Antitraditionalism in the May Fourth Era*. Madison: University of Wisconsin Press, 1978.

Lin Yutang. "Chinese Realism and Humour." In *The Little Critic*, vol. 1, 86–95. Shanghai: Commercial Press, 1936.

Lin Zhiyuan. "Liu Yulao shusan Zhonghechang yishi" [Anecdotes from when Old Mr. Liu Yubo was evacuated to Zhonghe town]. *Shuangliu wenshi ziliao* 4 (1985): 150–53.

Ling Xingzhen. "Qingmo Minchu Chengdu Zhongwai xueshu wenhua jiaoliu" [Cultural exchange between Chengdu and the outside world in the late Qing and early republican eras]. *Sichuan shifan daxue xuebao (shehui kexue ban)* 26, no. 2 (April 1999): 117–25.

Lipkin, Zwia. *Useless to the State: "Social Problems" and Social Engineering in Nationalist Nanjing, 1927–1937*. Cambridge, MA: Harvard University Asia Center, 2006.

Little, Alicia. *Intimate China: The Chinese As I Have Seen Them*. London: Hutchinson, 1899.

Little, Archibald John. *Gleanings from Fifty Years in China*. London: Sampson Low, Marston, 1910.
Liu Jingzhi. "Zhang Ruifang, Sun Daolin, yu Ba Jin de *Jia*" [Zhang Ruifang, Sun Daolin, and Ba Jin's *Family*]. *Beijing qingnian bao*, November 25, 2003. http://www.china.com.cn/chinese/zhuanti/448990.htm (accessed August 25, 2015).
Liu Xianzhi. *Chengdu Man-Mengzu shilüe* [Outline history of Chengdu's Manchus and Mongols]. Chengdu: Chengdu Man-Meng renmin xuexi weiyuanhui, 1983.
Liu Xiaobo. "Ba Jin: The Limp White Flag." In *No Enemies, No Hatred: Selected Essays and Poems*, edited by Perry Link, Tianchi Martin-Liao, and Liu Xia, 137–45. Cambridge, MA: Harvard University Press, 2012.
Liu Zhonglai. *Lu Zuofu yu Minguo xiangcun jianshe yanjiu* [Research on Lu Zuofu and the rural reconstruction movement during the Republic]. Beijing: Renmin chubanshe, 2007.
Lu, Yan. *Re-Understanding Japan: Chinese Perspectives, 1895–1945*. Honolulu: University of Hawai'i Press for the Association of Asian Studies, 2004.
Ma, Ling. "Negotiating Guilt: Abortion, Law, and Society in Early Twentieth-Century China." PhD diss., University at Buffalo, 2016.
Macauley, Melissa. *Social Power and Legal Culture: Litigation Masters in Late Imperial China*. Stanford, CA: Stanford University Press, 1998.
Madsen, Richard. "Secularism, Religious Change, and Social Conflict in Asia." In *Rethinking Secularism*, edited by Craig Calhoun, Mark Juergensmeyer, and Jonathan VanAntwerpen, 248–69. Oxford: Oxford University Press, 2011.
Manela, Erez. *The Wilsonian Moment: Self-Determination and the International Origins of Anticolonial Nationalism*. Oxford: Oxford University Press, 2009.
Mann, Susan. "Grooming a Daughter for Marriage: Brides and Wives in the Mid-Ch'ing Period." In *Marriage and Inequality in Chinese Society*, edited by Rubie S. Watson and Patricia Buckley Ebrey, 204–30. Berkeley: University of California Press, 1991.
———. *Precious Records: Women in China's Long Eighteenth Century*. Stanford, CA: Stanford University Press, 1997.
———. *The Talented Women of the Zhang Family*. Berkeley: University of California Press, 2007.
Mao, Nathan K. *Pa Chin*. Boston: Twayne, 1978.
McCord, Edward A. *The Power of the Gun: The Emergence of Modern Chinese Warlordism*. Berkeley: University of California Press, 1993.
McElderry, Andrea. "Doing Business with Strangers: Guarantors as an Extension of Personal Ties in Chinese Business." In *Constructing China: the Interaction of Culture and Economics*, edited by Kenneth G. Lieberthal, Shuen-fu Lin, and Ernest P. Young, 147–70. Ann Arbor: Center for Chinese Studies, University of Michigan, 1997.
Meijer, Marinus J. "Slavery at the End of the Ch'ing Dynasty." In *Essays on China's Legal Tradition*, edited by Jerome Alan Cohen, R. Randle Edwards, and Fu-mei Chang Chen, 327–58. Princeton, NJ: Princeton University Press, 1980.
Morse, William Reginald. *Three Crosses in the Purple Mist: An Adventure in Medical Education under the Eaves of the Roof of the World*. Shanghai: Mission Book Company, 1928.
Mühlhahn, Klaus. *Criminal Justice in China: A History*. Cambridge, MA: Harvard University Press, 2009.
Naquin, Susan, and Evelyn S. Rawski. *Chinese Society in the Eighteenth Century*. New Haven, CT: Yale University Press, 1987.

Ng, Kenny Kwok-kwan. *The Lost Geopoetic Horizon of Li Jieren: The Crisis of Writing Chengdu in Revolutionary China*. Leiden: Brill, 2015.
Overmyer, Daniel L., and Shin-Yi Chao, eds. *Ethnography in China Today: A Critical Assessment of Methods and Results*. Taipei: Yuan-Liou, 2002.
Pedersen, Susan. "The Maternalist Moment in British Colonial Policy: The Controversy over 'Child Slavery' in Hong Kong 1917–1941." *Past and Present*, no. 171 (May 2001): 161–202.
Perry, Elizabeth. *Shanghai on Strike: The Politics of Chinese Labor*. Stanford, CA: Stanford University Press, 1995.
Poon, Shuk-Wah. *Negotiating Religion in Modern China: State and Common People in Guangzhou, 1900–1937*. Hong Kong: Chinese University of Hong Kong Press, 2011.
Pruitt, Ida. *A Daughter of Han: The Autobiography of a Chinese Working Woman*. Stanford, CA: Stanford University Press, 1967.
Ran Yunfei. *Wu Yu he ta shenghuo de Minguo shidai, 1911–1949* [Wu Yu and the republican era he lived in]. Ji'nan: Shandong renmin chubanshe, 2009.
Rankin, Mary Backus. *Early Chinese Revolutionaries: Radical Intellectuals in Shanghai and Chekiang, 1902–1911*. Cambridge, MA: Harvard University Press, 1971.
Ransmeier, Johanna Sirera. "'No Other Choice': The Sale of People in Late Qing and Republican Beijing, 1870–1935." PhD diss., Yale University, 2008.
Reinhardt, Anne. "'Decolonisation' on the Periphery: Liu Xiang and Shipping Rights Recovery at Chongqing, 1926–38." *Journal of Imperial and Commonwealth History* 36, no. 2 (2008): 259–74.
Rogaski, Ruth. *Hygienic Modernity: Meanings of Health and Disease in Treaty-Port China*. Berkeley: University of California Press, 2004.
Ropp, Paul S., Paola Zamperini, and Harriet T. Zurndorfer, eds. *Passionate Women: Female Suicide in Late Imperial China*. Leiden: Brill, 2001.
Rowe, William T. *Saving the World: Chen Hongmou and Elite Consciousness in Eighteenth-Century China*. Stanford, CA: Stanford University Press, 2001.
Schwarcz, Vera. *The Chinese Enlightenment: Intellectuals and the Legacy of the May Fourth Movement of 1919*. Berkeley: University of California Press, 1986.
———. *Place and Memory in the Singing Crane Garden*. Philadelphia: University of Pennsylvania Press, 2014.
Schonebaum, Andrew, and Tina Lu, eds. *Approaches to Teaching* The Story of the Stone (Dream of the Red Chamber). New York: Modern Languages Association, 2012.
Service, Grace B. *Golden Inches: The China Memoir of Grace Service*. Edited by John S. Service. Berkeley: University of California Press, 1989.
Shao, Qin. *Culturing Modernity: The Nantong Model, 1890–1930*. Stanford, CA: Stanford University Press, 2004.
Shao Ying. "Chubanjia Fan Kongzhou" [The publisher Fan Kongzhou]. *Chengdu zhi tongxun* 3 (1986): 58.
Shaw, Craig. "Ba Jin's Dream: Sentiment and Social Criticism in *Jia*." PhD diss., Princeton University, 1993.
———. "Changes in *The Family*: Reflections on Ba Jin's Revisions of *Jia*." *Journal of the Chinese Language Teachers Association* 34, no. 2 (May 1999): 21–36.
Shen Congwen. "Xiaoxiao." Translated by Eugene Chen Eoyang. In *The Columbia Anthology of Modern Chinese Literature*, edited by Joseph S. M. Lau and Howard Goldblatt, 97–110. New York: Columbia University Press, 1995.

Shu Xincheng. *Shuyou xinying* [Reflections on my travels in Sichuan]. Shanghai: Zhonghua shuju, 1934.

———. *Wo he jiaoyu* [Myself and education]. Shanghai: Zhonghua shuju, 1945.

Shue, Vivienne. "The Quality of Mercy: Confucian Charity and the Mixed Metaphors of Modernity in Tianjin." *Modern China* 32, no. 4 (October 2006): 411–52.

Sichuan daxue xiaoshi bianxiezu, ed. *Sichuan daxue shi gao* [Draft history of Sichuan University]. Chengdu: Sichuan daxue chubanshe, 1985.

"Sichuan yinianlai dashiji" [Significant events in Sichuan over the past year]. In *Li Jieren quanji*, vol. 7, 57–77. Chengdu: Sichuan wenyi chubanshe, 2011. First published in *Chuanbao xinnian zengkan* [Sichuan journal New Year's extra], January 1, 1919.

Sichuansheng difangzhi bianzuan weiyuanhui, ed. *Sichuansheng zhi: renwu zhi* [Annals of Sichuan Province: Biographies]. Chengdu: Sichuan renmin chubanshe, 2001.

Sichuansheng wenshiguan, ed. *Chengdu chengfang guji kao* [A study of the old walls and neighborhoods of Chengdu]. Chengdu: Sichuan renmin chubanshe, 1987.

———. *Sichuan junfa shiliao* [Historical materials on Sichuan warlords]. 5 vols. Chengdu: Sichuan renmin chubanshe, 1981–1988.

Sinn, Elizabeth. "Chinese Patriarchy and the Protection of Women in 19th-Century Hong Kong." In *Women and Chinese Patriarchy: Submission, Servitude, and Escape*, edited by Maria Jaschok and Suzanne Miers. London: Zed, 1994.

Slack, Edward R. *Opium, State, and Society: China's Narco-Economy and the Guomindang, 1924–1937*. Honolulu: University of Hawai'i Press, 2001.

Smith, Richard J. "Ritual in Ch'ing Culture." In *Orthodoxy in Late Imperial China*, edited by Kwang-Ching Liu, 281–310. Berkeley: University of California Press, 1990.

Sommer, Matthew H. *Sex, Law, and Society in Late Imperial China*. Stanford, CA: Stanford University Press, 2000.

Spence, Jonathan. *To Change China: Western Advisers in China*. New York: Penguin, 1980.

———. *The Search for Modern China*. New York: Norton, 1990.

Stapleton, Kristin. *Civilizing Chengdu: Chinese Urban Reform, 1895–1937*. Cambridge, MA: Harvard University Asia Center, 2000.

———. "Generational and Cultural Fissures in the May Fourth Movement: Wu Yu (1872–1949) and the Politics of Family Reform." In *Beyond the May Fourth Paradigm: In Search of Chinese Modernity*, edited by Kai-wing Chow et al., 131–48.

———. "Hu Lanqi: Rebellious Woman, Revolutionary Soldier, Discarded Heroine, Triumphant Survivor." In *The Human Tradition in Modern China*, edited by Kenneth Hammond and Kristin Stapleton, 157–76. Lanham, MD: Rowman & Littlefield, 2008.

———. "Urban Politics in an Age of 'Secret Societies': The Cases of Shanghai and Chengdu." *Republican China* 22, no. 1 (November 1996): 23–64.

Strand, David. *Rickshaw Beijing: City People and Politics in the 1920s*. Berkeley: University of California Press, 1989.

———. *An Unfinished Republic: Leading by Word and Deed in Modern China*. Berkeley: University of California Press, 2011.

Su Jianxin and Tao Min, eds. "Xuantong yuannian jin'ge'en renkou maimai shiliao" [Historical materials on the prohibition of purchase and sale of people in the third year of the Xuantong reign]. *Lishi dang'an* 1 (1995): 68–71.

Su, Tsung. "New Women versus Old Mores: A Study of Women Characters in Ba Jin's Torrents Trilogy." *Chinese Studies in History* 23, issue 3 (Spring 1990): 54–67.

Sun Lianghao and Chen Jianwei. "Nüxing ziwo yishi de 'juexing' yu 'chenlun'—*Honglou-meng* yu *Jia* zhong de nüxing xingxiang toushi" [The "awakening" and "sinking" of female self-awareness—perspectives of female characters in *Dream of the Red Chamber* and *Family*]. *Journal of Wenzhou Normal College* 24, no. 3 (June 2003): 29–35.
Sun, Lung-kee. "The Politics of the Hair and the Issue of the Bob in Modern China." *Fashion Theory* 1, no. 4 (November 1997): 353–65.
Sun Xiaofen. *Sichuan de Kejiaren yu Kejia wenhua* [Sichuan's Hakkas and Hakka culture]. Chengdu: Sichuan daxue chubanshe, 2000.
Sun Xujun, Jiang Song, and Chen Weidong. *Sichuan minsu daguan* [Overview of Sichuan folklore]. Chengdu: Sichuan renmin chubanshe, 1989.
Sutton, Donald S. *Provincial Militarism and the Chinese Republic: The Yunnan Army, 1905–25.* Ann Arbor: University of Michigan Press, 1980.
Tan Xingguo. *Shuzhong wenzhang guan tianxia: BaShu wenxueshi gao* [The literature of Sichuan is the world's best: A draft literary history of the Ba and Shu regions]. Chengdu: Sichuan renmin chubanshe, 2001.
———. *Zoujin Ba Jin de shijie* [Entering Ba Jin's world]. Chengdu: Sichuan wenyi chubanshe, 2003.
Tang Zhenchang. "Wu Yu yanjiu" [Research on Wu Yu]. *Lishixue* 4 (1979).
Tao Liangsheng. "Yin Zhongxi yu Cihuitang" [Yin Zhongxi and the Hall of Mercy]. *Chengdu wenshi ziliao xuanji* 3 (November 1982): 106–21.
Taylor, Jay. *Generalissimo: Chiang Kai-shek and the Struggle for Modern China*. Cambridge, MA: Harvard Belknap Press, 2011.
Thompson, John Stuart. *Revolutionizing China*. Indianapolis: Bobbs-Merrill, 1913.
Tran, Lisa. "The Concubine in Republican China: Social Perception and Legal Construction." *Études Chinoises: Bulletin de l'Association Françaises d'Études Chinoises* 28 (2009): 191–223.
Unschuld, Paul U. *Medicine in China: A History of Ideas*. Berkeley: University of California Press, 1985.
Wakeman, Frederic E. *Policing Shanghai, 1927–1937*. Berkeley: University of California Press, 1996.
Waldron, Arthur. "The Warlord: Twentieth-Century Chinese Understandings of Violence, Militarism, and Imperialism." *American Historical Review* 96, no. 4 (October 1991): 1073–86.
Waltner, Ann. *Getting an Heir: Adoption and the Construction of Kinship in Late Imperial China*. Honolulu: University of Hawai'i Press, 1990.
Wang, Di. *The Teahouse: Small Business, Everyday Culture, and Public Politics in Chengdu, 1900–1950*. Stanford, CA: Stanford University Press, 2008.
———. *Street Culture in Chengdu: Public Space, Urban Commoners, and Local Politics, 1870–1930*. Stanford, CA: Stanford University Press, 2003.
Wang Lüping. *Sichuan baokan wushinian jicheng* [Fifty years of Sichuan periodicals]. Chengdu: Sichuan daxue chubanshe, 2011.
———. *Sichuan jindai xinwen shi* [A history of Sichuan's modern newspapers]. Chengdu: Sichuan daxue chubanshe, 2007.
Wang Lüping and Cheng Qi. *Sichuan baokan jilan* [Survey of Sichuan periodicals], vol. 1. Chengdu: Chengdu keji daxue chubanshe, 1993.
Wang Qingyue and Deng Shouming. "Qingnian Chen Yi zai Chengdu xunqiu 'gongye jiuguo' de fendou licheng" [Progress of the struggle of the young Chen Yi's quest to

"save the nation through industry" in Chengdu]. *Chengdu dianzi jixie gaodeng zhuanke xuexiao xuebao* 13, no. 3 (November 2010): 1–4.
Wang Shouxi. "Yuan Shiyao." In *Sichuan jinxiandai renwu zhuan*, edited by Ren Yimin, vol. 2, 26–31. Chengdu: Sichuan daxue chubanshe, 1987.
Wang Zheng. *Women in the Chinese Enlightenment: Oral and Textual Histories*. Berkeley: University of California Press, 1999.
Wasserstrom, Jeffrey N. *Student Protests in Twentieth-Century China: The View from Shanghai*. Stanford, CA: Stanford University Press, 1991.
Watson, James L. "Transactions in People: The Chinese Market in Slaves, Servants, and Heirs." In *Asian and African Systems of Slavery*, edited by James L. Watson, 223–50. Berkeley: University of California Press, 1980.
Watson, Rubie S. "Wives, Concubines, and Maids: Servitude and Kinship in the Hong Kong Region, 1900–1940." In *Marriage and Inequality in Chinese Society*, edited by Rubie S. Watson and Patricia Buckley Ebrey, 231–55. Berkeley: University of California Press, 1991.
Wei Qingyuan, Wu Qiyan, and Lu Su. *Qingdai nubi zhidu* [The Qing-dynasty slave system]. Beijing: Zhonghua renmin daxue chubanshe, 1982.
Wei Yingtao, ed. *Sichuan jindaishi gao* [Draft history of modern Sichuan]. Chengdu: Sichuan renmin chubanshe, 1990.
Wen Yu (pseud.). "Muqian Zhongguo zhi nubi jiefang wenti" [The problem of liberation from servitude in contemporary China]. *Dongfang zazhi* 29, no. 5 (November 1, 1932), 6–8 of the subsection on "Women and the Family."
Widler, Elly. *Six Months Prisoner of the Szechwan Military*. Shanghai: China Press, 1924.
Widmer, Ellen. "Qu Qiubai and Russian Literature." In *Modern Chinese Literature in the May Fourth Era*, edited by Merle Goldman, 103–25. Cambridge, MA: Harvard University Press, 1977.
Willmott, Cory. "The Paradox of Gender among West China Missionary Collectors." *Social Science and Missions* 25 (2012): 129–64.
Witke, Roxane. "Mao Tse-tung, Women and Suicide." In *Women in China*, edited by Marilyn B. Young, 7–31. Ann Arbor: University of Michigan Center for Chinese Studies, 1973.
Wolf, Arthur P., and Hill Gates. "Modeling Chinese Marriage Regimes." *Journal of Family History* 23, no. 1 (1998): 90–99.
Wright, Tim. "Distant Thunder: The Regional Economies of Southwest China and the Impact of the Great Depression." *Modern Asian Studies* 34, no. 3 (July 2000): 697–738.
Wu Shaobo. "Bisheng congshi jiaoyu shiye de Xu Jiong" [Xu Jiong (Zixiu), a lifetime of work in education]. In *Sichuan jinxiandai wenhua renwu*, edited by Sichuansheng wenshiguan and Sichuansheng zhengxie wenshi ziliao yanjiu weiyuanhui, vol. 2, 277–84. Chengdu: Sichuan renmin chubanshe, 1989.
Wu, Weiping, and Piper Gaubatz. *The Chinese City*. New York: Routledge, 2013.
Wu, Yi-Li. *Reproducing Women: Medicine, Metaphor, and Childbirth in Late Imperial China*. Berkeley: University of California Press, 2010.
Wu Yu. *Wu Yu riji* [Wu Yu's diaries]. Edited by Rong Mengyuan. 2 vols. Chengdu: Sichuan renmin chubanshe, 1986.
Xie Bingying. *A Woman Soldier's Own Story*. Translated by Lily Chia Brissman and Barry Brissman. New York: Berkeley Books, 2003.

Xie Fang. "Fan Kongzhou." In *Sichuan jinxiandai renwu zhuan*, edited by Ren Yimin, vol. 4, 177–82. Chengdu: Sichuan daxue chubanshe, 1987.
Xiong Yuezhi. "George Washington's Image in China and Its Impact on the 1911 Revolution." *Journal of Modern Chinese History* 6, no. 1 (2012): 45–63. doi:10.1080/17535654.2012.670514.
Xiong Zhuoyun. "Fandong tongzhi shiqi de Chengdu jingcha" [Chengdu's police in the time of reactionary authority]. *Sichuan wenshi ziliao xuanji* 16 (May 1965): 101–20.
Xu, Xiaoqun. *Chinese Professionals and the Republican State: The Rise of Professional Associations in Shanghai, 1912–1937*. Cambridge: Cambridge University Press, 2001.
Xu Zixiu. "Dacheng Zhongxuexiao kaixue yanjiang" [Speech at the opening of the Dacheng Middle School]. *Dachenghui conglu*, 3 (1922).
Yang Bingde, ed. *Zhongguo jindai chengshi yu jianzhu, 1840–1949* [China's modern cities and architecture]. Beijing: Zhongguo jianzhu gongye chubanshe, 1993.
Yang Shiyuan. "Wu Yuzhang." In *Sichuan jinxiandai renwu zhuan*, edited by Ren Yimin, vol. 1, 1–7. Chengdu: Sichuan daxue chubanshe, 1987.
Ye Chunkai. "Jiefang qian Chengdu guancai pu yitiao jie" [Chengdu's coffin street in the days before liberation (1949)]. *Longmenzhen* 1 (1996): 96–101.
Yeh, Catherine Vance. "Where Is the Center of Cultural Production? The Rise of the Actor to National Stardom and the Beijing/Shanghai Challenge (1860s–1910s)." *Late Imperial China* 25, no. 2 (2004): 74–118.
You Xin (pseud.). "Di sibailiushiqi ci de Chuan zhan" [The 467th Sichuan war]. *Dongfang zazhi* 29 (November 1, 1932): 4.
Zarrow, Peter. *Anarchism and Chinese Culture*. New York: Columbia University Press, 1990.
———. *China in War and Revolution, 1895–1949*. New York: Routledge, 2005.
Zelin, Madeleine. "Chinese Business Practice in the Late Imperial Period." *Enterprise & Society* 14, no. 4 (December 2013): 769–93.
———. *The Merchants of Zigong: Industrial Entrepreneurship in Early Modern China*. New York: Columbia University Press, 2005.
———. "The Rise and Fall of the Fu-Rong Salt-Yard Elite: Merchant Dominance in Late Qing China." In *Chinese Local Elites and Patterns of Dominance*, edited by Joseph Esherick and Mary Backus Rankin, 82–109. Berkeley: University of California Press, 1990.
Zhang Huichang. "Yi, san, bianjun yu san, qi, ershiyi shi zhi zhan" [The first, third, and border armies and the battle of the third, seventh, and twenty-first divisions]. In Sichuansheng wenshiguan, ed., *Sichuan junfa shiliao*, vol. 3, 49–57.
Zhang Jin. *Quanli chongtu yu bianqe—1926–1937 nian Chongqing chengshi xiandaihua yanjiu* [Power, conflict, and reform: Research on Chongqing's modernization, 1926–1937]. Chongqing: Chongqing chubanshe, 2003.
Zhang Liyuan. "Dai Jitao." *Sichuan jinxiandai renwu zhuan*, edited by Ren Yimin, vol. 3, 139–145. Chengdu: Sichuan daxue chubanshe, 1987.
Zhong Maoxuan. *Liu Shiliang waizhuan* [Unofficial history of Liu Shiliang]. Chengdu: Sichuan renmin chubanshe, 1984.
Zhonggong Sichuan shengwei dangshi gongzuo weiyuanhui, ed. *Wusi yundong zai Sichuan* [The May Fourth movement in Sichuan]. Chengdu: Sichuan daxue chubanshe, 1989.
Zhonghua minguo wuniandu Sichuan sheng neiwu tongji baogaoshu [Sichuan statistical report for the fifth year of the Republic]. Chengdu: Sichuan shengzhang gongshu neiwuting, 1920.

Zhou Fudao and Ma Xuanwei. *Xiong Kewu zhuan* [Biography of Xiong Kewu]. Chongqing: Chongqing chubanshe, 1989.

Zhou Kaiqing. *Minguo Chuanshi jiyao (Zhonghua minguo jiyuanqian yinian zhi ershiwu nian)* [Chronicle of Sichuan events in the republican period, vol. 1 (1911–1936)]. Taipei: Sichuan wenxian yanjiushe, 1974.

———. "Zhang Yuejun xiansheng yu Sichuan" [Zhang Qun and Sichuan]. In *Kaiqing wencun*, 80–97. Taipei: Chuan Kang Yu wenwuguan, 1990.

Index

actors, 121, 122, 173; female impersonators, 64, 65, 114–15, 173
agriculture, 100–104
Amusing Accounts (Yuxianlu), 62, 63, 64, 65, 122, 188
anarchism, 201–2, 247n43; Ba Jin as anarchist, 10, 12, 161, 185, 186, 192–95, 199, 202, 212–13, 222, 235n23, 245nn15,16, 246nn19,26,27; Equity Society (Junshe), 10, 195, 202, 244n77; Goldman, 10, 161, 193–94, 196, 213; Kropotkin, 10, 193, 196, 222, 246n19
ancestor worship, 22, 77, 110
anti-imperialist sentiments, 133, 145, 187, 188, 199, 208–9, 216, 223, 248n64
Anti-Rightist movement, 228n15
Autumn (Qiu), 2, 17, 123, 126, 227n1; arranged marriage in, 165; Ba Jin on, 109–10, 244n1; Chen Jianyun in, 236n1; Chen Yitai (Miss Chen) in, 22, 181; commercial arcade in, 84; Cuihuan in, 9, 18; Equity Society in, 195; Gao Juehui in, 242n19; Gao Juemin in, 67, 87, 94, 184, 195, 244n1; Gao Juexin in, 9, 18, 67, 80, 84, 87, 109, 114–15, 181, 234n3, 237n24, 242n32; Gao Shuzhen's suicide in, 163, 164, 242n31; vs. *Garden of Repose*, 237n27; Madam Wang in, 112, 242n31; publication, 11, 223; Qian'er in, 18, 25, 112, 237n24; Qin in, 163, 170–71, 243n32, 244n77; sale of Gao family residence in, 67, 100; Zhang Bixiu in, 109, 114–15, 236n4; Zhang Huiru in, 94; Zhao Botao in, 54, 60. See also *Turbulent Stream*

Ba Jin: as anarchist, 10, 12, 161, 185, 186, 192–95, 199, 202, 212–13, 222, 235n23, 245nn15,16, 246nn19,26,27; on *Autumn*, 109–10, 244n1; biographies of, 227n9, 231n4; birth, 221; on characters in *Turbulent Stream*, 18; on Cuifeng, 21; during Cultural Revolution, 4, 12, 224; death, 13, 224; democratic values of, 147; on *Family*, 2, 7, 8, 18, 31, 75, 113, 163, 184, 228n1, 232n9; family home, 66, 68–69, 71; on family rituals, 49, 76–77, 79–80, 81; in France, 161, 194, 213, 223, 235n23; on friendship, 8, 227n11; vs. Gao Juehui, 8, 184–85; vs. Gao Juemin, 184–85; *Garden of Repose*, 237n27; influences on, 7, 10–12, 18, 42–43, 68, 193–94, 218, 227n12, 228n1, 243n58; vs. Li Jieren, 6–7, 38, 56–57, 88, 212, 227n8; on Li Jieren, 227n8; and May Fourth movement, 188, 190, 192, 195, 218; memoirs, 192, 194, 231n4, 233n47; during 1989 political turmoil, 228n16; Nobel Prize nominations, 13; photograph of, 9, 197; relationship with Cao Yu, 11; relationship with Chen (carpenter), 95; relationship with Chen Yunzhen/Xiao Shan, 9, 12, 223; relationship with Emma Goldman, 10, 194; relationship with Lu Jianbo, 245n15; relationship with Li Yaomei, 8, 11, 109–10, 196, 198, 236n55;

269

relationship with Wu Xianyou, 94, 206; relationship with Wu Yu, 26, 59, 81, 194, 228n6; relationship with Yuan Shiyao, 202, 203; in Shanghai, 10, 11, 12, 13, 223; on *Spring*, 244n1; views on change, 16; views on Confucianism, 8, 13, 15, 56, 57, 65, 216; views on gentry, 49–50, 56–58, 65, 145, 146, 148, 194; views on male-female relationship, 9; views on material civilization, 208; views on militarists, 56, 148, 184; views on patriarchal families, 2–3, 5, 8, 13, 15, 48, 194, 215, 216, 218–19, 249n1; views on slave girls and concubines, 44; views on street warfare, 136; views on young generation, 2–3, 8, 9–10; vs. Xu Zixiu, 65, 81; youth in Chengdu, 1, 7–8, 10, 18, 21,74, 77, 95, 126, 143, 158–59, 184, 190, 192–96, 222, 234n9, 241n6. *See also Turbulent Stream*
Ba Jin Research Association, 228n19
Bannermen (*qiren*), 55, 69–70, 118, 205
Beech, Joseph, 145, 206, 209, 238n10
Before the Dawn, 195
beggars, 113–14, 117, 122, 125
Beijing, 3, 10, 100, 150, 183, 235n26; Beiyang government, 139; economic conditions, 117–18; May Fourth incident in, 1, 2, 187, 190, 191, 201, 222, 245n10; national government in, 131, 139; National Museum of Modern Chinese Literature, 13; slave girls in, 24, 25; workhouses in, 117; YMCA in, 117–18
Beijing opera, 106
Beiyang Army, 139
Bernhardt, Kathryn, 181
binü, 19, 22, 27, 228n2. *See also* slave girls
Bi-weekly (Banyue), 194–95, 200, 222, 246nn24,25
"blood glow" (*xueguang*), 42, 75, 79
Bodde, Derk: *Law in Imperial China*, 231n8
Bolshevik Revolution, 198, 201
bound feet, 22–23, 156, 162–64, 179, 242nn27–29,30
Boxer uprising, 72
boycotts of Japanese goods, 147, 190, 199, 222, 245n13
Brook, Timothy: *Opium Regimes*, 236n40
Buck, Pearl: *The Good Earth*, 111
Buddhism, 57, 67, 89, 172, 247n44; karma and reincarnation in, 78, 116; and poverty, 116; and Wu Yu, 43, 73–74

Cai E, 134, 135, 137
Cao Xueqin. *See Dream of the Red Chamber*
Cao Yu, 11, 12, 17, 223
censuses, 88–90, 126
Chang, Eileen, 228n2; translation of *binü*, 19
Chang, Natasha: *Bound Feet and Western Dress*, 244n66
Chang Yu-i, 244n66
Changzhou: Zhang family of, 158
Chao, Shin-Yi: *Ethnography in China Today*, 231n65
Chen, Janet, 117
Chen Duxiu, 10
Chen Jianwei, 228n1
Chen Jiongming, 238n9
Chen Sihe, 53, 236n55; *Ren'ge de fazhan*, 227n9, 231n4, 236n55
Chen Weixin, 204, 207, 211, 213, 222, 248n58
Chen Yi (foreign minister of PRC), 207–8, 238n6
Chen Yi (military and civil governor of Sichuan), 134, 135, 238n6
Chen Yunzhen. *See* Xiao Shan
Chen Zuxiang, 234n5
Cheng, Yi Meng, 228n1
Chengdu: Chamber of Commerce, 62, 104, 143, 147, 172, 188, 190, 209; Chunxi Road, 86, 87, 92, 98, 99, 105–6, 108, 183, 222, 234n11; city wall, 33, 35; climate, 230n43; coffin industry, 97–98; commercial arcade in, 84–86, 87, 98, 104, 109, 206, 234n5, 245n8; Communist Party in, 96–97, 185, 202–3; concubines in, 1, 21, 39, 40, 43, 44, 57, 228n6, 230n37; crime in, 125; Dianthus Garden, 163; East Gate, 97, 123; East Parade Ground, 107–8; economic conditions, 15, 22, 31–33, 47, 83, 84–87, 88–89, 90–109, 110, 118–24, 183, 204; elders and sages in, 56–57, 59–61, 64, 65, 67, 123, 132, 144, 201, 238n9; employment of women in, 180; entertainers in, 121–22; European consulates in, 144–45, 205, 207; female vs. male

population in, 124–25, 126; Friends Middle School, 93; Fuxing Street, 98, 99, 100; gentry in, 15, 48, 53–62, 64–65, 67, 69–71, 72–77, 78, 156, 167–68, 175, 219, 231n6; Great East Street, 190; guilds/trade associations in, 90, 96, 140; handicraft sector, 91, 103–4, 118; infrastructure and architecture, 15, 33, 36, 67–71, 73, 84–86, 87, 91–93, 104, 105–109, 127, 129, 143–44, 172, 186, 206–8, 234n11, 236n48; labor activism in, 96–97; life expectancy, 126; map of, 34; May Fourth movement in, 15–16, 48, 112, 145, 148, 184, 186–92, 199–200, 219, 222; militarists in, *see* militarists; municipal government, 108–9, 122–23, 127, 129; Nationalist Party in, 185; occupations and place of employment in, 88–89; police force, 28–29, 45, 87, 88, 89–90, 108, 121, 122, 124, 125, 127, 129, 146, 151, 164, 172–73, 199–200, 206, 221, 222, 246n25; Popular Education Institute, 211, 223; population diversity, 204–5; population growth, 118; poverty in, 15, 87, 112, 117, 118–19, 124, 125, 126–27, 216, 219; printing industry, 104; as provincial capital, 7, 31, 173; Railroad Protection movement in, 69, 161, 201; reformatory (*jiliangsuo*) for sex workers, 122, 123–24; Revolution of 1911 in, 133, 135, 161, 188; salt industry, 103, 105; sanitation, 127–28; service sector, 88, 89–90, 92, 119; as setting for *Turbulent Stream*, 3–4, 5–7, 14, 15–16, 20, 132, 133, 215, 216, 219–20; vs. Shanghai, 3, 5, 216, 220; Shaocheng area, 69–70, 107, 171–72, 205; Shaocheng Park, 69, 148, 149, 170, 190, 202, 203, 211, 221, 222, 232n32; Sichuan Teachers College, 175–77, 202, 203, 247n47; slave girls in, 26–31, 33–36, 42, 44; social change in, 3, 14, 16; social class in, 112, 118–25; social mobility in, 112, 118; social surveys of, 88; South Gate, 33, 36, 57, 68; street warfare in, 15, 135–36, 141–47, 222, 223, 232n9, 240n45; tradesmen and apprentices, 91–96, 97, 118, 235n23; Wangjianglou Park, 241n10; West China Union University, 206; Western medicine in, 72, 74–75, 76, 233nn47,48; workhouses in, 117; Xue Tao Well, 241n10; YMCA, 36, 37, 73, 92–93, 117, 118, 145, 204, 206–7, 208, 211, 221, 234n9, 248n58

Chengdu University, 56–57, 65, 202, 223, 247n47

Chiang Kai-shek, 192, 211, 225, 246n34; Nationalist government of, 11, 150, 192, 199, 223, 247n37; and Nationalist Party, 138, 147, 150, 199; New Life movement of, 61; policies regarding Communists, 97, 199, 203, 223

"chicken feather inns" (*jimaodian*), 127

China Writers' Association, 12

Chinese Communist Party (Gongchandang; CCP), 147, 192, 201, 209, 217–18; in Chengdu, 96–97, 185, 202–3; founded in Shanghai, 187, 222; and local histories, 96; and May Fourth movement, 13–14; New Fourth Army, 208; Northern Expedition, 199, 200, 203, 223; and social changes, 47, 98, 217–18; United Front with Nationalist Party, 198–99, 202, 222, 223, 247n46. *See also* Mao Zedong

Chinese Volunteer Army, 11

Chinese Youth Party (Qingnian dang), 187, 199, 202–3, 223

Chongqing, 98, 138, 194–95, 242n28; American consulate in, 144–45, 151, 205, 238n10, 239n27; as port city, 31, 32–33, 140; as wartime capital, 11, 223

Chow, Rey, 79–80

Christian missionaries, 33, 36–39, 72, 74, 157–58, 163, 169, 233n41, 241n5; *West China Missionary News*, 143, 242n29; West China Union University founded by, 73, 93, 206, 221. *See also* Service, Robert

Chu, Patricia: *Assimilating Asians*, 229n12

Cihai ("ocean of words"), 175

Citizens' Gazette (Guomin gongbao), 191

cities. *See* Beijing, Chengdu, Chongqing, Guangzhou, Nanchong, Nanjing, Nantong, Shanghai

civil service examination system, 50–53, 54, 57, 59, 72, 121, 123, 150, 201, 231n2

Cixi, Empress Dowager, 178–79, 221

Classic of Changes (Yijing/I-Ching), 115

clothing, 94, 98–99, 218

commercial arcades, 30–31, 36, 84–86
Communist International (Comintern), 198
concubines, 14–15, 17–18, 19, 22, 26, 28, 80, 159, 168, 216–17, 229n23, 230n53; in Chengdu, 20–21, 39, 40, 43, 44, 57, 228n6, 230n37; Miss Chen in *Turbulent Stream*, 39, 40, 42, 75, 78, 116, 121, 122, 181; vs. slave girls, 39–42, 230n53
Confucianism, 7, 43, 80, 150, 221, 227n3; *Analects*, 50, 54; Ba Jin's views on, 8, 13, 15, 56, 57, 65, 216; Confucian canon/classical texts, 10, 50, 51, 54, 55, 56, 58, 59–61, 116, 157; criticisms of, 2, 3, 8, 13, 14, 15, 26, 56, 57, 58–59, 81, 143, 156, 194, 216, 218; and family rituals, 77, 78–79, 81, 218; filial piety, 57, 78, 79, 113, 119, 180, 194, 218, 231n16, 233n57; harmony in, 78, 79; and poverty, 115, 116; women in, 178; of Xu Zixiu, 59–61, 78, 178–79
Confucian Society, 178
Confucian Temple, 143
courtesans, 121–22, 164
Cultural Revolution, 2, 4, 224, 228n16
cultural values: revolution in, 7, 15–16, 58–59, 175–78, 218

Dacheng Academy, 60, 61, 178–79
Dacheng Association, 60, 179
Dai Jitao, 61, 200, 201, 202, 204, 213, 222, 238n9, 247n44
Dai Kan, 134, 135, 141–42
Daoism, 43, 56, 57, 67, 89, 116, 172, 198
Deng Xiaoping, 218
Destruction, 10
Di Wang, 121, 125, 172, 232n32
Dikötter, Frank, 99, 102; *Exotic Commodities*, 227n6, 233n43; *Narcotic Culture*, 236n40, 237n36, 241n5
Dirlik, Arif, 194; *Anarchism in the Chinese Revolution*, 235n23
disease and illness, 126–27
Dong Zhongshu, 232n16
dragon dances, 119–20, 237n19
Dream of the Red Chamber: downfall of Jia family, 111; funds of Jia family, 244n72; Grand View Garden, 68; Jia Baoyu, 68; Qingwen in, 228n1; vs. *Turbulent Stream*, 18, 68, 111, 218, 228n1, 244n72
Dujiangyan, 143

Eastern Miscellany (Dongfang zazhi), 46–47; "Chronicle of the Life of Big Uncle Soldier Chen Zhenwu", 152–54, 240n49; "The 467th Sichuan War", 133
Eastern Times (Shibao), 11, 196
Equity Society (Junshe), 10, 195, 202, 244n77
Esherick, Joseph: *Chinese Local Elites*, 231n1
Esperanto, 202
eugenics, 169
exorcists, 43–44, 75, 78, 79, 81, 115

family. *See* family rituals; nuclear family; patriarchal family
Family (Jia), 1–2, 21, 36, 188, 227n1; Ba Jin on, 2, 7, 8, 18, 31, 75, 113, 163, 184, 228n1, 232n9; Chen Yitai (Miss Chen) in, 39, 42, 116; dragon dance in, 119–20; vs. *Dream of the Red Chamber*, 228n1; English translation, 2, 11, 19, 224, 225; Equity Society in, 195; film version (1953), 223; film version (1956), 2, 12, 113, 114, 223; footbinding in, 162; Gao Juehui in, 31, 49, 57, 79, 112–13, 116, 118, 164–65, 192, 194, 195, 196, 234n1, 236n55; Gao Juemin in, 31, 49, 232n13, 236n55; Gao Juexin in, 53, 109, 113, 164–65, 236n55; Gao patriarch in, 17, 20, 27, 39, 42, 43, 48, 54, 57, 79, 80, 82–83, 111, 113, 116, 126; Gao Sheng in, 113, 125; Gao Shuzhen in, 158–59, 162, 163; graphic-novel version, 12, 224, 225; vs. Ibsen's *Doll's House*, 161; Mingfeng in, 14–15, 17–19, 20, 21, 24, 25, 27, 31, 37, 38, 39, 40, 42, 44, 47, 54, 68, 112, 114, 116, 129, 216, 226, 228n1, 230n44, 236n55; New Year's celebration in, 67, 81, 111, 119–20; popularity of, 2, 4, 11, 13; poverty in, 112–14; publication, 8, 11, 59, 110, 144, 223; Qin in, 155–56, 159, 170, 236n55, 238n41; revisions of, 4, 11–12, 185, 192, 223, 241n16, 245n13; vs. *Spring*, 8; stage adaptation, 11, 12, 17, 223; street warfare in, 131, 138, 141, 144, 154, 156, 232n9; students and soldiers in, 148; TV miniseries adaptation, 13, 218, 224. *See also Turbulent Stream*

family rituals, 22, 67, 76–81; ancestor worship, 22, 77, 110; Ba Jin on, 49, 76–77, 79–80, 81
Fang Bao, 22
Fan Kongzhou, 62, 104–5, 143, 172, 188–89, 209
fashion. *See* clothing, hairstyles
fate (*ming*), 42, 43, 44, 116, 231n61
federalism, 138, 140, 200–201, 222, 238n9
female impersonators, 64, 65
Feng, Jin, 240n1
Feng Yuxiang, 152, 200
Fengshui, 115–16
Finnane, Antonia, 99
Fisac, Taciana, 241n16
footbinding, 22–23, 156, 162–64, 179, 242nn27–29,30
Foreign Languages School, 58, 157, 182, 184
fortune-tellers, 43, 180
Four Books for Women, 158
Franking, Mae, 249n1
Fu Chongju, 70, 76, 125; *Chengdu tonglan*, 231n6, 234n12, 242n27; on exorcists, 43–44; on footbinding, 163–64; *Popular Pictorial (Tongsu huabao)*, 159, 160
Fukuoka Asian Culture Prize, 13
Fung, Edmund S. K.: *Intellectual Foundations of Chinese Modernity*, 227n5
Furth, Charlotte, 169

Gamble, Sidney, 117–18
Gandhi, Mahatma, 246n30
Gao Sibo, 96–97
Gates, Hill, 21, 164, 229n13, 242n30
gender: gender equality, 175; gender politics, 147; gender roles, 95, 158. *See also* women
gentry: arranged marriages among, 54, 113, 155, 164–68, 181, 222; attitudes regarding actors and prostitutes, 121–22; attitudes regarding female chastity, 124; attitudes regarding foreigners, 72, 233nn42,43; attitudes regarding poverty, 115, 117; Ba Jin's views on, 49–50, 56–58, 65, 145, 146, 148, 194; classical education of, 50–51, 53, 58, 59–60; courtyard-style compounds, 67–68, 127–28; elders and sages in Chengdu, 56–57, 59–61, 64, 65, 67, 123, 132, 144, 201, 238n9; inheritance among, 181–82; involvement in commerce and industry, 50; land ownership by, 50, 53, 100–103; meaning of *shenshi*, 49–50, 231n1; philanthropy among, 117; poetry among, 61–62, 81, 158, 232n24; relations with militarists, 55–57, 102, 110, 132, 140, 144, 145, 148, 175; women among, 15, 155–71, 172, 179, 219
Ginling College, 209
Girl from Hunan, 229n12
Glosser, Susan, 165
GMD. *See* Nationalist Party
Goldman, Andrea, 64
Goldman, Emma, 10, 161, 193–94, 196, 213
Gone with the Wind: historical accuracy of, 6
Gonghe (Republican) Party, 246n33
Gowned Brothers (Paoge), 125, 146–47, 173–74, 175, 178, 203–4, 222, 239n34
Great Depression, 104, 236n44
Guangxu emperor, 59, 178, 221
Guangyuan, 221
Guangzhou, 138, 139, 183, 198
guilds/trade associations, 90, 96
Guizhou Province: militarists' troops from, 135, 141–42, 144, 222, 232n9
Gunde, Richard, 100–101

Hakkas, 242n27
hairstyles, 37, 171; women's short, 4, 99, 172, 174, 182–83, 195, 244n77
Hall of Mercy (Cihuitang), 123–24
Han Dynasty, 50, 241n12
Hangzhou, 52
Han Suyin: *Crippled Tree*, 235n23
Hardoon, Silas, 105
Harrison, Henrietta: *Man Awakened from Dreams*, 231n2
Hart, Sir Robert, 87
Helde, George, 92–93, 208
Help, The: historical accuracy of, 6, 227n7
hereditary slavery, 20
Heroine from Eastern Europe, The (*Dong Ou nü haojie*), 161
Hersey, John: *The Call*, 233n41
Hewlett, Meyrick, 86–87, 145, 237n19
Hirayama, Nagatomi, 203
Historical Materials on Sichuan Warlords, 133
Hong Kong: British colonial government, 23, 45, 73, 221; concubines in, 40–41;

Po Leung Kuk/Baoliangju, 45; slave girls in, 23, 26, 40–41, 46, 229n23, 249n4
Hu Huaichen, 46
Hu Lanqi, 164, 171, 172, 178, 182–83, 221; arranged marriage of, 167–68, 170, 222; education, 157, 179–80, 239n33; on footbinding, 242n27; on Qiu Jin, 159; and Yang Sen, 41, 174, 210, 222
Huaixuan Academy, 57, 65, 67, 221
Huang Chao, 61
Huang Juegao, 141, 142, 143
Huang Wenxuan, 233n57
Hubbard, George, 91, 119, 127

Ibsen, Henrik: *A Doll's House*, 156, 159, 161, 241n16
imperialism, 133, 145, 179, 187–88, 199, 208–209, 212

Japan: boycotts of, 147, 190, 199, 222, 245n13; Chinese students in, 137, 150, 159, 200, 201; Chinese travel to, 73; economic policies, 84; relations with China, 98, 104, 185, 187, 199, 206, 208, 209, 211, 212, 221; and Versailles Treaty, 187
Jaschok, Maria, 22, 26, 40–41, 229n23
Jiang Mengbi, 105, 234n5
Jiangnan region, 241n9
jianshe (economic development), 186, 207–8, 213, 216

Kang, Wenqing: *Obsession*, 236n4
Kang Youwei, 58, 59, 60, 150, 178, 221
Kapp, Robert, 139
kidnappings, 20, 23, 24, 28, 30, 114–15
Kilborn, Omar, 233n42, 242n27,29
Kilborn, Retta, 163, 233n47, 242n27
Knight, Deirdre Sabina, 231n61
Ko, Dorothy, 156, 157; on footbinding, 162, 163
Korean War, 4, 11
Kropotkin, Peter, 196; *An Appeal to Youth*, 10, 193, 222, 246n19; *Ethics: Origin and Development*, 10
Kuo, Margaret: *Intolerable Cruelty*, 243n40

land ownership: by gentry, 50, 53, 100–103; in *Turbulent Stream*, 100, 188; by Wu Yu, 101

Lang, Olga, 161, 192, 212, 227n11, 244n1, 246nn19,27; *Pa Chin*, 227n9, 227n12, 245n15
Lanza, Fabio, 240n39
Lary, Diana, 151–52
Lenin, V. I., 202
Levenson, Joseph: on Liao Ping, 232n18
Li, Xiaoxiong, 126
Li Daohe, 53, 221, 231n5
Li Daojiang, 85
Li Guoqing, 126
Li Jieren, 62, 75, 104, 150, 161, 199, 222, 223, 240nn39,40, 245n9; vs. Ba Jin, 6–7, 38, 56, 88, 152, 154, 227n8; in Chengdu, 188–89, 212; "Chronicle of the Life of Big Uncle Soldier Chen Zhenwu", 152–54, 240n49; *Dabo*, 230n51, 232n14; depiction of gentry, 56–57; as editor of *Sichuan Journal*, 188; photograph of, 189; relationship with Liu Yubo, 232n14; relationship with Lu Zuofu, 209–10, 212; relationship with Shu Xincheng, 176, 245n10
Li Wenxi, 51, 221
Li Yaolin, 8, 9, 71, 222
Li Yaomei, 51, 84, 85, 87, 197; relationship with Ba Jin, 8, 11, 109–10, 196, 198, 236n55; suicide of, 110, 196
Li Yong, 51, 52–53, 56
Li Zhi, 126
Li Zicheng, 61
Liang Qichao, 244n65
Liao Ping, 58, 181, 232n18
life expectancy, 126, 238n38
Lim, Janet, 26
Lin, Yueh-hwa: *Golden Wing*, 235n36
Lin Yutang: on Chinese rituals of mourning, 80–81
Lin Zhiyuan, 65, 67
Little, Alicia (Mrs. Archibald Little), 163, 242nn27,28
Little, Archibald John, 171–72
Liu Bannong, 196, 198; "Philosophy of the Bow" (*Zuoyi zhuyi*), 198
Liu Bogu, 26
Liu Chengxun, 140, 198, 201; in Chengdu, 134, 136, 138, 139, 145, 148, 151, 200, 207
Liu Cunhou, 134, 139, 145; in Chengdu, 136, 137, 138, 140, 141, 142, 148
Liu Family Manor, 236n41
Liu Fang, 176, 178, 244n62

Liu Shiliang, 143
Liu Wencai, 102, 139
Liu Wenhui, 102, 143, 146, 238n12; in Chengdu, 136, 138, 139, 140, 144
Liu Xiang (militarist), 102, 104, 146, 203–4, 212, 223; in Chengdu, 139, 140, 144; in Chongqing, 134, 140, 211
Liu Xiang (scholar): *Lives of Virtuous Women (Lienüzhuan)*, 158–59, 241n12
Liu Xianzhi, 248n52
Liu Xiaobo, 228n16
Liu Yubo, 58, 65, 67, 68–69, 232n14; concubine of, 20–21, 26, 57
Liu Zhitang, 57, 58, 221
Long March, 202, 223
Longmenzhen, 78, 97, 98
Lu Ban, 90
Lü Chao, 134
Lu Xun: "A Madman's Diary", 242n32; "True Story of Ah Q", 240n49
Lu Zuofu, 104, 204, 209–12, 213, 223
Luo Peijin, 134, 135, 141, 142
Luo Ruiqing, 202
Luzhou, 210, 222

Madsen, Richard, 79
Manchus, 162–63, 205
Mann, Susan, 157; *Talented Women of the Zhang Family*, 241n9
Mao Dun, 12
Mao Zedong, 2, 12, 102, 165, 217
marriage: arranged marriages among gentry, 54, 113, 155, 164–68, 181, 222; arranged marriages of slave girls, 21, 27, 28, 39, 46, 95, 165, 174; bride price, 124; child brides, 22, 229n12; among cousins, 166; widow remarriage, 124, 171
Marxism, 194, 202, 247n43
Mass Education movement, 207, 237n13, 248n58
"Materials on Culture and History", 96–97
May Fourth movement, 3, 4, 5, 13–14, 46, 47, 132, 147, 215; arranged marriages criticized during, 165–66, 169; and Ba Jin, 188, 190, 192, 195, 218; in Chengdu, 15–16, 48, 145, 148, 186–92, 219, 245n6; and ideology (*zhuyi*), 61; May Fourth incident in Beijing, 1, 2, 187, 190, 191, 201, 222, 245n10
May Thirtieth incident, 208, 248n64

Meiji Japan, 33, 132
Mencius, 50, 115
militarists, 33, 118, 131–40; Ba Jin's views on, 56, 148, 184; in Chengdu, 132, 135–40, 141–47, 222, 223; commerce and development, 104, 105, 106, 109, 110, 140, 186, 207, 211; crackdown on Communists, 96–97, 203; criticism of 10, 105, 143, 203; finances of, 102, 103, 105, 140; and opium, 102; origins, 55, 132; political ideas of, 150, 203, 204; recruitment of soldiers, 15, 151–54; relations with foreigners, 144–45, 206, 207; relations with gentry, 55, 56, 102, 110, 132, 140, 144, 145, 148, 175; relations with Gowned Brothers, 173–4, 175; relations with students, 96–97, 130, 132, 147–50, 203, 222, 240n37; as warlords (*junfa*), 131, 132, 143. *See also* Dai Kan, Liu Chengxun, Liu Cunhou, Liu Wenhui, Liu Xiang, Luo Peijin, Xiong Kewu, Yang Sen
Ming dynasty, 61, 74, 75, 178, 232n16
minsheng, 116
Minsheng Industrial Company, 104, 204, 212, 223
Mongols, 205
Morris, Clarence: *Law in Imperial China*, 231n8
Morse, William Reginald, 170
Mühlhahn, Klaus, 231n8
mui-jai, 22, 228n2, 229n9, 230n53
Muslims, 89, 205

Nanchong, 201–2
Nanjing, 132, 150, 199, 201, 223
Nantong, 201
Nationalist Party (Guomindang; GMD), 61, 139, 185, 187, 198–200, 202–3, 211, 238n9, 246n34; and Chiang Kai-shek, 138, 147, 150, 199; Nationalist government, 11, 46, 139, 150, 192, 199, 200, 203, 223, 247n37; Northern Expedition, 199, 200, 203, 223; and Sun Yat-sen, 198; United Front with Communist Party, 198–99, 202, 222, 223, 247n46
National Road-Building Association, 174–75, 204, 207
Natural Foot Society, 163–64, 242nn27,28

New Culture movement, 1, 3, 6, 13, 14, 219, 222, 232n14; and Wu Yu, 2, 26, 43
New Life movement, 61
New Women (*xin nüxing*), 155–57, 173, 174, 182–83, 216
New Youth, 10, 62, 167, 187, 194, 196–97, 222, 243n32
Ning, Old Mrs., 23, 25, 38–39, 41, 43, 120
North China Herald, 190, 240n37, 248n64
Northern Expedition, 199, 200, 203, 223
nuclear families, 217

opium: addiction, 23, 113–14, 125–26, 236n40, 237n36, 241n5; production, 102, 152
orphanages, 117, 123, 124
Overmyer, Daniel: *Ethnography in China Today*, 231n65

patriarchal families: attitudes toward, 67, 168, 217, 249n1; Ba Jin's views on, 2–3, 5, 8, 13, 15, 48, 194, 215, 216, 218–19; criticisms of, 1, 2–3, 5, 13, 14, 15, 26, 43, 47, 48, 167, 194, 215, 218, 219; difficulty of reforming, 216–17; members defined, 21, 166, 229n7; as patricorporations, 21; relationship to poverty, 110, 111, 113
peddlers, 119
Peking University, 222
People's Republic of China (PRC): Anti-Rightist movement, 228n15; Cultural Revolution, 2, 4, 224, 228n16; and local histories, 96; social changes in, 4, 47, 98, 217–18
Perovskaia, Sofia, 161
Perry, Elizabeth: *Shanghai on Strike*, 235n26
Popular Pictorial (Tongsu huabao), 159, 160
poverty: attitudes regarding causes, 115–18; in Chengdu, 15, 87, 112, 117, 118–19, 124, 125, 126–27, 216, 219; and Confucianism, 115, 116; and disease, 126–27; relationship to family support, 110, 111, 113; in *Turbulent Stream*, 111–15, 116, 118
Progressive Politics Party (Zhengjindang), 198, 246n33
Pruitt, Ida, 23, 25, 43
public space and women, 170–78, 183

public toilets, 128–29
Puyi, 142

Qin empire, 88
Qing dynasty, 7, 22, 54–55, 57–58, 74, 75, 107, 146, 150, 180, 204, 232n16, 241nn9,15; Bannermen (*qiren*), 55, 69–70, 205; civil service examination system during, 50–53, 54, 57, 59, 72, 121, 123, 150, 201, 231n2; economic policies, 84; Empress Dowager Cixi, 178–79; Guangxu emperor, 59, 178, 221; legal system, 19–20, 25–26, 39, 44–46, 54, 121, 173, 216, 231n8; military academies during, 118, 132, 133, 135, 137, 147; *minsheng* during, 116; New Policies reforms, 221; new schools under, 72; policies regarding official positions, 231n6; policies regarding opium, 125; population growth under, 23; post office bureaucracy, 87; poverty during, 116–17; railroad nationalization during, 55, 69, 161, 172, 201; relations with Britain, 221; relations with Japan, 221; vs. Republic of China, 28, 30, 33, 45–46, 122, 125, 171, 172, 216–17; salt industry under, 103; Western-influenced reforms, 72–73; women during, 158, 163, 172, 178; Yongzheng emperor, 20, 228nn4,5
Qiu Jin, 159
Qufu, 218

Railroad Protection movement, 55, 69, 161, 172, 201
Rankin, Mary Backus: *Chinese Local Elites*, 231n1
Ransmeier, Johanna, 21, 24
Ran Yunfei, 26, 71, 74, 228n6, 230n37
Records of Freedom (Ziyoulu), 194
Republic of China: "Beiyang" government, 139; Confucianism in, 59–60; government in Beijing, 131, 139; government in Nanjing, 132, 150, 199, 223; legal system, 216, 243n40; vs. Qing dynasty, 28, 30, 33, 45–46, 122, 125, 171, 172, 216–17; relations with Britain, 209; relations with Japan, 98, 104, 185, 187, 199, 206, 208, 209, 211, 212; Revolution of 1911, 49, 55, 99, 133, 135, 137, 173, 187, 201, 232n14, 248n52; and Versailles Treaty, 187,

190, 191, 206. *See also* Chiang Kai-shek; Nationalist Party; Sun Yat-sen; Yuan Shikai
Revolutionary Alliance, 135, 137, 139, 201
rickshaws, 35–36, 88, 105, 119, 234n11
Romance of the Three Kingdoms, 235n30
Rowntree, Fred, 206
rumors and gossip, 25, 159, 241n15
Russian Revolution of 1905, 195

Sacco, Nicola, 213
sales of human beings, 19–20, 22–24, 26–31, 33, 44–47, 216–17, 228n5, 230n46
salt industry, 103, 105
Sanger, Margaret, 169
sedan chairs, 35, 49, 86, 88, 112–13, 119, 170
Service, Grace, 37–38, 117
Service, John, 233n48
Service, Robert, 37, 73, 117, 145, 206, 207, 221
sexuality, 114, 169, 175, 177
sex workers, 121–22, 124, 125
Shandong province, 25
Shanghai, 100, 161, 165, 195, 196, 217, 235n26, 240n37, 247n37; Ba Jin in, 10, 11, 12, 13, 223; vs. Chengdu, 3, 5, 216, 220; Chinese Communist Party founded in, 187, 222; Commercial Press, 207; economic conditions, 90, 104; entertainment culture in, 121–22; foreign concessions, 73; International Settlement police, 208; Nanjing Road, 86, 105, 106; women in, 179, 180, 183; workhouses in, 117
Shanghai Women's Bank, 244n66
Shanghai Writers' Federation, 11
Shapiro, Sidney: translation of *Family*, 11, 19, 225
Shaw, Craig, 227n12
Shen Congwen: "Xiaoxiao", 229n12
Shu Xincheng, 175–77, 206, 243n61, 245n8
Sichuan Educational Association, 59
Sichuan Industrial College, 207–8
Sichuan Journal (Chuanbao), 188, 189–90, 245nn8,12
Sichuan Masses (Sichuan qunbao), 188–89, 209
Sichuan Province, 31–32, 51, 52–55, 57–58, 61, 98, 104, 144, 186, 204–5,

239n27; census of 1916, 126; Chengdu as capital of, 7, 31, 173; Chengdu County, 124, 237n30; Chongqing region, 53; Dayi County, 139; during Great Depression, 236n44; Guangyuan County, 53, 231n5; Hakkas in, 242n27; Huayang County, 124, 237n30; militarists in, 132–40, 141–47, 150, 198, 199, 202, 203–4, 222, 232n9; Military Academy, 135, 137, 138; nativism in, 185, 204; opera in, 62, 64–65, 84, 114–15, 173; opium in, 102, 126; Provincial Assembly, 54, 55, 138, 148, 172, 201, 221, 238n9; provincial police, 190, 199–200, 222; Railroad Protection movement in, 69, 161, 201, 222; salt industry, 103, 105; *Selected Materials on Culture and History*, 96–97; white turbans in, 99, 235n30; Xinfan County, 101, 235n36. *See also* Chengdu; Chongqing
Sichuan University, 247n47
silk production, 86, 90, 101–2, 158, 236n44
Singapore, 24, 26
Sinn, Elizabeth, 45, 46
Slack, Edward R.: *Opium, State, and Society*, 236n40
slave girls, 14–15, 17–47, 80, 120, 216–17, 228n2, 230nn46,51; birth families, 20, 21, 22, 23–24, 42, 111–12, 217, 229n23; and commercial economy, 22; vs. concubines, 39–42, 230n53; as conspicuous consumption, 22; contracts, 20, 27–31, 44, 45, 85, 95, 228n5; duties of, 38–39; and era of reform, 44–47; marriage of, 21, 27, 28, 39, 46, 95, 165, 174; physical punishment of, 24–25; sexual exploitation of, 18, 25–26
Smith, Richard: on family rituals, 77–78, 81
social class, 112, 118–25, 228n4
social mobility, 112, 118, 129–30, 152, 219
Sommer, Matthew H., 25; *Sex, Law, and Society*, 228nn2,4
Song dynasty, 60, 61
South Sichuan Teachers College (Chuannan shifan xuexiao), 210
Soviet Union, 217
Spence, Jonathan: *The Gate of Heavenly Peace*, 186

278 INDEX

Spring (Chun), 2, 17, 227n1, 243n56; arranged marriage in, 165; bandits in, 100; Equity Society in, 195; vs. *Family*, 8; family ritual in, 76–77; Gao Juemin in, 184, 192, 195, 234n9, 244n1; Gao Juexin in, 74, 234n9; Gao Shuying in, 155, 161, 168, 240n1, 241n15; Hai'er's death in, 126; Madam Zhou in, 42, 182; publication, 11, 223; Qin in, 156, 170, 178; rumors in, 241n15; Western medicine in, 74; Xi'er in, 39; Zhou Botao in, 54; Zhou family in, 76–77. See also *Turbulent Stream*
Standard Oil Company, 144, 239n24
Stevenson, Robert Louis: *Kidnapped*, 114; *Treasure Island*, 49, 62
Strand, David: *Rickshaw Beijing*, 235n26
students, 240n39, 248n64; and boycotts of Japanese goods, 147, 190, 199, 222, 245n13; protest against British, 209; women as, 157–58, 172, 173–74, 175–77, 179 80, 223, 241n9
Sun Chuanfang, 137
Sun Daolin, 12
Sun Shaojing, 150, 240n40
Sun Yat-sen, 188, 199, 200, 225, 246n34; and Nationalist Party, 147, 198; Revolutionary Alliance of, 135, 137, 139, 201; Three Principles of the People, 147, 150, 212
Suzhou, 52

Tagore, Rabindranath, 208
Taiping War, 32–33, 51, 221
Tan, Amy: *The Joy Luck Club*, 229n12
Tan Xingguo: *Zoujin Ba Jin de shijie*, 227n9
Tang Jiyao, 137
Tang Qunying, 161
Tang dynasty, 50, 61, 158; Xuanzong emperor, 236n4
taxation, 33, 51–52, 58, 129
Taylor, Charles, 79
Teacher Cao, 171, 172, 179–80
Thompson, John Stuart, 238n4
Three-Character Classic, 157, 241n6
Tian Hengqiu, 174–75, 179
Tibetans, 205
ti-yong ("essence-application"), 58, 73
Tolstoy, Leo, 196, 198, 246n30
Tran, Lisa, 229n7
Truth Society (Shishe), 194

Turbulent Stream: arranged marriages in, 164–65; Chengdu setting, 3–4, 5–7, 14, 15–16, 20, 132, 133, 215, 216, 219–20; during Cultural Revolution, 2, 4, 12; vs. *Dream of the Red Chamber*, 18, 68, 111, 218, 228n1, 244n72; emotional impact, 6; Gao family residence in, 67–68; historical accuracy of, 3–4, 5–7, 14–16, 18, 24, 31, 40, 42, 47, 54, 57, 60, 61, 64, 72, 80, 109, 112, 120, 126, 133, 148, 151, 154, 157, 158, 163, 169, 173, 177, 178, 182–83, 187, 204, 216, 219; land ownership in, 100, 188; May Fourth movement in, 187, 215; opium in, 113–14; political activism in, 184–86; popularity of, 2, 4, 5–6, 12, 155–56, 218–19; poverty in, 111–15, 116, 118; publication, 7, 8, 11; and "Qun", 4; Sichuan opera in, 62, 114; sources of tension in, 131; TV miniseries adaptation, 2, 12–13, 73, 218, 224; and women's place in public life, 170–78; and young women, 155–56. See also *Autumn*; *Family*; *Spring*; *Turbulent Stream* characters
Turbulent Stream characters: Chen Jianyun, 113, 225, 236n1; Chen Yitai (Miss Chen), 39, 40, 42, 75, 116, 121, 122, 181; Chunlan, 18, 25, 225; "Commander", 136, 148; Cuihuan, 9, 18, 31, 110, 225; Feng Leshan, 54, 57, 59, 60, 61, 62, 114, 178, 225; Gao Hai'er, 126; Gao Juehui, 5, 7–8, 17, 24, 31, 48, 49–50, 57, 59, 62, 68, 79, 83, 94, 99, 112–13, 116, 118, 120, 131, 148, 157, 158, 162, 164–65, 182, 184–85, 186, 192, 194, 196, 213, 215–16, 225, 234n1, 236n55, 240n1, 242n19, 244n1; Gao Juemin, 8, 24, 31, 49–50, 54, 59, 67, 71, 87, 94, 112, 113, 157, 167, 184–85, 186, 192, 195, 225, 232n13, 234n9, 236n55, 244n1; Gao Juexin, 2–3, 8, 9, 12, 18, 30–31, 36, 39, 40, 53, 67, 73, 74, 79, 80, 82, 83, 84, 85–86, 87, 94, 97, 100, 109, 110, 114–15, 126, 158, 162, 164–65, 167, 169, 181, 182, 186, 196, 225, 234nn3,9, 236n55, 237n24, 242n32, 244n72; Gao Ke'an, 18, 22, 112, 114, 115, 122, 126, 181, 225, 236n4, 237n24; Gao Keding, 18, 25, 39, 115, 119, 120, 164, 170, 181, 225, 236n4; Gao Keming, 79, 226;

Gao patriarch (Gao Laotaiye), 15, 17, 20, 22, 26, 27, 39, 42, 43, 54, 56, 57, 61, 62, 65, 71, 75, 77, 78, 79, 80, 81, 82–83, 84, 111, 113, 116, 126, 155, 165, 166, 180, 181, 182, 234n1; Gao Sheng, 113, 125; Gao Shuhua, 181, 226, 244n77; Gao Shuying, 5, 155, 161, 168, 226, 240n1, 241n15; Gao Shuzhen, 158–59, 162, 163, 164, 226, 242n31; Gao Zhong, 120; "General Zhang", 136; He Sao, 226; Huang Ma, 24; Liu Sheng, 100; Madam Shen, 164, 242n31; Madam Wang, 112, 242n31; Mei, 83, 164, 165, 167, 226; Mingfeng, 14–15, 17–19, 20, 21, 24, 25, 27, 31, 37, 38, 39, 40, 42, 44, 47, 54, 68, 112, 114, 116, 129, 216, 226, 228n1, 230n44, 236n55; Monday, 115, 122, 164, 170; Mrs. Zhang, 127, 182; Qian'er, 18, 25, 112, 226, 237n24; Qin, 99, 127, 155–56, 157, 159, 161, 163, 167, 170–71, 178, 180, 181, 182, 215, 226, 236n55, 238n41, 240n1, 243n32, 244n77; Ruijue, 12, 42, 75, 79, 83, 158, 162, 165, 169, 182, 226; Tang Sao, 226; Wan'er, 17–18, 31, 39, 54, 226; Wu Yu/Wu Youling, 26; Xi'er, 18, 25, 39, 40, 164, 226; Yuan Shiyao, 202; Zhang Bixiu, 64, 109, 114–15, 121, 126, 226, 236n4; Zhang Huiru, 94, 195, 206, 226, 246n24; Zhang Sao, 21, 226; Zheng Guoguang, 232n9; Zhou Botao, 54, 57, 60, 61, 232n9; Zhou Hui, 74, 80, 165, 226; Zhou Mei, 165, 226, 242n32; Zhou Shi (Madam Zhou), 42, 116, 182, 226; Zhou Yun, 243n32

United Front, 198–99, 202, 222, 223, 247n46
urban reform and development, 216, 220, 222; *See also* Lu Zuofu, Sun Shaojing, Yan Yangchu

Vanzetti, Bartolomeo, 213
Versailles Treaty, 187, 190, 191, 206
Voice of the Common People (Pingmin zhi sheng), 195

wages, 19, 30–31, 84, 93–94, 97–98
Wakabayashi, Bob Tadashi: *Opium Regimes*, 236n40
Wang Guangqi, 189–90, 245n10

Wang Lüping, 246n28
Wang Youmu, 202, 247n43
Wang Zheng, 179; *Women in the Chinese Enlightenment*, 240n1, 241n3
Wanxian incident, 209, 223
warfare, 4, 11, 23, 32–33, 52, 55–56, 78, 187, 208, 211–12; impact on Chengdu, 141–147; impact on the Sichuan economy, 103–108; impact on women, 156, 173–178; reasons for its prevalence in Sichuan, 132–140
Watson, James, 22, 23, 228n5, 229nn9,15,23
Watson, Rubie, 230n53
West China Missionary News, 143, 242n29
West China Union University, 145, 170, 238n10; dental medicine at, 74; founded, 73, 93, 206, 221; survey of manual laborers at, 93–94, 95, 124
Wilde, Oscar: *Lady Windermere's Fan*, 241n16
Wilson, Woodrow, 187
Wolf, Arthur, 229n13
women: childbirth, 75, 169–70; education of, 157–61, 170, 172, 173–74, 175–76, 179–80, 182, 223, 241n9; employment of, 179–80; fate (*ming*) invoked by, 42, 43, 44, 116, 231n61; female teachers, 179–80; footbinding of, 22–23, 156, 162–64, 179, 242nn27–29,30; and legal system, 243n40; New Women (*xin nüxing*), 155–57, 173, 174, 182–83, 216; and public space, 170–78; during Qing dynasty, 158, 172, 178; short hair among, 4, 99, 172, 174, 182–83, 195, 244n77. *See also* concubines; marriage; slave girls
Women's World (Nüjiebao), 172
World War I, 205–6, 245n12; Versailles Treaty, 187, 190, 191, 206
Wright, Tim, 236n44
Wu, Yi-Li, 75
Wu Tianming: *King of Masks (Bianlian)*, 230n46
Wu Xianyou, 94, 195, 246nn24,25, 247n43
Wu Yu, 30, 61, 201, 223, 243n32; attitudes regarding militarists, 143; *Autumn Waters (Qiushuiji)*, 62, 104; and Buddhism, 43, 73–74; concubines of, 39, 43, 228n6, 230n37; daughters of, 73, 158, 168–69, 174, 178, 180,

181–82, 243n47; diary of, 26–27, 101, 118, 119, 150, 169, 169–70, 182, 230nn38,43, 231n6, 235n36, 240n45; on employment of women, 180; and inheritance, 181–82; land ownership by, 101; and New Culture movement, 2, 26, 43; "One Family's Bitter Story", 59, 221; on patriarchal families, 194; and Progressive Politics Party, 198, 246n33; relationship with Ba Jin, 2, 26, 39, 58, 59, 69, 81, 91, 143, 158, 194, 221, 222, 228n6; relationship with Daoxiu, 169–70; relationship with father, 40, 59, 98, 168, 221; relationship with Sun Shaojing, 150; relationship with Xu Zixiu, 59–60; relationship with Zeng Lan, 143, 167, 168, 169, 181; residence of, 70–71, 91–92, 99, 100, 101; slave girls of, 26–27, 33, 37, 230nn37,38; views regarding Confucianism, 58–59; will of, 181–82; as Wu Youling, 230n36
Wu Yuzhang, 200, 201, 202, 204, 213, 222, 247n46
wushi, 42. *See also* exorcists

Xiao Shan, 9, 12, 223
Xie Bingying, 41
Xikang, 238n12
Xiong Kewu, 134, 139, 198, 199–200, 208, 238n9; in Chengdu, 136, 140, 147, 188; early life, 137–38; photograph of, 137
Xiong Zhuoyun, 237n36
Xue Tao, 158, 241n10
Xu Zhimo, 244n66
Xu Zixiu, 64, 69, 73, 78, 199; vs. Ba Jin, 65, 81; Confucianism of, 59–61, 78, 178–79; relationship with Wu Yu, 59–60; students of, 61, 200, 238n9; views on women, 178–79
Xuanzong emperor, 236n4

Yan Xishan, 137
Yan Yangchu (James Yen), 207, 212, 237n13
Yan'an, 223, 247n46
Yang Guifei, 236n4

Yang Sen, 92, 134, 179, 209; in Chengdu, 86, 105, 140, 153, 157, 174–75, 177, 202, 206, 207, 211, 212, 222, 234n11, 243n58; Chunxi Road project, 86, 105; and Hu Lanqi, 41, 174, 210, 222; and Shu Xincheng, 176, 177, 206
Yang Shukan, 134, 147, 188, 190, 199–200
Yangzi river trade, 140, 211, 212, 242n28
yatou, 19, 37, 228n2
Yeh, Catherine Vance, 121
Yellow Emperor's Inner Classic, 74
Yen, James. *See* Yan Yangchu
Yenching University, 209
Yi ethnic group, 243n52
Yin Changling, 122, 124
Yongzheng emperor, 20, 228nn4,5
Yosano Akiko, 161
Young China Association, 176, 222, 240n40, 245n10
Yu Fenggang, 105–6, 110
Yuan Shikai, 132, 133; death of, 135, 222; as president, 172, 198, 201 238n4; rebellions against, 135, 137, 138
Yuan Shiyao, 201–2, 203
Yun Daiying, 110, 168
Yunnan Province: militarists' troops from, 135, 136, 141, 142, 145, 222; Military Academy, 137, 141
Yusi, 244n61

Zelin, Madeleine, 103
Zeng Lan, 143, 167, 168, 169, 181
Zeng Qi, 199
Zhang Jian, 201, 247n42
Zhang Lan, 134, 201–2, 203, 247n42
Zhang Qun, 61, 199–200, 204, 206, 222, 247nn37,38
Zhang Ruifang, 12
Zhang Zhidong, 57–58, 221
Zhao Xi, 64
Zhejiang, 205, 231n6
Zhou Kaiqing: *Minguo Chuanshi jiyao*, 134
Zhou period, 50
Zhu De, 147
Zhuge Liang, 235n30
Zola, Émile: novels about Rougon-Macquart family, 10–11
Zunjing Academy, 58, 59, 60, 201, 221